John B. S. Greene

The Hebrew Migration from Egypt

John B. S. Greene

The Hebrew Migration from Egypt

ISBN/EAN: 9783337237264

Printed in Europe, USA, Canada, Australia, Japan

Cover: Foto ©ninafisch / pixelio.de

More available books at **www.hansebooks.com**

THE
HEBREW MIGRATION
FROM EGYPT

"It were better to have no opinion of God at all than such an opinion as is unworthy of Him; for the one is unbelief, the other is contumely . . . . and as the contumely is greater towards God, so the danger is greater towards men."—BACON.

LONDON
TRÜBNER AND CO., LUDGATE HILL
1879

PREFACE.

IT may, perhaps, be convenient to preface this treatise by a few words. It is an attempt to give an intelligible, and, at the same time, a historically true account of the Hebrew settlement in Egypt, the servitude, with the subsequent movement, of the liberated captives to the region on the east of the Jordan—a movement which, for want of a better term, I have called a migration.

In fulfilling this task, I have confined myself to an examination of the early Hebrew traditions, as set forth in records still preserved to us, comparing the inferences deducible therefrom with the opinions entertained in Palestine down to the fourth century of the Christian era, and with local traditions, which can be carried back from the present day to the time of the Jewish dispersion.

I have found it necessary to introduce this inquiry with some general remarks on the nature of the religion of the Hebrew nomads. So much light has been thrown of late years upon this interesting subject by the Dutch and German schools, that the views I have expressed will not surprise those who have followed the recent progress of Biblical criticism. It is, however, right I should add, that with the great bulk of this portion of Dutch and German literature I am unfamiliar. It may be, that in the course of this work I have expressed opinions which, though original in the sense of not having been borrowed, may already have found expression elsewhere. If such should be the case, I trust I shall be acquitted of dishonesty. I have invariably acknowledged my indebtedness when I have availed myself of the labours of others.

I have passed unnoticed the multitudinous works of those who have taken the liberated Hebrews into the Sinaitic peninsula, and speculated according to their fancies on the wanderings in the Desert. I trust that I shall not be considered discourteous on this account. My views differ so completely from theirs, that no good purpose would have been served by directing attention to opinions only for the purpose of assailing them. Whether the version of the Hebrew migration given by me or that hitherto received should command acceptance, must in the last resort depend on the original historical materials upon which the story must be founded.

November, 1879.

CONTENTS.

	PAGE
INTRODUCTION	1

Objects of the inquiry—Leading features of Hebrew traditions—The religion of the Hebrew nomads—Its Henotheism—No belief in a Future State—The Tetragrammaton—Errors arising from its interpretation as Lord—Materials for this inquiry.

CHAPTER I.

THE SETTLEMENT IN EGYPT—THE BONDAGE 26

The accounts given by Manetho—Period of sojourn in Egypt, and date of Exodus—How the settlement began—The story of Joseph—Its true interpretation.

CHAPTER II.

THE DEPARTURE FROM EGYPT 47

Possible cause of liberation of the Captives—The passage of the Red Sea—Not mentioned in the early traditions of the Exodus—Probable origin of legend—Brugsch Bey's views respecting scene of the occurrence—The *Jam Suph*—Interpretation of name—Its locality—Jephthah's account of the migration from Egypt.

CHAPTER III.

THE REGION FROM WHICH THE EXODUS TOOK PLACE . . . 87

Places named in Hebrew traditions—Variety of suggestions for their identification—Brugsch Bey's views—The region of the Captivity probably in the neighbourhood of Zoan-Tanis.

CHAPTER IV.

THE COMPOSITION OF THE EMIGRANTS 102

Israel and Judah always distinct—Their rivalry—Early traditions in which "Beni-Israel" and "Hebrews" are respectively mentioned—Allusions to the "Hebrews" in the historical books—The "Mixed Multitude"—The visit to Egypt by a tribe of shepherds—The Shasu from the land of Aduma.

CHAPTER V.

THE REGION TRAVERSED BY THE EMIGRANTS—THE MOUNT OF ELOHIM 122

Accepted account of the migration—The Book of Numbers—The Tih and the Sinaitic Peninsula—The Araba—The Mount of Elohim—Allusions to it subsequent to the settlement in Palestine—The Song of Deborah—The Blessing of Moses—Habakkuk—The Parable of Elijah—St. Paul—The limits of Arabia—Josephus' description of Mount Sinai, and account of the flight of Moses from Egypt—The Troglodytes—Midian.

CHAPTER VI.

THE EARLY TRADITIONS OF THE MIGRATION 161

The flight of Moses to Midian—Situation of Midian—The route from Rameses to the Mount of Elohim—The *midbhar* of Shur—Marah—Elim-Elath—The Sinaitic Peninsula—Egyptian occupation—Sarbut-el-Khadem—Diversity of opinion respecting the true Sinai—The Hajj route across the Tih—Abiar Alaina, Marah—*Midbhar* of Sin—The Araba The names given to the Mount of Elohim—Sinai—Choreb—Paran—The battle with the Amalekites—Philological characteristics of names of places in traditions of the migration.

CHAPTER VII.

THE VALLEY OF MOSES 209

The Nabathæan capital—The *Sik*—Ain Mûsa—Aaron's Plains—The Deir—Mount Hor—Earliest traditions respecting Mount Seir—The Kenites.

CHAPTER VIII.

THE LOCAL TRADITIONS OF EDOM 228

Eusebius and Jerome—The *Onomàsticon*—Choreb—Hor—Kadesh—Pharan—Petra—The rock struck by Moses—The Peutinger Table—The Targumists—Kadesh-Rekam-Petra—The Waters of Contradiction—Ignorance of Eusebius and Jerome respecting the precise situation of Mount of Elohim—The Crusaders—The expeditions of Baldwin into Arabia Tertia—Fulcher of Chartres—Albert of Aix—Arabian and Egyptian authorities—Expedition of Sultan Bibors to Petra—"Villages of the Children of Israel."

CHAPTER IX.

EDOM—JUDAH 259

Saul's campaign against the Amalekites—The scenes of David's adventures, when pursued by Saul—En-gedi—The city of Palms—The boundaries of Judah—The position of Kadesh.

CHAPTER X.

THE TRADITIONS OF THE PATRIARCHS 287

The Hebrew settlement in Edom—The Negeb—No settlement in Palestine—Identity of traditions of Abraham and Isaac—The league with Abimelech—The wells of Esek and Sitnah—Hagar—Beer-lahai-roi—Gerar—Bered—Gedor—ThePhelisti—The Simeonite emigration—The *nachal* Gerar—Beer-sheba—Haran—The Canaan of the Patriarchs—Egyptian records—Shur.

CHAPTER XI.

THE ROUTE FROM ELIM—THE MOUNT OF ELOHIM 316

The Araba—Kibroth-hat-Taavah—El Daba—Rephidim—Hazeroth—The *Sik*—The *Har-ha-Har*—The Shechinah—Death of Miriam—Oblivion into which the Mount of Elohim fell—Semitic conceptions of localisation of Deity—Deuteronomist's account of Aaron's death—The wells of Beni-Jaakan—The phenomenon of the burning bush.

CHAPTER XII.

THE STAY AT KADESH AND THE JOURNEY ROUND EDOM . . . 343

The contemplated invasion of Southern Canaan—The report of the Spies—Dissatisfaction of the people—The invasion of Canaan and defeat of the Hebrews—The unsuccessful negotiations with the King of Edom—The route from Kadesh to Moab—The dispossession of the Amorites—No details of this conquest preserved in Cis-Jordanic traditions—Apostasy of the emigrants in Moab—Its explanation.

CHAPTER XIII.

THE TRANS-JORDANIC SETTLEMENT 359

The story of the partition between Reuben, Gad, and half Manasseh—Its Cis-Jordanic origin—How the settlement was really effected—The subsequent movement across the Jordan—The first-born of Israel retained possession of the left bank—Reuben—Manasseh—Confusion arising in later times from misunderstanding tribal designations—The Cis-Jordanic version of the settlement on the east of the Jordan.

CHAPTER XIV.

THE WANDERINGS 374

The wanderings in the Desert had no place in the traditions of the migration—How the belief subsequently arose—The difference between the Cis- and Trans-Jordanic versions respecting the boundary line separating "the Wilderness" from "the Promised Land"—The introductory portion of the Book of Joshua—Interpretation of the words which have been translated "wander"—The "forty years," and the supply of manna.

CHAPTER XV.

THE TRANS- AND CIS-JORDANIC TRADITIONS RESPECTING THE DEATH OF MOSES 392

The Mount Abarim—The land of Moab—The *nachal* Zered—The Arnon—Story of Elijah and the ravens—The *nachal Ha-Arabim* The Valley of Willows—Mount Nebo—The narrative of Balaam and Balak—Fragment of ancient Itinerary of places on the border of the Wilderness—Shittim—The Pisgah—The topography of region south of the Arnon—Cis-Jordanic version of original story of death of Moses.

CHAPTER XVI.

CONCLUSION 416

The only reliable materials for construction of story of the migration—Earliest sources of history—The story-tellers and bards—Heterogeneous elements of Jewish history—The land of the Hebrews—Religion of the Hebrews and its influence on their early traditions—The stories told and preserved must have been intelligible—Original story of the settlement in Egypt and migration—Its subsequent modifications—The Mount of Elohim—The land in which it must have stood—The three stages of the migration—Final amalgamation of distinct traditions and consequent confusion—Mischievous consequences flowing from accepted mode of dealing with the Pentateuch.

MAP TO ILLUSTRATE HEBREW MIGRATION . . . . *Frontispiece*

MAP OF PETRA 216

THE HEBREW MIGRATION

FROM

EGYPT.

INTRODUCTION.

THE story of the Exodus is one of the oldest in the world. It is also one of the least understood. That this should be so has arisen from a variety of causes. The story itself is told in a book which, it is alleged, contains exclusively the Word of God; and writings placed on so lofty a pinnacle necessarily stand beyond the pale of human criticism. It has also been the accepted belief that the Books* in which the story we refer to is to be found were written by Moses; that he occupied the exceptional position of a divinely-appointed historian; and it has consequently been not illogically inferred that the materials must be so far homogeneous and the narrative so far continuous, that the same stories cannot be told in different forms, nor the same events recorded as having happened at different places and different times. Any objections based on the improbability or the unintelligibility of the story as presented under this mode of treatment are overruled as equally irrelevant and untenable, since nothing can be advanced by man which can shake the accuracy of statements presumably made by God. If the narrative of Moses is fragmentary, unconnected, and in places contradictory;

---

* The Pentateuch, or Five Books of Moses—Genesis, Exodus, Leviticus, Numbers, and Deuteronomy.

and if it apparently represents the Deity and His chosen people in colours which are irreconcilable with the assumed moral excellence of the one and the supposed sanity of the other, it is concluded that the distorted picture is the result of our want of appreciation, or it may be our lack of faith. The consequence is, that the accepted version of the Hebrew migration from Egypt to the region on the east of the Jordan labours under the greatest defect which can attach to a historical production. As measured by ordinary canons, it is totally incomprehensible.

It is, however, legitimate to ask whether this most interesting story is as unintelligible as it is represented, and to inquire whether the materials placed at our disposal are not amply sufficient for the construction of a narrative which will not shock by its distorted representation of the ways of Providence, and will not repel by its hopeless improbability. The alleged wanderings of the Israelites have hitherto been shrouded in a mystery which is supposed to be impenetrable. The object of the present inquiry will be to lift the cloud.

For many reasons it is worth while to attempt to solve a mystery which has hitherto been regarded as inscrutable. Historical accuracy is of importance in all matters, great and small; but its attainment is specially desirable in connection with an event which exercised so great an influence on the future of mankind as the migration of the Hebrews from Egypt to Canaan. Great advantage also arises from an accurate conception of the materials out of which the early history of the people of Israel came to be formed, and the manner in which those materials came in time to be welded together; the opportunity for forming such conceptions being pre-eminently afforded by the carefully preserved traditions of the most salient events which occurred between the departure from Egypt and the arrival in the Trans-Jordanic region. But especially is such a task worth undertaking with the view of rendering justice to the Deity to whom men—and these, for the most part, pious men—attribute the most capricious and preposterous conduct in achieving a work which was the turning-point in the national existence of a people declared to be specially His own. Whether the Almighty interposed more directly in the movement by which the Hebrews quitted Egypt and ultimately settled in Canaan, than in the invasion of England by the Normans, or in the discovery of America by Columbus, is a question with which it is unnecessary to deal in this inquiry. But whether His interposition was general or special, it is equally desirable to demonstrate from the records of the people of Israel that in their opinion the conduct of their protecting God was neither so vacillating nor so irrational as it is now almost universally believed to have been. If there be any point more strongly dwelt upon than another in the accepted version of the " Wanderings" it is that God personally interposed for the guidance of the host by means of a pillar of fire by night and a pillar of cloud by day; and we are asked to marvel at this extraordinary solicitude upon His part for His chosen people, who it is inferred would have lost their way but for this miraculous assistance. And yet in the same breath we are taught that this Heaven-guided people were led to and fro for nearly forty years in a region which may be roughly estimated at one hundred miles square, adjacent to Canaan and to Egypt, and furnishing the only line of communication between the latter powerful kingdom and the East—a region which they could at any time have quitted in less than a week; and further, that they were conducted in this miraculous manner " nowhere." for no other purpose than that of letting them die out.*

---

* Numbers xiv. 29-33.

Whatever may have been the shortcomings of the Israelites, and however wanting in faith, they would not only have been justified in abandoning a protecting God who treated them in this manner; but they would most assuredly have done so, and have returned to the flesh-pots of Egypt, instead of wearily trudging about in the wilderness until they perished. It is only just to the memory of the Hebrews to say that there is nothing in the traditions they have left us to support the belief that they were ever treated, or even thought they were treated, in so scurvy a fashion. It was reserved for the ingenuity and the piety of a later age to make the Creator of Heaven and Earth play the part of a will-o'-the-wisp.

One of the results of modern Biblical criticism has been to establish the non-Mosaic authorship of the Pentateuch. There are many who are unconvinced, or who affect to be unconvinced, fearing to make a concession which might endanger the foundation upon which rests the claim of the Scriptures to be regarded as the Word of God. Others, more thoughtful or more honest, admit that the work of many hands in the creation, and the compilation of the Books of the Law, is too apparent to allow of contradiction; but urge that the fact of their not having been written by Moses is nevertheless reconcilable with the doctrine of Inspiration in the literal sense of that most elastic word Without expressing an opinion upon this knotty point, it will perhaps be admitted even by those who believe that God "caused all Holy Scriptures to be written for our learning," that men are not relieved from the responsibility of exercising the intelligence with which God has endowed them in order to ascertain how they came to be written, and what it is they mean.

And the fulfilment of this duty is necessary, not only for the attainment of historical truth, but in order to make amends to the Deity whose character is so habitually maligned by well-meaning men who quietly fold their hands, and sheltering themselves behind the statue of a "Divine historian," coolly throw the responsibility of their calumnies on the Being whom they traduce. Only one illustration out of many is supplied by the accepted story of the manner in which the Hebrews were led from Egypt to Canaan. It is possible the Deity may regard with indifference or contempt the imputations of cruelty, deceit, vacillation, and injustice so freely lavished upon Him by His "servants;" but still it would seem only prudent to endeavour to regard Him in a more favourable light. When a conscientious, painstaking man conceives himself compelled to convict the Almighty out of His own mouth of some astounding piece of rascality, he would do well to ask himself whether he has heard aright, or whether it is really the Deity who has spoken, instead of holding up the crime to the admiration of mankind, and thereby sapping the foundations upon which all religion and morality must ultimately rest. Men cannot play fast-and-loose with the principles of truth and justice without necessarily demoralising those who listen to them, and the pages of history furnish only too abundant illustrations of the evil consequences of presenting a cruel, vindictive, and treacherous Deity for the admiration and imitation of mankind. The sophism that God's justice is not as man's justice does not need refutation. Unless there be a common standing-ground for the judge and the accused at that final tribunal before which we must all appear, Divine Justice, so far as the human race is concerned, would be a mockery and a snare.

If we place for a moment on one side the assumption that the Books ascribed to Moses were written by him, and if we take into consideration the social condition of the Israelites on quitting Egypt, the then low standard of education and the ignorance of the art of alphabetical writing even in Egypt, we should be led to conclude that the events connected with the journeyings of the Israelites were not simultaneously recorded in a consecutive history. We should, in fact, anticipate that the recollection of the most notable events was preserved in traditions which in later times came to be committed to writing. In these traditions we should not expect to meet with more than general allusions to remarkable occurrences, we should look for no attempt at chronology, and we should not be surprised if, in the event of the progress of the expedition having undergone a protracted check, the non-eventful current of a nomadic existence supplied during that time no materials worthy of preservation in the recollections of the people.

But possessing as we do a knowledge of the diverse elements of which the Jewish nation came to be composed; the existence in early times of distinct tribes; the settlements effected on opposite sides of the Jordan; and, at a later period, the establishment of the two great and antagonistic nations of Judah and Israel; we should not be astonished if we found in the records handed down to us traditions apparently dissimilar, but really identical—stories told with more or less variation, and exhibiting differences, sometimes merely of dialect, which betrayed not necessarily different origins, but a diversity of channels through which they were transmitted.

But as, in process of time, these traditions were committed to writing—that duty being, in all probability, discharged by men of the priestly caste—we should expect the records to assume what may be termed a priestly tinge. Events of great importance, departures on momentous journeys, arrivals at places which became the scenes of memorable incidents, would be assumed to have happened on the occasion of particular festivals; and thus the history would become invested with an apparent minuteness and accuracy of detail which from its traditional origin it could never have possessed.

One other and pre-eminently striking feature might with confidence be looked for in these traditions. The great historical fact could never be forgotten by the Hebrew settlers on both sides of the Jordan—that they had quitted Egypt as slaves, and forced their way into their new home as conquerors; and it lay at the foundation of their religious belief that their protecting God had given them this land in compliance with a solemn covenant. Looking back therefore on the past from the standpoint of the present, there would arise an irresistible tendency to mould their traditions into shapes conformable with this belief. But there were many stern and unpalatable facts which no ingenuity could reconcile with the assumption that their God, in leading them out of Egypt, and conducting them into the land which He had sworn to give them, had not only taken the control of the expedition into His own hands, but had used His presumably invincible power to give effect to His designs. It was impossible to blink the fact that, notwithstanding the alleged daily visible interposition of the Deity, the Hebrews made neither a more rapid nor a more successful advance than might have been expected if God had left them to their own unaided resources. In truth, it was quite the other way. Less than a week would have sufficed for the liberated captives, after quitting Egypt, to enter the smiling vineyards and mellow cornfields of Philistia; and, as they are said to have marshalled six hundred thousand fighting men,* which, with women, children, young and old, must have raised the number of the emigrants to between two and three millions, the materials for a successful invasion were

---

* Exodus xii. 37.

ready at hand, even throwing out of account the direct cooperation of the Almighty. It was, however, only too notorious that the Israelites did not march directly towards the land of promise; and this came to be explained by the *naïve* assumption that God was apprehensive that, if brought into immediate conflict with their enemies, His chosen people would be terrified and return to Egypt, thereby frustrating His great design.* It was also a fact indelibly impressed upon the memory of the people, that the interval which elapsed between the Exodus from Egypt and the crossing of the Jordan was so considerable, that the generation which quitted Egypt died out before the land of promise was reached; and it became necessary to explain a circumstance so apparently irreconcilable with the design and with the antecedent conduct of the protecting Deity by assuming that the perverseness and querulousness and want of faith on the part of the liberated captives were so great, that the boon especially intended for them was, on reconsideration by the Deity, withheld and given to their children—not even Moses nor Aaron escaping this manifestation of the Divine displeasure. But as the precise length of this interval was forgotten, the non-existence at that period of any era to furnish a basis of computation, and the monotonous tenour of a nomadic life rendering it equally difficult and apparently useless to preserve a record of time, tradition availed itself of a general form of expression to fix the period passed in the wilderness, and called it forty years.†

---

* Exodus xiii. 17.

† Bredow, in his preface to "Syncellus," thus explains the use of the word "forty" in the Hebrew language, to express an unknown but considerable period : " Causam hujus modi loquendi, non in casu cui quidem in usu dicendi nimium arbitrium est, sed in etymologia reperire posse arbitror. Nam אַרְבָּעִים *arbaheem*, quadraginta et אַרְבָּה *arbeh*, multitudo ab eadem origine רַב *rab*, multum, deducenda esse videntur. Fortasse principio multitudinem non stricte finitam significant

But if the result of a careful examination of the records preserved to us of this portion of Jewish history is to establish that all the materials we possess are stamped with those characteristics which we would have looked for on the assumption that it was not written by Moses or a cotemporary, and was not a connected and consecutive narrative; if we find that it is made up of disjointed fragments bearing a strong family likeness; if we hear the same stories told, or the same events recorded, with only such trifling differences as might be expected in a later compilation of the traditions of a people composed of different elements; if throughout we notice the colouring which can alone be imparted when the past and not the present is depicted, and which is suggested by the wisdom which follows the event; if, in a word, we find that the whole considered in its entirety presents

---

paulatim vero nomen certi numeri factum est, quanquam significatione infinitæ multitudinis non omissa." Bredow cites a great many instances in which the number "forty" is employed in the Old Testament, but still more may be found by referring to Cruden's *Concordance*, or to *The Englishman's Hebrew and Chaldee Concordance* —a most valuable book. In some cases the indefinite sense in which the word is used is intrinsically apparent; as, for example, when the life of Moses is divided into three periods of forty years. He was forty when he fled from Egypt, eighty when he returned to liberate Israel, and a hundred-and-twenty when he died. Again, Israel is said to have enjoyed peace forty years after the Mesopotamian captivity (Judges iii. 11); forty years after the victory of Deborah (Judges v. 31); and forty years after the subjection of the Midianites (Judges viii. 28). In other instances, the number forty, if taken literally, is hopelessly inconsistent with admitted facts; as, *e.g.*, where Absalom is said to have come to David after "forty" years (2 Sam. xv. 7). A similar illustration to the last is afforded in the brief inscription on the Moabite stone, where it is said that "Omri, the king of Israel, took the land of Medeba, and the enemy occupied it in his days, and in the days of his son, forty years." But according to the Book of Kings, Omri reigned only twelve years, and Ahab his son twenty-two years (1 Kings xvi. 23–29); so that we have here a proof that the word was used as late as the ninth century B.C. in the Jordanic region in a broad and indefinite sense.—Ginsburg, *The Moabite Stone*, 1871.

such a confusion of times, events, and places (not to speak of legislation) as to render it, humanly speaking, impossible that any one could ever have intended it to furnish a consecutive or consistent narrative; then we should be compelled to conclude that the common assumption that it is such a narrative, and was the work of a single hand, is erroneous; and if we desired to gather a clear idea of the events of which it treated, we should equally be compelled to deal with its materials as we found them, and as we should unquestionably deal with them in any ordinary records.

It would be outside the scope of this essay to enter into a detailed explanation of the religion of the people, the course of whose journeyings we propose to follow from the Nile to the Jordan. But as it is difficult to form a correct idea of the general tone of the records we are about to examine without at least some broad conceptions upon this point, it may be convenient to offer the following observations.

The religion of the Hebrews, at the period of which we are about to treat, and for long centuries afterwards, was in one sense Polytheistic, in another sense Henotheistic, but in no sense Monotheistic. Polytheism is the belief in the existence of many gods. Henotheism is the worship of one god out of a number, whose existence and powers are nevertheless unquestioned. Monotheism is the belief in, and worship of, one God, to the absolute exclusion of any other deity.* The Israelites never dreamt of denying that other tribes or nations had their gods. It was part of their belief that each nation or people had its protecting god or gods, and that the obligations existing respectively between the protectors and the protected were matters exclusively of national concern. The flippancy with which Naomi, when

---

* See on these distinctions, Max Müller, *Chips from a German Workshop*, i. 353, 354.

returning from Moab to her home in Judah, tells her daughters-in-law to return to their people and their Gods, and the levity with which Ruth declares that she will never part from her mother-in-law—" Thy people shall be my people, and thy God my God,"*—only so strike us because the language of the two women is measured by our own standard of religious thought. But it never occurred to Naomi to suggest to her daughters-in-law to worship false gods, or what she considered to be such, or to Ruth to express her readiness to exchange her religion for the presumably different religion of Naomi. They only severally gave expression to the acknowledged principle that residence with a "people" necessarily involved the service of that people's Gods. The choice of a people carried with it the acceptance of the national deity. "Qui sentit commodum sentire debet et onus," was a maxim which lay at the very foundation of the Semitic religions. A stranger could not benefit by the prosperity of a people without serving the Gods to whom that prosperity was believed to be due.

The religious obligations of the Semitic tribes were carefully prescribed by covenants, and foremost amongst the obligations imposed upon the Israelites was the duty of worshipping no other God in the presence of the protecting deity.† It never occurred to the Israelites that their God

---

* Ruth i. 10–16. The same word *Eloah* (the poetic form of Elohim), is used by Naomi when speaking of the "Gods" of Moab, as by Ruth when declaring her willingness to accept the country and the "Gods" of Naomi's choice.

† The literal translation of the concluding words of the First Commandment, "Thou shalt have no other God before me," is "before my face." When an Israelite was, for example, in Moab, he was no longer "coram deo suo," and he could worship the Elohim of Moab without offence. Indeed, but for this qualification, which there is every reason to believe was recognised by all the Semitic tribes, commercial and social intercourse would have been impossible between

would punish the individuals of a different people because they did not serve him,* or because they worshipped their own deities, since from the Hebrew standpoint there was no obligation upon their part to do the one, or to abstain from the other.† But they did expect that when their own interests and those of others conflicted, their God would make his power felt in their behalf, and that when they made war on their neighbours in order to dispossess them of their territory, he would fight their battles for them, and discomfit their enemies.‡

---

members of different "nations." Care must be taken, however, not to confound the presence of an individual, or even of a number of individuals in a "strange" land, with the temporary presence of a "people" or "tribe" in such a land. The materiality of this distinction will become apparent in the course of this inquiry. David fully recognised this intimate connection between residence with a people and the worship of that people's Elohim, when appealing to Saul to readmit him to his friendship, and to permit him to return. "They have driven me out this day from abiding in the inheritance of Jahveh, saying, Go serve other Gods."—1 Sam. xxvi. 19.

* Jahveh, the protecting God of Israel, is frequently represented as being angry with his people; and in like manner, in the inscription on the Moabite Stone, Chemosh, the god of Moab, is stated to have been angry with his people, and to have punished them by handing them over to their enemies.—*The Moabite Stone*, Ginsburg. The feeling of anger which the Monotheist believes is excited in the breast of the Deity cy the wickedness of any of his creatures, was never attributed by the Israelites to their protecting God, save through their own default. Jahveh might wreak vengeance on a strange people, but not for offences committed against him, but to punish it for wrongs done to Israel.

† The Monotheistic gloss that the Cannanites, and the many other 'ites whom the Hebrews are credited with exterminating, were thus dealt with because they were idolaters and served other gods than the God of the Israelites, is without the shadow of a shade of support in the Hebrew records. More truly good, pious, and enlightened men have made shipwreck upon this rock than probably upon any other.

‡ This quaint belief, which was by no means illogical under a system of Henotheistic Polytheism, when the people who were despoiled and exterminated were not the people of the God who made his power felt at their expense, has been engrafted on Monotheism with very ludicrous results. When, for example, one Monotheistic people makes war on another with the object of "annexing" a portion of its territory, if

This belief in a special protecting deity had, however, an irresistible tendency to intensify the anthropomorphism which all men, more or less, manifest in their conceptions of the Almighty. The protecting God became clothed with the characteristics of humanity. He rejoiced with his people in their prosperity, he grieved with them in their adversity. He was by turns vindictive and indulgent, easily irritated, no less easily appeased. At times blind in his fury, at others amenable to the voice of reason and ready to admit the cogency of argument.* But the Israelites specially delighted to think of their deity as a warrior using his might to crush and annihilate their enemies, or exercising his power to modify or suspend the laws of Nature for their special benefit, or for the discomfiture of their adversaries. The belief that these laws could be thus suspended was at that period universal, but was specially rife amongst the nomadic tribes,† and the Israelites were far

---

the raid is successful, "Te Deums" are sung, and heartfelt thanks expressed to the Deity for His all-powerful aid ; but if unsuccessful, it is at once concluded that the Divine co-operation in the contemplated rapine and robbery was withheld on account of the antecedent backsliding of the aggressors. The "Te Deums" are then sung by the other side.

* Numbers xiv. 13-20.

† All travellers concur in stating that none are more credulous in this respect than the Bedouin tribes, and none more easily imposed on by an affected possession of magical powers. Palmer relates an anecdote which fairly illustrates the credulity of the denizens of the desert. "Taking advantage of this incident (the capture of a snake), we determined to amuse the Arabs and ourselves, by giving them an entertainment of magic; so after dinner we displayed the box containing the jar of spirit in which we had preserved the reptile, and opening it with great mystery and pomp, produced an excellent toy imitation of a serpent which we had purchased at Cremer's, and allowed it to curl and writhe in the light of a magnesium torch, to the huge delight of the Arabs, who did not for a moment suspect any deception. So convinced were they of the reality of the exhibition, that not one amongst them could be found hardy enough to carry the locked box

from claiming for their protecting deity exclusive powers in this respect. The effect of this condition of mind was to invest with the marvellous even the most natural occurrences. The unexpected discovery of a spring by the thirsty wayfarers on their journey from Egypt, was referred to the direct interposition of the deity; the supply of a novel article of food, only to be found in the desert, became a supernatural boon granted for their special behoof.

The belief in the unremitting personal intervention of the national God not only led to his glorification when the cause of the people triumphed, but to the comparative exaltation of those who had vainly sought to oppose it. Cheap victories do not redound to the glory of the conquerors, and it became necessary to show that the vanquished were foemen worthy of the victor's steel. There was nothing irreverent, according to a Hebrew's conceptions, in pitting his God against the powerful monarch of Egypt supported by his Gods; or in presuming that the former would be actuated not only by a love of his people, but by an intelligible *amour propre* in exerting himself to obtain the victory. And even now, although we know how it will end, it is impossible to read without interest the narrative of the Homeric struggle on the issue of which the liberation of the Hebrews is said to have depended. The respective Gods of Israel and of Egypt armed their champions with the necessary means of working miracles, and to the Pharaoh

---

back again into the tent. . . . . This piece of trifling gained us an immense reputation in the desert, and as we passed from tribe to tribe the story was repeated with various additions, until some time after we heard one Sheikh declaring to a knot of Azazimeh Arabs who had visited our camp, that Captain Drake was in the constant habit of watching serpents' holes, and that having enticed the inmate out of his concealment, he made a practice of placing it in his bosom and occasionally producing it for the pleasure of allowing it to bite his face."—*Desert of the Exodus*, p. 310.

was assigned the office of assessor in this singular trial of strength. For some time the issue was doubtful. The marvels of Moses and Aaron were successfully capped by those of the magicians;* and the Pharaoh, puzzled and bewildered, not unnaturally found himself unable to decide between the rival thaumaturgists. But this seeming equality of strength was only imagined in order that more abundant opportunities might be afforded to the God of the Hebrews of displaying his superiority, and again and again he was supposed to have used his influence to blind the perceptive faculties of the Pharaoh to the end, that still more astounding proofs should be given of his supernatural powers. In all this there was nothing to shock the religious or the moral sense of an ignorant and a barbarous people. It never occurred to them that feats which alone seemed wonderful when connected with human agency, became puerile and contemptible when associated with the Creator of Heaven and of Earth; for the simple reason that they looked on their God as only one of several Elohim.† It never struck them that it was equally inconsistent with divine and human justice that an innocent people should be made to suffer for

---

* Exodus vii. 11, 22; viii. 7, 18.

† אֱלֹהִים *Elohim*, the plural of אֱלוֹהַּ *Eloah*. The singular is but rarely used, and chiefly in poetry. It has been suggested that *Elohim*, Gods, is simply the " plural of majesty," and so came to be applied to the one God, whilst others find in its use an indication of the Trinity. The real explanation is to be found in the Polytheistic notions of the early Hebrews. When their religion became purified, it was presumed that whenever " Elohim" was applied to the God of Israel, the one God could alone have been meant. The word Elohim is constantly used to denote " the gods" of other nations; or, as they are termed, " false gods." The operations of Nature were various and many, and the causes which produced them were to the Semitic mind divine and awe-inspiring. Hence the word Elohim came to be applied to those divine and incomprehensible powers. The etymology of the word is very obscure, and has given rise to much speculation.

the obstinacy and perverseness of a monarch, that obstinacy and perverseness being actually occasioned by supernatural influence, against which it was naturally useless for the unfortunate ruler to contend. According to their ideas, when contrasting in later times their position in Canaan with the state of servitude to which their ancestors had been condemned in Egypt, it seemed indispensable that the departure from the latter country should have been brought about by the direct interposition of their protecting deity, and it was due to him to make his part in the transaction as striking as possible. It was necessary that the liberation should be effected with an outstretched arm, and that the Egyptian and other nations should be made to know that the God of the Hebrews was the most powerful of all Gods. They would have dismissed as hypercritical and irrelevant the objection that, despite these exhibitions of supernatural power, the Gods of Egypt were not deposed, nor did the religion of the people of that country sustain any perceptible change; and they would have been but little embarrassed had they been told that the Exodus with its many portents, ending in the destruction of an Egyptian king and an Egyptian army, had left behind it no traces in the annals of the Pharaohs.

In forming a general opinion of the religion of the Hebrews, for the purpose of rightly estimating the character of the traditions which will engage our attention, it is essential to bear in mind that this people had no belief in a future state of reward and punishment. Their God could reward them with length of days, by giving them the victory over their enemies, by making them prosperous, contented and happy; or he could punish them by cutting them off, by giving them over into the hands of their adversaries, by making them suffer through pestilence or famine, and by rendering their condition generally miserable or intolerable. He might also execute his vengeance through successive generations, " visiting the sins of the fathers upon the children." But his power in dealing with them, whether for good or evil, was limited by the grave. If the Hebrews were unable in time of tribulation to console themselves by anticipating the pleasures of Heaven, they were at all events spared all apprehensions of the pains of Hell.*

A creed in the sense in which that term is understood by Christian sects found no place in the religion of the Hebrew shepherds. They never doubted the existence of the Elohim any more than they doubted the various phenomena of Nature which they witnessed in constant operation before their eyes. They had not reached that point of intellectual development when philosophy becomes confounded with religion, when the reason must be subordinated to the will, when divine favour is thought to be alone attainable by professing to know the unknowable, and to be firmly convinced of what is beyond the range of human comprehension; when the involuntary operations of the mind may supply the fitting grounds for divine punishment, and when the highest efforts to fashion human conduct in supposed conformity with the will of the Almighty can merit no reward. The Hebrew nomads were only rude barbarians, who thought that if they observed their duties to their protecting God, he would recompense them for their fidelity.†

With these conceptions of the mode in which divine justice was administered, it is not difficult to understand how,

---

* It will be recollected that even at the commencement of the Christian era the Sadducees, one of whom was then High Priest, denied the immortality of the soul (Matt. xxii. 23). They took their stand on the law as laid down in the Pentateuch. The Pharisees, who held the opposite view, were compelled to rely upon "traditions" which they alleged had been handed down from the time of Moses.

† Exod. xxiii. 20, 26.

when the traditions of the migration came to be moulded into shape, they should have assumed their present complexion. The vicissitudes were numerous, victory did not always crown the arms of the divinely protected people, pestilence thinned their ranks. Their original plan of entering the land which their God had sworn to give to them was frustrated; they were compelled to travel many weary miles, to traverse or to skirt the territories of numerous tribes, some of which treated them as friends, whilst others dealt with them as foes; and finally, a considerable period elapsed before a new generation made its home amongst the hills which their fathers might have seen on the distant horizon when quitting for ever the land of Goshen. All this needed explanation, and it was found in the presumed misconduct of those who had been victoriously led out of Egypt. It was treasured up in the dim memories of those who entered Canaan, that the half-hearted captives were terrified when they found themselves compelled to accept the hardships of life in the desert. They clamoured to be led back to Egypt, where, if they were hard worked, they had at least a sufficiency to eat and drink. Their sanitary condition, when leaving Egypt, there is every reason to believe was far from good; and whatever may have been their numbers, the relative mortality was no doubt considerable. But whether they were hungry or thirsty, dying of pestilence, or harried by their enemies, the explanation from the Hebrew standpoint was equally simple and unanswerable—they must have deserved it. Their God would never have so treated them unless they had displeased him, and therefore they, and not he, were to blame because the land of promise was not entered with greater speed or under more favourable circumstances. By this train of reasoning the belief in the majesty and power of the protecting deity was maintained unimpaired.

What was the name by which the Hebrews knew the deity under whose protecting care they quitted Egypt and entered Canaan? This question will probably never be answered with certainty. The tradition has been recorded that the name by which the deity was known to the parent stock from which Israel sprang was different from that by which he was called in later times; and it is stated that this change was made when Moses received his mission.* This statement should, however, be received with caution. If the latest name of Israel's God was, as some contend, of Canaanitish extraction, it is still perfectly intelligible that it should be relegated back to the period when the people of Israel quitting Egypt first made their appearance in the field of history, on the eve of the covenant with their protecting God. It is certainly a significant fact that Amos, a prophet of the eighth century B.C., deliberately charged the Israelites with worshipping whilst in the wilderness a deity named Chiun, who has been identified with Saturn.† The question thus raised is, however, too wide and important to be discussed here, and involves other considerations besides a mere change of name. It may be convenient to take for granted that the name by which their deity was known to the Israelites whilst in the wilderness was Jahveh.

The pronunciation and vocalisation of the Tetragrammaton are lost in oblivion.‡ The pious aversion to uttering the sacred name, which seems to have arisen subsequent to the Babylonian captivity, and to have been based on a forced construction of the Third Commandment, became subsequently so intensified, that as it was unlawful for any one to

---

* Exod. vi. 3.   † Amos v. 26.
‡ יהוה J H V H. Every possible mode of expression has been suggested. The most common amongst Hebrew scholars, though its correctness cannot be established, is Jahveh. The initial letter being pronounced Y, as it should be, for example, in Jacob, Jeroboam, &c.

utter it, and as the early Hebrew text was wanting in the vowel points, the true pronunciation was irrecoverably lost. The Masorites attached to the name the vowel points of *Adonai* (Lord) in order that the latter name should be substituted by the reader in the synagogue. To this circumstance is due the modern reading—Jehovah. That this is not the true pronunciation—or, at least, that which was intended by the Masorites—is evident from the fact that when the Tetragrammaton and Adonai came in conjunction, the former received the vowel points of *Elohim* (God).

This undefinable dread of uttering the name of the Blessed One led, however, to very curious results; and had the effect, in no inconsiderable degree, of altering the complexion of the sacred history of Israel. The Greek translators in the third century B.C. acted in accordance with the spirit of the Jewish people; and, instead of transcribing the name, substituted the rendering κυρίος (Lord); and this example was followed in the Vulgate, and, in modern times, in the numerous translations of the Scriptures into the various languages of the world. To this course no objection could be offered, if the name conveyed in early times the same ideas as were attached to it when the liberated Jews returned from Babylon. But this was not the case.

It is profitless to speculate on the etymology of the Tetragrammaton. All we know for certain is, that it was the distinctive proper name which the Israelites gave to their deity, just as the Moabites gave to theirs the name of Chemosh.* No one will seriously contend that anything turns on the particular name by which the Almighty is known; and whatever may be their distinctions of creed—Christians, Jews, Mohammedans, and in fact all Monotheists—neces-

---

* Num. xxi. 29; Judges xi. 24.

sarily worship the same God, though under different names. It must, however, be apparent that if, for example, the Moabites, whose national god was Chemosh; whose religion, there is every reason to believe, closely resembled that of the Israelites;* and who presented the same mixture of Henotheism and Polytheism, had undergone the same process of purification as their Jewish kinsmen, and become Monotheists—Chemosh would probably have continued to be the name given by them to the One God, and it would have been as good a name as any other. But if, as in the case of the Israelites, the ideas of the Moabites respecting the national deity had become thus spiritualised and extended, it would have been manifestly productive of error, in dealing with the history of that nation, to give invariably to the name Chemosh that which was only its later and purer signification. But this is precisely the error which is committed in treating the earlier history of Israel, and to which the non-reproduction of the name of Israel's God has in a large degree contributed. The substitution of the words "Lord" and "God," which convey ideas now universally understood, naturally create the impression that, when the Israelites referred to their deity, or put words into his mouth, they regarded him in the same light. Such an impression is erroneous. In dealing with this portion of the history of Israel, we have only to do with Jahveh, the tutelary deity of that people.†

---

* Ruth i. 15, 16; Judges xi. 24. The Henotheistic principle, the exclusively national character with which the deity was invested, and the apparent similarity in other respects in the religions of the Semitic tribes in and around Palestine, are strongly shown in the Idyl of Ruth. Chemosh relatively to the Moabites is placed by Jephthah on the same footing as Jahveh to the Israelites.—Judges xi. 24.

† A further illustration is afforded by a legend which attached to a sacred stone that stood on the right bank of Jordan, called the stone of Bohan Ben Reuben. It was said to have been placed there by the

It would also be beyond the scope of this treatise to seek to determine the precise times when the several traditions bearing upon that portion of the history of Israel which is about to engage our attention were committed to writing, and were put together in the form in which we now see them in the Books of Exodus and Numbers. We should be careful, however, not to confound their commission to writing with their compilation. The former took place at various periods after the art of writing was acquired by the settlers in Canaan. The compilation of the scattered records was probably effected at Babylon, from which place Ezra returned with the Book of the Law in his hand.* It is sufficient to remark that the compilation took place long after much in the early traditions had become unintelligible. It would seem as if the compiler had before him a mass of documents which he felt himself obliged to turn to account. Some of these related to current history, others to legislation; some furnished comparatively later glosses on early incidents and usages; others gave conflicting versions of the same events. But the compiler, whether from veneration for his materials, or want of critical discernment, or unacquaintance with the early history of his people, evidently felt himself debarred from exercising the right of selection, and with an ostentatious disregard for continuity mingled them in an extremely arbitrary fashion. Again and again is the thread of the narrative with which he happens to be

---

Trans-Jordanic tribes on their return from the invasion of Canaan, lest in aftertimes the settlers in the Cis-Jordanic regions might say that those who dwelt on the opposite side of the river had nothing to do with Jahveh, God of Israel—"For Jahveh hath made Jordan a border between us and you, ye children of Reuben and children of Gad; ye have no part in Jahveh."—Jos. xxii, 24, 25.

* Ezra vii. 14. Rabbinical tradition ascribes to Ezra the compilation of the Old Testament, and it is said that he performed the difficult task under the inspiration of God.

dealing interrupted in order to wedge in some fragment of legislation, whilst elsewhere, having before him two different records of the same event, he sets them both down, leaving to his readers to accept both, or possibly to reject either. Notwithstanding the confusion which such a course of procedure necessarily tended to create, the compiler is entitled to the thanks of posterity for having adopted it. Instead of one we have several authorities in support of the events referred to, and in what are termed "undesigned coincidences" we acquire corroborative evidence of statements which would otherwise rest on the testimony of a single witness.

We must not suppose, however, that we have all, or even approximately all, the materials which originally existed for constructing this portion of the history of Israel. The prophetic writings are replete with references to the past, for whose confirmation we look in vain in the Pentateuch. When, for example, Amos asks the question,[*] "Have ye offered unto me sacrifices and offerings in the wilderness forty years, O House of Israel?" and then adds, "But ye have borne the tabernacle of your Moloch and Chiun your images, the star of your god, which ye made to yourselves;" it is evident that in the eighth century B.C. much was known of the religious usages of the Israelites when on their way from Egypt to Canaan which was subsequently forgotten, or over which it was deemed expedient to draw a veil. Many of the early traditions were possibly lost, or with succeeding years received accretions which it became difficult to detach from the original nuclei, or may have become so distorted

---

[*] Amos v. 25, 26. A vast amount of ingenuity has been expended, mainly by German and Dutch biblical critics, on the rendering and interpretation of this passage. Among the latter, Tiele has treated the subject very exhaustively in his *Vergelijkende Geschiedenis*, p. 539 *et seq*. See also the authorities he refers to. Kuenen treats it with his usual ability in his *Religion of Israel*, i. 265, 266. Goldziher, *Mythology among the Hebrews*, p. 220, 221.

as to lead to their ultimate rejection. Reference is made in an early record to the "Book of the Wars of Jahveh,"* which doubtless contained much that has not been preserved, and which would have thrown considerable light on the early history of the Israelites and their kindred tribes. In fact, though we possess much more than we could have hoped for if the compiler had been more discriminating, still we possess far less than is requisite in order to draw a complete picture of the Israelites during the period immediately preceding their settlement in Canaan.

Before addressing ourselves to our task, a few words of caution may not be out of place. Those who believe themselves in a position to correct error, and to shake long-established convictions, whether in respect to things great or small, are pre-eminently exposed to the danger of deceiving themselves and thereby deceiving others. They are unconsciously tempted to distort facts, and to strain conclusions in support of their views. The feeling that to avoid being dull they must keep out of the beaten track operates as a never-ceasing temptation to furnish continual surprises. They may wish to act honestly ; but whenever an awkward obstacle presents itself on their path, it requires an effort to carry out their good intentions, and that effort is not always crowned with success. The attainment of truth is their avowed object, but they are irresistibly led to regard "truth" and the conclusions they seek to establish, as identical; and keeping before their eyes only the goal towards which they are hastening, if they find their progress barred, they do not hesitate to walk round the obstacle they are bound to remove, if no other way is open to them of

---

* Num. xxi. 14. It may be remarked that the latter portion of the verse is very incorrectly translated in the Authorized Version. There is no reference whatever to the Red Sea.

attaining the prize which they regard as rightfully their own.

It will therefore be expedient for those who follow such an inquiry as the present, to exercise unflagging vigilance; to err rather on the side of distrust than of confidence; to accept no conclusions that are not borne out by evidence; to view with suspicion inferences which are strained or opposed to surrounding probabilities; and to test, as far as is possible, the strength of each separate link, with profound indifference whether the result may be the snapping of the entire chain. In other words, let us endeavour to attain truth, whatever form that truth may assume, exclusively for its own sake.

CHAPTER I.

THAT a tribe of Semitic descent and nomadic habits was enabled to exchange a state of servitude in Egypt for the freedom of the desert, between the fourteenth and seventeenth centuries before the Christian era, may be regarded as a historical fact. It is true that Egyptologists have hitherto failed to discover, either on sculptured stone or written papyrus, any mention of this occurrence; but although this circumstance may tend to confirm our doubts respecting the extraordinary circumstances under which the Exodus is alleged to have taken place, it does not militate against the actual happening of an event which from an Egyptian point of view would have been regarded of such trivial importance, and so little deserving of record, as the escape or liberation of a number of slaves.

Josephus, in his well-known vindication of the antiquity of his people, cites an Egyptian historian as a witness that the Jews quitted Egypt under the leadership of Moses. Manetho, who lived in the third century before the Christian era, wrote a history of the Egyptians, which has long since perished, and is only known to us by a few scattered fragments preserved in the writings of others, who either at first or second hand made quotations from his work.* According to the account given by Manetho, Egypt was for upwards of five hundred years subject to the rule of some shepherd

---

* A list of the Egyptian dynasties taken from Manetho appears in the Epitome of Africanus in "Syncellus," and is referred to by Eusebius. The fragments respecting the shepherd kings and the Exodus are given in Josephus, *Contra Apion.*

tribes, at the end of which time the kings of Thebais and other places in Egypt revolted, and the rule of the Hyksos, or shepherd kings, was overthrown. The remnant of the shepherds thereupon withdrew to a place named Avaris, which contained an area of ten thousand acres, and surrounded it by a high and strong wall. Avaris was then besieged by King Thmosis, but unsuccessfully, and thereupon the besiegers and besieged came to terms. The conditions were that the shepherds should leave Egypt, and be permitted to proceed unharmed in whatever direction they pleased. In accordance with this arrangement, the shepherds, "not fewer in number than two hundred and forty thousand, departed, with their families and effects, and took their journey from Egypt through the wilderness for Syria; but being in fear of the Assyrians, who had then the dominion over Asia, they built a city in that country now known as Judæa, and that large enough to contain this great number of men, and called it Jerusalem."*

From this passage Josephus concluded that the Israelites were descended from the Hyksos, and that at one period their ancestors were the masters of Egypt. The conclusion, however gratifying to the vanity of the Jewish historian, and calculated to impose on those who were unacquainted with the traditions of the people of Israel must, however, be discarded as groundless. If the Israelites had been the masters and not the slaves of the Egyptians, they would have preserved in their traditions the memory of so glorious a period in their national history, and could never have looked back on their sojourn in Egypt as a period of intolerable servitude. They would also have taken with them to Canaan the religion which we know was that of the Egyptians; or, if their own religion differed in any important

---

* Josephus, *Contra Apion*, i. 14.

respects from it, they must have left behind them in Egypt some vestige of their creed and ritual.

Josephus, who entertains no doubt that this account was taken by Manetho from the sacred records of the Egyptians, and therefore eminently reliable, also gives us another version of the Exodus from the same author, which, however, he rejects as based on mere rumours and reports, and "no better than incredible fables."

According to this narrative, Amenophis, who reigned some four centuries subsequent to the expulsion of the Hyksos, was desirous of seeing the gods, and was informed by a priest that he might do so if he removed all leprous and unclean persons out of Egypt. He proceeded to carry this injunction into effect, and caused some eighty thousand of these people to be removed to the quarries on the east bank of the Nile. Some priests were, however, amongst them, and their ill-treatment and the indignity passed upon them angered the gods. The king subsequently allowed the eighty thousand unclean persons to dwell in the city of Avaris, and there they chose for their leader one of the priests of Heliopolis named Osarsiph, who made laws for them in opposition to the usages of the Egyptians. He then incited them to revolt, and having made an alliance with the Hyksos in Canaan, he overran Egypt and drove Amenophis with his army into Ethiopia. At the end of thirteen years Amenophis returned, and the lepers with their allies were routed and pursued to the confines of Syria. Manetho adds that the priest, Osarsiph, changed his name, and was called Moses.*

Josephus is extremely indignant with Manetho for giving such an absurd story a place in history, and proceeds to demonstrate that the historian "trifles and tells arrant lies."

---

* Josephus, *Contra Apion*, i. 26.

Posterity is, however, thankful to Josephus for having preserved the fiction he contemned, and has detected in it a closer resemblance to the Jewish tradition than that discovered by the Jewish historian in the narrative of the overthrow and departure of the Hyksos.

Manetho was not exempt from the failings of other historians, and, in the absence of any information respecting the sources from which he derived his facts, we must be careful lest we credit him with a knowledge which he did not possess. He lived at the time when the Pentateuch was translated into Greek, and may have been personally acquainted with some of those to whom Ptolemy entrusted this important and difficult task. However that may be, the long-established intercourse between Egypt and Judæa afforded abundant opportunities to the Egyptian historian for learning that the Jews believed that they had quitted Egypt as slaves; and, under the leadership of Moses, had crossed the desert, and after many vicissitudes had penetrated Canaan. Manetho found nothing in the Egyptian records to corroborate the Jewish version of the circumstances under which the Exodus took place; for if he had done so, and had related it, we may feel confident Josephus would have eagerly referred to it; but he doubtless did find a statement respecting the removal of the unclean persons to the right bank of the Nile; their employment at servile work; their election of a chief, a priest of Heliopolis, named Osarsiph; their revolt, and their subsequent departure across the desert. From these data Manetho would conclude that the Osarsiph of the Egyptian records was the Moses of the Pentateuch, and being as desirous of finding a corroboration of the Egyptian materials of his history in the records of a neighbouring nation as Josephus was of strengthening the Jewish statement of the departure from Egypt by an appeal to Manetho, he not improbably set down as a fact what was after all but his own conjecture. And the same objection would equally apply to the statement that Osarsiph made laws for the rebels which were opposed to the usages of the Egyptians. As the Egyptians regarded all others than themselves as unclean, it must not be concluded that the leprous and unclean persons whose removal was ordered by Amenophis were all actually diseased. If they were members of a Bedouin tribe which had settled in Egypt they would have come within this opprobrious designation.*

If we have here the Egyptian version of the Exodus, it must be admitted that in the main there are some striking points of similarity to the Jewish account. The strangers, according to the former, are placed on the eastern bank of the Nile, and are employed as slaves. The gods are indignant because some priests are amongst them who are driven across the river and compelled to work in the quarries. A priest of Heliopolis incites them to revolt, becomes their leader, and secures their independence. He forms an alliance with the shepherds who had been driven out of Egypt centuries before; with the aid of these allies he overruns Egypt, holds possession of it for thirteen years; but ultimately the rebels, together with the shepherds, are driven forth into the desert. In the Jewish account the Israelites are kept in slavery on the eastern frontier. Moses becomes their leader, and according to a Jewish tradition preserved in the speech attributed to Stephen, he "was educated in all the wisdom of the Egyptians."† The anger of Jahveh is manifested in consequence of the treatment to which the Israelites are subjected, and under Moses they revolt against the Egyptian authority, whilst in the connection between Moses and Jethro,‡ and the assistance received by

---

† Acts vii. 22.   * Gen. xliii. 32; xlvi. 34.
‡ Exod. ii. 18; iii. 1; iv. 18; Judges i. 16.

the Israelites from the tribe of which he was the sheikh, we detect indications of an alliance between the revolted Israelites and a nomadic tribe which Manetho confounds with the Hyksos or shepherds, to whom he incorrectly attributes some centuries previously the building of Jerusalem. There is nothing in the Jewish tradition to support the statement that Osarsiph, or Moses, together with his followers and allies, overthrew the established government and ruled Egypt for several years. In respect to this discrepancy, we are inclined to think that Manetho confounded two different traditions of what was probably a single event—namely, the connection of the Hyksos with the city of Avaris; and he attributed to the insurgents under Osarsiph an achievement which in earlier times marked the conclusion of the rule of the shepherd kings.

But although the testimony given by Manetho in the second fragment preserved by Josephus possesses a certain value, our belief in the Exodus of the Israelites from Egypt as a historical fact must rest chiefly on the concurrent testimony of Jewish historians and prophets that such an event took place. The memory of the occurrence was preserved in the traditions of the people of Israel, and it is impossible to suppose that such a belief could ever have been so generally established if it did not rest on a substratum of fact. That the tribe which ultimately came to be regarded as the parent stock of the Jewish nation should have fallen into subjection to the Egyptians, to whom, by the vicissitudes of a nomadic existence, it had been driven to apply for food, was not an improbable contingency. That it should have succeeded in recovering its liberty is also intelligible, without supposing that the laws of Nature were completely subverted, and that the Egyptian people were one and all most severely punished by the Almighty because their king exercised what no one at that day would have dreamt of denying to be his legitimate right over the subject people.

What was the date of the Exodus, and what was the length of the sojourn of the children of Israel in Egypt, are questions on whose solution a vast amount of ingenuity has been expended, but with the most conflicting results. It is doubtful if either of these points will ever be satisfactorily settled; but, at all events, pending the results of further researches in Egypt, we must content ourselves with accepting such conclusions as recommend themselves by their probability.

Nearly all the authorities concur in assigning the foundation of Solomon's Temple to the latter portion of the eleventh century before our era. Hales places it as early as 1027 B.C.; Usher at 1012; and Bunsen and others at 1004. It is probable that these dates are approximately correct. The variance between the extremes is less than a quarter of a century. It is, however, stated that Solomon began to build the Temple in the 480th year after the Israelites quitted Egypt;* and, if this statement could be relied upon, we should have no difficulty in concluding that the Exodus took place, in round numbers, about 1500 B.C. For many reasons, however, partly drawn from the Old Testament and partly from other sources, this estimate of the interval between the Exodus and the building of the Temple must be rejected.†

The variance in the dates assigned to the Exodus by different authorities is very considerable. Some place it as

---

* 1 Kings vi. 1. In the LXX. version it is the 440th year.

† Kuenen justly calls attention to the suspicion which attaches to the round number 480 = 40 × 12. *R. I.* 1.118. There is no evidence in the Old Testament records that in the reign of Solomon the Jews possessed the means of calculating the time which had elapsed since the Exodus. For the purposes of founding an era some starting-point, however

early as the middle of the seventeenth century B.C.; whilst others maintain that it took place as late as the close of the fourteenth. Those who follow Usher in accepting the authority of 1 Kings vi. 1, conclude that the Exodus occurred in the commencement of the fifteenth century; whilst others, as the result of independent calculations, or of inferences drawn from Egyptian records and a supposed identification of the particular Pharaoh in whose reign the Israelites quitted Egypt, arrive at dates varying to the extent we have described.

After duly weighing all the authorities, the balance of probability seems to incline in favour of the date assigned by Bunsen, Lepsius, and others—namely, *circa* 1320 B.C. This conclusion rests in no small degree on the identification of the King Amenophis (so named in the list of Manetho) with Mineptah II., a Pharaoh of the nineteenth dynasty. This Mineptah, of whose existence independent evidence has been brought to light by Egyptologists, succeeded Rameses or Ramses II., the successor of Seti, the first king of the nineteenth dynasty. Mention is made of the Israelites having built the cities of Pithom and Ramses;[*] and, although evidence of the existence of these cities in the time of Seti is supposed to have been discovered in papyri, still it is thought that it was under Ramses Miamum or Ramses II., successor of Seti, that the oppression of the Israelites reached its greatest height; and that it was in the

---

arbitrary, must be fixed on. The Greeks counted from the commencement of the Olympic Games; the Romans from the building of their city. We reckon from the birth of Christ; the Mohammedans from the flight of the Prophet from Mecca. The Exodus would have supplied a very suitable commencement to a Jewish era, but unfortunately, except in this solitary instance (1 Kings vi. 1), it is never so employed in Jewish history, and this fact is fatal to the supposition that it was treated as such in Solomon's time.

* Exod. i. 11.

reign of Mineptah II., the successor of Ramses II., that the
Exodus took place. This Mineptah is believed to have lived
in the latter half of the fourteenth century. The Exodus is
accordingly placed, by those who accept these dates, near
the year 1320 B.C.*

The length of the sojourn of the Israelites in Egypt is equally
a matter of speculation. If we turn to the Old Testament
records the accounts are hopelessly irreconcilable. In the
Hebrew text it is stated that "the sojourning of the children
of Israel who dwelt in Egypt was four hundred and thirty
years."† In the Septuagint this passage is rendered "the
sojourn of the children of Israel that they sojourned
in Egypt and in the land of Canaan was four hundred
and thirty years." In the Samaritan version it runs,
"the sojourn of the children of Israel and their fathers
that they sojourned in the land of Canaan and in the
land of Egypt was four hundred and thirty years."‡ Elsewhere we find within the limits of a single chapter two
statements respecting the length of the sojourn which are
incompatible. In the narrative of the covenant made
between Jahveh and Abraham, the former is represented as
saying, "Know of a surety that thy seed shall be a stranger
in a land which is not theirs, and shall serve them, and they
shall afflict them four hundred years . . . . but in the fourth
generation they shall come hither again."§ Here the period

---

* Brugsch Bey places the accession of Mineptah II., the supposed
Pharaoh of the Exodus, in 1300 B.C., and his death in 1266; but he
admits that even proximate accuracy is unattainable in chronology at
this period. It is merely the result of a broad system of calculation,
which apparently throws forward the reign of Mineptah II. into the
thirteenth century.—*Egypt under the Pharaohs*, i. 37.

† Exod. xii. 40.

‡ St. Paul adopts the latter view when he fixes the period between
the covenant and the promulgation of the Law at 430 years (Gal.
iii. 17).

§ Gen. xv. 13-16.

of the servitude is fixed at four hundred years; but if this be correct, the number of generations must have been much in excess of four. If we endeavour to solve the difficulty by using the data supplied respecting the ages of the patriarchs, we arrive at the singular conclusion that the length of the sojourn in Egypt was precisely the half of 430 years. Abraham was 75 years old when he quitted Haran,* and 100 when Isaac was born;† Isaac was 60 at the birth of Jacob,‡ and the latter was 130 years of age at the time of his presentation to Pharaoh.§ From the departure of Abraham from Haran to the arrival of Jacob's family in Egypt was consequently 215 years (25 + 60 + 130),‖ and this would leave 215 years for the sojourn in Egypt. This is, however, irreconcilable with the statement in Gen. xv. 13; whilst, on the other hand, if we accept Gen. xv. 16, which states that the Israelites quitted Egypt in the fourth generation, it is impossible to believe that in so short a period the family of Jacob could have multiplied into the immense host (estimated at two millions and a half) which under the guidance of Moses quitted Egypt.¶

Except from a historical point of view the question is of but little importance, and perhaps the wisest course would be to confess our ignorance of the period which elapsed between the settlement of the parent stock of Israel in Egypt, and the recovery of its freedom, and temporary resumption of a nomadic life. It is extremely doubtful whether even by Moses or his followers the

---

* Gen. xii. 4. † xxi. 5. ‡ xxv. 26. § xlvii. 9.
‖ The presumption which would arise in favour of the accuracy of 430 not being a round number, is, as Kuenen points out, shaken by this coincidence, *R. I.* i. 162. See Bunsen, *Egypt's Place in History*. i. 180; Lepsius, *Chron. der Egypter*.
¶ The Bishop of Natal has dealt with this and many other kindred points in his invaluable work on the Pentateuch.

precise length of the sojourn could have been determined.

The settlement on the eastern frontier of Egypt of a portion of the tribes which found their way westward across the desert, was probably gradual. The vicissitudes incidental to nomadic existence frequently compelled the wandering shepherds to seek food from the sedentary population of Egypt, and it will not surprise us to find that they purchased existence at the price of freedom. They did not willingly sell themselves into slavery, but circumstances compelled them to accept a condition of things which had a tendency to render them dependent. They were compelled to give some equivalent for the food of which they stood in need.* Temporary assistance they might secure by bartering their cattle for corn, and the tribes might once more return to enjoy the freedom and encounter the perils inseparable from life in the wilderness. Contact with an agricultural population would, however, foster a desire to settle in their vicinity, and thus it happened that some of the nomads took up their abode in the districts bordering on the delta of the Nile.† In the beginning their temporary settlements might

---

* The nomads were known to the Egyptians by the generic name Shasu. They were the sons of the desert, the Bedouins, the "shepherds." "The land of Edom," writes Brugsch Bey, "and the neighbouring hill country was the home of the principal races of the Shasu, which, in the fifteenth and, sixteenth centuries before our era, left their mountains to fall upon Egypt, with weapons in their hands, or in a friendly manner followed by their flocks and herds to beg sustenance for themselves and for their cattle, and to seek an entrance into the rich pastures of the land of Succoth" (the east of the Delta).—*Egypt under the Pharaohs*, i. 216.

† This district is called the land of Goshen. Much pains have been expended on determining its precise locality, but unsuccessfully, for the simple reason that it had no determinate limits. I am inclined to think it was a descriptive and not a distinctive name. It is observable that the border land on the confines of Egypt, and the border land on the southern frontier of Palestine, are equally termed "Goshen."

be effected without any loss of independence. The tents could be struck at a moment's notice, and the tribe might regain the open desert. But in process of time, some attracted by the comforts of a settled existence would attach themselves more and more closely, and more and more permanently, to the sedentary population, and, abandoning their nomadic life, would take up a position necessarily involving political dependence. From political dependence to slavery was, however, three thousand years ago, but a step, and those who exchanged the desert for the land of Goshen frequently purchased with their liberty the greater security they acquired against perishing of famine.

In the narrative of Joseph and his brethren we have the traditional view of the manner in which this process was effected on the north-eastern frontier of Egypt.[*] Famine compels some of the nomads to seek food in Egypt. They settle in the neutral zone which separates the desert from

---

(For the former see Gen. xlv. 10; xlvi. 28, 34; xlvii. 27; l. 8; Exod. ix. 26. For the latter, Jos. x. 41; xi. 16). The name may be derived from גֶּשֶׁם *Geshem*—violent rain. The land of Goshen would then, from a Bedouin's point of view, mean the land where, as in the region about Hebron, rain, or in the vicinity of the Nile, inundations furnished an abundant supply of water for vegetable life, when the adjoining deserts were parched with drought. The LXX. render the name Γεσέμ.

[*] We possess a curious record of the reign of Mineptah II., the supposed Pharaoh of the Exodus, which furnishes a striking proof of the manner in which the nomads sought for and obtained, in time of famine, sustenance for themselves and their flocks. "Another matter for the satisfaction of my master's heart. We have carried into effect the passage of the tribes of the Shasu, from the land of Aduma (Edom), through the fortress of Mineptah Hotephima, which is situated in Thuku, to the lakes of the city Pi-tum of Mineptah Hotephima, which are situated in the land of Thuku, in order to feed themselves and their herds on the possessions of Pharaoh, who is there a beneficent sun for all peoples." This is the report of a high Egyptian official, and but for its late date might have been the notification by Joseph of the reception of his famine-stricken kinsmen. "Pap. Anastasi," vi. pp. 4, 5, translated by Brugsch Bey, *Egypt*, ii. 127.

Egypt proper, and their example is subsequently imitated by others. In course of time the settlers gravitate towards the country on whose borders they dwell, and being unable to claim the political privileges (such as they were) of the Egyptians they sink into a state of servitude. The colossal works of the Pharaohs were effected by forced labour, of which the former nomads were compelled to contribute a considerable share. The connection with the desert tribes was never, however, totally discontinued. The settlers never forgot what their fathers once had been. The arrival from time to time of some great Sheikh with his followers made them long to recover the freedom they had bartered away, whilst some whose position was superior to that of the rest, whose liberty of action was uninterfered with, or again, some who succeeded in effecting their escape, formed relations with the members of the desert tribes. The story of the flight of Moses to Midian, and his marriage with the daughter of Reuel, or as he is also called Jethro,[*] may illustrate the link of connection maintained during the sojourn in Egypt between the nomads who had lost their liberty and their more fortunate kinsmen who continued to lead a pastoral life.

It is needless to point out that the narrative of Jacob's having sent ten of his sons from Canaan to Egypt to purchase corn is unhistorical.[†] If there had been a famine in Canaan whilst there was "plenty" in Egypt, it would have been absurd for ten persons to have undertaken the long and difficult journey between the two countries in order to bring back with them sufficient food for a family numbering about half a hundred individuals. When famine strikes a country it is not by such means that a few households can hope to preserve existence. The tradition in its earliest form

---

[*] Exod. ii. 15-21.   [†] Gen. xlii.

represented the nomads as seeking sustenance in Egypt; but when in later times Jacob and his children came to be fixed upon as the particular individuals who went there, it became necessary, inasmuch as Jacob was described as a settler in Canaan, to explain the migration of the entire family on the ground that there was a famine in that country. The narrative even in its present form is not, however, without value. It proves the impersonal character of the patriarch, and the historical inaccuracy of the statement that he or the nomadic tribes he may be taken to represent had ever effected a settlement in Canaan.*

In the history of Joseph in his character of a high Egyptian official, some incidents are mentioned which appear to indicate the manner in which the nomadic settlers on the frontier lost their liberty. If we accepted the narrative as literally accurate, Joseph, whether he was of Egyptian or Hebrew origin, would be justly open to condemnation as probably the most oppressive and iniquitous Minister that ever held the reins of government, and that is saying a great deal. According to the story, Joseph was one of the sons of Jacob, and had been sold into slavery in Egypt.† Whilst in prison on an unjust charge of soliciting the chastity of his master's wife, he interpreted correctly the dreams of two of his fellow-prisoners.‡ Some time afterwards Pharaoh had a remarkable dream, which his wise men and magicians were unable to solve; and Joseph having been sent for explained it to the king as indicating that seven years of plenty in Egypt would be succeeded by seven years of famine.§ Pharaoh, to mark his gratitude

---

* See Gen. xlvii. 3, 4. On their introduction to Pharaoh, the sons of Jacob are represented as saying, "Thy servants are shepherds, both we and our fathers. For to sojourn in the land have we come, for thy servants have no pasture for their flocks." This could not have been true of Canaan, the "land flowing with milk and honey."

† Gen. xxxvii. 28.   ‡ Gen. xl.   § Gen. xli. 1–36.

for such valuable information, made Joseph ruler over the land of Egypt, with full authority to turn to the best account the years of plenty and make suitable provision for the years of famine.* Joseph did so, and during the former period established depôts of corn throughout the land. As soon, however, as the period of famine set in, he turned his precautionary measures to very singular account. The famine being very severe, both in Egypt and in Canaan, "Joseph gathered up all the money that was in the land of Egypt and in the land of Canaan;"† or, in other words, he sold corn to those who needed it. As soon as "money failed in Egypt and in Canaan," "all the Egyptians"‡ came to Joseph and again demanded bread. Joseph consented to supply them, provided they gave him their cattle, their herds, and their beasts of burden.§ The famished Egyptians consented to these terms, and thereby obtained food for another year. At the end of this time, they were again obliged to present themselves before Joseph, and confessing that their "lord" having obtained all their money and all their flocks, nothing was left to them but their bodies and their lands, offered to sell themselves into slavery in order to avoid starvation.‖ Joseph closed with their offer, he "bought all the land of Egypt for Pharaoh, for the Egyptians sold every man his field because the famine prevailed over them, so the land became Pharaoh's; and as for the people he removed them to cities from one end of the borders of Egypt even to the other end thereof."¶

It does not need the knowledge we possess of the political condition of the Egyptians at this period, to feel satisfied that so stupendous a crime was never committed. The govern-

---

* Gen. xli. 38-45. † Gen. xlvii. 14. ‡ Gen. xlvii. 15.
§ Gen. xlvii. 16, 17. ‖ Gen. xlvii. 18, 19. ¶ Gen. xlvii. 20, 21.

ment of the Pharaohs was no doubt despotic in the fullest sense of the term, but the despotism was tempered by a religion which was far from contemptible, and by a system of morals which now, after the lapse of more than three thousand years, commands admiration. A little reflection and a careful examination of the text will satisfy us that we have in this singular narrative the nucleus of the tradition preserved by the people of Israel, of the manner in which their ancestors who settled on the Egyptian frontier lost their liberty, and passed into that state of servitude which became seared into their memory during their entire national existence.

A people preserves its own traditions, but it does not, at least in early times, retain the memory of events which only concern other nations. This particular narrative, as it is now presented to us, is a chapter of Egyptian and not of Jewish history. This circumstance would, even if it stood alone, excite our suspicion. When, however, we look at the text we see on how slight a foundation rests the supposition that the transaction referred to was one between Joseph and the Egyptian people.

It is stated that there was famine not only in Egypt but in Canaan, and that Joseph gathered up all the money in both countries. The narrative then continues, that "when the money failed in the land of Egypt and in the land of Canaan, all the Egyptians came to Joseph and said, Give us bread!"* But to make the sentence complete and the story consistent, the passage should have run, "all the Egyptians and all the Canaanites," &c. As, however, it would have been absurd to allege that the Canaanites had sold themselves into slavery, all further reference to them is omitted, and we are left in ignorance how they continued to support a famine which the narrative leads us to believe

---

* Gen. xlvii. 15.

pressed as long and as severely on them as on the Egyptians.*

On exegetical grounds no less than on that of the intrinsic impossibility of any people, especially the Egyptians, parting with their possessions and their liberty, in order to acquire corn which already belonged to them, we must treat the expression, "all the Egyptians," as one which found its way into the narrative, in order to make the story chime with the redactor's views of what must have occurred. From his standpoint, Joseph, the Egyptian Viceroy, but the son of Jacob and the progenitor of the powerful tribes of Ephraim and Manasseh, gave everything to the members of his own family when they were driven to seek food in Egypt, but made the harshest terms with the people in whose land the corn which he doled out had been actually produced. It was thus that, according to his view, Joseph *must* have acted, and he consequently moulded the tradition into the shape in which it is now presented to us.

But if we read between the lines, it is not difficult to ascertain the form in which the tradition was originally handed down. A tribe of nomads was compelled to seek food in Egypt. It was obliged to part with its money and its flocks, in order to procure the means of subsistence. Having thus given up its property, it was unable or unwilling to return to the desert; and it cast longing eyes on the border-land separating Egypt from the wilderness, and entered into negotiations with the Egyptian Government for permission to settle there. The conditions were no doubt severe, but such as the famished Bedouins were obliged to accept. They were allowed to settle in Goshen on condition that they should not personally acquire an absolute owner-

---

* If the famine ceased in Canaan, the motive for the emigration of Jacob's family from that country vanished.

ship in the land alloted to them,* and they were furnished with seed to sow the land placed at their disposal, on the terms of paying to the State one-fifth of the increase.† It may also have been part of the contract that the settlers should contribute largely to the construction of those marvellous monuments, which even to-day reveal to us the Egypt of the Pharaohs.‡

Such were, we have no doubt, the circumstances under which the tribe from which the children of Israel claimed descent came to settle on the confines of Egypt, and subsequently to lose its liberty. The process may, perhaps, have been more gradual than is here supposed, but whether the time occupied was long or short, the nomads driven from their pastures by hunger settled in Goshen on conditions which very speedily rendered them so completely subject to the Government that they could be removed at pleasure from place to place,§ and it only needed a more than ordinarily oppressive sovereign to render their position so intolerable that starvation in the wilderness might seem preferable to existence prolonged under such hard conditions. That the Governor of Lower Egypt, to whom they were indebted for permission to settle on the borders, and who provided them with the seed with which to utilise their newly-acquired possessions, should have lived in their grateful remembrance is not surprising, nor need it astonish us that in time their benefactor came to be regarded as of a common origin with themselves. They could pay him no higher compliment than to suppose that he was one of the sons of Israel, sold into captivity when a child, but raised to supreme power in Egypt by one of those caprices of fortune not uncommon in Oriental life. But when this belief came

---

* Gen. xlvii. 20. The law prohibiting aliens from holding property is to be found in most codes down to the present century.
† Gen. xlvii. 23, 24.   ‡ Gen. xlvii. 25.   § Gen. xlvii. 21.

to be established, and the tradition came to be transmitted to the pages of history, the conduct of the Egyptian Governor needed harmonising with the assumed character and nationality of Jacob's favourite son. The conditions under which the famine-stricken Hebrews were admitted to the land of Goshen, the parting with their herds and the bartering away of their liberty, were transferred to an impossible contract between the Egyptian Viceroy and the Egyptian people; whilst Jacob and his sons and their families were represented as having gratuitously received " a possession in the land of Egypt, in the best of the land, in the land of Rameses, as Pharaoh had commanded."*

Of the length of time passed in Egypt there is in the traditions preserved to us no indication. The Hebrews retained no recollection of the name of the Pharaoh who ruled Egypt when they entered it, nor of the name of his successor who was compelled by mighty portents to allow them to depart. This circumstance in itself shows that we are now dealing with traditions which at the time when they were committed to writing had already become obscured by the mists of so many centuries, that it was even then impossible to determine who were the exact Pharaohs whose hospitality the Israelites had accepted, and whose yoke they had thrown off. We are told in general terms that "the children of Israel were fruitful and multiplied, and waxed exceeding mighty"† and that "there arose a new king over Egypt who knew not Joseph;"‡ and that, alarmed at the increase of the Israelites, he "made their lives bitter with hard bondage"§ and instructed the Hebrew midwives (there were but two) to destroy all the male children at their birth.|| We have here not tradition but

---

* Gen. xlvii. 11.
† Exod. i. 7.   ‡ Exod. i. 8.   § Exod. i. 14 || Exod. i. 15, 16.

the explanation of a change in the condition of the Israelites which would otherwise have been unaccountable, considering the favourable circumstances under which their settlement took place "in the best of the land, as Pharaoh had commanded."* Although, according to what seems to have been the early tradition, the Governor to whom the Israelites were so much indebted died in a condition of prosperity, and was buried in accordance with Egyptian usages,† it is said that "a new king arose who knew not Joseph,"‡ and, as it would seem, in Joseph's lifetime conceived and carried out the design of reducing the free Israelites to a state of bondage, with the somewhat singular object of checking their increase. But what is more remarkable still is, that the Israelites, though they had "waxed exceeding mighty, and the land was filled with them,"§ do not seem to have resented this harsh and unjust treatment; or, notwithstanding their numbers and the terror with which they inspired "the new king," to have struck a single blow to vindicate their independence. The intrinsic inconsistency and improbability of this account, and the absence of all mention of any protest on the part of the Israelites against so tyrannical and unjust an act, consequently lead us not only to reject this explanation of the commencement of Israel's servitude as unhistorical, but tend to strengthen our conclusion that the bondage commenced under the circumstances we have just noted. A people preserves a lively recollection of its wrongs, and the period and incidents of their bitter servitude in Egypt were never forgotten by the Israelites. Their traditions told centuries afterwards of the heavy burdens which were imposed upon them,‖ and even preserved the memory of the system under which their head

---

* Gen. xlvii. 11. † Gen. l. 26. ‡ Exod. i. 8.
§ Exod. i. 7. ‖ Exod. i. 14.

men were made personally responsible for the amount of work done by those placed under their control, and of the cruel treatment to which they were submitted by the Egyptian taskmasters.* But there is not the faintest indication of any sense of injustice in compelling a people, hospitably invited by one of the Pharaohs to settle in his territory, and presumably free, to fulfil the duties of slaves. Moses, the appointed messenger of Jahveh, is nowhere represented as denouncing to Pharaoh a course of conduct which in the guise in which it is now presented to us was equally treacherous and iniquitous ; and even when Pharaoh increases the burdens of the unfortunate Israelites, the protest uttered by their representatives is directed, not against their unjust bondage, but against being required to make in the same time as many bricks, with straw gathered by themselves, as they had previously done when that commodity was supplied to them by their taskmasters.†

---

* Exod. v. 14.   † Exod. v. 15-19.

CHAPTER II.

THE story of the servitude of the Hebrews in Egypt, and of the circumstances under which their liberation was effected, is told in the form of a tolerably continuous narrative in the Book of Exodus. Whatever may have been their original position in the land of Goshen, they came ultimately to be treated as slaves; and such was their condition at the period when they severed their connection with the Egyptian people. But, without examining this singular narrative in detail, it is easy to understand how in after-times, when they attributed their liberation to the supernatural intervention of their God, the natural though startling phenomena which were peculiar to Egypt came to be regarded as the means adopted by Jahveh to convince the Pharaoh of the expediency of letting them go. There was, however, one fact connected with their departure which was indelibly fixed on their memory—namely, that they were not simply permitted to leave Egypt, but were "thrust out"—expelled, without a moment's warning. This is recognised in the words attributed to Jahveh when instructing Moses to demand their liberation, and is confirmed in the description of the straits to which the Israelites were put in the preparation of food after they were ejected: "Now shalt thou see what I will do to Pharaoh; for with a strong hand shall he let them go, and with a strong hand shall he drive them out of his land."* And later, before the slaughter of the first-born:

---

* Exod. vi. 1.

"Jahveh said unto Moses, Yet will I bring one plague more upon Pharaoh and upon Egypt: afterwards he will let you go hence. When he shall let you go, he shall surely thrust you out hence altogether."* And, as the result of this final manifestation of the power of the God of the Hebrews, "the Egyptians were urgent upon the people that they might send them out of the land in haste;" and "they were thrust out of Egypt, and could not tarry; neither had they prepared for themselves any victual."†

If the Israelites were correct in their recollection of having been expelled from Egypt, we detect here a strong confirmation of the identity of the event mentioned by Manetho in connection with the lepers and unclean persons, with the Exodus of the Israelites; and this becomes still further strengthened by the evidence that leprosy was rife amongst the liberated captives. But although thrust out from Egypt, it was natural that the Israelites should, after their settlement in Canaan, regard the expulsion as an unqualified blessing; and, though their fathers looked back with longing eyes on the flesh-pots they were compelled to relinquish, they found it easy, not only to represent their expulsion as having been brought about by the direct intervention of their protecting deity, but to condemn their forefathers for having, even when perishing in the wilderness, regarded their deliverance as a questionable blessing. It may well have been that, owing to the prevalence of pestilence or other causes, the Pharaoh was led to believe that the Gods were angry; and, in compliance with the advice of his ministers or priests, banished the Israelites. This connection between their departure and the supposed displeasure of the Gods was preserved in the Hebrew traditions, and ultimately, by a very easy transition, the assumed

---

* Exod. xi. 1.   † Exod. xii. 33–39.

evidences of such displeasure came to be referred to the direct interposition of Jahveh.*

Of the various miracles declared to have been worked in connection with the Exodus, perhaps the safe conduct of the Israelites through the Red Sea, with the submersion of the Pharaoh and his army, was the most striking and the most effective. Strictly speaking, there are no degrees in the miraculous, since all acts must be equally easy to an omnipotent Being. But the crossing of the Red Sea under the circumstances stated possessed features which, if any lesson is to be deduced from a miracle, would, one might have supposed, have completely convinced not only the Israelites but the Egyptians that the God in whose name and by whose authority Moses acted, was the greatest of the Elohim. Not only was "the sea made dry land," but " the waters were a wall unto them (the Israelites) on their right hand and on their left."† But even more marvellous than the drying-up of the depths of the sea were the faith manifested by the Israelites in venturing into such a chasm, and the unreasoning confidence which induced the Egyptians to follow them along such an appalling route. Overweening reliance in their protecting deity was, however, by no means a characteristic of the

---

* Diodorus states, though on what authority we know not, that in ancient times a pestilence which raged in Egypt was attributed to the wrath of the gods, caused by the strange worship of the great number of aliens then in the land. The latter were thereupon expelled; some, amongst whom were Danaus and Cadmus, going to Greece, whilst the main body, led by Moses, went to Judæa, and colonised it. It is to be regretted that Diodorus makes no mention of the source from which he obtained this curious narrative. It was probably Egyptian. The bracketing of Danaus and Cadmus with Moses should not lead us to treat the whole story as worthless. It seems to contain a nucleus of truth (Diod. xl.). Elsewhere the Jews are represented as a despicable race expelled from Egypt, and hateful to the gods on account of their cutaneous diseases (Diod. xxxiv.).—Browne, *Ordo Sæclorum*, 584.

† Exod. xiv. 22.

Israelites, and one would have thought that if they had the faith to follow Moses into the midst of the Red Sea, they deserved a better fate than that of perishing in the wilderness.

The passage of the Red Sea is for the most part treated in one of two ways. It is accepted as a miracle, and this mode of treatment has at all events the merit of great simplicity, or it is regarded as an occurrence capable of being explained without any presumed interference with the known laws of Nature. Those who hold the latter view suggest that the Israelites may have passed round the head of the Gulf of Suez on the seashore, when the tide was exceptionally low, and that the pursuing Egyptians may have been overtaken by the returning tide. There are others, again, who, whilst admitting that the Israelties were pursued, and that the Egyptian army was overwhelmed, maintain that the scene of the occurrence was not the Gulf of Suez.

There is yet another point of view from which the alleged passage of the Red Sea by the Israelites and the destruction of the Egyptian army may be regarded. It is open to grave doubt whether in the traditions of the Exodus any mention was made of this marvellous occurrence.

It is impossible to read the 11th, 12th, and 13th chapters of Exodus, or at least those portions which relate to the departure from Egypt, without being struck by the fact that they wind up the narrative to which the preceding chapters are devoted. That narrative is the story of Israel's oppression in Egypt, and Israel's complete liberation by the hands of Jahveh. Repeated manifestations of the supernatural power of Israel's God having failed to make a suitable impression on the Pharaoh (Jahveh having designedly afflicted the monarch with incurable obduracy), the time at length arrived when it became necessary to bring the protracted conflict to a close. Accordingly, Jahveh is represented as addressing Moses in the language already quoted:

"Yet will I bring one more plague upon Pharaoh and upon Egypt, afterwards he will let you go hence; when he shall let you go he shall surely thrust you out hence altogether."* In compliance with the divine commands, Moses told the Pharaoh that at midnight Jahveh would pass through Egypt and slay the first-born of man and beast of the Egyptians and their flocks, whilst sparing the Israelites and their cattle; and that in consequence of this exhibition of the divine displeasure, the king's servants would entreat him together with the people who followed him to quit Egypt, and thereupon he would go forth.† The Pharaoh refused, however, to let the people go, in order that Jahveh's wonders might be multiplied, and consequently the threat was carried into execution the same night. The first-born were slain, and "Pharaoh rose up in the night, he and all his servants, and all the Egyptians." Moses and Aaron were sent for "by night," and ordered to go forth together with the children of Israel. "The Egyptians were urgent upon the people that they might send them out of the land in haste;" and "the people took their dough before it was leavened, their kneading troughs being bound up in their clothes upon their shoulders," "because they were thrust out of Egypt and could not tarry."‡ The Israelites having thus been driven out of Egypt without a moment's preparation, a retrospective view of their stay in the land which they had now finally quitted is not inaptly introduced. The language employed is very significant: "Now the sojourning of the children of Israel who dwelt in Egypt was four hundred and thirty years, and it came to pass at the end of the four hundred and thirty years, even the self-same day it came to pass, that all the hosts of Jahveh went forth from the land of Egypt.§ It is

---

* Exod. xi. 1.   † Exod. xi. 4-8.   ‡ Exod. xii. 29-39.
§ This is repeated in the last verse of the chapter.

a night to be much observed unto Jahveh for bringing them out from the land of Egypt. This is that night to be observed of all the children of Israel in their generations."* Then follow two interpolations, one referring to the institution of the passover, and the other to the dedication of the first-born ; but connecting those religious usages with the complete liberation of the Israelites. "And Moses said unto the people, Remember the day in which ye came out from Egypt, out of the house of bondage ; for by strength of hand Jahveh brought you out from the place. There shall no leavened bread be eaten ;"† and, in relation to the dedication of the first-born : "And it came to pass when Pharaoh would hardly let us go that Jahveh slew all the first-born in the land of Egypt, both the first-born of man and the first-born of beast. Therefore I sacrifice to Jahveh all that opens the matrix, being males, but all the first-born of my children I redeem."‡ The thread of the original record, thus broken, is not resumed till we come to verse 20,§ which tells us that "they took their journey from Succoth, and encamped in Etham, on the edge of the wilderness." But the narrator evidently thought that this was a fitting place in which to foreshadow the somewhat singular route which it was known that the Israelites took on their way from Egypt to their future home, and to record the miraculous conditions under which they were guided on their road. "And it came to pass, when Pharaoh had let the people go, that God,‖ led them not through the way of the land of the Philistines, although that was near; for God said, Lest peradventure the people repent when they see war, and they return to Egypt. But God led the people about

---

* Exod. xii. 40-42. † Exod. xiii. 3. ‡ Exod. xiii. 15.
§ Exod. xiii. 20, seems originally to have followed in succession Exod. xii. 39. ‖ *Literally* Elohim.

through the way of the wilderness of the Red Sea; and the children of Israel went up harnessed out of the land of Egypt."* "And Jahveh went before them by day in a pillar of a cloud, to lead them the way; and by night in a pillar of fire, to give them light; to go by day and night. He took not away the pillar of the cloud by day, nor the pillar of fire by night, from before the people."†

It is difficult to imagine that the people who held the tradition which came to be embodied in this form could have known anything of the deliverance of Israel from the power of Egypt at the Red Sea. The departure from Egypt is treated as an accomplished fact, and is unequivocally referred to as what is regarded as the final manifestation of Jahveh's power, the destruction of the first-born. Jahveh is represented as solemnly pledging himself to Moses that one more plague would be efficacious—nay, that it would be so efficacious that Pharaoh would not merely let the people go, but would thrust them out altogether; and it is then stated that, according to Jahveh's word, they were thrust out in the night time, and compelled to depart without time being allowed for any preparations for their journey, and that the night was to be much observed unto Jahveh, for bringing them out from the land of Egypt. The sojourning in Egypt is thus treated as a thing of the past, and is computed as having lasted four hundred and thirty years. "And it came to pass, at the end of the four hundred and thirty years, even the self-same day it came to pass, that all the hosts of Jahveh went out from the land of Egypt."‡ The departure from Egypt having taken place, or in the words of the record, "when Pharaoh had let the people go," the migration towards Canaan commenced. The indications here given of the route subsequently taken, and of the

---

* Exod. xiii. 17, 18. † Exod. xiii. 21. ‡ Exod. xii. 41.

visible interposition of Jahveh when guiding the people on their way, demand very attentive consideration.

When the settlement on both banks of the Jordan was effected, and it became an established belief that the protecting deity had liberated Israel from captivity in Egypt in order to lead that people into the land which had been promised to the seed of Abraham, it became necessary to account for the fact that a very circuitous route was taken by Jahveh in leading his people from Egypt to their destination. An explanation was supplied by the suggestion that the recently liberated slaves would have been terrified, if without any preparation they had been obliged to engage in war with the Philistines, and would have returned to Egypt. The narrator accordingly states, that when "Pharaoh had let the people go (that is, when they had quitted Egypt), God led them not (the past tense is used) through the way of the land of the Philistines, although that was near," for the reason stated, "but God led the people about (past tense) through the way of the wilderness of the Red Sea, and the children of Israel went up harnessed out of Egypt."*

It is universally assumed that this statement that "God led the people about through the way of the wilderness of the Red Sea," indicates that the Israelites were led into the region bordering on the Gulf of Suez. A closer examination of the passage will show this not to be the case.

According to one of the traditions transmitted to us, which will at a later period engage our more particular attention, the Israelites, terrified by the reports brought to them by the spies whom they sent forth to explore the promised land, refused to adopt Caleb's counsel and "go up" against the inhabitants. Jahveh was very angry in con-

---

* Exod. xiii. 17, 18.

sequence of this disobedience, and threatened to "smite them with pestilence, and disinherit them." He was, however, dissuaded by Moses from carrying his threat into effect, and apparently abandoning his intention of leading the people into Caanan by the route followed by the spies, gave the order to Moses, "To-morrow turn you, and get you into the wilderness by the way of the Red Sea."* We find the same tradition, though told in somewhat different language, elsewhere, the same order being given, "Turn you, and take your journey into the wilderness by the way of the Red Sea;"† and the narrative continues, "Then we turned, and took our journey into the wilderness by the way of the Red Sea, as Jahveh spake unto me, and we compassed Mount Seir many days."‡ It is, however, universally conceded that "the wilderness" and "the way of the Red Sea," referred to in these passages, were in the neighbourhood not of the Gulf of Suez, the north-western arm—but of the Gulf of Akaba, the north-eastern arm of the Red Sea. It was by this route—and this is not disputed by any one—that the emigrants finally made their way to the promised land.

But, if with this fact fixed in our minds, we return to the concluding passages of the narrative of the Exodus we find a striking confirmation of our impression that the narrator regarded the severance between the Israelites and the Egyptians as complete, and having conducted the former to the edge of the wilderness, wound up the story by briefly surveying the direction followed and the means adopted by the protecting deity in leading the Israelites to their future home. "When Pharaoh had let the people go, God led them not (through) the way of the land of the Philistines, but God led the people about (through) the way of the

---

* Num. xiv. 6-25.   † Deut. i. 40.   ‡ Deut. ii. 1.

wilderness of the Red Sea" (that is, by the head of the Gulf of Akaba); "and Jahveh went before them by day in a pillar of cloud .... and by night in a pillar of fire ... he took not away the pillar of cloud by day nor the pillar of fire by night from before the people."

It is noticeable, even to the English reader, that a different form of expression is used in reference to the leading of the people by "the way of the land of the Philistines" and by "the way of the wilderness of the Red Sea." In allusion to the latter it is said that "God led the people about." The Hebrew word signifies to "lead round about,"* and we shall be struck with the applicability of such an expression to the movement of the Israelites when we proceed to consider more particularly the course taken during the migration to Canaan.

The expression "led round about," is incomprehensible, if it be assumed that the narrator wished to describe the movement of the Israelites from the place of their captivity in Egypt to the western shores of the Gulf of Suez. If their starting-point was west of the meridian of Suez—that is to say, of the line of the present Suez Canal— the direction taken by the captives, even if they made for this gulf, would in any case have been direct and not circuitous; but if it was to the east of the district now traversed by the canal, they must have penetrated still farther into Egypt, as a preliminary step to quitting it, a course which they were neither so stupid, nor even for the purpose of supplying their deity with an occasion for the display of his supernatural powers, so docile as to adopt.

The mention made by the narrator of the supernatural means of guidance afforded by Jahveh to his people affords a further proof that he had before his eyes, not the journey

---

* יַסֵב *Yaheb* caus. from סָבַב *Sabab*.

of the Israelites within Egyptian territory, but through the desolate region they were compelled to traverse in order to reach their promised home. On the western side of the Suez Gulf the Israelites would have found themselves not only still in Egypt, but in a region sufficiently well known to render their miraculous guidance wholly superfluous, whilst the distance to be traversed before the seashore was reached must, in any case, have been inconsiderable. The language used by the narrator in connection with the pillar of cloud and the pillar of fire, has, however, clearly no reference to the journey from Rameses to Succoth, and thence to the place of encampment on the edge of the wilderness.* It is at this latter point that he considers the journeyings of the Hebrews through what to them was an unknown region, to have commenced ; it is from thence that Jahveh plays the part of a visible guide, and he does so by day and by night during a period which the narrator does not attempt to define, but which he evidently regards as considerable, far greater than would have been necessary to enable the Israelites to reach what is generally assumed to have been their next station, the encampment by the shore of the Red Sea.

Let us now turn our attention to the story of the passage of the Red Sea. It is contained in the 14th chapter of Exodus. We notice, in the first place, that it is not only not a continuation of the narrative in the preceding chapter, but that it commences with an apology for, or explanation of, a change of route which no one accepting the preceding statement would have expected. The former narrative, it will be recollected, had taken the Israelites out of Egypt, or rather, having accounted for their being thrust out, had calculated to a day the period of their stay in that

---

* Exod. xiii. 20.

country, and had conducted them to an encampment in Etham on the edge of *the wilderness (ham-midbhar)*, this term clearly denoting on the mind of the narrator a region outside the limits of Egyptian territory. The accuracy of this narrative was too generally accepted to be called in question, and it was therefore essential, in order to make the passage of the Red Sea in the presence of a pursuing army and the destruction of the latter intelligible, to account for the Israelites, notwithstanding their arrival at the edge of the wilderness, finding their way to the Egyptian side of the Red Sea, and also to explain the attempt of the Egyptian monarch to retake the people whom he had cast out.

The narrative is accordingly introduced with a statement that Jahveh ordered Moses to direct the Israelites to turn—or, literally, to "return,"—and to encamp between Migdol and the sea, the effect of which operation would be to induce Pharaoh to say of them, "They are entangled in the land, the wilderness hath shut them in."* The obvious folly of such a movement on the part of a people desirous of quitting Egypt needed explanation, and Jahveh is made to declare that his object in exposing his people to apparent danger, is to have a further opportunity of "being honoured upon Pharaoh and upon all his host, that the Egyptians might know" that he was Jahveh.† The bait was swallowed by the hapless monarch, who had in fact no choice in the matter, as Jahveh once more hardened his heart; and it having been "told to the king that the people had fled"‡ he and his servants repented them of having liberated their Hebrew slaves, and a strong force at once went in pursuit, the army being led by the king in person. The details of what subsequently occurred need not occupy our attention.

In dealing with this narrative, in respect to its claim to

---

* Exod. xiv. 3.   † Exod. xiv. 4.   ‡ Exod. xiv. 5.

occupy a place in the traditions of the Exodus, we are struck by its incongruity with the story which the latter embody. The destruction of the Egyptian monarch with his army in the sea, furnishes an anticlimax to the slaughter of the first-born. Again, this act of divine vengeance, unlike "the plagues," is absolutely purposeless, save for the sake of gratifying the inordinate vanity of Jahveh. The scheme of the story of Israel's servitude and liberation which we have recently considered is logical and harmonious throughout. A request is, in the first instance, made of the Pharaoh to allow the Hebrews to depart and make a three days' journey into the wilderness, in order to sacrifice to their God. This request is refused, and it thereupon becomes necessary to convince the king that the God of the Hebrews is so powerful that he can insist upon his wishes being attended to. A succession of "plagues" is the result, but between each chastisement the Pharaoh is apparently afforded a *locus pœnitentiæ*. His heart is invariably hardened, so that these opportunities of giving way are delusive; but it is nowhere suggested that if he had "hearkened" to Moses and "let the people go," he and his people would nevertheless have been made the objects of Jahveh's vindictiveness. The "plagues" are a means to an end, that end being the liberation of Israel; and that end is declared to have been accomplished, as well it might be, when the manifestation of Jahveh's power culminated in the instantaneous destruction of "all the first-born in the land of Egypt, from the first-born of Pharaoh that sat on his throne, unto the first-born of the captive that was in the dungeon, and all the first-born of cattle."* We are not considering whether anything of the kind ever took place, but whether those who believed that it did take place, and who made this unexampled proof of divine power

---

* Exod. xii. 29.

and divine vengeance the cause of Israel's liberation from Egypt would have destroyed the whole force and moral of this story, and brought the liberated people back again for the sake of taking them through a sea which did not lie in their path, and of submerging, together with his army, the king who a day or two previously had not only felt the terrific weight of Jahveh's arm in the universal destruction of the first-born throughout the kingdom, but had by freeing—nay, thrusting out—his people given a conclusive acknowledgment of his superiority to the Gods of Egypt.

It is further noticeable that in seeking to account for the institution of the religious rites of the feast of unleavened bread, the paschal lamb, and the dedication of the first-born a connection is drawn between the circumstances under which the liberation from Egyptian servitude was alleged to have taken place and those usages. We are not now concerned with the cogency of these explanations; it is sufficient to point out that, whether rightly or wrongly, the festival of unleavened bread, the sacrifice of the paschal lamb, and the dedication of the first-born, came to be associated in the minds of the settlers in Palestine with occurrences supposed to have signalised the departure of their ancestors from Egypt. It is, however, a very significant fact, that the final triumph of Jahveh over the Egyptians at the Red Sea, and the miraculous conduct of the Israelites through its depths (supposing such a tradition to have been generally accepted), did not, like the sprinkling of blood on the door-posts, the slaughter of the Egyptian first-born, and the hurried departure of the captives with their unleavened bread, find a commemoration in any religious rite, or give occasion for any ceremonial usage which would have tended to keep that great event alive in the memory of the people. When the traditions of the Exodus came to be moulded into the form in which we now find them, under the influence of the paramount idea that the liberation of Israel from "the house of bondage" was the inauguration of Israel's independent existence and adoption as Jahveh's people, it is easy to understand how attempts should be made to account for the institution of rites whose origin was even then lost in the oblivion of the nomadism from which they sprang, and to connect their introduction with the crowning act of Israel's conversion into a free people. If such a conclusion recommends itself, it furnishes an additional reason for disallowing to the narrative of the passage of the Red Sea a place in the story of the Exodus.

If, however, the story of this extraordinary event was accepted in early times by the children of Israel, it is a most remarkable fact that it is not referred to, except in records of a comparatively late date. The prophets, if we except the later Isaiah, who lived at the time of the liberation of the Jews by Cyrus,* apparently knew nothing of this miraculous occurrence, though they make frequent allusions to the liberation from Egypt and the sojourn in the wilderness. Unequivocal reference is made to the passage of the Red Sea in only a few places. Thus in a speech attributed to Joshua, that leader reminds the Israelites with great particularity of the incidents connected with their preservation from the pursuing Egyptians, and the submersion of the latter in the sea.† The reference to this occurrence in Deuteronomy is equally unmistakable.‡ In

---

* Only the most uncompromising champions of what is taken for orthodoxy now venture to deny that the Book of Isaiah is the work of two persons, the one a contemporary of Hezekiah, cir. B.C. 725; the other of Cyrus, cir. B.C. 536 [c. c. i.-xxxix. constitute the work of the former, c.c. xl.-lxvi. that of the latter]. How the two works came to be bracketed together we have no means of telling. Perhaps the prophets bore the same name. The second in order, called "the Great Unknown," is, for the sake of distinction, generally termed the later Isaiah.

† Josh. xxiv. 6.   ‡ Deut. xi. 4.

some of the Psalms also, the poet manifests his acquaintance with the details of the story.* Isaiah, the contemporary of Cyrus, used language which indicates familiarity with the statement that Moses divided the sea ;† and Nehemiah, who quitted Babylon in the latter half of the fifth century, treats the story as authentic.‡ It should also be stated that the author of the Itinerary in Numbers declares that the Israelites passed through the midst of the sea.§

None of these authorities can, however, be shown to be earlier than the close of the seventh century B.C., and most of them are much later. If Joshua addressed to his followers the speech ascribed to him, the question would be settled, because if he quitted Egypt with the Israelites, he must have had amongst his hearers some at least who were eye-witnesses of the miracle. But one of the results of recent Biblical criticism is to demonstrate that the concluding, like the introductory, chapters of the Book of Joshua are compositions of a very late date. The Book of Deuteronomy (with the exception of the opening and concluding portions) is shown to be a work of the close of the seventh century, immediately preceding the fall of the Jewish monarchy.|| The date of the Psalms referred to is unknown, but everything points to the period of the Babylonian exile. The

---

* Psalms lxvi. 6 ; lxxviii. 13 ; cvi. 9.
† Isaiah lxiii. 12-13. ‡ Neh. ix. 11. § Num. xxxiii. 8.
|| "There is one point upon which there exists now almost unanimous agreement among the critics of the liberal school—namely, the age of Deuteronomy;" which is placed in' the latter half of the seventh century B.C.—Colenso, *Pentateuch*, vi. 24. The Bishop of Natal believes it to have been written either in the latter part of Manasseh's reign, or in the early part of Josiah's. Graf says that "among the most generally admitted results of the historical criticism of the Old Testament, for all who do not take up a position of antagonism against these results altogether, may be reckoned the composition of Deuteronomy in the reign of Josiah." "The Book of Deuteronomy, from internal evidence, cannot have been written earlier than the seventh century before the present era, and is probably the 'Book of the

apparent corroboration by the second Isaiah and Nehemiah does not call for comment, because unquestionably in their time the story had secured, probably through the Deuteronomist, an unassailable position in the sacred history of Israel. The testimony of the author of the Itinerary* is valueless, because, as we shall have occasion to show at a future stage of our inquiry, he lived long posterior to the epoch whose events he professed to record. The conclusion already forced upon us that the story of the passage of the Red Sea occupied no place in the original traditions of the Exodus is therefore indirectly confirmed by the absence of all allusion to it in records of unmistakable antiquity.

The first portion of Exod. xv. contains a song of triumph ascribed to Moses, but which, with the exception of the introductory verse, is the product of a comparatively late period. Somewhat similar passages to those in this Psalm have been found in the Book of Job and in the writings of the Prophets Habbakuk, Isaiah, and Jeremiah, but its antiquity must be antecedently established in order to justify the inference that the individuals referred to borrowed its language. But, independently of this preliminary objection, it is somewhat singular that in the points of correspondence relied on there is obviously no reference to the miracle said to have been worked at the Red Sea. When, for example, the poet, in giving instances of the omnipotence of God, speaks of Him as the Being who "stretches out the north over the empty place, and hangeth the earth upon nothing,"† who "bindeth up the waters in thick clouds,"‡ who "com-

---

Law,' or Book of the Covenant found in the Temple during the reign of Josiah." (2 Kings xxii. 8; xxiii. 2)—Kalisch, *Leviticus*, pt. i. 43. See also Kuenen's *Religion of Israel*. Certain portions of the book, especially in the introductory and concluding chapters, consist of much older records, which were subsequently incorporated by a compiler, probably during, or subsequent to, the Babylonian captivity.

* Num. xxxiii. † Job xxvi. 7. ‡ Job xxvi. 8.

passeth the water within bounds,"* and who " divided the sea with his power,"† it is evident that reference is made to the works of creation. When one of the Psalmists exclaims in the same strain, " Thou didst divide the sea by thy strength,"‡ "thou didst chase the fountain and the flood, thou driedst up mighty rivers," "thou hast prepared the light and the sun, thou hast set all the borders of the earth, thou hast made summer and winter,"§ it is equally apparent that he is not referring to a solitary and capricious exercise of divine power. And, in like manner, when the later Isaiah appeals to those who have " forgotten Jahveh their maker, that stretched forth the heavens and laid the foundation of the earth," and adds "but I am Jahveh, thy God, that divided the sea whose waves roared, Jahveh of Hosts is his name,"‖ it is idle to suggest that the prophet is referring to the passage of the Red Sea. Very similar language is used by the earlier prophet Jeremiah, where no one can doubt that allusion is made to the power daily exercised by God over the deep. " Thus saith Jahveh, which giveth the sun for a light by day and the ordinances of the moon and stars for a light by night, which divide the sea when the waves thereof roar, Jahveh of Hosts is his name."¶ Again, when Habakkuk, in an extremely beautiful song of praise, asks, " Was Jahveh displeased against the rivers? was thine anger against the rivers? was thy wrath against the sea, that thou didst ride upon thy horses and thy chariots of salvation? The mountains saw thee, and they trembled; the overflowing of the waters passed by, the deep uttered his voice, and lifted up his hands on high,"** it is not only preposterous to suggest that the prophet has the passage of the Red Sea in his mind, but it brings him into undeserved contempt by suggesting

---

* Job xxvi. 10. † Job xxvi. 12. ‡ Ps. lxxiv. 13. § Ps. lxxiv. 15-17.
‖ Isaiah li. 13 15. ¶ Jer. xxxi. 35. ** Hab. iii. 8-10.

that the concluding words refer to the walls of water formed on each side of the retreating Israelites. The song generally attributed to Moses must be referred to a far later period of Israel's religious development, and be classified with those Psalms in which when singing the praises of Jahveh the poet conjures up the memories of what he believes to be the events of the past. The language which he puts into the mouth of the "enemy," "I will divide the spoil; my lust shall be satisfied upon them; I will draw my sword, my hand shall destroy them."* leads one to conclude that in his poetic ardour he overlooked the fact that the released captives could have possessed nothing and taken nothing with them when "thrust out" save by the sufferance of the Egyptian monarch, and that the object of the supposed pursuit was not to destroy the fugitives with the sword, but to regain possession of useful slaves.

In the narrative of the pursuit of the Israelites by the Egyptians through the sea,† it is somewhat curious that the name of the sea where the miraculous occurrence took place is nowhere mentioned. And this is all the more remarkable and important when we recollect the isolated character of the fragment, and its total want of connection with the narrative which precedes it. Nor can it be said that mention having been made of the Red Sea in the previous chapter,‡ it became unnecessary to repeat the designation, for the reference there made is, as we have shown, to the route by which the Israelites ultimately made their way to Canaan, and not to the neighbourhood in which they found themselves on quitting Egypt. The circumstance that the narrator, in order to take the Israelites to the sea, found it indispensable to make them "turn about" from

---

* Exod. xv. 9.   † Exod. xiv.
‡ Exod. xiii. 18.

F

their original course* affords a further proof that the Red Sea spoken of in the former narrative was not in his mind.

If we have satisfied ourselves that the passage of the Red Sea had no place in the traditions of the Exodus, it becomes of no practical importance to ascertain how the legend arose, or where the occurrence was supposed to have taken place. Before dismissing the subject, it may, however, be worth while to make a few remarks upon these points.

According to the narrator, Jahveh said to Moses, "Speak unto the children of Israel that they turn and encamp before Pi-hahiroth,† between Migdol and the sea, over against Baal-zephon: before it shall ye encamp by the sea." If we could determine the locality of any of these places, we should have no difficulty in ascertaining the precise sea that was present to the narrator's mind.

It is very doubtful whether Pi-hahiroth is a proper name. It literally means "the mouth of caverns," and is never again mentioned except in the Itinerary in Numbers xxxiii.‡ It renders us no assistance. It is different with Migdol. This word signifies in Hebrew a "tower," but there is no reason to doubt that it was a distinctive name given to a well-known Egyptian city. Migdol is referred to by the

---

* Exod. xiv. 2; Num. xxxiii. 6-8. The author of the Itinerary unconsciously renders this very clear, for he makes the Israelites quit Etham to reach a point from whence, by crossing the Red Sea, they again entered the wilderness of Etham.

† The Septuagint rendering of the name as it occurs here is τῆς ἐπαύλεως, but in Num. xxxiii. 7 it is given as ἐπί τὸ στόμα Εἰρώθ, and in the following verse Εἰρώθ.

‡ According to the text in its present form the author of the Itinerary calls the place Pi-hahiroth in verse 7, and simply Hahiroth in verse 8. The Septuagint translation takes the same form. (See preceding note.)

prophets Jeremiah and Ezekiel,* and was evidently known to them as a town on the north-eastern frontier of Egypt. The words of Ezekiel, "I will make the land of Egypt utterly waste from Migdol to Syene, even unto the borders of Ethiopia," indicate that he regarded the former as the extreme north, and the latter—which has been identified as Assouan†—as the extreme south of Egypt. In the Itinerary of Antoninus Martyr, a town named Magdolo is mentioned as distant from Pelusium twelve Roman miles on the road to Serapeum, which latter place was near the western shore of the Suez Gulf. Pelusium was, however, an Egyptian frontier town of considerable strength under the twenty-sixth dynasty, in the seventh century B.C., and was situated close to the Mediterranean, to the east of the Pelusiac mouth of the Nile; and there seems good reason for supposing that Migdol was substantially identified with Pelusium by the prophets whom we have quoted. However this may be, the reference made by Jeremiah to the adjoining districts, in which the Jewish captives (his contemporaries) were interned, leaves no doubt that the Migdol mentioned by him was in the neighbourhood of the Mediterranean, and on the Egyptian frontier looking towards Syria.

But although it is universally conceded that the Migdol of the Hebrew prophets and the Magdolo of later authorities was in the immediate neighbourhood of Pelusium, it is urged that a second Migdol existed in the vicinity of the Suez Gulf; and that it was between the latter town and the

---

* Jer. xliv. 1; xlvi. 14. Ezek. xxix. 10; xxx. 12. The rendering in the Authorised Version, "from the tower to Syene," in both these passages in Ezekiel, is confessedly incorrect. The word Migdol is not preceded by the definite article, which would be required to give it the signification "the tower."

† Assouan is on the Nile, immediately below the first cataract.

Red Sea that the Hebrews encamped previous to their miraculous delivery from the pursuing Egyptians. It is true no evidence of the existence of such a Migdol is attainable;* but it would be dangerous to attach much importance to the fact that no traces of what may have been an insignificant town are discoverable after the lapse of three thousand years. The negative evidence assumes, however, considerable weight when, as is stated, the researches of Egyptologists fail to discover any records of a second town of that name. In dealing with the locality of the region from which the Exodus took place, we shall have occasion to refer once more to the probable site of Migdol.

A few years since an English Egyptologist,† when deciphering one of the papyri in the British Museum, found a reference to a deity styled Baali-zapouna, which is supposed, not without reason, to be identical with the Baalzephon mentioned in the Book of Exodus. The name is Semitic, and not Egyptian, and signifies "The Lord of the North." Further investigation by Brugsch Bey has led that eminent Egyptologist to the conclusion that a lofty headland on the shore of the Mediterranean to the east of the ancient Pelusium, known as Mount Casius, was dedicated to the worship of this deity. If this conclusion be correct—and the evidence in support of it is unquestionably very weighty —the inference would be irresistible that the Migdol referred to in Exodus was the Migdol of the Prophets, and that "the sea," between which and the town the Israelites were ordered to encamp, was the Mediterranean. Brugsch

---

* En remarquant que ce Migdol (that near Pelusium) est la seule place de ce nom que j'ai rencontrée dans les textes géographiques parmi un nombre de plus de trois milles noms propres géographiques, il en résulte de là, la probabilité que le Migdol du prophète Ezéchiel ne diffère pas du Migdol de l'Exode.—Brugsch Bey, *L'Exode et les Monuments Egyptiens*, 20.

† Mr. Goodwin.

Bey, however, goes farther; for he professes to identify Pi-hahiroth with the "Khirot," or lagunes, of which, on the papyri, Baali-zapouna was declared to be lord. These "Khirot" were swamps, or lakes, which in the vicinity of Mount Casius skirted the Mediterranean Sea. On these data Brugsch Bey has propounded an explanation of the passage of the Red Sea which is deserving of notice.

In ancient times, if we may trust the evidence of historians, a sheet of water existed on the south side of Mount Casius, and separated by a well-defined but narrow strip of land from the Mediterranean Sea. Diodorus Siculus declares, though on what authority we know not, that it was two hundred stadia in length, comparatively narrow, but of a prodigious depth. This was the Serbonian lake.* It is also mentioned by Herodotus† as being in the vicinity of Mount Casius, and as the place where Typhon (Zephon) was reported to have been concealed. This lake no longer exists. It has been filled by the drifting sands of the adjoining desert.

If we may further trust the testimony of Diodorus, the neighbourhood of the Serbonian lake was fraught with considerable danger to unwary travellers, and even proved fatal to armies. The narrowness of the lake, and the treacherous nature of the soil forming its borders, led the incautious to advance into quagmires from which they afterwards found it impossible to extricate themselves; and thus it happened, according to Diodorus, that whole armies had been swallowed up.‡ Elsewhere he mentions that the Persian king, Artaxerxes, when about to invade Egypt, lost a portion of his army in this region owing to his ignorance of the dangerous locality.

Strabo states that when he was at Alexandria an

---

* Diod. Sic. i. 30.   † Her. iii. 5,   ‡ Diod. xvi. 46.

exceptionally high tide occurred in the neighbourhood of Pelusium, which had the effect of inundating the adjoining country, converting the headland of Mount Casius into an island, and rendering it possible for ships to sail over the road leading to Palestine.*

Brugsch Bey, relying on these authorities, suggests that the Israelites, having encamped between Migdol and the sea (the Mediterranean) opposite the lagunes (Pi-hahiroth) advanced towards Mount Casius along the narrow tongue of land separating the lake from the sea, which he states at that time furnished the route from Egypt to Palestine; that they were pursued along this route by the Pharaoh and his army; and that at the time when they reached the headland in safety, a high tide, similar to that mentioned by Strabo, swept across the road then occupied by the Egyptian army, and overwhelmed the latter. That this occurrence was described in the history of Israel as the passage of the Red Sea is explained by Dr. Brugsch in the following manner:— The Serbonian lake was remarkable for its growth of reeds, and *Jam Suph* in Hebrew, which is translated the "Red Sea," should be rendered, at least in this instance, the "sea of reeds" or "of weeds." By the *Jam Suph*, in which, according to the Biblical records, the Egyptians were overwhelmed, and through which the Israelites were conducted in safety, was meant the Serbonian lake.

Brugsch Bey treats the destruction of the Egyptian army as a historical fact, though he affords a rationalistic explanation of the supposed miracle. His theory may therefore be fairly dealt with on the basis which he himself supplies.†

Whatever may be the value of the testimony of Diodorus

---

* Strab. i. 58.

† "Le m'racle il est vrai cesse alors d'être un miracle: Mais avouerons le en toute sincérité la Providence divine maintient toujours sa place et son autorité."—*L'Exode et les Mon. Egypt*, 32.

Siculus to the loss of entire armies in the Serbonian lake, it is substantially discarded by Dr. Brugsch as irrelevant to the issue before him. This is not very apparent to the ordinary reader, and the voluminous quotation* from Diodorus has unquestionably a tendency to create an impression that he was in some sort a corroborative witness of the Biblical account of the destruction of the Egyptian army. If armies ever were lost through marching incautiously into this Serbonian bog, it may be affirmed with absolute certainty that those of Egypt were not among the number. It is at least conceivable that a Persian king, invading Egypt, might lose some of his troops under the circumstances mentioned by Diodorus; but it is totally incredible that an Egyptian ruler should lead his army into a lake or quagmire on his own frontier, the position of which was well known, and whose perils were even then indicated by a name (Khirot) familiar to every resident in the country. Dr. Brugsch doubtless felt this difficulty; and contenting himself with the favourable, though delusive, impression Diodorus could not fail to create, prudently abstained from any application of his testimony.

It is on the evidence given by Strabo of the exceptionally high tide near Pelusium that Dr. Brugsch exclusively relies as affording a plausible explanation of the destruction of the Egyptian army. What occurred at one time might have occurred at another, and it may be frankly conceded that if the Egyptian army was surprised by such a tide as that spoken of by Strabo, a great catastrophe would doubtless have been the consequence.

But if we accept this explanation, and treat the Biblical account of the destruction of Pharaoh and his army when in pursuit of the Israelites as having some foundation in fact,

---

* *L'Exode et les Mon. Egypt*, 29.

we are met by a number of difficulties. We have to account for the presence of the Israelites on the route leading direct to Philistia, and leading nowhere else, notwithstanding the distinct statement that this route was avoided; and we have to explain how the submersion of an army by the waters of the Mediterranean could be regarded either then, or at any future time, as a swallowing up in a lake of reeds. Even supposing that the retreating captives called the narrow papyrus-covered lake which lay on their right as they treaded the narrow causeway to Mount Casius the *Jam Suph*, they could not have been blind to the apparently limitless extent of the great and, at the time, possibly turbulent sea which stretched away in every direction on their left. They might have been led to fancy that their God had cleft for them a way through the waters to enable them to pass through on dry land, but those waters would assuredly have never been regarded as those of the marshy lagune which separated them by only a trifling distance from the adjoining desert. And, finally, when from the headland of Mount Casius they saw the mighty waves of the Mediterranean enveloping their pursuers, they could not by any intelligible mental operation have concluded that their destruction was accomplished by the stagnant marsh which became itself swallowed up in the advancing sea.

But what shall we say to the suggestion that the Israelites gave to the Serbonian lake the name of the *Jam Suph*. If this name occurred nowhere else in the Scriptural records, it might no doubt be urged with some plausibility that a lake overgrown with reeds was called by this appellation. But the name is of tolerably frequent occurrence, and Dr. Brugsch would frankly admit that elsewhere than in reference to the destruction of the Egyptian army it is applied to a sea far distant from the Serbonian lake.

It is a somewhat singular fact that no sufficient, at all events no perfectly satisfactory, explanation has been afforded of the designations given respectively by the Phœnicians and the Greeks to the Gulf which washes the western shores of Arabia and the south-eastern coast of Egypt. When skirting the southern spurs of the Idumæan range, on their way to the Trans-Jordanic region, we are told that the Israelites passed by the way of the *Jam Suph*,* and at a later period, when the Jewish monarchy was at the zenith of its glory, King Solomon had a fleet of ships at Ezion Gaber, at the head of the *Jam Suph*, in the land of Edom.† That reference is made in these passages to what is now known as the Red Sea is not contested by any one; but why the Semites should have called it the *Jam Suph*, and the Greeks ἡ ἐρυθρὰ θάλασσα,‡ which latter designation is rendered the "Red Sea," raises difficulties which have never been satisfactorily solved.

Into a consideration of this difficult question it would not be necessary to enter for the purpose of discussing Dr. Brugsch's view, because it is sufficient to point out that whatever may have been the reasons which prompted the Hebrews to call what is now known as the Red Sea the *Jam Suph*, it is preposterous to suppose that they would have given the same name to an insignificant swamp on the Egyptian frontier. Wherever the name was used as a distinctive appellation, it must have been applied to one and the same sea. And it is all the more singular that Dr. Brugsch has not noticed, or if he noticed has not combated this difficulty, inasmuch as he conducts the Israelites from Mount Casius, in a south-westerly direction by way of the Bitter Lakes, one of which he identifies as Marah,§ to the head of the Isthmus of Suez, and justifies this erratic course as being a fulfilment of the

---

* Deut. ii. 1; Num. xiv. 25. † 1 Kings ix. 26.
‡ Her. i. 1; Diod. Sic. iii. 28. § *L'Exode*, 34.

providential design that "God led the people about through the way of the wilderness of the Red Sea," or, as he translates the passage, "by the way of the wilderness towards the sea of reeds." In other words, having been miraculously preserved at the *Jam Suph*, "the sea of reeds," afterwards known as the Serbonian lake, the Israelites were conducted to another *Jam Suph*, the Suez Gulf of the Red Sea.

It has been necessary to examine Dr. Brugsch's theory in detail and to state the grounds for rejecting it, because he is unquestionably entitled to the credit of showing that the Migdol of the narrative in Exodus was the Migdol close to Pelusium, and that the scene of the encampment of the Israelites present to the narrator's mind lay between that town and the Mediterranean Sea.

If we are correct in refusing to give to the story of the passage of the Red Sea a place in the traditions of the Exodus, we nevertheless cannot deny that at least as early as the seventh century B.C. it commanded respect in the kingdom of Judah, and received a place in history. If, however, the Hebrews were, according to the conception of the framer of the original narrative, encamped on the shores of the Mediterranean on the eve of their deliverance from the king of Egypt and his army, it is desirable, if possible, to discover how the belief subsequently came to be established that the scene of the miracle was the Red Sea.

We have already noticed the all-important fact, that in the prosaic account in Exodus* no mention is made of the "Red Sea." The narrator invariably uses the term "the sea," and this no longer surprises us if we have satisfied ourselves that according to his idea the Hebrews were encamped close to the Mediterranean. When we turn to the Psalm ascribed to Moses, we find that the expression *Jam Suph*

---

* Exod. xiv.

only occurs once,* that it is wanting in the nucleus of the song variously ascribed by tradition to Moses† and to Miriam,‡ and that even in the gloss which follows the Psalm and explains its subject no distinctive name is given to the sea where Pharaoh and his army were said to have perished.§ All these omissions are very remarkable, and they cannot with any appearance of probability be considered accidental.

It would assist us greatly in our investigation if we could determine with some approach to certainty how it was the Red Sea came to be called the *Jam Suph*. The generally accepted view is that *Suph* means "weeds," and that the Red Sea received this title from its quantity of sea-weed. In other passages in the Scriptures, *Suph* is believed with much plausibility to mean "rushes" or "reeds," and it is concluded that when connected with the word *Jam* it means a sea remarkable for the quantity of its vegetable productions.||

---

* Exod. xv. 4.   † Exod. xv. 2.   ‡ Exod. xv. 21.   § Exod. xv. 19.

|| ים סוף *Jam Suph*, which is universally rendered the Red Sea, is supposed to mean literally the sea of weeds. This conclusion has been arrived at because elsewhere in the Hebrew records the word *Suph* signifies, or is believed to signify, reeds or weeds (Exod. ii. 3–5; Isaiah xix. 6; Jon. ii. 5). This inference is supposed to be corroborated by the Coptic name given to the Red Sea, *Schari*, which is interpreted "reedy," or "weedy;" σαρι, according to Theophrastus (*Hist. Plant.* iv. 9) having that signification (Pliny xiii. 23–45). Others, however, have apparently on good grounds questioned this rendering of the Coptic word (*Journ. Asiatique*, 1834, i. p. 349; Peyron, *Lex. Copt.* 304; Gesenius, *Thesaurus, s. v.*). Misled by the title "sea of weeds" some writers have brought themselves to believe that the Red Sea was remarkable for its abundance of sea-weed; but observant travellers have failed to notice this peculiarity. Assuming that the word *Suph* is correctly translated "flags," or "weeds" (in Exod. ii. 3–5, and Isaiah xix. 6), it is fairly open to question whether it can be rendered "weeds" in Jon. ii. 5. In the Authorised Version this passage is as follows: "The depths closed me round about; the weeds were wrapped about my head." In the Septuagint we have, "The lowest deep compassed me, my head went down to the bottom of the mountains;" and Jerome renders the passage "Pelagus operuit caput meum." It is certainly not easy to imagine how Jonah, whilst in the whale's belly,

It may well seem presumptuous to challenge an interpretation supported by a great *consensus* of authority, but still when we recollect how frequently the origin of names has been lost in antiquity, we may be excused for hesitating to accept on etymological grounds an explanation which otherwise has nothing to recommend it. The sea in question, there is no reason to doubt, was known to the nomadic tribes as the *Jam Suph* long before the Hebrews entered Egypt; and if the word *Suph* was descriptive, it is not unreasonable to suppose that it was descriptive of something which would be pre-eminently striking to the senses of the denizens of the desert. The evidence of travellers does not, however, support the suggestion that the Red Sea is remarkable for an excessive supply of sea-weed, nor does it seem likely, even if it were so, that such a circumstance would make much impression on a Bedouin's mind.

We find elsewhere in the Old Testament, and notably in the poem ascribed to an inhabitant of a land in close proximity to the north-eastern arm of the Red Sea, a term which certainly might by a very intelligible process be combined

could fancy "weeds" being wrapped about his head (on this point see some quaint remarks by Gnarin, a Benedictine monk, in his *Lex. Heb. et Chahl. s.v.*, סוף); besides, the Mediterranean, and not the *Jam Suph*, was the scene of his adventure. I do not think that a sufficient cause has been shown for concluding that by *Jam Suph* the Hebrews meant the weedy sea. We must rather look for the meaning in סופה, Suphah, "the whirlwind," for the reasons stated above; or in סוף, Soph, signifying the "end" or "extremity" (2 Chron. xx. 16; Daniel iv. 11 (8)). Captain Burton states that according to the Bedouins the eastern Gulf of the Red Sea is called Ya'kkab el Bahr, not, as is generally supposed, after the steep defile which here descends from the Tih to the seashore, but because at this point the sea "heels," or terminates (*Midian Revisited*, i. 229). If this be so, the present name of the Gulf may be an Arabic rendering of *Jam Soph*, if סוף was used in the early traditions of the Exodus to signify the "end" of the sea, or the point where it turned back from the land. The high authority of Ibn Ezra may be cited in support of the latter construction.

with the word "sea." That term is *Suphah*, and signifies a whirlwind or a tempest. In the Book of Job it occurs several times, and in one passage the poet exclaims, "Out of the south cometh the whirlwind (*Suphah*), and cold out of the north."* It is also used by the Prophets Isaiah† and Hosea‡, and in the Book of Proverbs,§ and always in the same sense.

Now let us inquire whether there was any special reason why an inhabitant of Idumæa should have regarded the south as a region of whirlwinds, or why the gulf stretching southwards from Edom should have been called the *Jam Suph* in the sense of the Sea of Tempests.

The Gulf of Akaba, known to the ancients as the Ælanitic Gulf, and forming the north-eastern tongue of the Red Sea, is a narrow gorge bounded on both sides by precipitous mountains, rising occasionally to the height of two thousand feet.‖ This gorge is the natural continuation of the great valley of the Araba, which, lying between the cliffs of the table-land of the Tih on the west and the mountains of Idumæa on the east, extends from the head of the Gulf until it somewhat abruptly and precipitously drops into the basin of the Dead Sea. Under such conditions the frequency of storms in the Gulf of Akaba might with confidence be anticipated by any one versed in

---

* Job xxxvii. 9; also in xxi. 18; xxvii. 20. Job lived in the land of Uz, which was on the eastern slopes of the Idumæan hills, and to the north-east of the head of the Red Sea.

† Isaiah xvii. 13.   ‡ Hos. viii. 7.   § Prov. x. 25.

‖ The Gulf of Akaba has the appearance of a narrow deep ravine extending nearly a hundred miles in a straight direction, and the circumjacent hills rise in some places two thousand feet perpendicularly from the shore (Wellsted, *Arabia*, ii. 108). The valley of the Araba supplies a funnel, through which an intermittent but powerful draught of the colder air from the north is frequently turned on, whilst the clefts in the mountains lining the Gulf act as so many windsails.

the science of physical geography, and as a matter of fact there is probably no sea which possesses a worse reputation in this respect, or is beset with greater dangers to the navigator.*

That these atmospheric disturbances should have failed to attract the attention of those frequenting the shores of the Œlanitic Gulf is unlikely, and if it be conceded that the Semitic tribes gave it a descriptive name, and if we find that such name was identical with that which they applied to tempests, we have at least some grounds on which to base the conclusion that by the *Jam Suph* the Hebrews meant the Sea of the Supha, the Sea of Tempests—the Tempestuous Sea.

If we now return to the Song of Moses, we may perhaps find an explanation of the apparent occurrence in one place, and in one place only, of mention of the Red Sea. The bard sings—" Pharaoh's chariots and his host hath he cast

---

* All accounts agree as to the prevalence of storms in this Gulf. "The Gulf of Akaba is unfit for navigation, owing to the almost incessant and violent north winds and the numerous reefs. During the recent survey the *Palinurus* was blown from her anchors three different times" (*Horsburgh's Sailing Directions*, quoted on map of Arabia Petræa in Keith Johnston's *National Atlas*). See Wellsted's description of the storms in the Gulf when engaged on this survey, *Arabia*, ii. 113–131, 135, 136. He thus explains their prevalence and severity: "On looking over a map of this portion of the globe, we perceive that one straight and continuous valley extends from the Dead Sea to the entrance of the Gulf of Akaba. The northerly wind which prevails during the greater part of the year naturally takes the direction of the valley. Finding no other outlet, however, than its southern termination, it acquires there its extraordinary force and strength, and although the body of water exposed to its influence is not greater than in some large rivers, yet having none of their sinuosities, the course of its waves is unintercepted to the entrance of the Straits, and finding but a small outlet the water returns by a violent effort in a powerful current" (ii. 133). Capt. Burton gives a vivid description of this "Spitfire Gulf," as he calls it (*Midian Revisited*, i. 247-264). See also his daily record of Observations in this Gulf (*App*. ii. 290-294).

into the sea; his chosen captains also are drowned in the *Jam Suph*."* May we not be wrong in rendering the concluding words "Red Sea," and in inferring that the bard here made use of a proper name? Is it not at least as probable that in employing the parallelism so universal in Hebrew poetry, and in repeating in the second stanza of the verse the idea already expressed in the first, he simply varied it by substituting for "the sea," "the tempestuous sea?" But if this be so, we may have here the key which explains how, in later times, when nothing remained but the naked story in which the sea was unnamed, and the song of triumph in which it was apparently once named, the idea should have arisen that the *Jam Suph*, properly so-called, which was undoubtedly associated with the journeyings from Egypt to Canaan,† was the scene of the miraculous occurrence which was recorded.

If we yield to the temptation of endeavouring to ascertain the origin of the story of the passage of the Israelites on dry land through the midst of the sea, and of the destruction of the pursuing host of Egyptians, we venture on an inquiry so extremely speculative that any conclusions, whatever they might be, would possess no real value. We know how great a part the physical peculiarities of a country plays in the creation of legendary lore; how a rent in a cliff is attributed to the falchion of some doughty giant or demi-god; and how a water-fed depression on a mountain-top is made to supply an approximate drinking-bowl for the devil. It is very probable that in the communication between Egypt and southern Palestine, subsequent to the Hebrew settlement, the Jewish travellers were struck by the peculiarity of the route which, where it intervened between the Mediterranean and the Serbonian lake, had the appearance

---

* Exod. xv. 4. † Num. xiv. 25; Deut. ii. 1.

of passing through the midst of the sea. That it should have been made by Jahveh to assist the Hebrews in their escape from Egypt was an inference equally natural and tempting, and the story of the destruction of Pharaoh and his army either came to be evolved out of an ambiguous cry of triumph, which by some was attributed to Moses and by others to Miriam,* or was based on some comparatively insignificant occurrence which the bard and the story-teller magnified into the form in which we now see it.

The question how the legend came to originate is, however, of very subordinate interest. The main point to be kept in mind is that, so far as we have any opportunity of judging, the story of the passage of the Red Sea had no place in the original traditions of the Exodus. Those who made their way to the Trans-Jordanic region before entering Canaan were ignorant of this miraculous interposition of their God on their behalf. They had no knowledge of the encampment between Migdol and the sea, or of their passage on dry land between upreared walls of water. When the story of their departure from Egypt came to be duly formulated, it told how, after repeated manifestations of Jahveh's power at the expense of the Egyptians, they were finally thrust out; how they quitted Egypt in haste, and how they encamped in the edge of the wilderness previous to commencing their protracted and arduous journeyings. It told how they were amicably received by the Midianite tribe of which Jethro was the Sheikh; and how when he was informed of "all that Jahveh had done to Pharaoh and the Egyptians for Israel's sake," he said: "Blessed be Jahveh, who hath delivered you out of the hand of the Egyptians, and out of the hand of Pharaoh; who hath delivered the people from under the hand of the Egyptians,"† no allusion, direct or

---

* Exod. xv. 1, 21.   † Exod. xviii. 10.

indirect, having been made either by his informants or himself to the stupendous miracle at the Red Sea. The story told how, when they quitted Egypt, they were not led into the promised land by Philistia, though it was near, but by a circuitous route by way of the *Jam Suph*, which inferentially was distant; and it told how, after many years of trials and privations, they at last reached their promised home.

And it is curious how this story, the details of which it will be our duty to examine, finds a confirmation in a record of unquestionable antiquity. In his fruitless negotiations with the king of the Ammonites, Jephthah gave a singularly clear and succinct review of the course followed by the Israelites from the time of their departure from Egypt until their conquest of the territory of the Amorites—the territory then claimed by the king of Ammon. "When Israel came up from Egypt, and walked through the wilderness unto the *Jam Suph*, and came to Kadesh,"* messengers were sent to the king of Edom and to the king of Moab soliciting, in vain, permission for Israel to pass through their territories. In consequence of their refusal, Israel was compelled to abide in Kadesh, but ultimately compassed Edom and Moab, and having failed to obtain permission from Sihon, king of the Amorites, to pass through his dominions, made war on him and dispossessed him. Now it is very noticeable that Jephthah here follows the same route which is shadowed forth in the concluding verses of Exodus xiii., which wind up the narrative of the Exodus, and which is elsewhere referred to with more particularity: "When Israel quitted Egypt, and walked through the wilderness unto the *Jam Suph*." Is it conceivable that by "the wilderness" Jephthah could have meant the perfectly well known, doubtless well populated, and undeniably Egyptian territory which inter-

---

* Jud. xi. 16.

vened between the city of Rameses and the shore of the Suez Gulf? But if he did not mean, and by no possibility could have meant, the region on the west side of the Gulf of Suez, he must have referred to that lying on the east of the Egyptian frontier; and by the *Jam Suph*, to which Israel walked through the wilderness, he must equally have meant that portion of what is now called the Red Sea to which reference is beyond all question made in the Books of Numbers and of Deuteronomy, which it is no less apparent is alluded to in Exodus xiii., which was not far distant from Kadesh, and which is to-day known as the Gulf of Akaba. But if this is the only possible interpretation which can be put on the language attributed to Jephthah, is it conceivable that he was acquainted with the reputed passage of Israel through the Red Sea? It may be urged with great cogency that there was no more necessity for Jephthah to refer to this incident in his negotiations with the king of the Ammonites than to any of the others, no less miraculous in their kind, which tradition associated with Israel's sojourn in the desert. But whilst freely admitting this, we still must ask how it was possible that Jephthah, if he knew of the passage of the Red Sea, could represent Israel as quitting Egypt and walking through *the wilderness* in order to arrive at a sea identified by him as the same, and called by him by the same name, as that in which Israel's miraculous deliverance took place? Nor are we justified in attempting to overcome this difficulty by crediting Jephthah, not only with the knowledge we possess that the Red Sea bifurcates into the Gulfs of Suez and Akaba, but by further assuming that the term *Jam Suph* was applied by the Israelites to the entire Gulf, which we now call the Red Sea. So far as we have any evidence to guide us, *Jam Suph* was exclusively applied by the Hebrews to the Gulf of Akaba, and possibly to the limitless waste of waters into which it opened. There is but one solitary instance in the Hebrew records in which the Gulf of Suez is unmistakably referred to, and it is there called "the Egyptian Sea." It is Isaiah, who "prophesied" in the kingdom of Judah about the middle of the eighth century B.C., who thus designates it.* On the other hand, we find the *Jam Suph* named as a boundary, when it is apparent the Gulf of Akaba† can alone be referred to, and where, if the name was used in the extended sense now given to it, its description as a landmark would have been equally erroneous and delusive. In the course of our investigation of the story of Israel's "wanderings," we shall find further grounds for our conclusion that the denomination *Jam Suph* was exclusively applied to the Gulf of Akaba, which it would be inconvenient now to anticipate. If Jephthah believed that Israel had crossed any portion of what he knew as the *Jam Suph*, it is incomprehensible that he should have treated that sea without any qualification as marking an important step in Israel's journeyings, and affirmed that Israel, after quitting Egypt, had traversed the wilderness to reach it. It is impossible for any unprejudiced person to read the language ascribed to the Hebrew "Judge," and to compare it with the passages already referred to, without arriving at the conclusion that, according to the received traditions, at all events amongst those tribes which subsequently settled on the east of the Jordan, the captives in Egypt were thrust out, or at least permitted to depart peaceably, they set out on their way without any subsequent molestation, and not until they had crossed a region which they called "*the wilderness*" (*hammidbhar*) did they set eyes on the Red Sea (*Jam Suph*).

It would be interesting to ascertain, if possible, at what time the belief arose that the Hebrews passed through the

---

* Isa. xi. 15.   † Exod. xxiii. 31,

midst of the *Jam Suph*, properly so-called, and that Pharaoh and his army were overwhelmed in its waters. On the eastern side of the Jordan, and most probably also in the kingdom of Israel, this tradition had no place in any form whatever. No allusion, however remote or indirect, is made to the occurrence by the Prophets, the scene of whose labours was confined to the northern kingdom. In the kingdom of Judah, or before its foundation, amongst "the men of Judah," the legend in its original form placed the scene of the occurrence in what was called κατ' ἐξοχήν, "the sea," and sometimes "the Great Sea,"—the Mediterranean.* The striking event offered an appropriate subject for treatment by the bard, and was celebrated in the so-called Song of Moses.† In repeating himself in strict conformity with the canons of Hebrew poetry, he sang, "Pharaoh's chariots and his host hath he cast into the sea, his chosen captains also are drowned in the tempestuous sea" (*Jam Suph*). Time rolled on, and men undertook the task of writing history, with the aid of records, the meaning of which had become obscured, or occasionally even totally lost. That the Hebrews in their migration from Egypt had followed the direction indicated in Jephthah's address to the king of the Ammonites was a fact about which there could be no dispute. They unquestionably went by the way of the *Jam Suph*—the Gulf of Akaba—on their road to Canaan.‡ But the legend of the passage through the sea, with the subsequent destruction of the Egyptian army, could not be omitted from the narrative. It commanded credence in Judah, and it is exclusively to scribes and bards of the southern kingdom that we owe the later references to the marvellous incident; whilst it is to one of the Babylonian exiles that we are probably indebted for the compilation of the ancient records

---

* Exod. xiv. † Exod. xv. ‡ Num. xiv. 25; Deut. i. 40.

in the form in which we now possess them.* The general conception of the direction taken by the released captives had a tendency to exclude the idea that the miracle had been performed in "the Great Sea," and the ambiguous expression of a bard supplied a natural and obvious mode of connecting it with the sea by whose shore Jahveh had led his people to their promised home. The time when this change was wrought, so far as we have the means of judging, was subsequent to the fall of the northern kingdom, and on the eve of the overthrow of that of the south; whilst we must even pass on to the later days of the Babylonian exile to find the narrative assume its final form. Whether at this time the *Jam Suph* became identified, not with the Gulf of Akaba but with the Gulf of Suez—the Egyptian Sea—is a question involved in considerable doubt. The language in which the narrative is resumed after Miriam's Song would seem to place it beyond dispute that the *Jam Suph* is identified as the Suez Gulf, and that having passed through it the captives entered the wilderness: "So Moses† brought Israel from the Red Sea, and they went out into the wilderness of Shur, and they went three days in the wilderness and found no water." But placing geographical ignorance out of account, everything indicates that the introductory sentence is simply‡ used as a bracket. When

---

* Ezra vii. 6, 11, 14, 21.   † Exod. xv. 22.   *Literally* "And Moses."
‡ We must be careful to avoid crediting the ancients with our knowledge of geography. Maps were unknown in Palestine, and the Hebrew scribes had no more idea of the configuration of the coast-line of the Red Sea, with its two gulfs, than we have of the precise boundaries of the lands adjoining the Arctic Sea. One is apt unconsciously to suppose that those with whose writings we are now dealing had present to their mind the Gulfs of Suez and Akaba, and could not by any possibility confound one with the other. But this was not so. All that was known was that a sea washed the eastern shores of Egypt, and it was called in Judæa the Egyptian Sea

we proceed at a later stage to consider the locality of the wilderness of Shur, we shall find that it was not contiguous to the Suez Gulf. The grammatical construction of the sentence, "So Moses brought Israel from the Red Sea, and they went," &c., is strained, if not incorrect. The words, "And they went out into the wilderness of Shur," &c., must be treated as the continuation of the narrative of the Exodus from Egypt: "And the children of Israel journeyed from Rameses to Succoth,"* "and encamped in Etham, on the edge of the wilderness,"† "and they went out into the wilderness of Shur, and they went three days in the wilderness and found no water."‡

(Isa. xi. 15), and that a sea reached the southern extremity of Edom, and it was called the *Jam Suph*, but probably very few were aware that these seas united into a greater one. How erroneous were the ideas entertained, even so late as the beginning of this century, respecting the configuration of the upper end of the Red Sea, is shown by the representation in maps of that period of the Gulf of Akaba splitting into two distinct arms, similar to the bifurcation of the Red Sea into the Gulfs of Suez and Akaba.

* Exod. xii. 37–39.   † Exod. xiii. 20.   ‡ Exod. xv. 22.

CHAPTER III.

IS it possible to ascertain the particular region of Egypt which was the scene of the Hebrews' servitude—or, at least, the locality from which, according to tradition, the Exodus took place? This is by no means easy; and, until Egyptology has made further advances, and Egyptologists evince greater unanimity than they have hitherto done in their interpretation of the relics which the most ancient of known kingdoms has left behind it, and in the inferences they draw from them, we must content ourselves with such conclusions as appear to recommend themselves by their greater probability.

At the commencement of the narrative of the servitude in Egypt it is stated that the Israelites were employed in building the treasure or store cities, Pithom and Raamses;* and as there is no question that the latter was identical with the Rameses from which the Exodus took place,† we may confine our attention to determining, if possible, the locality of one or both of the two cities in whose construction the forced labour of the Hebrews was turned to account by the Egyptian Government.

In dealing with this part of our subject, we are compelled to place ourselves almost unreservedly in the hands of Egyptologists. We must accept with thanks, and by a process somewhat akin to faith, believe whatever they are good enough to tell us. But Egyptology is still in its infancy.

---

* Exod. i. 11. † Exod. xii. 37.

The vast mine of Egyptian memorials is scarcely penetrated much less explored; and when we so often see the certainties of the day overthrown by the discoveries of the morrow, we may be excused if we temper our faith with a little caution. Nor is the wisdom of such a course less apparent when we notice how frequently Egyptologists fail in convincing each other. When the teachers disagree, the disciples may be pardoned if they maintain an attitude of reserve.

Various sites have been assigned to Rameses. It has been identified with On, the later Heliopolis; with old Cairo, and with Memphis; whilst Lepsius placed it at Abu Kesheyd, in the Wady Tumeylat—the valley through which ran the canal which in ancient times connected the waters of the Nile with those of the Gulf of Suez by way of the Lake Timsah. On the strength of a passage in the Septuagint Version,* it has been thought to be the same as Heroöpolis; and the latter city has been variously placed in the valley of the old canal, and between Lake Timsah and the Suez Gulf. Other authorities, no less entitled to respect, place Rameses in the west portion of the Wady Tumeylat, and reject the hypothesis advanced by Lepsius, and supported by Ebers, that it stood on the site of Abu Kesheyd, in the eastern division of that valley. Pithom, like Rameses, has also been a good deal pushed about. Some have identified it with the Patumos which Herodotus placed on the Great Canal,† which city they regarded as the same as the Thoum mentioned in the Itinerary of Antoninus. Others have declared it to be Heroöpolis, and place it near the head of the Great Bitter Lake; whilst equally eminent scholars, though admitting the identity of Pithom with Heroöpolis, give a site to the latter city as far south as Suez.

* Gen. xlvi. 28. καθ' Ἡρώων πόλιν, εἰς γῆν Ῥαμεσσῆ. † Herod. ii. 158.

Speaking generally, the drift of these speculations is to place the region occupied by the Hebrews at the time of the Exodus to the south-west of the modern town of Ismaila. Those who, accepting the Mohammedan view, identify Rameses with Memphis, or who, with Josephus, suppose it to have been the same as Latopolis (old Cairo),* fix the place of departure of the Israelites at a point almost due west of the head of the Gulf of Suez.

The most recent theory respecting the site of Rameses is that propounded by Brugsch Bey. He affirms, and certainly in no hesitating tone, that the Rameses of the Exodus is identical with the Zoan of later Hebrew authorities, the Tanis of the Greeks, and known in the time of the Pharaohs as Pi-rāmses, the city of Ramses. Zoan was situated on the right bank of the Tanaitic branch of the Nile, and is now but a short distance from the southern border of Lake Menzaleh. In ancient times the Tanaitic, like the still more eastern arm of the Nile the Pelusiac, found its way to the Mediterranean through a low-lying but fertile district, and the plain extending in a north-eastern course from the city between the two branches of the Nile, appears to have been the "field of Zoan," to which allusion is made in one of the Psalms.†

At Zoan, or Zan as it is now called by the Arabs, have been found the ruins and the relics of what was undoubtedly at one time a great city. Broken or prostrate columns, statues, steles, and obelisks of Syenite granite, testify to the grandeur of this Egyptian town, and to the recklessness and magnificence of the monarchs who conveyed from the border of Ethiopia the stupendous monuments whose fragments are now seen close to the waters of the Mediterranean. A ruined gateway of granite bearing the cartouche of Ramses II. indicates

---

* *A. J.* ii. 15, 1.   † Ps. lxxviii. 12, 43.

what was once the entrance to a spacious temple; and the obelisks, of which there are ten if not twelve, a number unexampled in any other Egyptian city, bear the shield of the same monarch. Nor are the traces of the contributions of other Pharaohs wanting. The cartouches of Usurtasen III. and of Mineptah II., the successor of Ramses II., are to be seen on some of the sculptured remains. The former testifies to the existence of the city under a ruler whose epoch cannot be determined; the latter brings before our eyes the monarch in whose reign it is now generally believed that the Exodus took place.

With much particularity of detail, and with a conclusiveness which to those who are unacquainted with the ancient Egyptian language, seems perhaps suspiciously complete, Brugsch Bey demonstrates the identity of Pithom, Succoth, and Etham with places in the neighbourhood of Zoan, and having thus established his premises, confidently appeals to the world to accept his conclusion that Zoan was the Pi-ramses, the city of Ramses, which the captive Hebrews assisted in building during the reign of Ramses II. Pithom, he alleges, was the principal town in the district of Sukot, the town being so called because it was dedicated to the solar god Tom, who was also specially worshipped at On (Heliopolis),* the district receiving the essentially Semitic name which signifies "tents," from the circumstance of its being frequently made the camping ground of the nomadic tribes of the adjoining desert.† Etham is the Hebrew pronunciation of the Egyptian Khetam, which signifies "fortress,"‡ of which there were many in Egypt, but notably one frequently alluded to in the province of Zor (Zoan), whilst Migdol is placed on the site of Magdola, a few miles south of Pelusium, and is identified with the present Tel-

---

* *L'Exode*, 15. † Ibid., 12. ‡ Ibid., 25.

es-Semout,* the ancient Egyptian name having been Samout, which, like the Hebrew Migdol, signifies "a tower." But Brugsch Bey carries his case even farther, for he translates from a papyrus in the British Museum a letter giving an account of the pursuit of two slaves by an Egyptian officer, in which the latter mentions *seriatim* the places visited by the Hebrews on quitting Rameses. This official quitted the royal palace on the ninth day of the month, he arrived on the tenth at the barrier of Sukot, on the twelfth he reached Khetam, and there he was told by some persons who came from the neighbourhood of the lakes of Suph that the fugitives had passed through the country of "the wall" to the north of Migdol of the king Seti Mineptah. Like the Hebrews, the Egyptian official quitted Rameses and passed by way of Succoth to Etham, where he heard that those of whom he was in pursuit had also, like the Hebrews, turned and made their way to the north of Migdol towards the region of the *Jam Suph*. It occasions no surprise that Brugsch Bey should attribute the preservation of this precious letter to the intervention of Providence.†

But, unfortunately, those who are best qualified to appreciate the nature of the evidence given by Brugsch Bey refuse to accept either his facts or his conclusions,‡ and therefore the question of the place from which the Hebrews took their departure, and the direction which they followed

---

* *L'Exode*, 20.

† "Un heureux hasard—disons plutôt la Providence divine—nous a conservé dans un des papyrus du Musée Britannique le souvenir le plus précieux de l'Epoque contemporaine du séjour des Hebreux en Egypte."—*L'Exode*, 27.

‡ Dr. Birch, in referring to Brugsch Bey's theory that the Exodus took place towards the Mediterranean, observes: "The difficulties of reconciling the Scriptural account as to the time passed in the transit, as well as that of allowing the philological coincidence of some of the Hebrew and Egyptian names, have caused this brilliant discovery of the supposed direction of the Exodus not to be universally admitted

on their way to "the edge of the wilderness" cannot be regarded as conclusively disposed of.

The author of Psalm lxxviii. uses an expression which raises a strong presumption that, according to tradition, the marvels which preceded the liberation of Israel were worked in the neighbourhood of Zoan. "Marvellous things did he in the sight of their fathers in the land of Egypt, in the field of Zoan;" and in a subsequent verse, "How he had wrought his signs in Egypt and his wonders on the field of Zoan." Now, as there is no question of the identity of Zoan and Tanis and the modern Zan, it would follow, if the Psalmist correctly represented the tradition, and if the tradition was itself correct, that the place of abode of the captive Hebrews must have been in the region adjoining the north-eastern frontier of Egypt. There is, however, a possibility that the Psalmist was inaccurate. Zoan was unquestionably a city of considerable political importance some two centuries after the Exodus, when it became the capital under the twenty-first dynasty. Pi-biseth or Bubastis appears to have been the seat of government under the following dynasty, but Zoan again became the residence of the Pharaohs with the accession of the twenty-third dynasty at the close of the ninth century B.C. It is evidently so spoken of by the earlier Isaiah,* and it is one of the cities marked out for destruction by Ezekiel.† It is therefore quite possible that the author of Psalm lxxviii., if he lived at a time when Zoan was the capital of the Egyptian kings, might have assumed that the city, which was the residence of the Pharaoh and

---

by those who have studied the antiquities of Egypt or Biblical geography."—*Egypt*, 135. Dr. Birch identifies Pithom and Rameses with the fortresses Pa-Khatem-en-Tsaru, or the citadel of Tanis, and Paramessu, which were erected on the line of the great wall constructed between On and Pelusium.—*Egypt*, 125.

* Isaiah xix. 13; xxx. 4. † Ezek. xxx. 14.

his court at the time of the Exodus, was the same which in his own time was well known to be the capital of the Egyptian empire. This element of uncertainty cannot therefore be thrown out of account in estimating the value of the evidence of the Psalmist.

According to the received tradition, the Hebrew colony whose departure from Egypt now engages our attention, was originally permitted to settle in a district which was called the land of Goshen. It is generally admitted that this district lay on the north-eastern frontier of Egypt, and probably comprehended the pasture-land which there stretched between Zoan and Pelusium, part of which the subsidence of the Mediterranean coast has since converted into a lake during one portion of the year, and a desert during the remainder. This region is spoken of as "the land of Rameses,"* and it is not unreasonable to conclude was, according to tradition, identical with that from which the Hebrews ultimately took their departure. If, however, the land of Goshen and the land of Rameses were identical, and if the departure from Rameses was either from "the land of Rameses" or from the city bearing the same name, but which was almost certainly in "the land," we have not only very strong evidence that the Exodus took place from north-eastern Egypt, but we have very powerful confirmation of the accuracy of the Psalmist in naming "the field of Zoan" as the scene of the wonders which were said to have preceded the liberation of Israel.

In the fragments from Manetho preserved to us by Josephus, mention is made of a town called Avaris. Manetho states that this city was built by the Hyksos† who

---

* Gen. xlvii. 11.

† The name Hyksos is said to be compounded of Hyk or Hak, a ruler, and Shasu, the appellation given by the Egyptians to the nomad tribes—that is, the shepherds. Manetho, cited by Josephus, *Contra Apion*, i. 14.

made themselves masters of Lower Egypt, and that when their rule was subsequently overthrown this city was the last stronghold from which they were driven. This is to some extent confirmed by a papyrus in the British Museum, in which it is recorded that Egypt fell into the hands of the lepers; that king Rasekuen ruled only in Upper Egypt; that the lepers possessed On (Heliopolis); whilst their ruler established his court at Haouar (Avaris).* The shepherds, or lepers, were expelled by Aahmes or Amosis, the first king of the eighteenth dynasty; and as it appears that several naval actions took place on the waters of Haouar, it is concluded that this city was on the Tanaitic branch of the Nile. Avaris was captured in the third naval engagement, and the Hyksos were expelled.

Manetho also speaks of Avaris as the town to which at a much later period king Amenophis removed the lepers whom he had previously employed in the quarries on the east bank of the Nile, and who took for their leader Osarsiph, the priest of On. They are said to have revolted, and with the aid of the expelled Hyksos to have ravaged Egypt during a period of thirteen years, when they were subdued and driven out of the country.

Some years since, M. de Rougè established, on what seem to be substantial grounds, the identity of Zoan and Avaris. Zoan is the Semitic equivalent of the Egyptian Ha-awar or Pa-awar, and signifies "the place of departure." How it came by this name cannot be determined with certainty. It may have been so called because from its contiguity to the frontier it was the place from which caravans set out for the East, or because it was the city from which the Hyksos took their final departure. Again, it may have received its Semitic appellation as being the spot from which

---

* Birch, *Egypt*, 75.

the Exodus took place. If the name Ha-awar be as old as the time of the shepherds, the latter gloss is untenable; but it is at least remarkable that no mention is made of Ha-awar or Zoan by either of those names in the traditions of the Exodus, if that city or either of them (if they were distinct) had been connected with the departure of the Israelites. In the account of the sending forth of the spies from the Hebrew camp in the desert, it is stated that they came to Hebron, the name of which city previous to the settlement in Canaan was Kirjath-Arba.* Although this prolepsis sufficiently indicates the composition of the record in its present form subsequent to the Hebrew incursion, a still later writer has added, though on what authority we know not, the statement that Hebron was built seven years before Zoan. Hebron is, however, referred to in connection with Abraham, and hence it would follow that Zoan must have been built previous to the Hebrew settlement in Goshen. But even admitting the antiquity of Zoan, the time at which it received its Semitic name would still remain uncertain. It might have been called Zoan by the Hyksos, or by the Hebrews during their stay in Egypt; but it is at least singular that, although all the evidence indicates that it stood in the region occupied by the Hebrews previous to their departure, and although its monumental remains prove that it was a city of great importance in the reigns of Rameses II. and his successor Mineptah—the supposed Pharaoh of the Exodus—it is never mentioned *eo nomine* in the traditions we are now examining. Those traditions speak of the city of Raamses, and the departure from Rameses, names we should expect to find employed if the Hebrews inhabited the neighbourhood of a city which Ramses II. undoubtedly took great trouble to adorn, and

---

* Num. xiii. 22.

which it is stated was at one time called by the Egyptians Pi-rāmessu. If, however, the Semitic name Zoan had then been borne by this city, it seems not unreasonable to conclude that the Hebrews would have used it in preference to "Rameses;" but when we find that they did not do so, and when we further find that in later times the plain around this great city was regarded as the scene of the marvels which preceded the Exodus, and that the city was called by the Semitic name Zoan, it raises a possibility, some might perhaps be inclined to think a probability, that the name became a standing memorial as well in the Hebrew as in the Egyptian language, Zoan (Ha-awar), of that great event which marked the severance between Israel and Egypt.

There seem therefore to be, on the whole, probable grounds for concluding that the Hebrew colony which was either "thrust out" of Egypt, or permitted to depart, inhabited the region lying between the Tanaitic branch of the Nile and "the wilderness;" that its members were engaged in forced labour, either in the city which was then, or subsequently came to be, known as Zoan, or in other Egyptian towns or fortresses in the same region; and that when they took their departure they followed the ordinary easterly route leading directly to the *midbhar*, or "wilderness," which lay outside the Egyptian frontier. In other words, they quitted Egypt, as might naturally be expected, by the shortest road. The chief grounds upon which Biblical scholars have hitherto placed Rameses farther south—namely, in the valley of the ancient canal, or in the neighbourhood of Memphis—have been supplied by the necessity of giving a rational explanation of the march to the western coast of the Suez Gulf in order to supply an occasion for "the passage of the Red Sea." It was universally felt that it would have been a little too absurd to suggest that Moses would have led the children of Israel from the field of Zoan, which lay close to the Mediterranean, due south through Egyptian territory, some eighty or ninety miles (even if he had been permitted to do so), for the mere sake of placing a broad Gulf between them and the region towards which he was leading them; when, by following an easterly course, not more than twenty miles needed to be traversed to cross the Egyptian frontier. It is alleged that in ancient times the waters of the Gulf of Suez flowed into the great Bitter Lake; but it may well be doubted whether what was known as "the Egyptian Sea"* was deemed to extend farther north than the site of the modern Suez. Assuming that Rameses was in the valley of the ancient canal, the southerly march on the western side of the Bitter Lake, and of the extension more or less broad and deep of the Suez Gulf, would still be unaccountable on any rational grounds. If, on the other hand, Rameses was in the neighbourhood of Memphis, then a very slight deflection to the south would have brought the Israelites to the shore of the Gulf. The imperative necessity of crossing the Red Sea has heretofore, despite all the evidence pointing in another direction, irresistibly dragged the Hebrews into a region of Egypt which it is nowhere stated or suggested that they ever visited. Even those who would not dream of questioning the authority of the Psalmist surmount the difficulty raised by his testimony by suggesting that the earlier plagues may have been witnessed in the neighbourhood of Zoan, but that the Pharaoh moved his court subsequently to a city farther south, from which latter point the Exodus took place.

When the Israelites quitted Rameses, they "journeyed to Succoth;" and when "they took their journey from Succoth" they "encamped in Etham, in the edge of the wilderness." If we accept the views of Brugsch Bey, we shall have no

---

* Isaiah xi. 15.

H

hesitation in identifying Succoth with the Egyptian Sukot, a district lying to the east of Zoan, and Etham with the Khetam or fortress which, according to this Egyptologist, stood on the Pelusiac bank of the Nile, in the close neighbourhood of the town Tabenet, of which mention is made by Herodotus* as Daphne, and which to-day is known as Tell-Defennah. Outside Khetam lay the open country south of Migdol, stretching towards the wilderness.

It is impossible, however, to shut our eyes to the exclusively Semitic character of the words "Succoth" and "Etham;" and although we should not feel surprised if places in a district which we have reason to believe were occupied during a long period by the Hebrews received Semitic names, we must view with some suspicion an explanation which, whilst admitting that Succoth is pure Semitic, accounts for the use of Etham by assuming it to be a Hebrew pronunciation of the Egyptian "Khetam." There is still another reason why we should hesitate to lay much stress on this philological demonstration of the route of the Hebrews. The Egyptian Suku,† or Sukot, was a name given to an entire district, in the Sethroitic Nome, lying between the Tanaitic and Pelusiac branches of the Nile—this name, signifying "tents," being so given, according to Dr. Brugsch, in consequence of the encampments of the nomadic tribes which were permitted to settle there‡. But if this were so, we should not expect the name of an extensive district to be named as a stage in the journey. In order to obviate this difficulty, Brugsch suggests that the place referred to as Succoth was Segor, or Segol, "the close" of Succoth—a kind of fortress commanding the communications between the district of Zoan-Rameses and that of Succoth§.

It would perhaps be safer to admit our uncertainty

* Her. ii. 30–107. † Egyptologists read this name Thuku.
‡ L'Exode, 25. § Ibid.

respecting these two places, even though we should be satisfied that the Exodus took place from the region about Zoan. The names Succoth and Etham present certain characteristics, which in the course of our inquiry we shall find are common to many of the names preserved in the earliest traditions of the " journeying" toward Canaan. That Succoth was descriptive and meant " tents" there can be no doubt, but whether the place was so called by the Hebrews from their having found themselves obliged to erect tents, or leafy bowers, for their accommodation, or whether the the name was already of old standing, we cannot say. But Etham we cannot safely accept as a reproduction of the Egyptian Khetam. The latter word was extremely common, signifying simply " fortress," and whatever direction the Israelites had taken on quitting Egypt, a convenient Khetam might have been found to fit in with the Etham, in the edge of the wilderness. It seems probable that Etham is not a proper name. It is very noticeable that the word is not preceded by the preposition " to," as is the case with Succoth, the preceding station, and Marah and Elim, the next stages noted in the journeyings. They " encamped in Etham, in the edge of the wilderness." May not this word be an obsolete archaism, signifying "the neighbouring" or "adjoining places." The passage would then run, " and encamped in the neighbouring places in the edge of the wilderness."* It is remarkable that Etham is nowhere else mentioned save by the author of the Itinerary in Numbers xxxiii., who, as

---

* אֵתָם Etham, seems to have been formed in an early dialect from אֵת Eth, " near," and would signify the " near places." I am certainly at a loss to understand how Brugsch Bey renders Etham as the equivalent of the Egyptian Khetam, as in the table of equivalents of the Egyptian and Hebrew characters the initial letter of Khetam is given by him as the Greek χ and the Hebrew ח, and in English is rendered Kh.—*Egypt*, ii. 321. Etham, on the other hand, commences with a vowel, or a letter having a vowel sound.

will subsequently be shown, is wholly unreliable. Besides, we know from a number of sources that the wilderness, trending eastwards from the Egyptian frontier, was called the wilderness of Shur, and is so styled in the same record in which the word Etham occurs.

In the fact that only one halting stage is recorded between the place of the Hebrews' captivity and the edge of *the* wilderness (*ham-midbhar*), tends to confirm the conclusion that the Exodus took place from that part of Egypt adjoining the north-eastern frontier. If it be correctly stated that at the time of the Exodus the waters of the Suez Gulf extended to the great Bitter Lake, or possibly to Lake Timsah, the route from Egypt to the East must have run between the last-named lake, or probably between the more northern Lake of Balah, and the Pelusiac branch of the Nile. Through this comparatively narrow isthmus there is every reason to believe that the Israelites passed, in order to reach "the edge of the wilderness;" and if they succeeded in doing so, having encamped only once on the road, the place of their departure could not have been far distant.

It will be seen therefore that the broad view propounded by Brugsch Bey has much to support it. Whether the city of Zoan-Tanis was the treasure city Raamses which the Hebrews were engaged in building, or was some smaller town or fortress, we leave to Egyptologists to determine. We believe that the land of Goshen or of Rameses, where, according to tradition, the Hebrews were allowed to settle, was the same from which the Exodus took place, and was situated on the north-eastern frontier of Egypt; and that on taking their departure the Hebrews directed their steps between that portion of the Pelusiac arm of the Nile which has long since been effaced by Lake Menzaleh, and what are now known as the Bitter Lakes towards the broad and inhospitable region known to them as "the wilderness."

Such a route would have taken them at no great distance from Migdol, and hence the facility with which the legend of the passage of "the Sea," the Mediterranean, came to be engrafted on the original tradition. We must, however, decline to accept the identification of the Sethroitic Nome under the name of Suku with Succoth, and one of the many Egyptian Khetam "fortresses," with "Etham, in the edge of the wilderness." But this is comparatively unimportant. In conducting such an inquiry as the present it may be convenient to keep in mind that we are separated by an interval of more than thirty centuries from the events recorded; and that during that time, even assuming that the traditions remained unaltered, some changes must have taken place in topical nomenclature. We shall do well to recollect that we are not following the track of an advancing army with a special correspondent's letter in one hand, and an Ordnance map in the other. We must not assume that we are bound to identify every halting-place, nor should we think that our character for acumen and accuracy will be forfeited if we fail to track the Israelites from stage to stage with unerring precision. If we would achieve the possible, we must not strain at the impossible. We must not only rest content, but shall have every reason to be content, if we succeed in obtaining a broad and generally correct view of the direction taken by the Hebrews in the course of a migration which was destined to exercise so great an influence on the human race.

CHAPTER IV.

BEFORE following the released captives into the desert it would seem an almost indispensable preliminary to determine, with some approach to certainty, their numbers and their race. As regards the former our information is certainly precise, but overwhelming reasons oblige us to reject the statement that the fighting men numbered six hundred thousand,* which would give between two and three millions as the number of all the captives who quitted Egypt. In dealing with figures Orientals are proverbially reckless, and the Hebrews proved no exception to this rule. No nomadic tribe would have ventured to attack so formidable a host, much less have succeeded in defeating it. No leader with such a force at his back would have brooked a refusal of permission to pass through the Idumæan valleys.† In fine, if the Hebrews marshalled such an enormous army, it is inexplicable that they did not at once attempt to penetrate Canaan by the nearest route, or when they did make the attempt that they did not sweep before them the mountaineers who barred the way.‡

A different question arises when we inquire who were the people who were thrust out of Egypt. According to the generally accepted view, the twelve sons of Jacob settled with their families in Egypt, and those who were led out of that country were their descendants. It is also an accepted belief that on quitting Egypt the released captives were

---

* Exod. xii. 37.   † Num. xx. 18.   ‡ Num. xiv. 45; Deut. i. 44.

divided into distinct tribes—thirteen in number—two tribes, Ephraim and Manasseh, having sprung from the loins of Joseph. Much of this we must, however, discard.

Assuming that those who quitted Egypt were the reputed descendants of Jacob, to whom also the name of Israel was given, then the multitude would properly be termed the Beni-Israel—the children of Israel. But we cannot ignore the fact that, previous to the fall of the northern monarchy at the hands of the Assyrians at the close of the eighth century B.C., the style of Beni-Israel was exclusively borne by those who were the subjects of the northern kingdom, and, previous to the establishment of the foundation of the monarchy, more especially by the members of the tribes of Ephraim and Manasseh. The rival tribe of Judah makes a brief appearance on the scene in connection with the invasion of Canaan; it then passes into obscurity. It is not referred to in the Song of Deborah.* We have a slight glimpse of it in captivity to the Philistines, in the story of Samson;† it emerges at the time of the foundation of the monarchy, the crowns of Israel and Judah are united on David's head, only to be separated on the accession of his grandson Rehoboam, and from that date to the time of the overthrow of the kingdom of Israel an unceasing antagonism existed between the two peoples. It is difficult to imagine that during the subsistence of the northern kingdom its people would have admitted the claim of those of the southern to be " children of Israel." Israel regarded Judah with a contempt which it was at no pains to conceal.‡

---

* Judges v. † Judges xv. 11.
‡ The epitome given in 2 Kings xiv. of the reign " of the good king" Amaziah of Judah, throws a singular light on the relationship, political and religious, which subsisted between the two sections of what are popularly known as "the children of Israel," about a century before the overthrow of the northern kingdom. Amaziah having con-

In dealing with the records of the Hebrew migration from Egypt it will be necessary, at all events, to avoid starting with the assumption that the children of Israel and those of Judah were so inseparably connected from the time of their quitting Egypt until the severance of the monarchy on the death of Solomon, that the traditions of the one

---

ceived the idea of ravaging Edom mobilised his army, which amounted to three hundred thousand men. This force being thought insufficient, he hired an additional hundred thousand men from the king of Israel for a hundred talents of silver. When about to commence the campaign, "a man of God" informed Amaziah that the war would not be successful if he received the co-operation of the Israelites, for "Jahveh was not with Israel." The king reluctantly followed the seer's advice, dismissed his mercenaries, and successfully ravaged Edom, slaying ten thousand in battle, and taking ten thousand alive, whom he butchered by casting them down from the top of a rock. The Israelites who were sent home were, however, so much dissatisfied, that they fell upon the cities of Judah and smote three thousand of them (the figures in this narrative are perfectly dazzling) and took much spoil. The pious king returned in triumph from Edom, bringing with him the gods of the Edomites, and "set them up to be his gods." (His biographer admits that though "he did that which was right in the sight of Jahveh," it was "not with a perfect heart.") Elated by his victory over the Edomites, the king of Judah sent a message to the king of Israel, "Come, let us look one another in the face," which would seem to have been the Hebrew way of provoking war when a *casus belli* happened to be wanting. The reply of the king of Israel was certainly not what in the language of modern diplomacy would be termed "reassuring." It ran—"The thistle that was in Lebanon sent to the cedar that was in Lebanon, saying, Give thy daughter to my son to wife: and there passed by a wild beast that was in Lebanon, and trod down the thistle." Then followed advice to the king of Judah to be content with his victory over the Edomites, and not to "meddle to his hurt," lest "he should fall, and Judah with him." The delicate metaphor of the cedar and the thistle was, however, too much for Amaziah; he repeated his challenge to the king of Israel to come and look him in the face. The latter accepted the challenge, invaded Judah, the kings looked each other in the face at Beth-shemesh, and the army of the king of Judah was routed. The sequel of the story is curious. The king of Israel took Jerusalem by assault, and sacked the Temple, carrying off "all the gold and silver, and all the vessels that were found in the house of Jahveh."

would necessarily tally in every respect with those of the other, and that in the records of the tribes which formed the northern kingdom the expression "children of Israel" would necessarily be intended to include those who colonised the southern portion of Canaan. Assuming that the ancestors of those who subsequently occupied Palestine from Mount Hermon to the southern slopes of the hills of Judah quitted Egypt together, it may seem of little consequence whether they were known collectively as Israelites or not. But it is of some importance to ascertain whether, in the records we possess, the term "children of Israel" is used in the extended sense in which it is popularly employed. That in later times Judah deemed itself of the house of Israel is beyond all doubt, and that some centuries after the disappearance of Israel proper it claimed to be the heir and sole representative of the people of Israel, is a great historical fact. But before the subjugation of the northern kingdom the distinction between Israel and Judah was, save during the brief period when the kingdoms were united under David and Solomon, as sharp and well-defined as it was well possible to be, between two people who shared the belief that they had been led out of captivity in Egypt, and by the aid of the same protecting God had obtained possession of the land in which they had established themselves. In presence of the story which makes Jacob (Israel) the common ancestor of all who quitted Egypt, it is impossible to account for some of the tribes in after-times arrogating exclusively to themselves the proud title of "Israel," and for the people of Judah acquiescing in this special appropriation of a common designation. We are, however, confronted by the fact that such was the case, and we are necessarily driven to suspect that if the records of Israel had not been transmitted to us through the hands of Judah this singular fact might be satisfactorily explained. The consideration of this interesting question does not, however, come within the scope of the present inquiry.

In the account of the departure from Egypt, it is stated that when "the children of Israel journeyed from Rameses" "a mixed multitude went up also with them, and flocks and herds, even very much cattle."* Elsewhere we find this "mixed multitude" again referred to. Whilst in the wilderness it is stated that "the mixed multitude that was among them fell a lusting: and the children of Israel also wept again, and said, Who shall give us flesh to eat?"† Who were those who are spoken of as a "mixed multitude?"

It is universally assumed that as the children of Israel are supposed to have included all the descendants of Jacob—that is to say, the thirteen tribes—the "mixed multitude" must have comprehended Egyptians and others, not of Israelitish descent, who elected to unite their lot with that of the departing captives. But for many reasons this is extremely improbable. It was in presumed obedience to the God of the Hebrews, and with the ostensible object of worshipping the God of the Hebrews, that the Exodus took place; and it is therefore very unlikely that any save Hebrews would have desired, or would have been permitted, to quit Egypt with the emancipated slaves. Independently of this natural presumption, it is noticeable that no allusion is made subsequently to the presence of any other than a Hebrew with the departing host; nor does any one of the "mixed multitude" which quitted Egypt, if it was composed of others than those whose deliverance was accomplished by Jahveh, leave any trace in the histories of Israel and Judah. The "mixed multitude," nevertheless, although no pointed allusion is apparently made to any of those who composed it, played a not unimportant part in the migration towards Canaan. It

---

* Exod. xii. 38.   † Num. xi. 4.

is sufficiently numerous to be spoken of as accompanying the children of Israel on their departure, and it is rather invidiously referred to as having set the bad example subsequently followed by the children of Israel, of lusting after more solid food than manna. It is impossible to imagine that it was composed of men of a race different from that of the "children of Israel."

The allusions made to "the Hebrews" in the earlier portion of the narrative of the bondage in Egypt, might perhaps appear to offer to some extent a solution of the question before us. Israel here seems to be included amongst the Hebrews, whilst the latter are not regarded as necessarily Israelites. The sufferings of the Hebrews are incidental to, and consequent upon, those of the Israelites. The latter were prosperous and flourishing when "a king arose who knew not Joseph."* But Joseph had then been a long time dead; it is therefore evident that Joseph is here treated as a synonym for Israel, as in later times the tribes of Manasseh and Ephraim, his sons, were regarded as specially constituting the Beni-Israel. No notice whatever is taken of the other sons of Jacob, who on the invitation of Joseph and under his protection were said to have settled in Egypt. It is the "children of Israel" who fill the land;† it is they who excite the alarm of the Pharaoh, lest they become "more and mightier" than the Egyptians;‡ it is against them that the king adopts strong measures by setting taskmasters over them and making "their lives bitter with hard bondage."§ This is the tradition of Israel, and it is throughout marked by the consciousness that the descendants of Joseph constituted the *élite* and the bulk of the stock of Abraham in Egypt. But there were others besides Israelites in bondage, though the latter in their traditions thought proper to ignore them. There were

---

* Exod. i. 8.   † Exod. i. 7.   ‡ Exod. i. 9.   § Exod. i. 11-14.

others whose posterity in after-times claimed with the children of Israel descent from a common ancestor, who relied on the covenant which tradition declared that the Elohim had made with their father Abraham. These were "Hebrews;" they embraced not only the descendants of Joseph but all of Terahitic descent,[*] as well those held in captivity in Egypt as those who had never parted with their liberty and were even at the time of the Exodus in possession of the lands which the Elohim of the Hebrews had given them. Joseph himself is represented as declaring that he had been "stolen out of the land of the Hebrews."[†] He was "the Hebrew" boy, falsely accused of soliciting the chastity of Potiphar's wife.

When, previous to the settlement in Canaan a severance took place between those who ultimately became known respectively as "Israel" and "Judah," their traditions assumed in many particulars different complexions. The former, owing to causes which can only be adequately dealt with in an examination of the Hebrew settlement in Canaan, claimed the title of Beni-Israel, whilst the latter were content to bear the generic designation of Hebrews in addition to the patronymic styles of their tribes. The former, consciously or unconsciously, moulded their traditions so as to make it appear that when they quitted Egypt they bore the appellation of Beni-Israel; the latter, being exposed to no such influences, recollected that in common with their brethren, from whom they became subsequently separated, they bore the name of Hebrews.

Now in the opening chapters of the Book of Exodus we discover clear traces of the two classes of tradition to which we refer. The narrative of the bondage in Egypt begins at Exodus i. 7, and continues without interruption to verse 14.

---

[*] Gen. xii. 27-31.   [†] Gen. xl. 15.

At the latter verse, however, a break occurs, and we find that the compiler has found it expedient to make use of a different record. In Exodus i. 7-14 we read a statement that "the children of Israel were fruitful and increased abundantly," and "waxed exceeding mighty;" that "a king arose who knew not Joseph;" and that apprehensive lest they should multiply and join the enemies of Egypt he "set taskmasters over them to afflict them with their burdens," and "made their lives bitter with hard bondage." In this record it is noticeable that the captives are spoken of exclusively as the children or people of Israel, and are so styled even by the Pharaoh, and that the mode of checking their increase was by afflicting them with burdens, an expedient which, it is added, proved wholly ineffectual.

In the concluding verses of the chapter (verses 15-22) we find not only a different account of the means adopted to check the multiplication of the captives, but we look in vain for any allusion to the "children of Israel." The oppressed people are now spoken of exclusively as "Hebrews." In an abrupt and disconnected manner the king of Egypt is described as speaking to the "Hebrew" midwives, Shiphrah and Puah, and directing them when they do their office to the "Hebrew" women to kill the male offspring. The midwives, however, disobeyed the king, excusing themselves on the ground that owing to a constitutional difference between the "Hebrew" and the Egyptian women, their services were anticipated by Nature before their arrival. The result was that "the people multiplied and waxed very mighty;" and the king then "charged all his people" that every male child should be cast into the river.

The next chapter contains an epitome of the life of Moses from his birth to his flight to Midian, and marriage with the daughter of Reuel. In this narrative we are also struck by the singular circumstance that no mention is made of the "children of Israel," but that the captives are invariably referred to as "Hebrews." The parents of Moses are described as of the tribe of Levi. The mother exposes her child in the river, and when the child is seen by Pharaoh's daughter, she exclaims, "This is one of the Hebrew children."* His sister, who watches the child, then appears, and asks the Princess, "Shall I go and call to thee a nurse of the Hebrew women?" and the latter having assented, the mother, a Levite woman, is brought and engaged to nurse the child. Years afterwards, when Moses was grown, it is said he saw an Egyptian smiting "a Hebrew, one of his brethren," and on the following day he saw "two men of the Hebrews" striving together, when having interposed, he was reminded of the murder he had committed on the previous day, and he thereupon fled to Midian.

In this narrative, as in that of the Pharaoh and the midwives, with which it is closely connected, we see in the different designations given to the captives conclusive evidence that the traditions embodied in it grew up and were moulded amongst people different from, and at the time apparently unconnected with, those who called themselves the children of Israel. It would also seem that the tribe of Levi, which is now reckoned amongst the "children of Israel," did not in

---

* There is a visible connection between the story of the finding of Moses, and the singular order attributed to Pharaoh to despatch the male Hebrew children by casting them into the river. Both traditions have had a common source, but one of them in time became modified. The finding of Moses in the river was at first explained by attributing to Pharaoh the order referred to, and hence his daughter on seeing the child concluded it was a Hebrew child. Another version then grew up that the mother put the child in the river, not in compliance with the Royal decree, but in order to save him from destruction.

early times claim that proud distinction.* The "Israelitish" record, broken by the compiler at Exod. i. 14, to interweave the "Hebrew" narratives of Pharaoh's design to check the multiplication of the captives, not by hard bondage but by killing the male children, and of Moses' early life, is resumed at Exod. ii. 23, and continued to the end of the chapter. The appellation "Hebrew" vanishes, whilst that of the "children of Israel" is restored. In direct continuation of the narrative, Exod. i. 7-14, it is said that "it came to pass that the king of Egypt died, and the children of Israel sighed by reason of the bondage, and they cried, and their cry came up unto God by reason of the bondage," "and God looked upon the children of Israel, and had respect for them." There is no suggestion of any complaint of the far more serious hardship of the wholesale slaughter of their male children. It would thence appear that in the traditions of "Israel" the story of Pharaoh's destruction of the male offspring of his captives had no place.

The expression "Hebrews" occurs five times in the Book of Exodus, exclusive of the instances already noticed, and in all these cases is employed as descriptive of the Elohim who demands the liberation of those who were kept in bondage in Egypt. It is "the God of the Hebrews," in whose name Moses and Aaron speak,† when demanding permission for the children of Israel to go a three days' journey into the wilderness to serve their God. When Pharaoh asks, who is Jahveh? the envoys reply, "The God of the Hebrews has sent us,"‡ and it is over and over again stated that "the God of the Hebrews" is not only the God of Jacob but is the God of Abraham and Isaac, and, by implication, of all their descendants. We see therefore that even in

---

* But it is at least as probable that this reference to the tribe of Levi is the work of a later writer.

† Exod. iii. 18.   ‡ Exod. v. 3.

traditions which furnish intrinsic evidence of having been derived from Israel, the liberating God is styled, not exclusively the God of Israel, but the God of the Hebrews, and that it is in this larger and more comprehensive character that he interposes. But this interposition in the larger character tends to fortify our conclusion, that from an Israelite's point of view there were non-Israelites in Egypt, whose liberation their God was equally anxious to secure, descendants of Abraham, to whom the generic appellation Hebrews was applied. If, however, we place ourselves in the position of those who settled in southern Palestine, and who subsequently were known as "the men of Judah," we can equally understand how, in accordance with their traditions also, the liberating deity was the God of the Hebrews, whilst the people liberated bore the same comprehensive title.

The designation "Hebrews" next appears several times in the records of the events preceding the foundation of the monarchy of Judah, and then vanishes completely. We shall refer briefly to those instances in which the word is used, because they throw some light upon the point under consideration.

In the accounts given of the wars with the Philistines which resulted in the liberation of Israel and Judah from their oppression, frequent allusion is made by the Philistines to their adversaries, but invariably as Hebrews. "What meaneth the noise of this great shout in the camp of the Hebrews?"* "O ye Philistines, be ye not servants unto the Hebrews as they have been unto you."† "There was no smith found throughout all the land of Israel, for the Philistines said, Lest the Hebrews make them swords or spears."‡ "And the Philistines said, Behold the Hebrews

---

* 1 Sam. iv. 6. † 1 Sam. iv. 9. ‡ 1 Sam. xiii. 19.

come forth out of the holes where they have hid themselves;"* apparently in connection with the previous statement that "the men of Israel saw they were in a strait, and the people did hide themselves in caves, and in thickets, and in rocks, and in high places, and in pits;"† and on the eve of the battle in which Saul was slain, the princes of the Philistines asked in reference to David and his followers, whose aid had been accepted by Achish, "What do these Hebrews here? .... make this fellow return .... lest in the battle he be an adversary unto us."‡

We find, however, that the designation "Hebrews" is not employed by the Philistines alone. Saul and his son Jonathan having attacked the enemy with a force of three thousand men, and captured a garrison, thereupon "Saul blew the trumpet throughout all the land, saying, 'Let the Hebrews hear."§ The Philistines afterwards marshalled a mighty host and advanced against Saul, the result of which was that "when the men of Israel saw that they were in a strait, they hid themselves in caves," &c "and some of the Hebrews went over Jordan to the land of Gad and Gilead."|| In the succeeding chapter, in an account of a battle with the Philistines, it is stated that "the Hebrews that were with the Philistines before that time, which went up with them into the camp, even they also turned to be with the Israelites .... likewise all the men of Israel which had hid themselves in Mount Ephraim," &c.¶

It would appear therefore from these passages, that at a comparatively early period—namely, before the establishment of the monarchy—those who constituted what are termed the tribes of Israel were known by the Philistines collectively and individually as Hebrews, whilst those who

---

* 1 Sam. xiv. 11. † 1 Sam. xiii. 6. ‡ 1 Sam. xxix. 3 4.
§ 1 Sam. xiii. 3. || 1 Sam. xiii. 7. ¶ 1 Sam. xiv. 21, 22.

claimed the title of "children of Israel" gave the same designation to those who were united with them by ties of lineage, by similarity of traditions, and by the same strong motives to cast off the oppressor's yoke, but who at the same time were not deemed " Beni-Israel." It is easy therefore to understand how, during David's reign, even a Benjamite was found to lead a rebellion to the cry, " Every man to his tents, O Israel .... we have no part in David, neither have we inheritance in the son of Jesse ;"* and to succeed in inducing " every man of Israel"† to separate himself from David and from the men of Judah; and how at a later period, on the accession of Rehoboam, " when all Israel saw that the king hearkened not unto them," the people uttered the same cry and the same disavowal, the final severance from Judah took place ; " but as for the children of Israel which dwelt in the cities of Judah, Rehoboam reigned over them."‡

This digression has been necessary in order to show that, although the two great nations of the Hebrew race which settled in Palestine had common traditions of the servitude from which their fathers were liberated, each section came to be known by a special title which was not claimed by the other; that the generic appellation, although given by the Philistines equally to the members of the tribe of Judah, who had long been subject to them, and to the Israelites, was apparently employed by the latter to designate men of a common race, who were united with them in casting off the yoke of the Philistines, and who most unquestionably were the people of Judah.

The contradistinction between the two great families of Israel and Judah was not then the result of political differences arising on the death of Solomon, but ran back to a

---

* 2 Sam. xx. 1.   † 2 Sam. xx 2.   ‡ 1 Kings xii. 16, 17.

much earlier period. When their common ancestors quitted Egypt together, there is no reason to doubt that they acknowledged a common lineage, and that they enjoyed the equality springing from a common servitude, though certain tribal distinctions may have existed amongst them. At this period they were content to be known in their entirety as Hebrews. Subsequently the body of emigrants was split up. One portion colonised the region east of the Jordan and northern Palestine, whilst another section effected a settlement in the south. During the long period which intervened between the invasion of Canaan and the struggle for independence which resulted in the foundation of the kingdoms of Israel and Judah, these two great sections were completely disconnected. The Judges of Israel exercise no dominion over the men of Judah, nor do the latter co-operate with the Beni-Israel in their constantly recurring conflicts with their enemies. Deborah is apparently unaware of the existence of Judah, or at all events it does not occur to her to mention it in the spirit-stirring lyric* in which she refers by name to the tribes which either did take part or omitted to take part in the great struggle against the Canaanite forces under the command of Sisera. The tribe of Simeon, which united its fortunes with that of Judah,† and settled in southern Palestine, is equally unnoticed by the "mother of Israel." When at last Judah emerges from obscurity, we look in vain for its recognition as "Israelite." Its people, known to the Philistines, and apparently to their neighbours, the children of Israel, as "Hebrews," with the achievement of their independence designate themselves by a title based upon their traditions, and of which they are no less proud than their kinsmen of the north are of that of "Beni-Israel." They know nothing of the circumstances under which the

---

* Jud. v. † Jud. i. 3.

latter came to assume this title, and its validity or otherwise gives them very little concern. They are the "men of Judah," and as such are distinct from the "children of Israel." Whilst Samuel still lived we find Saul numbering "the children of Israel" and "the men of Judah" separately.* When David vanquishes Goliath, "the men of Israel and of Judah arose and shouted."† When Saul is slain, the "men of Judah," without any communication with the "children of Israel," anoint David king over the house of Judah;‡ whilst Ishbosheth, the son of Saul, is simultaneously, and without any protest from Judah, made king over "all Israel."§ A few years later, when Ishbosheth was murdered, "all the elders of Israel came to the king to Hebron ; and king David made a league with them in Hebron before Jahveh : and they anointed David king over Israel."‖ And finally, when Israel, wearied by the exactions of Solomon, failed to secure any promises of amendment from his successor Rehoboam, it separated itself from Judah, taking with it the title with which it had never parted, and leaving Judah in undisturbed, and apparently contented, enjoyment of the designation by which its people

---

* 1 Sam xi. 8.   † 1 Sam. xvii 52.   ‡ 2 Sam. ii. 4.   § 2 Sam. ii. 10.
‖ 2 Sam. v. 3. This league is referred to by Rehoboam's son Abijah, on his accession to the throne of Judah, 2 Chron. xiii. He declared war against Jeroboam, and brought into the field an army of four hundred thousand men, whilst the forces of Israel amounted to "eight hundred thousand chosen men, mighty men of valour." Before the battle Abijah made an ineffectual appeal to "Jeroboam and all Israel" to acknowledge the fact that "Jahveh, God of Israel, gave the kingdom over Israel to David for ever, even to him and to his sons, by a covenant of salt." In the battle which ensued Abijah was victorious, and "there fell down slain of Israel five hundred thousand chosen men." Considering that the territory of Israel and Judah, taken together, did not much exceed one hundred and twenty miles in length, by about forty in breadth, the extravagance of these figures is apparent, but it is impossible to deny a tribute of admiration to the audacity of the historian who employed them. The older writer, to whom we are

were known before the union of the two kingdoms had taken place.

Although we may satisfy ourselves that the captives in Egypt were known by a common generic title, the "Hebrews" —in some sort the equivalent of the Egyptian expression, "Shasu"—and that the distinctive appellations, Israel and Judah, were the creations of a much later age, still, in seeking to appreciate fully the meaning of the expression "a mixed multitude," we must consider the possibility of the captives having been accompanied by men of a common race with themselves, but who had not, like them, been reduced to servitude.

We have already, in connection with the Hebrew settlement in Egypt, directed attention to a very singular document of the reign of Mineptah II., the supposed Pharaoh of the Exodus.* It briefly states that permission has been accorded to some tribes of the Shasu, from the land of Aduma, to enter the land of Thuku to obtain sustenance for themselves and their herds. We are therefore tempted to inquire whether we may not have, in the Shasu here referred to, "the mixed multitude" of the traditions of Israel?

When, subsequent to the settlements on both sides of the Jordan, the descendants of those who had been kept in servitude in Egypt conjured up in their traditions the

---

indebted for the record in the Book of Kings, though he alludes to the war between Judah and Israel, makes no allusion to this wonderful battle (1 Kings xv. 1, 8). Israel maintained its independence notwithstanding the crushing defeat, but we are told in a general way that "Abijah waxed mighty, and married fourteen wives, and begat twenty-two sons and sixteen daughters" (2 Chron. xiii. 21), a degree of domestic prosperity which, however, seems rather dearly purchased by the slaughter of half a million of men. It was not, however, unworthy of mention, when it is kept in mind that Abijah only reigned a little over two years (1 Kings xv. 1–9). The earlier historian is silent as to Abijah's prowess both in love and war.

* See *ante*, p. 37.

triumphant manner in which their God had led them out of the house of bondage, it was certainly not unnatural that their liberation, and the surrounding circumstances so far as they exclusively concerned themselves, were alone deemed worthy of retaining a place in their memories. Assuming, for the sake of argument, that others of a common race, but who had not like them been reduced to slavery in Egypt, accompanied them across the wilderness, the fact might perhaps be recorded, but it would be treated as of trifling importance. In the traditions of the several sections into which the descendants of the captives were ultimately split up, it might be that one section came after a time to treat the others as deserving no higher or more distinctive appellation than that of a "mixed multitude;" but if the entire body of captives was accompanied by a tribe which had not shared their sorrows, then another explanation of the term "mixed multitude" would present itself.

And there are many circumstances which would lead us to conclude that the captives did not quit Egypt unaccompanied. According to the story in its present shape, Moses returned from Midian alone, and with the co-operation of his brother, and by virtue of the gift of thaumaturgy, succeeded in compelling the Pharaoh to liberate his Hebrew slaves. We cannot, however, accept this account as historical. It is in the remotest degree improbable that one of the despised Shasu—in the company of whom to partake of food was reckoned an abomination amongst the Egyptians*—crossing the frontier unaccompanied, could have been permitted to maintain with the mighty sovereign of Egypt the intimate personal intercourse of which we have so detailed an account in the Book of Exodus, or even that he could, through the intervention of Egyptian officials, have exercised

* Gen. xliii. 32; xlvi. 34.

an influence sufficiently powerful to obtain the liberation of a large body of slaves. But the case assumes a different complexion if we suppose that Moses came as the Sheikh of a pastoral tribe, with numerous followers, and accompanied by herds of cattle. It might well be that distress compelled the tribe to seek sustenance on the Delta, and that the Sheikh came as a supplicant to beg, or more probably to purchase, food for his people and pasturage for their flocks. But it is perfectly intelligible that, between the Shasu from the desert and the Shasu detained in captivity, there should exist strong ties of sympathy, and that an effort should be made by the former to obtain the liberation of the latter, an effort which special circumstances then existing might conspire to aid. And if we attentively study the tradition of the grounds upon which Pharaoh was requested to let the people go, we may discover how extremely probable it is that what was ultimately accomplished was done through the intervention of a friendly tribe which happened at the time to visit the Egyptian frontier.

The motive of departure advanced by Moses was that the captives should make a brief journey into the wilderness in compliance with the command of the God of the Hebrews, to offer him sacrifices, and thereby avert the danger of his " falling upon them with pestilence or with the sword."* That such a request should have been preferred by the Sheikh of a tribe received under the circumstances set forth in the document to which we have referred, is in the highest degree probable, whilst the likelihood of its being granted by the Egyptian ruler would depend upon surrounding circumstances. The sanitary condition of the captives at the time of the Exodus, there is every reason to believe, was very indifferent. The frequent allusions to leprosy indicate the presence amongst

---

* Exod. v. iii.

them of that terrible disease ; and it is not only possible, but highly probable, that representations should have been made on the one hand and should have been entertained on the other, which rested on the expediency of affording to the captives the opportunity of offering sacrifice to their God on a mountain, distant a few days' journey from the Egyptian frontier. If the request was granted, the released captives would accompany their liberators. Together with "the Shasu from the land of Aduma" they would turn their steps towards "the land of the Hebrews," from which, according to one tradition, the progenitor of the Beni-Israel was stolen.* In the words of the record still preserved to us; "a mixed multitude went up also with them; and flocks and herds, even very much cattle."† The difficulty of reconciling the presence of herds with the servile status of the Hebrews and the oppression to which they were subjected, then disappears, and we discover a ready explanation, not only of the heterogeneous elements of which the departing tribes were composed, but of the material wealth which the captives had the appearance of possessing at the very moment of their release from a terrible servitude. We must not be too hasty in arriving at conclusions, but it is excusable to entertain a very strong belief that in this papyrus scroll, now more than three thousand years old, is preserved the record of the arrival and reception of the Sheikh through whose instrumentality Israel was delivered from the house of bondage, and under whose guidance the Hebrews were led through the desert which interposed between Egypt and their future home.

As it is principally the object of this inquiry to ascertain the route followed by the Hebrews in their migration from Egypt to the Trans-Jordanic region, no reference will be made

---

* Gen. xl. 15.   † Exod. xii. 38.

to any of the events alleged to have happened in "the wilderness," or to any of the chief actors, except so far as may be necessary to elucidate the subject engaging our attention. What was the religious *cultus* of the Hebrews in the desert, what were the changes which it underwent, and what the circumstances under which those changes were effected, are questions of an importance which demands that they should be treated separately. Nor, for similar reasons, shall we touch upon the personal history of Moses, or on the parts which he played as a legislator and as a leader. We shall assume, for all the purposes of our search, that Moses filled the positions popularly assigned to him.

CHAPTER V.

NO portion of sacred history has excited greater emulation on the part of pious and industrious men, with a view to its complete elucidation, than the story of "the wanderings" of the Israelites. Every passage in the Pentateuch bearing on this important subject has been carefully studied; the name of every place has been duly recorded; whilst those who have been enabled to visit the Sinaitic peninsula and Idumæa, have, with the Bible in their hands in place of a guide-book, sought to follow in the track of the released captives, and have in some places established such an identity of names, and in others such an identity of physical characteristics, as (to their own satisfaction, at least) to remove all doubt that the Israelites must have passed by these particular points on the way to their promised home. But there is one spot in the Itinerary where there is a break in the trail, and at this point even the most honest, painstaking, and ingenious are compelled to trust exclusively to their imagination. It is not very difficult to give a tolerably intelligible, though not necessarily accurate, description of the track followed from Egypt to a mountain in the Sinaitic peninsula. Nor does it impose a great task on the ingenuity or the imagination to follow in fancy the course of the Israelites from a mountain on the western border of Idumæa, known as Mount Hor, in a southerly direction, through a broad desert valley to the head of the eastern branch of the Red Sea, and thence by a north-easterly course to the Trans-Jordanic region. But unfortunately between the arrival at Mount Sinai and the departure from Mount Hor an interval of close on forty years is supposed to have occurred, and the difficulty is to give a rational account of the apparently purposeless wanderings of the Israelites during this long period. The attempt has been made scores of times, and those who take pleasure in viewing the revels of the human fancy will do well to compare the various maps designed and narratives told to illustrate the wanderings in the desert, which have from time to time been supplied for the instruction of both Jew and Gentile. In one particular, and in one alone, do these maps and narratives agree. They ascribe to the Heaven-conducted host an aimless, senseless moving to and fro through an inhospitable region, which is irreconcilable with the presumed sanity of the people.*

The accepted account of the "wanderings" of the Israelites in the desert, their arrival in the Trans-Jordanic region, their subsequent invasion of Canaan, and its partition amongst the twelve tribes, is familiar to every one. There are, however, many reasons why this account must be

---

* Professor Porter, who contributes the article, "The Wilderness of Wandering," to the third edition of *Kitto's Biblical Cyclopædia*, remarks: "It will be observed from a careful examination of the narratives that the more direct line of route to the point of ultimate destination was rarely, if ever, followed. The people appear to have directed their course now to the right, now to the left: they even turned back, and passed and repassed the same places, in obedience, no doubt, to their divine Guide. They also spent much more time than was required for the mere purposes of travel." Then follow some illustrations of the eccentricity of the course followed by the Israelites. "To some this may seem strange and inconsistent, but it is the theory most in accordance with the physical geography of the desert and the statements of the divine historian." It seems scarcely just to the Almighty to make Him responsible if a "theory" "seems strange and inconsistent," and to anticipate objections by references to "divine guidance" and the authority of "the divine historian." It is only fair to the Professor to say, that all who have attempted to construct the Itinerary of the Israelites from Sinai to Mount Hor, have been compelled to throw the divine ægis over their "incomprehensibilities."

rejected as unhistorical. The very numbers of the liberated captives startle us by their extraordinary magnitude. Accepting the Scriptural data, the Israelites must have numbered between two and three millions. Though the impossibility of such a multitude obtaining subsistence in the desert may be overcome by an appeal to the miraculous, even the most credulous might ask how provision was made for the large flocks and herds by which they were accompanied, and for whose subsistence the narrator fails to mention that any miraculous interposition took place.*

This host was said to have been divided into twelve—or, taking the subdivision of the descendants of Joseph into the separate clans of Ephraim and Manasseh—into thirteen tribes. These tribes, whatever may have been their rivalry, are nevertheless represented as acknowledging a common leader, and as constituting in their entirety a united people or nation welded together by a common religion and a common political purpose—the invasion and partition of "the promised land." The period of their sojourn in the wilderness is stated to have been forty years, during which time all those who had quitted Egypt perished, save Joshua and Caleb.† Of the events which happened during these forty years, with the exception of the first and the last of the series, we are told nothing. On their arrival in the Trans-Jordanic region they overcame the possessors of the territory on the eastern bank of the river, and its rich pasture-land was thereupon allotted to the tribes of Reuben and Gad, and half the tribe of Manasseh. On the eve of the invasion of the Cis-Jordanic region Moses is said to have died, and the leadership of the Israelites having devolved on Joshua, the united tribes under his guidance

---

* Bishop Colenso, *Pentateuch and Book of Joshua*. Part I.
† Those under twenty years of age at the Exodus were excepted.

crossed the Jordan, and prosecuted the invasion of Canaan with such success that he was enabled to allot to the different tribes their several portions of the conquered country; the Trans-Jordanic tribes of Reuben, Gad, and half of Manasseh, which had aided in the invasion, thereupon returning to their recently allotted homes on the eastern bank of the river.

If we accepted with unwavering confidence the minute historical details given in the Book of Numbers respecting the numbers, the composition, and the journeyings of the host which quitted Sinai under the leadership of Moses, we might endeavour to reconcile ourselves as best we could to the meagre information afforded us by the historian respecting the doings of the Israelites during a period which it is impossible to suppose was destitute of stirring incident, or unmarked by features which would have been replete with interest to the student of the religion of Israel. It is impossible to read the Book of Numbers without arriving at the conclusion that it omits much with which the Prophets of the seventh, eighth, and ninth centuries B.C. were well acquainted respecting the religious practices of the Hebrews before they entered Canaan; and that it contains much which tradition was but little likely to preserve, but which the mistaken zeal of a late compiler would be easily led to supply. The fourth Book of the Pentateuch is not, however, exclusively the production of the comparatively recent age in which the redactor lived. It contains embedded in it some very interesting records of considerable antiquity, the significance and historical importance of which had passed into oblivion at the time when the Book was compiled. We find, for example, repetitions, though under other forms, of traditions with which we have already been made familiar in the Book of Exodus. Different versions are given of the establishment of the tribunal of seventy

Elders,* of the flight of quails,† and of the miraculous supply of water at Meribah;‡ but we are surprised at noticing that, whereas in Exodus these events are recorded as preceding the arrival at Mount Sinai, they appear in the Book of Numbers to have occurred subsequent to the departure of the people from the neighbourhood of that mountain. The seditious conduct of Aaron and Miriam§ rests doubtless on an old tradition, but is hopelessly unintelligible upon the assumption that they stood to Moses in the relation of brother and sister, and that they were, like him, entrusted with a divine mission; whilst the tribute paid to the meekness of Moses, "above all the men which were upon the face of the earth,"|| indicates the compiler of a later age.

In reading the Book of Numbers we are struck by the difference of style in the writer when giving an account of the assembling of the tribes, the names of their respective chiefs, the numbers of those composing the tribes, the order observed on the march and in encampment, and of the journeyings and stations of the people until their arrival in the plains of Moab; and that when he is recounting some of the incidents which occurred in the wilderness. The former is clear, unhesitating, and explicit, and such as might be met with in official records published at the present day; the latter is disjointed, faltering, and in several instances unintelligible. Sometimes different versions of the same story are given; sometimes, by a process of blending the same language, is unnecessarily repeated. The cause of this difference is not difficult to find. Tradition preserved little or any materials for a minute history of the census of the population, their precise order of marching, or the names of all the places which they stopped at on their way to their future goal. The compiler, or it may be some priestly scribe, who

---

* Num. xi. 16, 17; Exod. xviii. 13-26. † Num. xi. 31-33; Exod. xvi. 13.
‡ Num. xx. 7-13; Exod. xvii. 5-7. § Num. xii. || Num. xii. 3.

preceded him, felt that this was an omission which should be supplied, and with a running pen produced that portion of the history which by its very minuteness of detail seems to indicate the work of an eye-witness. But it is observable that the portion to which we refer contains nothing which admits of either corroboration or refutation, and, we might add, nothing either interesting or instructive. Any person who chose to take the trouble might re-write this portion of the history, and altering the numbers of the members of the several tribes, the names of the leaders, the positions occupied by the tribes on the march and in the camp, and the names of the various halting-places of the travellers, yet produce a composition which, so far as we have any means of judging, would be equally veracious. But it is less easy to write a history of what was actually done by the Hebrews on their journeyings, in the absence of materials; and this task was abandoned by the writer who was so well acquainted with the order of the tribes on the line of march, and who could even enumerate the various halting-places, from the departure from Egypt to the arrival on the left bank of the Jordan.* It has been already observed that we know nothing of what occurred in the wilderness save during the first and the last of the forty years which were supposed to have elapsed between the Exodus and the arrival opposite Jericho; but it would perhaps be more correct to say that the compiler compressed the traditions preserved in the records at his disposal within the periods we have mentioned, because he did not know exactly where to put them, and naturally used them in the beginning and the ending of his story. The dates of none of the incidents alleged to have happened in the wilderness were fixed by tradition. Nor was anything approaching a consecutive history of the journeyings in the

---

* Num. xxxiii.

wilderness ever preserved. All that was really retained by tradition was the conviction that the time passed there was sufficiently long to permit of the death of nearly all who had quitted Egypt.

Before quitting "the edge of the wilderness," it will be advisable to acquaint ourselves, so far as possible, with the physical characteristics and general topography of the region we are about to penetrate. This task is, however, by no means so easy as might at first sight appear. There is every reason to believe that considerable changes have taken place since early times in the country stretching from the south of Palestine towards the Red Sea; and we can at best but speculate on the extent of those changes since the Exodus took place. We may find the traces of former cultivation and of human labour in districts which are now solitary wastes; but we cannot determine at what period the dismal transformation took place. Nor even in seeking to make ourselves acquainted with the present condition of the region lying between Egypt and Arabia, is the information at our command as ample as might be supposed. The Sinaitic peninsula has been carefully explored, but the same cannot be said of the plateau lying between it and southern Palestine. For centuries past it has been annually traversed by Egyptian pilgrims on their way to and from Mecca, but those who conduct or accompany the Hajj neither know nor care to know anything of the country outside their beaten track. Travellers who have crossed "the Tih"—for so this region is named—have generally allowed their attention to be so much engrossed by the "Holy Places," in Palestine or in the Sinaitic peninsula, to which or from which they were directing their steps, that they could spare little or none for the wild and desolate region which they simply associated in their minds with the scene of Israel's purposeless wanderings. This dearth of precise information respecting the topography of the Tih is fortunately of but little importance in the present inquiry.

The region penetrated by the Hebrews on quitting Egypt may be roughly described as triangular in shape, the apex pointing southwards, the base or northern boundary being formed by the Mediterranean, and the southern slopes of the hills of Judæa, the western side by the Gulf of Suez, together with the isthmus of the same name, and the eastern side by the Gulf of Akaba and a broad valley named the Araba. If a line be drawn across the triangle from the head of the Gulf of Suez to that of the Gulf of Akaba, a smaller triangle will be formed within the greater one, having the same apex, the sides of which will be formed by the two arms of the Red Sea which we have just named, and the base by the region lying between this imaginary line and the Mediterranean coast and Southern Palestine. The distance from the head of one Gulf to that of the other is about one hundred and twenty miles, and the line we have traced would roughly mark the direction of the route taken by those quitting Egypt who were desirous of proceeding to the head of the Gulf of Akaba. The caravan of pilgrims proceeds annually from Egypt by the route we have indicated on its way to Mecca.

The features of the entire region lying between the south of Judæa and the apex of the Sinaitic peninsula are very singular. The loose and shifting sands which are popularly connected with the idea of a desert, and so strikingly impress the traveller in Egypt, are almost unknown. From the shores of the Mediterranean and the spurs of the hills of Judæa a plateau extends in a southerly direction, at first interspersed with slight eminences, but gradually becoming deeply seamed by gullies; whilst the entire table-land becomes more and more elevated above the level of the sea. Towards the east these inequalities become most strongly

K

marked, the surface of the plateau being fissured by deep ravines, till at length the steppe comes to an abrupt termination in a range of precipitous cliffs running in a line nearly north and south, and forming the western wall of a wide and desert valley which lies at the foot of the Idumæan range.

The portion of this great plateau trending westward towards the Isthmus of Suez is less rugged in its features, and bears traces of having in former times been submitted to cultivation. The channels which drain the water-shed, and converge towards the Mediterranean, appear in past times to have been turned to account in establishing a system of artificial irrigation; and it is not only possible, but probable, that at the time of the Exodus the fields and vineyards of Judæa stretched much farther into what is now known as the Desert of Et Tih than they do at present. Even now, however, the region which we are describing is far from barren. Covered by a light soil, it produces a sufficiency of pasturage for the flocks of the six thousand Bedouins who form the estimated population of this region; whilst, in some favoured valleys and gullies, the labour of the agriculturist is not expended in vain. It is believed that wood was tolerably plentiful in the Tih in early times. The improvidence of the Bedouins, and the high prices paid by the Egyptians for fuel, have, however, caused it to vanish. With the disappearance of wood the climate of the Tih became less humid, and a further evil was thereby occasioned in diminishing the productiveness of the soil.

The southern border of the steppe, like the eastern, is marked by precipitous cliffs. Sweeping downwards from the head of the Gulf of Akaba it describes an arc, the further extremity of which approaches the head of the Suez Gulf. These cliffs attain their greatest altitude in the neighbourhood of the Eastern Gulf; and being composed chiefly of limestone they present to persons viewing them from the south the appearance of mountains of snow. The semilunar range thus formed by the abrupt termination of the plateau on the south is called the Jebel Et Tih.

The tract lying between this mountainous range and the coast-line formed by the two arms of the Red Sea, constitutes the Sinaitic region, in which stands the cluster of mountains whose several peaks advance rival claims to the honour of being the "Mount of God." Separated from Jebel Et Tih by a narrow belt of sand, the mountains forming the Sinaitic group rear themselves to heights varying between six thousand and nine thousand feet, whilst their spurs, particularly on the western side, support lesser eminences, and form the valleys and the passes through which these mountains are approached. The Sinaitic mountains are of granitic formation, and offer scarcely any vestige of verdure. Built up of bare naked crags they present a picture of utter desolation. By one traveller they have been termed "the Alps unclothed."* They are suggestive of chaos, not of creation.† Animal life is almost entirely absent from this dreary region. The silence is so complete that the slightest sound is audible at a considerable distance. The Bedouins, with excusable exaggeration, believe it possible to make the human voice heard from the mountain-tops across the Gulf of Akaba.

Into this barren, waterless, and apparently heaven-forsaken region, tradition to-day declares that the liberated Hebrews penetrated after quitting Egypt, and at the foot of one of these naked masses of rock, already hallowed in

---

* *Notes during a Visit to Egypt.* Sir F. Henniker, p. 214.
† "If I were to make a model of the end of the world, it would be from the valley of the convent of Mount Sinai."—*Ibid.* p. 225.

the Bedouin's mind as the abode of the Elohim,* assembled to hear from His very lips the dread commands of their protecting God.

The pleasure which men experience in viewing scenes which have acquired historic interest is perhaps second to none which depend on the imagination. This pleasure, however, becomes greatly enhanced by the addition of the element of religious enthusiasm. It is the same feeling which leads the Christian traveller to turn his steps towards the Holy Land, which supports the Moslem pilgrim on his weary march to Mecca, which prompts the lover of ancient history to explore the ruins of Egypt and of Rome, to scale the Acropolis at Athens, or standing in the Troad on the hill of Hissarlik to trace in fancy the windings of the Scamander, and survey the adjacent shores once furrowed by the keels of the Grecian ships. So universal, so inextinguishable is this craving to associate oneself, however distantly, with the scenes of the mighty past, and to touch or even to see objects which have been touched or seen by those who have long since passed away, but whose names remain imperishable, that the craving is supplied when the means of supply are notoriously wanting, and men must carefully abstain from inquiry lest their sagacity should entail the loss of a coveted pleasure. There is not an event in our Great Master's career the scene of which has not been carefully localised for the behoof of the pious pilgrim and the curious traveller. Shrines, grottoes, and churches mark the exact sites of every recorded action of his life, from his birth in the stable to his death on the cross. The sceptical, with facts in one hand and reason in the other, demolish the historical reputation of the Holy Places, without however adding to their own enjoyment. The credulous greedily, and the practical philosophically, accept what they

---

* Exod. iii. 1.

are told, and more or less readily conjure up the scenes with which the places are declared to be associated; whilst perhaps the more cautious turn their steps towards Nazareth, which beyond all contradiction they know was *his* home during the greater portion of his life ; or wander by the Sea of Galilee with the certain conviction that the scenes before their eyes must have again and again met *his* view whilst he was still on the threshold of his great Mission, and was laying the foundations of a religion which, even after the lapse of nearly two thousand years, the misdirected zeal of its votaries has proved ineffectual to destroy.

The identification of the "Mount of God" has perhaps a wider, if not a deeper, interest than that of any other spot referred to in sacred history. To the Jew, to the Christian, and, though in a less degree, to the Mohammedan, it must ever be a matter of concern to determine, if possible, the scene of the conclusion of the covenant between God and His chosen people. Beliefs productive of real pleasure and pious enjoyment should not be rudely or wantonly assailed ; and if we find ourselves compelled to give to the Mount of God a site different from that popularly assigned to it, it becomes a duty to state fully the grounds for doing so. Many would more readily give up a dogma than relinquish a shrine, and would repeal a commandment sooner than acknowledge that they had invested a mountain with a sanctity having no other foundation than that supplied by their own imagination.

In the general description of the physical characteristics of the great triangular-shaped region lying between Egypt and Edom, mention has been made of a broad and desert valley which separates the abrupt precipitous wall of the Tih plateau on the one side from the Idumæan range on the other. This valley bears to-day the name by which it may have been known to the Hebrews, the Araba ; and whatever else may be in doubt respecting the course of their peregrinations, it is absolutely certain that they marched (probably more than once) along this desert plain. The Araba is the direct continuation of the Jordan valley, which, starting from the mountain range of the Lebanon, follows a southerly direction till it terminates in the Dead Sea, from the southern extremity of which the Araba ascends by a series of wall-like terraces, until, having attained a height of nearly 600 feet above the sea-level, it gradually descends, till it disappears in the Gulf of Akaba. The valley of the Jordan, as is well known, begins to sink beneath the level of the ocean not far from the river's source, and the surface of the Dead Sea into which the river empties itself is upwards of 1300 feet below the level of the Mediterranean, whilst its bottom is 2600 beneath the same level. From these figures it will appear that from the highest point of the Araba to the shores of the Dead Sea is a fall of nearly 1900 feet, which is more or less abrupt; whilst the fall of nearly 600 feet from the same point to the Red Sea, being extended over a distance of nearly a hundred miles, is necessarily gradual. Were it not for the anomalous depression of the Jordan valley, which empties the river into a hole, that seems to have been occasioned by a falling in of the earth's crust, the Jordan would have found its way along the Araba, and passing between the limestone cliffs of the Tih on the right hand and the Idumæan mountains on the left, have flowed into the Eastern Gulf of the Red Sea. Whether in pre-historic times it actually did so, geologists may be able to determine.

The title of Araba was given in pre-Mosaic times to the lower portion of the Jordan valley; at the present day it is confined to its continuation south of the Dead Sea. The breadth of this valley varies between two and four miles. The surface is rugged in its southern portion, being marked by numerous sand-hills, whilst the northern is intersected by what have not inaptly been called dry watercourses. It is extremely barren, a scanty growth of tamarisks and acacia shrubs, sprouting in a mass of gravel and flint, furnishing almost the sole vegetation.* It is moreover waterless, the springs of Ain el Weibeh, situated in the upper third of the valley, being almost the only fountains whose existence have been deemed worthy of being recorded. On the west side it is flanked by the limestone cliff of the Tih, rising at places to a height of nearly two thousand feet, and intersected by ravines, which are for the most part impassable; and on the east by the mountainous range of Edom, penetrated by numerous valleys, which in past times furnished the highways by which that country was entered from the west.

Speaking generally, and subject to limitations to be noted hereafter, the land of Edom, or Seir as it is sometimes termed, given by the Elohim as an inheritance to the elder branch of the descendants of Abraham, was a narrow strip of territory lying between the Araba on the west and the great desert of Arabia on the east, its northern boundary resting on Moab and the Dead Sea, whilst its southern reached to the head of the Gulf of Akaba. Elath, a port

---

* " È una vasta pianura di sabbia sparsa di ciotolli, che si stende davanti a noi e si perde all' orizzonte in una sfumatura incerta di dune, di monti lontani velati di una cortina di rena sollevata dal vento. . . . . La pianura è monotona. Quà e là qualche acacia a cono rovesciato, qualche cespuglio di crocifera spinosa, ed un fiore curioso la *Philipia tubulosa*, che gli Arabi chiamano, *Tarthuth*. . . . . La valle o la pianura, giacchè, l'Arabah è valle perchè chiusa fra i monti, ma per la sua vastità, ha l'aspetto di una pianura, rimane per così dire divisa in due zone per il lungo. . . . . Il suolo è ricoperto per breve tratto di un 'erba che cresce a mazzi, chiamata dagli Arabi, *Halfi*."
—Arconati Visconti, *Diario di un Viaggio in Arabia Petraea*, Torino, 1872, 4to, pp. 327-330.

at this point of the Gulf, was in early times spoken of as in Idumæan territory. Solomon (Edom having previously been ravaged by David) subsequently converted it into a haven for his ships.*

The western boundary of Idumæa consists of a mountainous range, descending somewhat precipitously into the Araba, whilst on the east the mountain slopes become gradually transformed into fertile plains, until they are lost at the distance of from twenty to thirty miles in the sands of the Arabian desert. Geologists describe the Idumæan range as composed of porphyritic rock surmounted by sandstone, and the varied colours of the latter, ranging between yellow and red, have excited in all times the admiration of travellers, and are supposed to supply an explanation of the name by which the country was known.† The contrast between the sterility of the Araba and Tih and the fertility of Edom, becomes at once apparent as soon as the traveller penetrates one of the valleys issuing from the plain.‡

According to ancient tradition, Seir was originally inhabited by the Horites,§ who were vanquished, if not completely dispossessed, by the children of Esau.|| The

---

* 1 Kings ix. 26.   † Edom signifies red.

‡ "The first thing that struck me on turning out of the Araba up the defiles that lead to Petra, was that we had suddenly left the desert. Instead of the absolute nakedness of the Sinaitic valleys, we found ourselves walking on grass sprinkled with flowers, and the level platforms on each side were filled with sprouting corn" (Dean Stanley, *Sinai and Palestine*, p. 88). "The country is extremely fertile, and presents a favourable contrast to the sterile region on the opposite side of the Araba. Goodly streams flow through the valleys, which are filled with trees and flowers, while on the uplands to the east rich pasture-lands and corn-fields may everywhere be seen" (Palmer's *Desert of the Exodus*, ii. 430). See also Laborde, *Voyage de l'Arabie Pétrée*; and Arconati, *Diario di un Viaggio in Arabia Petræa*.

§ Gen. xiv. 26; xxxvi. 20. || Deut. ii. 12.

former were so called because they dwelt in caves. In strictness the name should be written Chorites, being derived from a word signifying a hole in the earth or in a rock—a cave or cavern.* The practices of the Chorites in this respect were adopted by their conquerors, and the cave dwellings of Petra still excite the surprise and provoke the speculation of the astonished traveller.

It is admitted on all hands that the mountain associated by Hebrew tradition with the conclusion of the covenant between Jahveh and his chosen people is situated between the meridians of Egypt and Idumaea; and we may add, almost equal unanimity exists in placing it in the Sinaitic region south of the semilunar wall of the Tih steppe.† Here, however, the unanimity disappears. The Sinaitic group is composed of several mountains, whilst these mountains are again subdivided into peaks and bluffs, and each has its supposed traditions and its claims to the title of being the true Sinai on which Moses conversed with God, and received from His hands the two tables of stone containing the Ten Commandments.

In ascertaining, or at least in seeking to ascertain, the precise locality of the Mount of God, we must, as in con-

---

* חוֹר *Chor*, hence חֹרִי *Chori*, a Horite. Job xxx. 6: 1 Sam. xiv. 11.

† Dr. Beke suggested, so far back as 1834, that Mount Sinai was to be found in the neighbourhood of Petra, but to its *eastward*. He arrived at this conclusion in a somewhat singular way. He contended that the land of Mizraim, in which the Hebrews were detained in bondage, was not Egypt, but lay in the Tih plateau, and that the Red Sea which they crossed was the Gulf of Akaba. He accordingly assigned a portion of their wandering to the Arabian desert. He also entertained the belief that Sinai would be found to be an extinct volcano. Shortly before his death he made a voyage to the Red Sea, and on landing at Akaba fixed on a mountain in its neighbourhood, Jebel Baghir, as being the true Sinai. It is not supposed that he made any converts to this view.—*Origines Biblicæ*, 1834, chap. viii. *Sinai in Arabia*. 1878.

ducting any other investigation, seek the best evidence, and be careful to avoid being misled by the apparent weight of a mass of testimony which may in truth consist of only a single atom, whose value is possibly worthless. If A, B, and C give accounts of a transaction of which they have had personal cognisance, and those accounts substantially correspond, the combined weight of their testimony, assuming them to be speaking in good faith, is greater than that of the testimony of either standing alone. But if B only repeats what he has been told by A, and C what he has been told by B, the value of their combined testimony depends solely on that of the evidence of A, the original narrator. An unbroken tradition of about fifteen centuries places the Mount of God in the Sinaitic peninsula, but the strength of the entire chain of tradition depends on the links forged in the early centuries of the Christian era, and their connection with the previous chain which spans over an equally great distance of time.*

In Hebrew tradition the Mount of God was known by two different names, Sinai and Horeb. Ewald was of opinion that the former was the more ancient of the two; but this is open to question. There seems, however, good reason for concluding that Sinai was the name used in Israel, whilst Horeb was the designation adopted in Judah. In the Song of Deborah, one of the most ancient fragments in the Old Testament, the prophetess of Israel uses the

---

* Dean Stanley, referring to the numerous sites connected with the history of Moses, especially by traditions having a Christian source, justly remarks: "When we remember how many of these sites have evidently been selected for the sake of convenience rather than of truth, it is not easy to trust a tradition that has descended through such channels even for fifteen hundred years, unless it can render good its claim to be the offspring of another which requires for its genuineness another fifteen hundred still."—*S. and P.* p. 33.

word Sinai. In the Blessing of Moses, interpolated between the thirty-second and thirty-fourth chapters of Deuteronomy, Sinai is spoken of as the dwelling-place of Jahveh. Elsewhere in Deuteronomy the Mountain of God is invariably called Horeb.* In the account given of the flight of the prophet Elijah from the vengeance of Jezebel, wife of the king of Israel, which is evidently from a Judaic source, the Mount is called Horeb,† and it is also thus named in Psalm cvi. In the book of Exodus we find both names, but they are not indifferently used in what appear to be the same narratives. Perhaps we should not very much err in concluding that in the traditions of the Israelitish section of the people the Mountain of God was known as Sinai, whilst in those of Judah it was styled Horeb. In the subsequent assimilation and fusing together of these traditions in the books of Exodus and Numbers, the original distinction became probably almost effaced, a consequence all the more likely to occur as the names were confessedly applied to the same mountain.

Considering the stupendous nature of the manifestations declared to have taken place at Mount Sinai, and that from this place Jahveh is supposed to have given to his people the comprehensive code which he intended to provide for their religious and social wants in all after-time, it must be admitted that the descendants of the emigrants from Egypt apparently manifested very little interest in this marvellous locality. The allusions made to the Mount of God subsequent to the settlement in Canaan are very scanty, and are couched exclusively in the language of poetry or rhapsody. No pilgrimages seem to have been undertaken to the celebrated Mount; and if we were to

---

* Deuteronomy is a work of the seventh century, and was produced in Judah, see *ante*, p. 62, *note*.
† 1 Kings xix. 8.

judge from the pages of Jewish history it would appear to have been forgotten. We should not, however, therefore conclude that there was not in fact a mountain credited with being the abode, or having been the abode, of God; but we might profitably ask ourselves whether it is probable that the people who settled in Canaan entertained the belief, which is now attributed to them, that their laws were delivered by God himself from a mountain not a hundred miles distant from their own frontier, and yet have evinced so little interest and curiosity about it. There is one instance in which the Mount of God is apparently referred to as a place accessible to the inhabitants of Judæa—namely, in the account given of the visit made to Horeb by the prophet Elijah.* Even this narrative is very far from prosaic; it abounds with the marvellous, and places the "man of God" and the "Mount of God" in a supernatural sphere. In dealing with the question of the locality of Mount Sinai we have therefore but scant materials, and must endeavour as best we can to ascertain the particular region in which the Mount of God was popularly believed in Israel and in Judah to be situated, and having done so, inquire whether such situation is reconcilable or irreconcilable with the traditions of the route taken by the Israelites on quitting Egypt.

In the Song of Deborah, a lyric which probably dates from the twelfth or thirteenth century before our era,† the prophetess is represented as celebrating a victory gained by Israel over the Canaanites, a victory which she attributes to the intervention of Jahveh. The protecting God is described by the poetess as quitting his abode to come to the assist-

---

* 1 Kings xix.
† Judges v. "D'après les calculs les plus modestes il peut remontre au douzième siècle avant notre ère."—Reuss. *La Bible. Nouv. Trad. Hist. des Israélites.* Introduct. p. 105.

ance of his people. "Jahveh, when thou wentest out of Seir, when thou marchedst out of the field of Edom, the earth trembled and the heavens dropped, the clouds also dropped water. The mountains melted from before Jahveh, even that Sinai (or Sinai itself) from before the God of Israel." Here we have a revival by the bard of the primitive belief of the nomads that the Elohim dwelt in a mountain, and beyond all doubt this mountain was believed to be in the Idumæan range. It is from Seir that Jahveh goes forth, it is from Edom that he marches to the aid of his people. His departure is attended with mighty portents: the earth trembles, the heavens drop, and the mountains melt, including Sinai itself. It is not perhaps an extravagant conclusion, that if all we knew of Sinai was that it was "the Mount of God" and reputed abode of Jahveh, and had no other evidence respecting its locality save Deborah's Song, we should unhesitatingly place it in Idumæa.

The Blessing of Moses,* a composition, at least in its present form, of a later epoch than the Song of Deborah, commences with the following words:—"Jahveh came from Sinai, and rose up from Seir unto them; he shined forth from Mount Paran, and he came with ten thousands of saints" (A. V.). In this passage, as in that to which attention has just been directed, we notice the apparent collocation of Sinai with Seir, if not indeed their absolute identification. It is one of the characteristics of Hebrew poetry to repeat the same idea, or to affirm the same statement, in successive stanzas. This parallelism is noticeable throughout the Psalms, where each verse consists of two stanzas, the latter being generally a recitation of the senti-

---

* Deut. xxxiii.

ment expressed in the former. In the verse just quoted from Deborah's Song, this peculiarity is well-marked :—

"Jahveh, when thou wentest out of Seir;
When thou marchedst out of the field of Edom."

As the identity of Seir with Edom is incontestable, it is evident that, in accordance with the canons of Hebrew poetry, the poetess simply repeated herself, though in somewhat different language. So also in the verses :—

"The earth trembled and the heavens dropped :
The clouds also dropped water.
The mountains melted from before Jahveh ;
Even that Sinai from before Jahveh, God of Israel."

The Blessing of Moses belongs to the same class of poetry, and is marked by the same characteristic, though in portions it has evidently suffered from later emendations :—

"Jahveh came from Sinai :
And arose from Seir unto them.
He shined forth from Mount Paran :
And he came from Meribah Kadesh."*

Here, in conformity with the canon we have just noticed, we should, in the absence of all conflicting evidence, and with minds perfectly unprejudiced, have no hesitation in identifying Sinai with Seir, just as in the Song of Deborah Seir and Edom were treated as synonymous.

In the passage just quoted the poet, pursuing the same train of thought expressed in Jahveh's proceeding from Sinai and arising out of Seir, adds—

"He shined forth from Mount Paran,
And he came from Meribah Kadesh."

The word Paran is derived from the Hebrew *Par* or *Phar*,

---

* This is Ewald's rendering of the passage, and it is generally considered to be correct (*Gesch. d. V. Israel*, ii. 257). See similar expressions in Num. xxvii. 14; Deut. xxxii. 51.

signifying a cave,* and Mount Paran consequently signifies "the Mount of Caves." Meribah Kadesh, or Meribah in Kadesh, is a place where it is stated that the people murmured for want of water, and where it was supplied miraculously by Moses. Meribah is said to signify strife or contention, and the place was so called, according to one tradition, because the people† (and according to another, because Moses and Aaron) trespassed there against Jahveh, and through want of faith contended against him.‡ Kadesh signifies "holy," and would seem to apply to the region in which the miracle was effected.

The conclusion we would therefore draw from the entire passage which has been quoted from the Blessing of Moses, is that, in the opinion of the poet, Sinai and Seir were substantially identical, and that Mount Paran or Mount of Caves and Meribah Kadesh, where according to tradition water was miraculously drawn from the rock, were so closely connected with each other and with Sinai and Seir, as to admit of being spoken of collectively as the region from which Jahveh "came," "rose up," and " shone forth."

The conclusion that Meribah Kadesh, the scene of the miraculous supply of water, was not only in the neighbourhood of Mount Paran but of Mount Sinai and Seir, becomes, however, considerably strengthened by the tradition that it was at Mount Horeb (the Mount of God) that the miraculous supply of water was obtained, and that the place

---

* The root of פָּארָן *Paran* is פָּאַר *Par*, but the word has two significations, "to adorn, to be beautiful," and "to dig, to bore." Some, accepting the former, regard Paran as a region abounding in foliage; others, adopting the latter derivation, treat the word as meaning a place noted for its caves. The latter is the more reasonable interpretation of the two, and will be found to be descriptive of the place known in the traditions of the Exodus as the *midbhar of Paran*.
    † Exod. xvii. 7.   ‡ Num. xx. 12: xxvii. 14.

where it was so obtained was called Massah (signifying temptation) and Meribah (strife).* Elsewhere we find this tradition repeated in another form, the place of the miracle being called Kadesh (the holy).† We shall have occasion subsequently to examine the identity of these traditions, and to disprove the assumption that the same miracle was believed to have been repeated at two different places after an interval of thirty-eight years under identical circumstances, such circumstances giving to the two places the same name.

Of the contiguity of Paran and Kadesh, if not of their identity, and of their being situated in the Idumæan region, we have abundant evidence. In what is known as "the Battle of the Kings," Chedorlaomer and his allies are said to have smitten "the Horites in their Mount Seir, unto El-paran (the tree of Paran), which is by the wilderness, and they (the allies) returned and came to En-Mishpat, which is Kadesh."‡ The tradition respecting the settlement of the elder branch of Abraham's descendants, which has come down to us in two forms,§ Ishmael representing that branch in the one and Esau in the other, assigns Paran and Seir as the region occupied by them. The spies who set out from Kadesh to explore Canaan, are said to have returned "unto the wilderness of Paran to Kadesh,"‖ the identity of which places is further confirmed by the Septuagint version of Num. xxxiii. 36, which states that "they (the children of Israel) removed from the wilderness of Zin and pitched in the wilderness of Paran, which is Kadesh;"¶ whilst the locality

---

* Exod. xvii. 6, 7. † Num. xx. 1-13. ‡ Gen. xiv. 6, 7.
§ Gen. xxi. 21; xxxvi. 1-8. ‖ Num. xiii. 26.
¶ The words contained in the Septuagint appear to have been accidentally omitted from the Hebrew text. Elsewhere the wilderness of Zin and that of Paran seem to be regarded as identical (compare Num. xii. 16 with xvii. 21); and both were identified with Kadesh (Num. xii. 16; xvii. 21-26; 33-36. A. V.).

of Kadesh is absolutely determined by the statement that it stood on the border of Edom, and was the place from which the Israelites despatched messengers requesting permission to pass through the Idumæan territory.* The immediate proximity of Sinai and Paran is indicated by the statement that when the children of Israel commenced their journey out of the wilderness of Sinai, the cloud rested in the wilderness of Paran.†

The extract made from the Song of Deborah is repeated almost literally in the 68th Psalm, with, however, the significant exception that, although Sinai is named, all mention of Seir and Edom as the place from which Jahveh went forth is omitted. This may have been due to the more spiritual view taken by the later poet of the abode of Jahveh, and an unwillingness to give support to the early superstition that God dwelt in the mountains of Seir.

Habakkuk, a prophet of the latter half of the seventh century B.C., uses the expression "God came from Teman, and the Holy One from Mount Paran,"‡ and though this is not to be interpreted literally, it is nevertheless a spiritual adoption of the primitive belief of Israel. Teman was, however, the southern part of Edom, which is to-day known as Es Sherah as distinguished from the northern, in the neighbourhood of the Dead Sea, known to the Israelites as Jebal, and called Gebalena by the Romans. The region of Teman included the Idumæan range as far north as Mount Hor.

The primitive belief that Jahveh dwelt in Seir also finds expression in the language of Isaiah, when, in pronouncing "the Burden of Dumah," he exclaims, "He calleth to me out of Seir, Watchman, what of the night?" The spiritual conception entertained of God by this

---

* Num. xx. 16. † Num. x. 12, 13. ‡ Hab. iii. 3.

prophet excludes the supposition that he believed Seir to be the abode of the Deity. He seems merely to have adopted language which would have been intelligible to his hearers.

There is one other passage in the utterances or writings of this prophet which deserves notice in connection with the subject under consideration. In announcing the retribution which would fall on the Assyrians for their oppression of Judah, the prophet exclaims: "Jahveh of hosts shall stir up a scourge for him according to the slaughter of Midian, at the rock of Oreb."* The English reader might suppose that Isaiah had dropped the initial letter, and was referring to the rock of Horeb from which the water was miraculously drawn; but this is, at all events, very doubtful. If the prophet refers to the execution of the Midianite prince Oreb by Gideon, upon the rock which thenceforth bore his name,† then the allusion is irrelevant to the present inquiry. But if reference is made to the slaughter of the Edomites a century previously by Amaziah, when ten thousand captives were said to have been thrown down from the top of a rock (Selah),‡ generally identified with the precipices overhanging Petra, then the mention of Oreb would furnish additional evidence of the rock of Horeb being in Seir. Independently, however, of the different etymology of the words,§ much more striking in Hebrew than in English, the passage is too ambiguous‖ to be used in the present investigation.

The only seeming historical allusion to the Mount of God subsequent to the settlement in Canaan is connected with

---

* Isa. x. 26.   † Jud. vii. 25.   ‡ 2 Kings xiv. 7; 2 Chron. xxv. 12.
§ חֹרֵב *Choreb*. עֹרֵב *Oreb*.
‖ The Septuagint rendering is ἐν τόπῳ θλίψεως; the corresponding words in Jud. vii. 25 are rendered ἐν Σούρ Ὠρήβ.

an event in the life of Elijah.* The prophet having fled from Samaria to escape the vengeance of Jezebel, is represented as having gone to Beersheba, a town in the south of Judah. There he left his servant, proceeded a day's journey into the wilderness (*midbhar*),† and sat down under a juniper-tree to die. An angel then appeared and supplied him with food, which having partaken of, he " went in the strength of that meat forty days and forty nights unto Horeb, the Mount of God." On reaching the mount he lodged in *the* cavern‡ there, when the word of Jahveh came to him and inquired with what object he had come. Having replied, he was told to "go forth, and stand upon the mount before Jahveh." Then followed certain manifestations. A strong wind rent the mountain, the wind being followed by an earthquake, the earthquake by a fire, and the fire by a still small voice. But Jahveh was not in the wind, nor in the earthquake, nor in the fire, but in the still small voice ; and Elijah, emerging from the cavern, received the commands of Jahveh.

This incomparably beautiful parable,§ the spiritual depth and bearing of which are overshadowed and ignored by those who persist in treating it as a prosaic statement of a succession of miraculous occurrences, renders us comparatively little assistance in its English guise. A journey of forty days was as little necessary to enable the prophet to reach

---

* 1 Kings xix. 1–18.
† *Midbhar* does not necessarily imply a barren desert. it may mean a plain fit for pasturing flocks.
‡ It is important to note that the definite article is used in the Hebrew text, evidently to denote a particular cavern hallowed by tradition, and probably referred to in Exod. xxxiii. 22.
§ " Pour bien apprécier ce quil y a de sublime dans cette parabole (car c'en est une et la plus belle de toute la littérature Hebraïque) il faut se rappeler que partout ailleurs dans l'Ancien Testament c'est dans la tempête que le Dieu d'Israël se révèle, et nulle part l'esprit du vraie prophetisme n'est point comme il l'est ici" (Reuss, *La Bible, N. T. H. des I.*, p. 493).

the mountains in the Sinaitic peninsula as those in Edom, and a person quitting Judah for either destination might equally pass by way of Beersheba. But it is not unworthy of notice that, before the time of Elijah, communication had been opened between Judah and Elath, or Ezion-gaber, at the head of the Gulf of Akaba,* and the caravan route followed in all probability the course adopted centuries later in the western Roman road between Haila (Elath) and Jerusalem,† and which cannot be far divergent from the track of modern travellers in proceeding from Hebron to the middle of the Araba. This route passes through the *midbhar* of Beersheba. On the other hand, we have no indication in ancient times of any route from Judah across the Tih plateau to the Sinaitic region; nor of the journey having been undertaken either for business, pleasure, or pious purposes, by any individuals whatever. It is, of course, quite possible to proceed direct across the plateau, following the windings of the Wadys, and to emerge through one of the passes in the southern wall of the Tih into the Sinaitic region, and many travellers have done so. But there is no evidence of such a journey having been undertaken in pre-Christian times.

It may be urged with plausibility that this is begging the entire question, and that this is precisely the journey which was undertaken by the prophet Elijah. The truth is, this account gives no apparent indication whatever of the locality of Horeb. That mountain might, so far as the narrative is concerned, be in Idumæa, in the Sinaitic peninsula, or on the banks of the Nile. But let us examine the narrative a little closer, and ascertain whether we rightly interpret the prophet's language.

One may be permitted to doubt whether the rendering, he "went in the strength of that meat forty days and forty nights

---

* 1 Kings ix. 26.
† *Tabula Itineraria Peutingeriana.* Ed. Mannert Lips, 1824.

unto Horeb, the Mount of God," is correct. The narrative, though spiritualised, is transparently modelled on the accepted tradition of Moses at Sinai. Moses saw a burning bush, Elijah beheld a fire; Moses hid his face, Elijah wrapped his head in his mantle. Moses was placed in a "cleft of the rock" when Jahveh passed by, Elijah stood in the entrance of *the* cave, which tradition doubtless affirmed to be "the cleft." The thunders and lightnings when Moses was on the mount had their counterpart, when Elijah was present, in the whirlwind and the earthquake. Moses remained in the mountain, without food, forty days and forty nights; and in order to make the parallel complete, the abode of Elijah, under the same circumstances, on the mount should have lasted the same period. If therefore all we knew on the latter point was that a similar fast was ascribed to Elijah, we would unhesitatingly conclude that the prophet, like Moses, fasted during the whole of that period upon the Mount of God.

The translation in the Authorised Version conveys the idea that the journey of Elijah from the wilderness of Beersheba to Mount Horeb occupied forty days and forty nights, during which time the prophet was miraculously sustained by the food supplied by the angel of Jahveh. Nothing is apparently said of the time he remained on the mount whilst he lodged in the cave, or of his means of subsistence whilst there; and his return journey is referred to as a matter of course, not necessitating miraculous intervention on the part of the Deity, or comment on that of the narrator. These apparent omissions give a certain incompleteness to the narrative in its accepted form.

The Hebrew text of the passage to which attention is now directed is in some respects peculiar. The verb rendered "he went," in the sense of journeying, is constantly used in the Old Testament to imply a continuing state of existence ;* whilst the preposition translated "unto" is frequently employed to convey the idea of duration, being perhaps more often applied to time than to space.†

It would therefore seem that the more correct rendering of this passage should be as follows: "And he arose and did eat and drink, and subsisted on the strength of that meat forty days and forty nights while on the Mount of God (Horeb), and he entered there‡ into *the* cave and lodged there." And this rendering is justified not only on the

---

* הָלַךְ *halech*. Like the French "aller." Illustrations of the idiomatic employment of this verb will easily suggest themselves.

† As regards the use of the verb in the sense referred to, there is a great abundance of illustrations. One "who walketh (liveth) uprightly" (Ps. xv. 2), who "walks according to the counsel of the wicked" (Ps. i. 1), who is "living in wind (vanity) and lying" (Mic. ii. 11); and with a similar signification, "the child Samuel grew on more and more" (1 Sam. ii. 26), "David waxed stronger and stronger" (2 Sam. iii. 1), "Mordecai waxed greater and greater" (Esther ix. 4), "Jehoshaphat waxed great exceedingly" (2 Chron. xvii. 12). See other illustrations *s. v.* הָלַךְ *halech*, Gesenius, *Lexicon* (*Heb. and Chald.*, and *Thesaurus*, &c.). With respect to the preposition here employed, its primitive and more general meaning would seem to be "during," or "while," or "as long as." Thus, "so long as the whoredoms of Jezebel (last)" (2 Kings ix. 22); and in a passage immediately preceding the narrative now under consideration, and evidently the work of the same writer, "and it came to pass in the meanwhile," or more literally, "while so and while so" (1 Kings xviii. 45), "during a moment" (Job xx. 5), "while they waited" (Jud. iii. 26), "until the morning" (Jud. vi. 31), "until the evening"(Lev. xv. 5)," within thirty days," &c. (Dan. vi. 8, 13). See *Lex. H. and C. s. v.* עַד *ad*. Gesenius observes, the "particle אֶל *el* and this differ properly in this respect: that אֶל signifies nothing but motion and direction *towards* some limit. עַד on the contrary signifies an actual arrival *quite to* such limit." The limit is excluded in the former, included in the latter. The Septuagint version renders the passage "ἕως ὄρους Χωρήβ;" ἕως implies the idea of duration, being rendered "until," "whilst," "as long as," and thus distinguished from πρός, the translation given to אֶל and signifying simply "to" a place.

‡ The A. V. gives, "and he came thither unto a cave." The Hebrew verb here employed בּוֹא *bou*, signifies "to come in," "to enter." See Gesenius, *s. v.* The Septuagint gives the true spirit of the passage, "καὶ εἰσῆλθεν ἐκεῖ εἰς τὸ σπήλαιον."

grounds just stated, but because it is the only one which relieves the parable of incompleteness, and perfects the pendant drawn on the lines of the original picture of Moses on the Mount of God.

But if this be the correct translation of the passage, it sheds indirectly considerable light on the probable locality of the Mount of God. The writer represents Elijah as leaving his servant at Beersheba, and proceeding a day's journey into the wilderness. There he received from the angel food which enabled him to fast forty days and forty nights on Mount Horeb. It is therefore reasonable to infer that the writer assumed the prophet to have reached a point which he believed to be not far distant from the mountain, since it was a suitable place for receiving the food which was to constitute his sole support during his protracted stay whilst there.* This point was, however, far distant from any of the mountains in the Sinaitic peninsula, whilst it was not far from the Idumæan range. Beersheba was the most southern point of Judah, and within two days' journey of the middle of the Araba. We do not look for extreme accuracy of detail in parables; we must be content with broad features. The writer represents Elijah as having quitted Judah and proceeded into the *midbhar*, a distance which is stated as a day's journey. All that was intended to be conveyed is that he journeyed to a point where, faint and exhausted, he lay down under a tree, expecting death. Such a journey, assuming that he had taken a south-eastern course, would have brought him in two days' time to the wide valley skirting the base of the Idumæan chain.

---

* It is assumed that the writer of the parable was acquainted with the precise locality of Mount Horeb, and that the Beersheba present to his mind was that which lay some four-and-twenty miles south of Hebron. But both these assumptions may be erroneous.

The main value which the narrative possesses in connection with the locality of the Mount of God rests on its consistency with the evidence already examined, which places Sinai in Seir, and its inconsistency with the general conception of the situation of that mountain in the south of the Sinaitic peninsula. One of the main features of the parable must be ignored, and the miraculous part be supposed to have taken place on the journey, and not on the mountain, in order to conduct the prophet to a region which, so far as we possess any information, was wholly unknown to the inhabitants of Judæa.

The narrative of Elijah's visit to Horeb is preserved by Josephus, and as told by the Jewish historian curiously confirms our impression that the mountain was in Idumæa. After mentioning the steps taken by Jezebel to slay Elijah, Josephus says that the latter "was affrighted, and fled to the city called Beersheba, which is situated at the utmost limits of the country belonging to the tribe of Judah *towards the land of Edom*, and there he left his servant and went away into the desert. He prayed also that he might die, for that he was not better than his fathers, nor need he be very desirous to live when they were dead. And he lay and slept under a certain tree, and when somebody awakened him and he was risen up, he found food set by him and water, so when he had eaten and recovered his strength by that his food, he came to that mountain which is called Sinai (τὸ Σίναιον), where it is related that Moses received his laws from God, and finding there a certain hollow cave he entered into it, and continued to make his abode in it."* Josephus, who was not overburdened with credulity, or at all events deemed it advisable in writing for the Gentile world to omit as much as possible of the marvellous, has, it

---

* *A. J.* viii. 13. 7.

will be seen, considerably toned down the original story. The angel of Jahveh becomes a "somebody," and nothing is said of the forty days' fast. But his reference to the relative situation of Beersheba to Edom would be unintelligible unless he understood that the prophet was directing his steps towards that country. In Elijah's time the dominions of the Edomites did not extend west of the Araba, between which and Beersheba stretched the north-eastern portion of the Tih steppe. Beersheba was "towards Edom;" that is to say, it lay in the route of a traveller quitting Judah for that country. It would seem therefore that Josephus represented the prophet as quitting Beersheba in the direction of Edom, "where he came to that mountain which is called Sinai."

There is only one reference in the writings of the New Testament to the locality of Mount Sinai, and it is of a very general character. St. Paul, in his Epistle to the Galatians, wrote: "For these are the two covenants; the one from the Mount Sinai, which gendereth to bondage, which is Agar. For this Agar is Mount Sinai in Arabia."* What country or region was referred to by the Apostle as Arabia?

In the writings of the Old Testament, Arabia is invariably identified with the east—that is, the east of the meridian of the Jordan valley. According to tradition, the descendants of Abraham through Hagar and Keturah migrated to the east country (Kedem)."† Ishmael (or perhaps, according to another form of the tradition, Esau) occupied Seir. Midian and the other sons of Keturah moved farther south, to the region on the eastern coast of the Gulf of Akaba and the Red Sea. In the story of the sale of Joseph by his brethren, the purchasers are indifferently spoken of as Ishmaelites and

---

* Gal. iv. 24, 25.   † Gen. xxv. 6.

Midianites.* The east country would therefore seem to have been the country lying to the east of the Araba and the Red Sea.

In the time of Solomon we first find any mention of Arabia. The kings of Arabia, or of Ereb, send him gifts.† Elsewhere the country and the people are occasionally referred to, but in every instance we are led to conclude that the region was deemed to lie to the east or south-east, and not to the south of Judæa. We have already noticed the allusion of Isaiah to the slaughter of Midian at the rock of Oreb. In his account of the massacre of the Edomites by Amaziah, Josephus states that the king "brought his prisoners to the great rock which is in Arabia, and threw them down headlong ;"‡ that is, from the precipices of Petra. In Hebrew, Arabia and Oreb are spelt with the same letters, though with a slight difference in the vowel points.§ It is not improbable that Isaiah wrote "the rock in Arabia,"|| meaning a place well known as late as the time of Josephus. However this may be, the name of Arabia was, down to the commencement of the Christian era, applied by the Jews to Idumæa and the region lying to its east and south; but, so far as we have any evidence, never to the country lying to the south of Palestine and enclosed between the two arms of the Red Sea.

The earliest Greek geographers only knew of an Arabia lying to the east of the meridian of the Jordan valley. Strabo and Eratosthenes give the name Arabia¶ to the great peninsula lying between the Red Sea and the Persian Gulf, together with the region on the north extending from Idumæa and Palestine on the west, to the Euphrates on the

---

* Gen. xxxvii. 28.

† 1 Kings x. 15; 2 Chron. ix. 14.   ‡ Jos. *A. J.* ix. 9. 1.

§ עֲרָב *Arabia*, עֹרֵב *Oreb*. The vowel points were supplied by the Masorites some centuries after the commencement of the Christian era.

|| Isa. x. 26.   ¶ Strab. xvi. 767 ; Diod. Siculus, ii. 48.

north-east. The peninsula they styled Arabia Felix, whilst the northern region, from its physical characteristics, was called Arabia Deserta. The same classification was adopted by Pliny.* In the second century Ptolemy introduced to the notice of the world a third Arabia,† to which he gave the name of Arabia Petræa, from Petra, the Idumæan metropolis; and in this third subdivision he seems to have included the Sinaitic peninsula and Idumæa. He had doubtless good grounds for placing Idumæa in Arabia, but the extension of the latter to the confines of Egypt and the Gulf of Suez was wholly arbitrary. Oriental geographers give the name Arabia to the great region between the Red Sea and the Persian Gulf, together with Idumæa and the deserts lying on its eastern side, whilst they assign the northern portion of Arabia Deserta to Syria, and give the Sinaitic peninsula and the Tih plateau to Egypt.

The earliest geographers of Arabia exclude the Sinaitic peninsula and the Tih plateau from their domain, and one of the most celebrated (Isstachri), who lived in the tenth century,‡ bases the exclusion on the grounds that water and pasturage were alike wanting in this region. The name Arabia Petræa, by which it is now known, is never applied to it by the natives even at the present day. This title was the result of an accident, and arose from the hasty application of the name of the ancient Petra, the Idumæan capital, to the whole country. Mohammed, though his followers advanced as far as the head of the Gulf of Akaba, never penetrated the Sinaitic peninsula. It was peopled, so far as it could be said to have been peopled at all, by Coptic Christians down to the middle of the seventh century, when it fell under the

---

* Plin. vi. 8, par. 32.   † Ptol. *Geographia*, v. 16.
‡ Isstachri. *Das Buch der Länder*, Hamburg. 1848, pp. 31, 32; also note 19, p. 140.

Moslem domination. A century previous to this event, Justinian built the great convent of Sinai, apparently as a memorial of himself and as a tribute to the piety and virtue of Theodora.* At this time the population consisted almost exclusively of monks and hermits. No Arabian had yet passed westward of the Idumaean hills.†

It will thus be seen that if St. Paul had spoken of the Sinaitic peninsula as Arabia, he would have committed a prolepsis ;‡ that is to say, he would have given it a name which it did not receive until a century after his death. But if he did not refer to the Sinaitic peninsula, he must have had Idumaea in his mind, because all the Hebrew traditions concur in stating that the covenant was made at the Mount of God before the Israelites had passed round Edom on their way to Moab, and save in the Sinaitic peninsula and the Tih there are no mountains between Egypt and Edom.

We have now (with the exception of the traditions of the Exodus) examined all the evidence to be found in Scriptural records bearing on the locality of Mount Sinai, and it points conclusively in one direction. Seir is the dwelling-place of

---

* Burchardt mentions an Arabic inscription over the gate of the convent, to the effect that Justinian built the convent in the thirteenth year of his reign as a memorial of himself and Theodora (*Syria*, p. 545). A Greek inscription to the same effect is also to be seen. "This holy convent of Mount Sinai, where God spoke to Moses, was built from the foundation by Justinian," &c. Copies of both inscriptions will be found in the Appendix to Lepsius' *Letters from Egypt*.

† Ritter, *Die Erdkunde*, xiv. 5-8.

‡ It is, of course, impossible for any one to commit a prolepsis. But when an apparent prolepsis occurs in any writing, it can only be explained in one of two ways : either the writing is of a later date than that which is supposed, or the writer's meaning is misunderstood. In the present instance the latter explanation is the true one. By Arabia, St. Paul did not mean, because he could not have meant, the Sinaitic peninsula.

Jahveh, Sinai is the Mount of God. In the eyes of the Poet, the Prophet, the Historian, and the Apostle, the two were so inseparable as to be absolutely identified both physically and metaphorically. These men may have been ignorant. They may have been under a delusion. The spirit of rhapsody may have led them to confuse places geographically distinct, and far removed the one from the other;* but unquestionably, if human language is to be interpreted by its only intelligible meaning, then one and all believed, and desired to convey the belief, that Mount Sinai was in Idumæa.

But there is no reason for supposing that any of the writers we have quoted had more than a general idea that the Mount of God was in the Idumæan range. Accepting the voice of tradition, they placed it in Seir; or, speaking more generally, in Arabia.†

Josephus, neither in his paraphrase of the Scriptures nor in his history of the Jewish wars, gives any direct information respecting the locality of the mountain, though he affects to speak of it as a place whose general characteristics were well known. "It is the highest of all the mountains there-

---

* The learned contributor of the Article "Paran," in Smith's *Bible Dictionary*, in commenting on the similarity of the language in the Song of Deborah (Jud. v. 4, 5), in the Blessing of Moses (Deut. xxxiii. 2), and in the book of the prophet Habakkuk (Hab. iii. 3), remarks: "We may almost regard this lofty rhapsody as a commonplace of the inspired song of triumph, in which the seer seems to leave earth so far beneath him that the preciseness of geographical detail is lost to his view." It does seem rather hard on the "seer" to suggest that he talked nonsense, because he lost sight of geographical details which no one heard of till many centuries after his death. Surely, even putting all claims to inspiration on one side, it would not be so very unreasonable to give these people credit for knowing what they were speaking about.

† This singular oblivion of the precise locality of Mount Sinai will be dealt with at a later stage of our inquiry.

abouts, and the best for pasturage, the herbage being there very good, and it had not been fed upon before" (the time of the appearance of God in the burning bush), "because of the opinion men had that God dwelt there, the shepherds not daring to ascend it."* And elsewhere he writes : "Mount Sinai is the highest of all the mountains that are in that country, and is not only very difficult to be ascended by men, on account of its vast altitude, but because of the sharpness of its precipices also ; nay, indeed, it cannot be looked at without pain of the eyes; and besides this, it was terrible and inaccessible, on account of the rumour that passed about that God dwelt there."† Josephus does not, however, say in what particular region the mountain stood, which he most undoubtedly would have done if he had ever seen it or even knew where to find it.

In giving an account of the escape of Moses from Egypt, he writes : "He took his flight through the desert, and when he came to the city of Midian, which lay upon the Red Sea (the Gulf of Akaba), and was so denominated from one of Abraham's sons by Keturah, he sat down by a well, and rested himself after his laborious journey."‡ Whilst Moses was there the seven virgin daughters of Raguel the priest came to the well to draw water, and, adds Josephus, "these virgins took care of their father's flocks, which sort of work it was customary and very familiar for women to do in the country of the Troglodytes."§ The Troglodytes (dwellers in caves) were, at least in this part of the world, to be found only in the mountains of Edom, and it would seem there-

---
* *A. J.* ii. 12. 1. † *A. J.* iii. 5. 1. ‡ *A. J.* ii. 11.
§ Τρωγλοδυτοί is the Greek counterpart of the Hebrew חרי Horites. Elsewhere, Josephus states that the Midianites "took possession of Troglodytis and the country of Arabia Felix, as far as it reaches to the Red Sea" (*A. J.* i. 15 ; ii. 9. 3). But Arabia Felix, according to every authority, ancient and modern, was to the east of the Red Sea and Ælanitic Gulf.

fore that Midian and Edom were identified in the mind of Josephus. In this country, occupied by "dwellers in caves," Moses took up his abode, and Raguel having married him to one of his daughters, gave him charge of his flocks. Josephus then continues: "Now Moses, when he had obtained the favour of Jethro, for that was one of the names of Raguel, stayed there and fed his flocks, but some time afterwards taking his station at the mountain called Sinai, he drove his flocks thither to feed them." The conclusion is irresistible that Sinai was, according to the belief of Josephus, in the country of the "dwellers in caves," where Raguel was priest or chief ruler, and that the people whom he ruled, though following pastoral pursuits, were not of nomadic habits. According to the idea of Josephus, Moses in flying from Egypt had to cross deserts to reach the country in which he made his home; but when "*there* finding his flock," "he took his station at the mountain called Sinai." In his paraphrase Josephus represents Moses as going to the city of Midian. The earlier form in which the tradition is handed down, that he went to the "land of Midian,"* is the more accurate, and this land unquestionably lay to the east of the Araba. Whether it included both Idumæa and the country lying between the Ælanitic Gulf and the Arabian deserts is a question of minor importance.†

In the account of the insurrection against the Roman authority, in which Simon of Gerasa took part, Josephus states that Simon "overran the Acrabattene toparchy and the places that reached as far as the great Idumæa, for he built a wall at a certain village called Nain, and at the

---

* Exod. ii. 15.
† It is very questionable whether the supposed differences between Ishmaelites, Edomites, and Midianites, and the assignment of different regions to the descendants of Ishmael, Esau, and Midian, rest upon any solid foundation. See next Chapter.

valley called Paran he enlarged many of the caves."* Paran, which we have seen to be so intimately connected with Sinai and Seir, was thus, according to the testimony of the Jewish historian, remarkable for its cave dwellings, and was situated in Idumæa.

Having now exposed all the evidence procurable on the vexed question of the locality of Sinai down to the time of the final dispersion of the Jews, it only remains to inquire whether the apparent conclusion that the Mount of God was in Edom is reconcilable with, or opposed to, the traditions of the Exodus.

---

* B. J. iv. 9. 4.

CHAPTER VI.

MOSES is represented in the Book of Exodus as flying from justice, and taking refuge in the land of Midian.* There he married the daughter of Reuel, the priest or prince of Midian, and whilst in charge of his father-in-law's herds, " he led the flock to the backside of the desert, and came to the Mountain of God, even to Horeb."†

Midian is said to have been one of the sons of Abraham and Keturah, and with the other children of the patriarch to have been sent away into the east country.‡ In other words, a people claiming descent from Abraham settled in the country to the east of the Araba. In another form the tradition represents the Ishmaelites as having taken the same direction;§ whilst in still a third, Esau, the eldest son of Isaac, is represented as settling in Edom.|| From the earliest times, however, the Ishmaelites and the Midianites appear to have been regarded as identical, for in the story of the sale of Joseph by his brethren, the merchantmen who were on their way from Gilead to Egypt are indifferently described as Ishmaelites and Midianites;¶ and in the account of the victory of Gideon over the Midianites, the latter are said to have worn golden earrings because they were Ishmaelites.** "Midianites" would seem therefore to have been, like "Ishmaelites," a generic term given to the great

---

* Exod. ii. 15. † Exod. iii. 1. ‡ Gen. xxv. 6.
§ Gen. xxi. 21; xxv. 12–18. || Gen. xxxvi. 1–8. ¶ Gen. xxxvii.
** Jud. viii. 24.

bulk of the people inhabiting the east country (the east of the Araba). They were the Beni-Kedem, the children of the East. In the narrative of Balaam, the son of Beor, the elders of Moab take counsel with the elders of Midian; but it is the king of Moab alone who sends the messengers, including the elders of Moab and of Midian, in search of the seer.* In the celebrated prophecy ascribed to Balaam, though vengeance is denounced on Moab and Edom, no reference is made to Midian.† Amalek is marked out for destruction, and when " he looked on the Kenites, he said, Strong is thy dwelling-place, and thou puttest thy trust in a rock, nevertheless the Kenite shall be wasted."‡ Elsewhere the Midianite priest, who was father-in-law to Moses, is spoken of as a Kenite,§ and we therefore have a confirmation of the statement of Josephus that the people of the land where Moses took up his abode were " dwellers in caves." In the account of the licentious worship of Baal-peor into which the Israelites were seduced, the daughters of Moab and the Midianitish women are evidently treated as identical.‖

Everything therefore indicates that the land of Midian, to which Moses is said to have fled, was to the east of the Araba, and it is at least singular that one of the names ascribed to Moses' father-in-law, Reuel,¶ was that of one of the descendants of Esau,** who, according to tradition, settled in Edom.††

Whilst tending Reuel's flock, Moses led it "to the backside of the desert" (*midbhar*), and then came to the Mount of God. The Hebrew word translated "the backside,"

---

* Num. xxii.   † Num. xxiv. 17, 18.   ‡ Num. xxiv. 20, 21.
§ Jud. i. 16.   ‖ Num. xxv.   ¶ Exod. ii. 18.   ** Gen. xxxvi. 10.
†† It is not suggested that a son of Esau was the father-in-law of Moses, but simply that one of the names, by which, according to tradition, the " priest of Midian" was known, was Edomitish.

signifies to the westward of the desert,* and all that can be fairly gathered from this passage is that the mountain was to the west of the usual pastures of the flock, and within easy distance of them. In order to place Horeb in the Sinaitic peninsula, it is necessary to extend the land of Midian, which on all hands is admitted to have been east of the meridian of the Araba, in a westward direction, so as to include the Sinaitic region. It is, in fact, suggested that Reuel or Jethro was the Sheikh of a nomadic tribe, who in search of pastures visited the Sinaitic mountains at the time when Moses fled from Egypt. This explanation of the difficulty of extending "the land of Midian" to the Sinaitic peninsula is plausible, but it is altogether unsupported by evidence. It is simply coined to meet the requirements of the Coptic tradition, which places the Mount of God in that region. It is also necessary to assume that the barren, desolate region which to-day meets the eye was sufficiently fertile in the Mosaic time to induce a powerful chief to quit the pastures of the east country, and settle amongst the Sinaitic mountains during the forty years supposed to have elapsed between the arrival of Moses and the theophany on the mount; and that having seen the Israelites arrive under the guidance of Moses, Reuel, accompanied by his people and his flocks, turned his back on the holy mountain with its adjacent pastures, "and went his way into his own land."†
It must be admitted that the narrative, viewed in this light, is beset with the greatest improbabilities.

Let us now follow the course taken by the Hebrews on quitting Egypt.

---

* אַחַר *achar*, also אָחוֹר *achor*. The spectator was supposed to be looking towards the east, hence that which stood behind was west, that to the right south, that to the left north, whilst " before" signified the east. Michaelis, *Diss. de locorum differentia, ratione anticœ, posticœ, dextræ, sinistræ.* Hale, 1735. Gesenius, *Lex. Heb.* s. v. אחר *achar*.

† Exod. xviii. 27; Num. x. 29, 30.

According to the tradition preserved in Exodus, the Israelites proceeded into the wilderness of Shur, and they went three days in the wilderness, "and found no water;"* they next arrived at Marah, where to their mortification the water was bitter;† and it is next recorded that "they came to Elim, where there were twelve wells of water and three-score palm-trees, and they encamped there by the waters;"‡ and on quitting Elim they "came into the wilderness of Sin, which is between Elim and Sinai."§ In this wilderness the Israelites murmured in consequence of want of food, and received manna and quails;‖ and on journeying from the wilderness of Sin "they pitched in Rephidim,"¶ where there was no water to drink, their consequent discontent being removed by the miraculous supply at Horeb, which was Sinai.** At this place, whilst encamped at the Mount of God, Jethro came to meet Moses, bringing with him Zipporah and her two sons; here Jethro offered sacrifice, and praised Jahveh as greater than all Gods, and here a solemn league was concluded "before God," between Aaron and the Israelitish elders and Jethro and his people.††

In the detailed account set forth in the thirty-third chapter of the Book of Numbers the same itinerary is followed. On crossing the Red Sea, the Israelites went three days' journey into the wilderness, here, however, called that of Etham, and pitched in Marah;‡‡ removed thence, and came to Elim, noted for its fountains and palm-trees,§§ and encamped by the Red Sea;‖‖ thence they moved into the wilderness of Sin.¶¶ Two camping-places are then mentioned—not recorded in Exodus—Dophkah and Alush.*** On quitting the

---

* Exod. xv. 22.   † Exod. xv. 23.   ‡ Exod. xv. 27.
§ Exod. xvi. 1.   ‖ Exod. xvi. 2–15.   ¶ Exod. xvii. 1.
** Exod. xvii. 6.   †† Exod. xviii. 1–12.   ‡‡ Num. xxxiii. 8.
§§ Num. xxxiii. 9.   ‖‖ Num. xxxiii. 10.   ¶¶ Num. xxxiii. 11.
*** Num. xxxiii. 12, 13.

latter the Israelites halted at Rephidim, where there was no water to drink; and having departed thence, encamped in the wilderness of Sinai.* A number of stages are then mentioned which, with very few exceptions, rest on the sole authority of the compiler of this itinerary, and are incapable of identification, until at length the travellers appear at Ezion-gaber, a port at the head of the Gulf of Akaba.† From this point they are conducted into the wilderness of Zin, which is Kadesh;‡ from Kadesh to Mount Hor, on the edge of the land of Edom,§ and thence they pass, by way of Zalmonah, Punon, and Oboth into Moab.|| This latter portion of the itinerary would apparently lead to the conclusion that at the end of their journeyings the Israelites proceeded by way of the Araba, from the head of the Ælanitic Gulf, past Mount Hor, and entered Moab by passing through northern Edom, or between it and the Dead Sea.

We find elsewhere no additional information respecting the journeyings of the Israelites between Egypt and Sinai, but what we are told of their route on quitting the holy mountain is not devoid of value. For the purpose of identifying a locality, evidence tending to fix a route from it is as valuable as evidence respecting a route towards it.

It is stated that "the children of Israel took their journeys out of the wilderness of Sinai, and the cloud rested in the wilderness of Paran."¶ Whilst encamped there, the spies were despatched, "and they searched the land from the wilderness of Zin unto Rehob, &c.;" and "they returned and came to all the congregation of Israel, unto the wilderness of Paran to Kadesh."** These statements would point to the conclusion that the wildernesses of

---

* Num. xxxiii. 14, 15. † Num. xxxiii. 35. ‡ Num.xxxiii. 36.
§ Num. xxxiii. 37. || Num. xxxiii. 41-48. ¶ Num. x. 12.
** Num. xiii. 21-26.

Sinai and of Paran and of Zin were in close proximity, and that Kadesh, which is here identified with the wilderness of Paran, and elsewhere with the wilderness of Zin,* was a convenient place relatively to Canaan from which the spies could set forth. Elsewhere, however, we are positively informed that Kadesh was on the border of Edom, and on its western side.† If it was from Kadesh that the spies were sent to explore Canaan, it was equally from Kadesh that messengers were despatched to request a free passage for the Israelites through Edom.

The evidence supplied by the opening chapters of the Book of Deuteronomy is singularly confirmatory of that we have just examined. We are told nothing of the journey from Egypt to Sinai, or Horeb as it is here called; but Moses is represented as reminding the Israelites of their journey on quitting the Mount of God: " When we departed from Horeb, we went through all that great and terrible wilderness which ye saw by the way of the mountain of the Amorites, and we came to Kadesh-barnea."‡ Here the spies were sent forth.§ The people murmured when they returned with their report;‖ an unsuccessful attack was made on the Amorites, who destroyed the Israelites in Seir, even unto Hormah.¶ After an abode in Kadesh of many days,** the Israelites " turned and took their journey into the wilderness by way of the Red Sea, and compassed Mount Seir many days;†† and " passed by from the children of Esau, which dwelt in Seir, through the way of the plain from Elath, and from Ezion-gaber, and passed by the way of the wilderness of Moab."‡‡ Here the journey from Horeb to Kadesh-barnea is said to have been through " a great and terrible wilderness," which was seen

* Num. xxxiii. 36. † Num. xx. 16. ‡ Deut. i. 19.
§ Deut. i. 22-25. ‖ Deut. i. 26. ¶ Deut. i. 43, 44.
** Deut. i. 46. †† Deut. ii. 1. ‡‡ Deut. ii. 8.

by way of the mountain of the Amorites, which latter was contiguous to the Idumæan mountains, because the victorious Amorites are reported as having pursued the Israelites into Seir.* Nothing is said of the time occupied in the journey from Horeb to Kadesh-barnea, nor are any stations mentioned between these places. A statement is made elsewhere, which is so singularly disconnected with the matter which precedes and follows it, that it has all the appearance of an interpolation by even a still later writer than the compiler of the introductory chapters of Deuteronomy: "There are eleven days' journey from Horeb by the way of Mount Seir unto Kadesh-barnea."† It would be interesting to know the circumstances under which this gloss was inserted, and where were situated the Horeb and the Kadesh-barnea which were present to the writer's mind.

Now, let us examine more attentively the account of the route taken by the Israelites on entering the wilderness, and ascertain whether here, if nowhere else, we can find any indications that the Mount of God stood in the Sinaitic peninsula. All the evidence hitherto has led us to place it in the Idumæan mountains. Is this evidence set aside or confirmed by all that tradition has preserved to us of the direction taken by the escaped captives on quitting Egypt?

According to the tradition in Exodus, the Israelites went three days into the wilderness of Shur, without finding water; they were more successful when they arrived at Marah, but the water was extremely bitter; and they then proceeded to Elim, where they found twelve fountains and seventy palm-trees, and "they encamped there by the waters."

---

* The word אֱמֹרִי *amori*, which is always used in the singular, Amorite, signifies "a dweller on the heights"—a highlander; it does not appear to have been always used as the designation of a distinct tribe.
† Deut. i. 2.

The same account is given in the Itinerary in the Book of Numbers, save that the wilderness of Shur is called that of Etham ; and the ambiguity of the statement that when at Elim the Israelites encamped by the waters, is cleared away by the information that Elim was by the Red Sea.

Where was the wilderness of Shur into which the Israelites made what is termed a three days' journey? On this point we possess information from several sources. The descendants of Ishmael are said to have "dwelt from Havilah unto Shur, that is before Egypt, as thou goest toward Assyria."* Abraham is said to have "dwelt between Kadesh and Shur, and sojourned in Gerar,"† Shur being necessarily on the west and Kadesh on the east of the region occupied by the patriarch. Saul is described as having "smote the Amalekites from Havilah until thou comest to Shur, that is over against Egypt ;"‡ and David is said to have "invaded" several tribes which had been in early times "the inhabitants of the land as thou goest to Shur, even unto the land of Egypt ;"§ that is to say, the country which the traveller would pass through on his road from Judah to Egypt. It is therefore clear that Shur stood somewhere to the east of Egypt. The wilderness of Shur must consequently have formed at least part of the region of the Tih, a position, we may add, which is generally, if not indeed universally, assigned to it.

The expression "three days' journey" must not be taken literally. Elsewhere we have seen it used to convey the idea of a journey occupying a brief but undefined term,‖ and

---

* Gen. xxv. 18. This passage is somewhat ambiguous. It means, as is most probable, that a traveller from Judæa to Assyria would descend the Araba, and thus have on his right hand between him and Egypt the plateau of Et Tih, known as the *midbhar* of Shur. If the traveller cross the Jordan on his way to Assyria, this reference to Shur and Egypt is unintelligible.
† Gen. xx. 1.   ‡ 1 Sam. xv. 7.   § 1 Sam. xxvii. 8.   ‖ Exod. v. 3.

probably corresponded to the English idiom of "a few days." Independently of this consideration, it is needless to say tradition does not preserve a record of minute divisions of time. All that we can reasonably conclude is, that the Hebrews journeyed in the wilderness of Shur for some days without finding water. As they did not go to Canaan by the nearest way, they must consequently have followed an easterly or a south-easterly course. The former would have led them across the Tih along a route varying, perhaps, but little from that followed annually by the Egyptian Hajj on the way to Mecca. The latter would have taken them into the Sinaitic peninsula. The "three days' journey" into the wilderness of Shur raises, however, a strong presumption that they must have taken the easterly route, because in order to enter the Sinaitic region they would have been compelled, immediately after crossing the Egyptian frontier, to turn southwards and pass between the Suez Gulf and the western declivities of that semilunar wall of the Tih plateau which has been described as stretching across the peninsula between the respective heads of the two Gulfs of the Red Sea.*

Having been for some days in want of water, the Israelites reached Marah, with its bitter spring, and the next place of sufficient importance on their journey to retain a place in their memory was Elim, with its fountains and its palm-trees, on the shores of the Red Sea. Where was Elim, the first place at which the Hebrews appear to have found a suitable camping-ground from the time that they entered the wilderness of Shur?

---

* "There can be no dispute as to the general track of the Israelites after the passage. If they were to enter the mountains (Sinaitic) at all, they must continue in the route of all travellers between the sea and the table-land of the Tih, till they entered the low hills of Ghurundel" (Stanley, *S. and P.*, p. 37). Nor can there be any dispute about this, if it be conceded that they entered the Sinaitic region.

The word Elim signifies "trees," or probably "palm-trees," being one of the plural forms of El, which is only once used in the singular, in the expression El Paran.* Another plural form of the same word is Elath, sometimes written Eloth.† Elim, as applied to a place, is only found in the passages in Exodus and Numbers to which we are now directing attention.‡ Elath is spoken of in Deuteronomy as one of the stations of the Israelites when encompassing Edom,§ and is more particularly described in the historical books as a port at the head of the eastern arm of the Red Sea.‖ No mention is made of Elath in the records which contain references to Elim, and none to Elim in those in which we find Elath spoken of. This is all the more remarkable in the list of the journeys in the Book of Numbers, from its apparent exhaustiveness and perspicuity of detail. The writer includes in the list of stations Eziongaber, which in Deuteronomy is placed in the neighbourhood of Elath, but nevertheless omits to mention the latter place.

Of the locality of the Elath referred to in Deuteronomy and the historical books there is no doubt whatever. Situated

---

* Gen. xiv. 6.

† אֵילִם Elim, אֵילָה Elath, אֵילוֹת Eloth, are so many plural forms of אֵל El, which amongst other significations has that of a *tree*, hence rendered in the plural a *palm grove*. This word has been regarded, even by those who seem never to have suspected the identity of Elim with Elath, as applicable to both places; Elim, on account of its seventy palm-trees; Elath, because the port at the head of the Gulf of Akaba was noted for the palm grove in the neighbourhood of the fortress (Fürst, *Lex. Heb.*, on meaning of both words). Gesenius notes also the applicability of the name Elim to the station at which the Israelites encamped, whilst in referring to Elath, besides noting the palm grove near the castle of Akaba, directs attention to the Arabic interpretation of 1 Kings ix. 26. "And Solomon built ships (*in sylva Wal*) in the grove Wal near the city of Elath" (Ges., *Thesaurus*, s. v. *Elath*).

‡ Exod. xv. 27; Num. xxxiii. 9. § Deut. ii. 8.

‖ 1 Kings ix. 26; 2 Kings xiv. 22; xvi. 6.

at the head of the Eastern Gulf of the Red Sea, known to the Greeks as 'Ελανα, and subsequently converted by the Romans into Haila or Æla, it gave the name to the gulf on whose shores it stood—Sinus Ælaniticus. It became a place of considerable importance in the reign of Solomon,[*] its value was recognised under the Roman rule, and during the Byzantine supremacy it was an Episcopal See. It was one of the few spots in the world where, in early times, Christians and Jews succeeded in living in amity, this friendly relationship being continued after the region fell under the Moslem sway.[†] Its commercial importance as a seaport has long been a thing of the past, and for several centuries it has been known only as a station of the Egyptian Hajj. The name has been changed from Aila to Akaba, the latter being also the designation given to the steep and gloomy defile which at this point cleaves the wall of the Tih, and through which the caravan descends from the table-land to the sea-shore. The gulf formerly known as the Ælanitic is now called that of Akaba.

Though all traces of the former greatness of Elath have vanished, the natural characteristics of the place vary but little from those by which it was known in the earliest times. A few hundred yards from the shore at present stands a dilapidated castle, which affords shelter to a garrison of some thirty or forty Egyptian soldiers. Close by is a grove of date-bearing palm-trees. The neighbourhood is extremely fertile, and, it is stated on ancient Arabian authority,[‡] was in more prosperous times distinguished by its

---

[*] In paraphrasing the account in 1 Kings ix. 26, Josephus writes, "The king built many ships in the Egyptian bay of the Red Sea, in a certain place called Ezion-gaber. It is now called Berenice, and is not far from the city of Eloth (Αἰλανή)." Josephus evidently regarded the Sinaitic peninsula as part of Egypt.

[†] Ritter, *Erdkunde*, xiv. 296.

[‡] Isstachri, cited by Ritter, *Erdkunde*, xiv. 302.

numerous gardens. Water is abundant. A deep well within the walls of the castle supplies the wants of the garrison, but the traveller who takes the trouble of scooping up the gravel of the beach is rewarded with a plentiful supply of fresh water. There are no streamlets from the neighbouring mountains on the east; the rainfall would seem to be absorbed in the gravelly soil before reaching the sea.*

If a person of ordinary intelligence, who had never heard of the Sinaitic peninsula, was forced to content himself with the evidence supplied by the records and the traditions of the Jewish people respecting the course taken by the Israelites on quitting Egypt, it is impossible to imagine he could arrive at any other conclusion than that Elim, with its fountains and its palm-trees, was the Elath of later times. The necessities of the hybrid Coptic legend, however, rendered it essential that the Israelites should be dragged down into the desolate region lying to the south of the Tih, and Elim with its fountains and palm-trees had to be discovered and placed by the shore of the Suez Gulf.

It would be foreign to our purpose to follow the wanderings, not of the Israelites, but of the many curious and pious persons who since Cosmas Indicopleustis† and Antoninus Martyr‡ have visited the Sinaitic peninsula and accepted with credulity the stories of ignorant monks, or by personal investigation brought themselves to believe that they had determined with precision the track of the released captives,

---

* Accounts of Akaba will be found in the works of Rüppell, Laborde, Robinson, Stanley, Ritter, Burton, and others. Stanley says: "Akaba stands on the site of the ancient Elath—the Palm Trees—so called from its beautiful grove" (S. and P. p. 84).

† Cosmas Indicopleustis, Christ. Topogr. sive Christianorum de mundo opinio, in Bern. de Montfaucon, Collectio Nova Patrum, &c. Paris, 1706.

‡ Itinera et Descriptiones Terræ Sanctæ. Genevæ, 1877.

and ascertained the exact stations at which they halted on their route. One and all set forth with a postulate the accuracy of which they never dreamed of questioning, and once landed in the Sinaitic region, that region was obliged to accommodate itself to the exigencies of the Jewish traditions. The land of Midian was carried westwards from beyond the Idumæan mountains and Ælanitic Gulf in order to enable the shepherd Moses to stray with his flock on the Mount of God. The Amalekites who inhabited the mountainous region at the south-west of the Dead Sea, were exceptionally transported across the Tih steppe in order to be vanquished by the Israelites,[*] within sight of the waters of Suez. The barren crags of the Sinaitic range were clothed in fancy with pristine verdure to tempt Jethro from the land, to which he subsequently returned, and to feed the flocks which accompanied the Israelites on quitting Egypt. In a word, whenever the narrative and the facts failed to correspond, the curious and the pious investigators unanimously decided that it was so much the worse for the facts. And to this conclusion they were necessarily driven by the premises from which they started.

And yet there was much which was calculated to arouse the suspicion that the retreating Hebrews could not have entered the Sinaitic peninsula. It is alike opposed to probability and to fact to assume that the territory of Egypt, and the dominion of the Pharaohs, terminated on the east at an imaginary line drawn from the head of the Gulf of Suez to the Mediterranean Sea. It is generally taken for granted that when the Israelites crossed the Red Sea they found themselves beyond the reach of molestation by their former oppressors, and free to roam through a region unoccupied, save by some wandering Bedouin tribe. It would

---

[*] Exod. xvii. 8-13.

seem to be supposed that the Egyptians never had the curiosity to pass round the head of the Suez Gulf, and to explore the opposite coast; or the enterprise to utilise its harbours, and to develop the resources, if any, of the adjoining littoral. It is, however, placed beyond the pale of dispute that they did both the one and the other many long centuries before the captivity of the Israelites commenced, and when the tradition of Abraham's visit to Egypt was still unknown to the Semitic tribes.

If the traveller from Suez bent on visiting the Sinaitic mountains deviates a very little from his course whilst passing between the south-western corner of the Tih and the shore of the Gulf of Suez, a very curious spectacle meets his view. A small valley bearing to his left in an easterly direction, will lead him to a somewhat steep hill. On ascending this hill, he will see what at first strikes him as a cemetery. The surface of the ground is covered with stones, from five to seven feet in length, some upright, some lying on the ground, the former standing on pediments. The stones are rectangular in shape, rounded at the top, and covered on all sides with hieroglyphics. In the midst of these steles are seen the ruins of a building. The shafts of the pillars which project above the rubbish, and the inner surface of the walls are deeply carved with Egyptian characters. Close by are three catacombs hewn out of the rock, apparently for the reception of mummies, the interior being also covered with hieroglyphics. To the east and west of the ruined temple are found large mounds of slag, the produce of smelting operations conducted at this place thousands of years ago, the copper mines which supplied the ore being found in the neighbouring mountains. This remarkable place is called Sarbut el Khadem.

Egyptologists declare that the oldest inscriptions found here carry us as far back as the twelfth Manethonic dynasty (the last of the old monarchy), anterior to 2000 B.C., whilst the latest stele exhibits the shields of the last king of the nineteenth dynasty, a monarch who reigned probably a short time after the Exodus of the Hebrews. Speaking generally, the copper mines in the mountainous region on the western side of the Sinaitic peninsula, through which the Israelites must have passed if they entered this country, were, according to the steles of Sarbut el Khadem, worked by the Egyptians for at least a thousand years before the Israelites quitted Egypt, and appear to have been continuously worked down to the very time of their departure.

To the south-west of Sarbut el Khadem, but separated from it by a hilly range, is a gorge called the Wady Maghara. This gorge opens into the broad valley known as the Wady Mokkateb, or "valley of inscriptions," which affords to the traveller the easiest route for penetrating the Sinaitic region, and would probably have been turned to account by the Israelites if they entered the peninsula. In the Wady Maghara are found the traces of copper mines worked in ancient times, whilst on the rocks overhanging the excavations made in search of ore have been discovered designs belonging to the earliest class of Egyptian antiquities. These prove, according to the statements of Egyptologists, that these mines were worked before the pyramids of Ghizeh were reared, or more than three thousand years before the Christian era!

It is therefore abundantly evident, if the Israelites having either passed round or crossed the head of the Gulf of Suez took a south-easterly direction and entered the Sinaitic region, they must have passed through territory occupied by the Egyptians. If the departure was hostile, it is scarcely conceivable that their leader would have taken them by this route, and still less so that they should have passed unmolested, or at least without some event happening in connection with the Egyptians worthy of being preserved in tradition. If the departure was permissive these difficulties do not arise, and we would simply be left to deal with the broad question whether the evidence indicates that the Israelites entered the peninsula. We cannot, however, avoid noticing the significant silence in the Mosaic books respecting the Egyptian occupation of the region which they traversed. This is considered by some conclusive that the hieroglyphic inscriptions at Sarbut el Khadem and in the Wady Maghara are of a later date than the Exodus. The unprejudiced will see in it another proof that the peninsula was never visited by the departing Israelites.*

However ingenious may be the explanations offered for the unopposed entrance of the Israelites through Egyptian territory into the heart of the Sinaitic peninsula, and for the silence of the Hebrew traditions respecting the Egyptian colonists, the difficulty raised by the reported victory of the Israelites over the Amalekites is not so easily disposed of. This battle is supposed to have been fought at Rephidim,† which was a station between Elim and Sinai. If, however, the latter mountain was in the peninsula which now bears the name, the battle must have been fought in

---

* Laborde was sorely exercised by the silence of Moses in this respect, and he therefore incontinently rejected the alleged antiquity of the memorials. Had they existed at the time of the Exodus, Laborde, with a not unjust appreciation of the Hebrew character, suggested that the Israelites would have plundered the colonists, overturned the memorials, and sung a song to celebrate their victory (*Comp. Geog. sur l'Exode*, Paris, 1841, fol. p. 131, app. pp. 9–17). Ritter was also staggered by the absence of any allusion to the Egyptian settlements, and thus explains the difficulty: " It was by no means necessary to suppose that the Israelites turned out of their way to Sarbut el Khadem—a point so difficult to reach; or if they took the lower route, that they went up the Wady Maghara as far as the Egyptian settlements there" (*Erdkunde*, xiv. 802).

† Exod. xvii. 8–16.

its western section, and within the region bounded on the north-east by the semilunar wall of the Tih, and on the west and south by the Suez Gulf. But this was the very region which is indisputably proved to have been occupied at the time by Egyptian colonists.

But who were these Amalekites, and what ground is there for believing that either on this or on any other occasion they were found in the Sinaitic peninsula? Amalek was, according to tradition, a grandson of Esau and one of the Dukes of Edom.* The connection with Edom was never completely lost, Josephus frequently treating Edomites and Amalekites as apparently identical.† The Amalekites, however, were to be found to the south-east of Canaan, for the spies on returning to Kadesh reported that they, together with the Canaanites, barred the route by which the Israelites at first proposed to enter the promised land.‡ In later times Saul conducted a campaign against them, and having first induced the Kenites, who were an Idumæan tribe, to sever their connection with the Amalekites, he " smote them from Havilah unto Shur, which is over against Egypt;"§ that is, throughout the great region traditionally assigned to the descendants of Ishmael.|| This is simply the language of Oriental exaggeration, and only means that the king of Israel fought a successful battle with some nomadic tribes under the leadership of the Amalekite king. It is not suggested that the campaign was carried into the Sinaitic peninsula. If the captive king and the herds were brought to the camp of the Israelites at Gilgal,¶ which was on the right bank of the Jordan, this victory could not have taken place at a great distance from that spot.**

---

* Gen. xxxvi. 12.   † *A. J.* ix. 9. 1–2.   ‡ Num. xiii. 29.
§ 1 Sam. xv. 7. || Gen. xxv. 18.   ¶ 1 Sam. xv. 12.
** A mount of the Amalekites is referred to during the period of the Judges as being in the land of Ephraim (Jud. xii. 15).

Now, after allowing the widest latitude for the assumed nomadic habits of the Amalekites, is it within the bounds of possibility that they should have been encountered by the Israelites at the entrance to the Sinaitic region south of the Tih, ready to give battle, without any apparent object, to a host, as we are asked to believe, numbering more than half a million fighting men; and that only a year later (if so much) this ubiquitous and irrepressible tribe, notwithstanding their defeat, again confronted the Israelites in the mountainous region to the south-east of Canaan, and utterly defeated them, "chasing them, as bees do, and destroying them in Seir, even unto Hormah?"* If, as is stated, a battle was fought between the Israelites and Amalekites not far from Mount Sinai, is it not evident from all we can gather respecting the Amalekites, the Egyptians, and the mountain, that the battle could not have been fought nor the mountain have been situated in the Sinaitic peninsula?

It might at least be expected that those who treat as indisputable the passage of the Israelites through the Sinaitic peninsula would be able to point with something approaching unanimity to the more noteworthy of the stations mentioned in the ancient narratives, that they would refer to the still existing traces of ancient names, and that they would with triumphant acclamation indicate the mountain which was honoured by the visible presence of the Almighty. It might also be not unreasonably hoped, that having led the Israelites from Egypt into the midst of the Sinaitic region, they would also lead them out again by a route of which some faint indications might be found in the Hebrew traditions. Singularly enough, however, not one of these modest expectations is realised.

Those who take the trouble of reading a few of the

* Numb. xiv. 45; Deut. i. 44.

multitudinous works on the Hebrew Exodus will be amply recompensed by the versatility displayed by the authors in determining each for himself the course taken by the Israelites. Marah, the station where the bitter water was found, is placed by some at Howara, by others at Ghurundel; whilst, according to a third authority, it is to be found at a place distinct from the two.* Elim, with its palm-trees and fountains, is unhesitatingly placed by one authority in the Wady Ghurundel ;† whilst another, no less celebrated, identifies it with the harbour of Abu Zelemah, on the eastern coast of the Gulf of Suez.‡ Some declare it is to be found in the Wady Useit; others are no less positive that it stood in the Wady Tayibeh. The Wady Feiran is confidently claimed, on the strength of some fancied resemblance in the name, as identical with the Pharan or Paran which, as we have seen, was in the immediate vicinity of Sinai, and the same authority has no hesitation in declaring that the neighbouring mountain—Serbal—was the Mount of God.§ Others go farther afield, and discover the true Sinai in one of the three summits of the Jebel Musa block— Om Shomar, St. Catherine, and Ras Sufsaveh. Each mountain has its traditions and its shrines, and it may with perfect truth be said that the claims preferred on behalf of one are quite as good as those advanced for any of the others.∥

Having, however arbitrarily, and with however little

---

* "Marah must be either Howâra or Ghurundel; Elim must be Ghurundel, Useit, or Tayibeh."—Stanley, *S. and P.*, p. 37.

† Robinson, *Bib. Res.*   ‡ Lepsius.

§ Lepsius' *Letters from Egypt*. Let. 33. Burchardt held the same opinion about Serbal.

∥ Captain Burton, not inaptly, thus sums up the claims of each of the various mountains in the Sinaitic peninsula to be "the true Sinai." "It is evident that Jebel Serbal dates only from the early days of Coptic Christianity, that Jebel Musa, its Greek rival, rose after the

unanimity, followed the track of the Israelites from the Red Sea to Mount Sinai, the most painstaking confess that they are unable to follow them any farther.* There is not even a pretence of identifying the course followed on the long and weary road, which must have been traversed by the Israelites if they made their way from any of the mountains in the Sinaitic peninsula to Kadesh, the place identified with the wilderness of Paran and of Zin, from which the spies set forth to explore the land, and where the Israelites awaited their return. The difficulty has been ascribed to reticence in the Hebrew traditions. The true explanation is to be found in the fact that there was no such journey undertaken. There was no story to tell.

Let us now join the Israelites at a stage in their journey which is accepted on all hands—the region at the head of the Gulf of Suez; and dismissing from our notice, as if it were non-existent, the Sinaitic peninsula, inquire whether not only an intelligible, but in many respects a circumstantial, account of their route is not supplied from their departure from Egypt to their arrival at Mount Sinai; and thence (after their attempt to enter Palestine) on their march round the south "coast" of Edom to the border of the Arabian desert, on their way to Moab.

Having reached the edge of the wilderness,† the Israelites entered the wilderness of Shur.‡ During "a three days'

---

visions of Helena in the fourth century while the building of the convent by Justinian belongs to A.D. 527. Ras Sufsaveh, its rival to the north, is an affair of yesterday, and may be called the invention of Robinson; and Jebel Katerina, to the south, is the property of Rüppell" (*Midian Revisited*, i. 237).

* "So far as concerns the route taken by the children of Israel, we are able to indicate with a feeling of certainty (?) but three or four stations, and trace them to Serbal *or* to Sinai; but after the time that they received the Law, their course is to us *terra incognita*, and rests on mere hypothesis" (Ritter, *Erdkunde*, xiv. 729).

† Exod. xiii. 20.   ‡ Exod. xv. 22.

journey" they sought in vain for water, and subsequently they came to Marah, with its bitter spring.* We cannot expect to discover with certainty each place preserved in the Hebrew traditions, but those who set store by striking resemblances will probably have no difficulty in satisfying themselves of the identity of the spot where the weary and parched Israelites found the bitter water.

In the year 1658 Thevenot crossed the plateau from Suez to Akaba, and gave an account of the Hajj stations. The entire journey occupied six days, of which sixty-seven hours were spent in travelling.† The first day, of seven and a half hours, no water was found; the second day, of ten hours, the result was the same; but the third day brought the traveller to Kalaat-el-Nakhl, which may be considered the half-way house of the caravan across the desert. Here was a palm grove, a castle for the protection of the pilgrims, and a well of excellent water. On the fourth day, of fourteen hours, Thevenot reached Abiar Alaina, where he noted that the water was bitter; on the fifth day he arrived at the top of the pass leading downwards to Akaba; and on the sixth he reached Akaba, the ancient Elath, on the head of the Gulf.‡

In 1721 Dr. Shaw made the journey from Suez to Akaba in five days. No water was obtained till the third day, when he arrived at Nakhl; and on the following day he reached a place he calls Ally. He adds, that on this day's journey no water was found.§

Dr. Pococke, afterwards Bishop of Meath, stated, on the

---

* Exod. xv. 23.
† This corresponds with the estimated time (sixty-eight hours) in the *Tabula Peutingeriana*.
‡ Quoted by Ritter, *Erdkunde*, xiv.
§ Thomas Shaw, D.D., *Travels in Barbary and the Levant*, p. 477. London: 1757.

authority of one who had accompanied the Egyptian Hajj fourteen times, that on the third day the caravan reached Newhail (Nakhl), where there was water. It halted there twenty-four hours. On the following day it reached Allahaih, where the water was only fit for beasts. The next day's march brought it to Soot, with no water; and on the following one it arrived at Achaba, where the water was plentiful and good.*

Burckhardt crossed the Tih steppe in 1812, from east to west, entering it through a defile opening into the middle of the Araba, and at a day's journey from Nakhl (on the east) he found the spring of Et Themed, the water of which had a sulphurous taste.

A list of the Hajj stations was given, in 1658, by the Turkish historian, Haji Khalifeh, who, as his title implies, made the pilgrimage to Mecca. They are thirteen in number between Cairo and Akaba, the caravan having apparently moved very slowly. Nakhl, with its castle and wells, is the seventh station; and the tenth station is Abiár-el-Alá, "the springs of the height."† The Turkish historian makes no comment on the quality of the water at these wells.

The stations of the Hajj at the present day are eight in number, between Suez and Akaba. The second station beyond Nakhl is Et Themed, where the water has a sulphurous taste. There can be no question that this is the same to which Burckhardt refers, and is probably identical with Abiár-el-Alá of the Haji Khalifeh, the Abiar Alaina

---

* R. Pococke, D.D., *Description of the East*, i. 265. London: 1743.

† Wellsted translates Abiár-el-Alá, "The exalted wells" (*Arabia*, 2, app.). The Haji makes mention of two wells at the place, one called Borch, and the other Aláni, but this is probably an error. Borch and Aláni forming together Abiar Alaina, the name by which the wells are now known.

of Thevenot and Ally of Shaw, and the Allahaih of Pococke.

Now, if the Israelites proceeded across the plateau, it is easy to understand how their three days' journey should have been made without water. Whether they refreshed themselves at Nakhl we have no means of knowing, because the tradition that they went three days' journey without water does not exclude the possibility, or even the probability, of their having obtained good water at the end of that time.* The next station which was preserved in their memory was that at which the water was extremely bitter. Is it not, to say the least, extremely probable that this was the spring referred to by Thevenot and Pococke and the Haji Khalifeh, the Abiar Alaina, Abiár-el-Alá, " the springs of the highlands ?"

It may be said that there is here no trace of the name by which the Israelites knew the bitter spring. This is true; but then the names of places not infrequently change after the lapse of thousands of years. The Israelites may have called the place Marah, and the denizens of the steppe may have been ignorant of the fact. Or, as is more probable, it may have been already known as Marah, and either the Israelites or the compilers of the traditions may have jumped to the conclusion that it was so called because the water was bitter.† There is, however, another conjecture. If the word Amorite is rightly deemed to signify generically a mountaineer, "Marah" may, like "Amorite," have been

---

* No stations are mentioned in the three days' journey.

† The authors and compilers of the Old Testament records are extremely unreliable on questions of philology, indeed it may be said that they are invariably wrong. מָרָה Marah, is thus apparently derived from מָרַר Marar, to be bitter. This seems improbable. Elsewhere words signifying "bitter," or "bitterness," contain the repetition of the letter Resh (Deut. xxxii. 32; Job xx. 25); "the gall of vipers" (Exod. xii. 8): "bitter herbs" (Gen. xlvi. 11; Exod. vi. 16; Num. xxvi. 57). Marah is not an uncommon name in the Tih steppe.

derived from an unused root,* signifying a height or elevation, and thus the name of the springs Abiár-el-Alá = Abiar Alaina, would be simply an Arabic rendering of the ancient Semitic title—the springs of the highlands. Too much stress should not, however, be placed on what may after all be only a fanciful analogy.†

It is sufficient for our purpose to show that if, as is here contended, the Israelites proceeded in a direct course across the Tih, the incidents of their journey would have been similar to those recorded in these traditions. In the first portion of their journey they would have looked in vain for water, and in the latter portion they would not improbably have come across the bitter springs well known to travellers and to pilgrims. After quitting Marah, the next notable place must have been Elath, at the head of the eastern arm of the Red Sea. The next station recorded in the Hebrew tradition is Elim.

If the objective point of the Israelites on quitting Egypt was the Mount of God, and if that mountain was in the Idumæan range, then the route from the north of the Bitter Lakes to the head of the Gulf of Akaba was preferable to

---

* אֱמֹר ĕmor. The initial vowel is very short. This is the view taken by Simonis with respect to the derivation of Amorite. See also s. v. Gesenius, Lex. Heb. and Chald. and Thesaurus.

† In connection with the well of Abiar Alaina, and the etymology of the name, it may strike many persons as a curious coincidence that the Bedouins have a tradition that the wood with which Moses sweetened the water was the aloe. The gum of the aloe is, however, as every one knows, extremely bitter, and it is not easy to imagine how the Bedouins could have got it into their heads that the aloe, of all woods, could have been used to remove the bitter taste of the water at Marah. But if Allai or Alaina, be the Arabic rendering of the Semitic Marah, a "height," or "highland," then it is conceivable that the Arabic name furnished the origin of the tradition that the aloe was the wood employed by Moses to render the water drinkable by his followers. Abiar signifies the well, or wells, from Bir, the Arabic closely following the Hebrew.

any other. It was one which was well known to the Egyptians in their communications with the east country,* it was less perilous for the Israelites than a more northerly course on the borders of Philistia, and it had the advantage of placing the released captives at the southern entrance to that broad but desolate valley (Araba) which led to the foot of the mountain to which they were directing their steps.

Having reached Elim, with its abundant supply of water and its pleasant palm groves, the Israelites probably rested for some days, and refreshed themselves after their weary journey across the Tih. They "encamped there by the waters" of the eastern arm of the Red Sea. To the south stretched the Ælanitic Gulf, whilst to the north opened out before their eyes a broad valley shut in on both sides by mountains.

On departing from Elim, "the congregation of the children of Israel came unto the wilderness of Sin, which is between Elim and Sinai."† Where was this wilderness which was situated between Elim and the Mount of God? Was it between some point on the eastern shore of the Gulf of Suez and one of the mountains in the Sinaitic peninsula, or was it between the head of the Ælanitic Gulf and some mountain in Idumæa? If we are right in identifying Elim with Elath, it must have been the latter. Let us consult the traditions.

It is impossible to avoid being sometimes struck in the Hebrew records by the repetition of names which bear a striking resemblance to each other, sometimes by reference to the same places under different names. That this should be the case in traditions flowing through different channels,

---

* Captain Burton remarks that this is the oldest route in the world, and still wants a detailed survey (*Midian Revisited*, i. 124).
† Exod. xvi. 1.

even though they had a common source, is not to be wondered at. We have seen how the Mount of God came to be known by the different names of Sinai and Horeb. We have found, to all appearances, how the resting-place whose memory had been preserved on account of its fountains and its trees, was called by the cognate though apparently dissimilar names Elim and Elath, and it certainly would not astonish us to discover that the name of the same wilderness had been handed down in two forms so closely resembling each other as Sin and Zin.

The first of these names is found in the tradition in the Book of Exodus.* On quitting Elim, the Israelites entered the wilderness of Sin; they there received manna and quails. "They journeyed from the wilderness of Sin,† according to their journeys;" "pitched in Rephidim;" murmured for want of water, and obtained the miraculous supply from the rock in Horeb, the place receiving the name of "Massah and Meribah because of the chiding of the children of Israel, and because they tempted Jahveh."‡ It is further recorded in this tradition that "the children of Israel came unto the wilderness of Sin on the fifteenth day of the second month after their departure out of the land of Egypt."§ As their departure was said to have taken place on the fifteenth day of the first month, their arrival in the wilderness of Sin would be a month after quitting Egypt. No mention is made of the wilderness of Zin in the Book of Exodus.||

* Exod. xvi.; xvii.
† This passage should perhaps more fitly be translated, "journeyed through the wilderness of Sin."
‡ Exod. xvii. 7.   § Exod. xvi. 1.
|| No reliance can be placed upon statements respecting certain occurrences having taken place on particular days. Such minutiæ are not preserved in traditions; but when in later times the traditions of the migration came to be moulded into shape, it was found convenient

In the Book of Numbers a tradition is recorded in which reference is made to the wilderness of Zin: "Then came the children of Israel, even the whole congregation, into the desert of Zin, in the first month, and the people abode in Kadesh, and Miriam died there."* Whilst in this place "there was no water for the congregation;" the people rebelled, and Moses, by command of Jahveh, smote the rock, and the water came forth abundantly. "This is the water of Meribah, because the children of Israel strove with Jahveh, and he was sanctified in them."†

Those who wilfully shut their eyes to the abundant proofs of the disconnected and fragmentary nature of the Pentateuch—who, despite the evidence of their senses, deny that the same stories are frequently told twice and sometimes three times over in somewhat different language, and who believe that the Mosaic books contain a well-connected and consecutive history—will have no hesitation in saying that the wilderness of Zin here referred to was not reached by the Israelites till nearly forty years after the departure from Egypt.‡ But let us see what the Hebrew records say upon this point.

According to the tradition in the Book of Numbers, "the congregation gathered themselves together against Moses and Aaron," in consequence of the want of water; they demanded why they had been brought into the wilderness with their cattle to die? and asked "wherefore have ye made us to come out of Egypt, to bring us into this evil place? it is no

---

to assume that arrivals and departures synchronized with the occurrence of the new or the full moon, dates of considerable importance in the religious calendar of the Hebrews.

* Num. xx. 1. † Num. xx. 13.

‡ According to the marginal chronological annotation of the Authorised Version, the events recorded in Num. xx. took place thirty-eight years after the Exodus. Curiously enough, no one knows who is responsible for the Authorised Version marginal chronology.

place of seed, or of figs, or of vines, or of pomegranates; neither is there any water to drink."* This was language natural enough in the mouths of people who had only a short time before quitted Egypt, but it is totally inconceivable as coming, not from the released captives (for they had, according to the accepted theory, almost entirely died out), but from the new generations, composed of those who quitted Egypt in early youth or had been born in the wilderness, and who at this very time, we are asked to believe, had passed close on forty years rambling objectlessly about within less than a week's journey of the country which they regretted having ever left, and to which they clamoured to return. Even if the story stopped here we should have little hesitation in concluding that this exhibition of popular discontent took place very shortly after the departure from Egypt, but all doubt is removed by the statement that the discontent was allayed by the miraculous supply of water from the smitten rock, and that the place was called Meribah because the Israelites strove with Jahveh. In the tradition in Exodus† we are told that this miracle was performed at Horeb—that is, at Sinai—and that the Israelites, having journeyed from or through the wilderness of Sin, were at Rephidim, and also that the place received the name of Meribah. The apparent difficulty arising in both traditions—the one making the scene of the discontent Rephidim and the other Kadesh, whilst in both the water is stated to have been supplied from the rock in Horeb—is easily explained by supposing that the Israelites were encamped in

---

* Num. xx. This is curiously confirmatory of the conclusion that the captives accompanied from Egypt another tribe, and were led to believe that on crossing the wilderness they would reach a fertile country. There is no tradition of any manifestation of discontent until after quitting Elim-Elath.
† Exod. xvii.

a valley or plain supplied by a stream which flowed from the smitten rock.* Both traditions, however, concur in stating that the water thus supplied was called the water of Meribah. It is simply puerile to suggest that two miracles, identical in their nature and in the circumstances which occasioned them, were performed at different times and places, and that the latter were nevertheless known afterwards by the same name.

It will no doubt be objected that in the Itinerary contained in Numbers mention is not only made of two distinct deserts of Sin and Zin, but they were to all appearance at a great distance from each other, and were visited by the Israelites at periods separated by a considerable interval of time. In this record the Israelites are represented as having entered the wilderness of Sin only a few days after crossing the Red Sea;† whereas they only reached the wilderness of Zin on the eve of Aaron's death, which it is stated took place in the fortieth year after the departure from Egypt.‡

We have already alluded to the suspicion with which this list of stations must be received. The compiler tells us nothing new or instructive; he adds nothing to the information we already possess through tradition; he sheds no light on what nevertheless must have been an eventful history. He introduces a number of new names, but he can tell us nothing connected with the places. He appears

---

* That this is the correct explanation appears from Exod. xvii. 5, 6. "And Jahveh said unto Moses, *Go on before the people*, and take with thee of the elders of Israel; and thy rod, wherewith thou smotest the river [note the absence of any allusion to the Red Sea having been smitten], take in thine hand, and go. Behold, I will stand before thee there upon the rock in Horeb; and thou shalt smite the rock, and there shall come water out of it, that the people may drink." The water from the rock flowed to Rephidim, where the people were encamped. See also Deut. ix. 21.

† Num. xxxiii. 8-11.   ‡ Num. xxxiii. 36-38.

to have been anxious to make the number of stations at which the Israelites encamped after crossing the Red Sea correspond with the traditional number of years passed in the wilderness. In using the records at his disposal, he aimed at establishing a verbal harmony without caring about substantial consistency, of which he seems to have been unable to form any judgment. Perhaps we shall not err in ascribing this curious work to a pious and industrious scribe resident in Babylon, and profoundly ignorant of the relative positions of the localities to which he referred. He treated the deserts of Sin and Zin as distinct and geographically far apart; but it is nevertheless easy to show, even from his own record, that they were, if not identical, certainly contiguous.

Having quitted Rephidim, which in the Exodus tradition appears to have been in or close by the wilderness of Sin, but which this scribe separates from that desert by two stations not elsewhere mentioned—Dophkah and Alush*— he states that the Israelites encamped in the wilderness of Sinai. Thence they proceeded to Kibroth-hattaavah and Hazeroth;† and from Hazeroth to a long series of places not elsewhere mentioned, until in the fortieth year after the Exodus they are brought to the wilderness of Zin.‡ But on turning to the old records which the author of the Itinerary had at his disposal, we find that Kibroth-hattaavah

---

* Num. xxxiii. 12, 13. Dophkah and Alush seem to be a transposition of Elim and Rephidim, and the places may have been thus arranged in some ancient record, now lost to us, of the return journey down the Araba from Mount Hor, previous to compassing Edom (Num. xxi. 4). It is noticeable that the name Dophkah in the Hebrew text דָּפְקָה was read by the LXX. רָפְקָה Ραφακα, and between Raphaka and Raphidim, as the LXX. transcribe Rephidim, there is a very close resemblance. אלוּשׁ Alush, is not only very like אילם Elim, but it was not improbably another variant of that word, similar to Elath.

† Num. xxxiii. 15–17.   ‡ Num. xxxiii. 36.

was so called because the people died there from eating quails, probably to excess,* and that these quails were "sent" in the wilderness of Sin, between Elim and Sinai.† We also learn that from Kibroth-hattaavah they proceeded to Hazeroth,‡ and thence to the wilderness of Paran,§ which is identified with the wilderness of Zin from which the spies were sent forth.‖ Of the wilderness of Paran or Zin or of Kadesh our author makes no mention after recording the departure from Hazeroth, because, according to his ideas of harmony, it was preferable to bring these places in at the conclusion of the traditional term of the stay in the wilderness. Having, however, stated that the Israelites proceeded from Kibroth-hattaavah, which was by all accounts in the desert of Sin, to Hazeroth, which was the next station to the desert of Paran or of Zin, he has written all that is necessary for our purpose to show that even by his own admission the deserts of Sin and Zin must have been contiguous.¶ As, however, the spies "searched the land from the wilderness of Zin unto Rehob," the wilderness of Sin, which was close by, if not identical with that of Zin, and which, we are authoritatively informed, was between Elim and Sinai, could not have been in the Sinaitic peninsula. The same train of reasoning equally leads to the conclusion that it must have been to the north of the head of the Ælanitic Gulf.**

* Num. xi. 34. † Exod. xvi. 14. ‡ Num. xi. 35. § Num. xii. 16.
‖ The valley of the Araba appears to have been known to the nomads as the *midbhar* of Sin or of Zin. The allusions to this *midbhar* subsequent to the arrival at Sinai deal with the upper portion, and as in the records in which they are contained the name Zin is invariably used, it would appear as if the name was confined to that region.
¶ Num. xiii. 21-26.
** One of the curious results of accepting the statements in the Itinerary, is that as the emigrants did not reach the *midbhar* of Zin until immediately before the death of Aaron, the spies who set out from this *midbhar* (Num. xiii. 21) could not have undertaken their mission until nearly forty years after the departure from Egypt

On quitting Elim the Israelites must have proceeded along the Araba. They had descended from the Tih plateau by a steep defile, and certainly did not retrace their steps. They had no inducement for following the eastern coast of the Gulf in a southerly direction, and there consequently only remained two routes between which to choose. One led to the eastward, round the southern spurs of the Idumæan range, by a valley known at the present day as the Wady el Yitm;* the other lay open between the wall of the Tih and the mountains of Edom—the broad valley of the Araba. The former, though turned to account by the Israelites at a later period of their migration, was now disregarded. The liberated captives marched up the Araba.

The valley, at its southern entrance, is about three miles broad, and conveys to a spectator standing on the shore of the Gulf the appearance of being covered with verdure. This idea is quickly dispelled on entering "the plain." The sandy and gravelly surface is found to be rather thickly sprinkled with tarfa bushes. Of grass or other vegetation there is none, and water is sought for in vain to refresh either man or beast. At certain seasons of the year the shrubs which grow on the sand-hills of the Araba produce a sweet substance, which by the Bedouins is termed "manu." This product is also found in the Sinaitic peninsula. It is not met with on the table-land of the Tih.†

(Num. xxxiii. 36-38). But the forty years' delay in the wilderness was supposed to have been the punishment for the disobedience of the Israelites on the return of the spies (Num. xiv.).

* The name is a corruption of El Yatim, according to Captain Burton, and should be thus written (*Midian Revisited*, i. 235).

† An exhaustive account of manna, its various kinds, the regions where and the plants on which it may be gathered, with references to the various authors who have written on the subject, will be found in Ritter's *Erdkunde*, xiv. pp. 665-695. See also the Biblical Dictionaries of Smith and of Kitto, with the authorities there referred to.

If we are right in our conclusions, this was the wilderness of Sin which lay between Elim and Sinai, and here for the first time the Israelites partook of manna. Now it is not very difficult to form a plausible conjecture how the wilderness came to receive this name.

The Mount of God, as has been already observed, was known according to one set of traditions as Sinai, and according to another as Horeb. With respect to the derivation of these words, the ablest scholars cannot speak with confidence. There is still a wide field for suggestion.

According to a tradition of great antiquity,* Jahveh appeared to Moses on the mount in a burning bush, and it would therefore not be very strange if the mountain was known by a name associating it with this miraculous occurrence. The Hebrew for "bush" is *seneh*, and the Mount of the Bush would as probably as not be Mount Sinai.† In the same manner the mountain might have been known in other traditions in connection with its caves, if it possessed this peculiarity, and be termed "Choreb," Mount Choreb (Horeb) being thus synonymous with Mount Paran.‡

Now the Israelites, or the nomads before them, could not

---

* Exod. iii. 2.

† סְנֶה *Seneh*, a "bush;" סִינַי *Sinai*, the name of the mountain. Gesenius thinks Sinai may be derived from an unused root סִין *Sin*, "to be muddy." He says "*Sinai*, perhaps 'clayey,' 'miry;'" but there is no suggestion in the Hebrew records that the Mount of God had these characteristics. Fürst derives the word from סִין *Sun*, a fissure (*Heb. and Chald. Lex.* s. v.), in reference to the divisions in the granitic mass in the Sinaitic peninsula, of which Jebel Catherine is the south-western peak. Buxtorf, as it seems to me, with much more probability, refers the name of the mountain to the bush סְנֶה *Seneh*, in which God appeared to Moses (*Lex. Chald. Talm. et Rabbinicum*, s.v. Fischer Lipsiæ, 1869-75).

‡ Gesenius identifies חֹרֵב *Choreb* with חֹרֶב *Choreb*, "dry," but it seems at least as likely that it is derived from חוֹר *Chor*, a hole or cavern; hence חֹרִי *Chori*, a Horite or cave-dweller. The word is used in the sense of a mausoleum or resting-place for the dead, if we accept the

fail to have been struck by the peculiarity of the Araba to which we have referred—the abundance of low bushes; and if they gave to the desert a name in connection with this characteristic, it would not improbably be "Sin." The other name by which this wilderness appears to have been known, "Zin," would have had the same signification.* The difference in spelling and pronunciation is easily accounted for by a difference of dialect. The Septuagint renders both words indifferently Σίν.

Having advanced up the Araba through the wilderness or *midbhar* of Sin, the Israelites found themselves shut in between the precipitous cliffs of the Tih on their left and the mountains of Edom on their right. When in this region an engagement is commonly supposed to have taken place with the Amalekites. If we accepted as conclusive of priority of time the order in which the event is spoken of in Exodus,† we should infer that this battle was fought previous to the arrival of the Israelites at Sinai. This is, however, extremely improbable, because we are told that when the Israelites encamped at the Mount of God, Jethro came to meet Moses, and in his thanksgiving to Jahveh dwelt upon

---

Masoretic *Keri* in 2 Chron. xxxiv. 25. This passage goes far to support the view I venture to express, that the name given to the mountain in southern Palestine was associated with artificial caves, which may have been used as habitations for the living, or final resting-places for the dead. (See Fürst. *Lex. Heb.* s. v.)

* צִין *Zini*, is interpreted in the Talmud, "Lesser Palms." According to the Talmudists the desert of Zin was so called after a mountain of the same name which was noted for its dwarf palms, *Bara Bathra*, fol. 69, 2. In the Targum of Palestine this mountain is called the Iron Mountain, and the "Desert of Zini" the "Desert of Palms." The palms of this mountain were so small that it was said they were only fit to make a bunch to hold in the hand at the Feast of Tabernacles, *Succah*, iii. 1; Lightfoot ii. 325. Subsequent to the settlement in Canaan, the name "midbhar of Zin" appears to have been given to the upper portion of the Araba (the Ghor), near the Dead Sea.

† Exod. xvii. 8.

the liberation from the hands of the Egyptians, whilst making no reference to the discomfiture of the Amalekites.* It is impossible, however, to suppose that if the latter event had then taken place, it would have been passed over in silence by Jethro when praising Jahveh for all that had been done for Israel. The point is of no practical moment, but it may be convenient now to add some remarks to those already made respecting the battle with the Amalekites in its bearings on the locality of the Mount of God.

We have accounts of two battles between the Israelites and the Amalekites; in the one the former are represented as having been victorious, in the other the latter defeated their adversaries. The first engagement would seem to have taken place at Rephidim, in or near the wilderness of Sin,† the second at or near Kadesh, in the wilderness of Zin.‡ In the latter, the Amalekites are said to have been assisted by the Canaanites, and there can be no doubt that this engagement and defeat of the Israelites arose from an attempt on the part of the latter to enter Canaan from the south-east. About this there seems no dispute.

But assuming that there were two battles fought at different times between the Israelites and the Amalekites, have we not the strongest confirmation that the desert of Sin in the one tradition and the desert of Zin in the other were identical, since it was in or near the one that the Israelite victory was said to have been won, whilst it was in or near the other that the defeat was reported to have been sustained? Is not this obvious solution preferable to the accepted theory which places the desert of Sin and Rephidim near the north-western entrance to the Sinaitic peninsula, and transports the Amalekites across the Tih steppe to fight a battle with the Israelites in territory which

---

* Exod. xviii. x.   † Exod. xvii. 8.   ‡ Num. xiv. 40-45.

there is every reason to believe was at the time occupied by the Egyptians, and then transports them back again in order to offer a successful resistance to the invasion of Canaan? Not the least curious feature in this supposed movement of the Amalekites, is that it must have taken place in the first year after the Exodus, through a region—the Tih steppe— which for thirty-eight years afterwards is commonly supposed to have been exclusively appropriated by the Israelites for the purposes of wandering about.

Josephus has something to tell us about the first battle, in which the Israelites were victorious, which is worthy of notice; not that he possessed much better sources of information than we do, but because it is instructive to learn what was the general conception formed by a Jew living at the beginning of the Christian era respecting the route followed by the Israelites on leaving Egypt. In his paraphrase of the "journeyings," from the crossing of the Red Sea (which, curiously enough, he puts on all-fours with the passage of Alexander through the Pamphylian Sea,*) to the arrival at Sinai, he says nothing to convey the idea that the Sinaitic peninsula (south of the Tih) was present to his mind as the region through which the released captives passed. His allusion to the supply of quails is, on the contrary, couched in language which apparently excludes the possibility of his belief that the so-called Sinaitic region was the scene of this providential intervention; for he says, "a little time after came a vast number of quails, which is a bird more plentiful in this Arabian Gulf than anywhere else, flying over the sea."† In using the expression Arabian Gulf, it may be suggested that the Jewish historian meant what is to-day known as the Red Sea, and that consequently his remark would apply with equal probability to the Heroopolitan (Suez) and to the

---

* *A. J.* ii. 16, 5. † *A. J.* iii. 1, 5.

Ælanitic (Akaba) Gulf. This is scarcely so. For the reasons already given respecting the conception entertained of Arabia in the first century, it is extremely improbable that he would have spoken of the Egyptian arm of the Red Sea as the Arabian Gulf, whilst the words " flying over the sea" appear to imply that, in his opinion, the quails came from Arabia and not from Egypt.*

But in his remarks upon the encounter between the Israelites and the Amalekites there can be no question that, according to his view, the battle was fought in the region south of the Dead Sea. In a narrative containing more than the ordinary amount of fringe with which Josephus delighted in adorning his stories, he tells his readers that the fame of the Hebrews having spread abroad in consequence of the circumstances under which they quitted Egypt, " the inhabitants of those countries" sent ambassadors to each other, with exhortations to take measures for their common defence : " Those who induced the rest to do so were such as inhabited Gobolitis and Petra ; they were called Amalekites."† Gobolitis was the name given to the region on the east of the Araba between the Dead Sea and Petra, and although we cannot accept as conclusive the statement of Josephus that the Amalekites at this time inhabited Gobolitis and Petra, still it is strong evidence that, in his opinion, the first battle with the Amalekites was fought in that neighbourhood, and consequently that this was the region in which, according to his ideas, the Israelites naturally found themselves when on quitting Elim they approached the Mount of God.

---

* It is stated in Num. xi. 31, that "a wind from Jahveh brought quails from the sea ;" but as, according to the generally accepted view, the Israelites had then long left the Gulf of Suez behind them, this must have been the Gulf of Akaba.

† A. J. iii. 2, 1. Gobolitis is identical with the later Gebalena. In the Samaritan Pentateuch it is substituted for Seir in Deut. xxxiii. 2.

Following the tradition in the Book of Exodus, the next event recorded is the meeting of Jethro, or Raguel, the priest of Midian, with Moses. Having " heard of all that God had done for Moses," he came with Zipporah and her two sons " unto Moses, where he encamped at the Mount of God."* The first part of the journey was now completed ; the Israelites had reached the mountain, where on seeking permission to quit Egypt they proposed to sacrifice to Jahveh their God. From what region did Jethro come to meet his son-in-law, bringing with him the wife and children of the latter ?

When this portion of the narrative is connected with the introduction which tells of Moses' flight to Midian, his reception by Jethro, his occupation as a shepherd, and his interview with Jahveh on the Mount of God, there can be no doubt that Jethro's " own land" was in the immediate neighbourhood of the mountain, and that a very short journey was necessary upon Jethro's part to enable him to join Moses when encamped at the foot of Sinai. Without recapitulating, however, what has been urged to show that Midian was unquestionably on the east of the Araba, and that the particular portion of Midian here referred to was that in which " cave-dwellers " were found, which is called Troglodytis by Josephus, and in the Biblical narrative is spoken of as the abode of the Kenites, whose priest was Jethro, we are struck by this curious fact. If we have followed the correct track of the Israelites thus far, and if we are right in placing Sinai in Seir, nothing can be more consistent with all the evidence hitherto examined than that Jethro, the Midianite or Kenite Sheikh, should come from Petra or its neighbourhood, and meet Moses and the Israelites in the Araba ; or, more probably still, in one of the valleys leading from the Araba into the Idumæan mountains,

---

* Exod. xviii. 1, 2.

into which, as will subsequently be shown, they entered in
quest of the water supplied by "the brook which descended
from the Mount of God."* But further, the indications
which have hitherto led us to trace the Israelites across the
Tih to Elim, and from thence along the Araba towards
Mount Sinai, receive overwhelming corroboration by the
circumstance that we discover Jethro, who at this point
meets the Israelites, precisely in the very locality where
following the Scriptural records and the account of Josephus
we should expect to find him.

One of the oldest traditions of the Jewish people referred
the institution of their supreme judicial council—the Sanhedrin—not to Moses, but to his father-in-law. There are
in effect three distinct accounts of the origin of this celebrated tribunal; but we shall probably not err in concluding that the version given in Exodus† is the most ancient,
and that the Israelites borrowed their system of administer-
ing justice from the friendly tribe which they encountered
in the neighbourhood of Mount Sinai, of which Jethro was
chief, and with which they made a league.‡

The three accounts of the institution of the Sanhedrin
concur in stating that it took place close to Sinai, but in
one it is referred to Jethro,§ in the second to Jahveh,|| and
in the third to Moses.¶ For the purposes of our present
inquiry it is, however, only necessary to notice that the

---

* Deut. ix. 21. † Exod. xviii. 13–26.
‡ The section of a tribe of the Shasu, which came from the land of
Aduma (vide ante, p. 37), and was hospitably received by the officer of
Mineptah II., was in all probability Kenite. On approaching its home
it was met by Jethro, the Sheikh of the entire tribe, accompanied by
the wife and children of Moses. The released captives who had
accompanied "the mixed multitude," the Kenites, were thereupon
presented to "the priest of Midian," and through their elders a treaty
of amity was concluded with Jethro and his people (Exod. xviii. 12).
§ Exod. xviii. 19. || Num. xi. 16. ¶ Deut. i. 9.

second account apparently makes the appointment of the seventy judges take place in the region where the quails were sent; whilst the third account places it at Horeb, previous to the departure from thence "by way of the mountain of the Amorites," "through the great and terrible wilderness," to Kadesh-barnea. As, however, there can be no question that the region referred to in the first account must be identical with that spoken of in the second and third accounts, we have further confirmation of our conclusion that Jethro met Moses in or near the Araba, in the neighbourhood of Kibroth-hattaavah.

It is impossible to avoid being struck by a very singular peculiarity in the names of the places at which the Hebrews rested during their journeying through "the wilderness." These names are descriptive of the places to which they are applied; they are such as might have been given by the travellers to spots as yet unnamed, or with whose names they were unfamiliar, and they very frequently occur in the plural form. In the examination of their etymology it will further be found that they are, without exception, archaic. Unlike "proper" names, they have roots from which their signification can be gathered, but they are for the most part roots which in later times became obsolete. It is impossible to resist the conclusion that we are here dealing with materials of great antiquity.

The very fact, however, that the places mentioned in these traditions received their names in this manner, should prepare us for at least the possibility of the same place receiving different descriptive names in different traditions, and also, *à fortiori*, of the same name being differently pronounced, and in course of time differently written, by the members of different sections of the same people. We may not doubt that those who quitted Egypt spoke the same language, but it is no less certain that after the settlement in Palestine, if not before, there were to be found differences of dialect and of *patois* which have left their traces in the records of some of their oldest traditions. That such differences existed does not, however, rest alone on the natural presumption of the philologist. It is evidenced by unmistakable proofs in the Hebrew language. In one remarkable instance the difference of *patois* between the tribes which settled on the opposite sides of the Jordan is the subject of special mention. It is worthy of note that the difference in this case lay in the use of sibilants.*

In the Book of Exodus the various halting-places of the Israelites noted between Rameses and the Mount of Elohim are as follows :—Succoth, Etham, Marah, Elim, the *midbhar* of Sin ("which is between Elim and Sinai"), Rephidim, and Horeb, also called Sinai, whence the water of Massah and Meribah was caused to flow for the people at Rephidim. From Rephidim the Israelites passed into the desert of Sinai, and pitched before the mount. We have omitted from this list the names of the places mentioned in the account of the *détour* made for the purpose of "the passage through the sea." Our reasons for doing so have been already fully stated.

In the traditions in the Book of Numbers, which deal with occurrences stated in the Book of Exodus to have happened previous to the arrival at the Mount of God, the following places are noted :—Taberah, Kibroth-hattaavah, Hazeroth, the *midbhar* of Paran (in which was Kadesh), the *midbhar* of Zin (the same as that of Paran, for Kadesh was also in it), the unnamed rock from which Moses caused the water to flow, the water however being called that of Meribah. No allusion is made in these traditions to the journeying of the Hebrews from the time of their quitting

---

* Jud. xii. 6.

Egypt to their arrival at the place where they obtained the supply of quails brought by "a wind from the sea." We must not necessarily conclude that it was wanting in the records which the compiler had at his disposal. It may have been present, but possibly, being substantially identical with that in Exodus, have been rejected as involving unnecessary repetition. But it is at least as probable, that even before his time these traditions had become pruned and moulded into their present shape. However this may be, they assumed a form calculated to create false impressions in the minds of those who were ignorant of the manner in which the traditions originated, and who were easily misled by differences of names whose original identity had become buried in the oblivion of centuries.

Let us now examine these names, and ascertain whether in their philological aspect they tend to confirm or to overthrow the conclusion we have already drawn respecting the identity or contiguity of many places hitherto regarded as distinct and far apart.

The names Succoth, Etham, and Marah call for no further comment. Their probable meanings have been already discussed. Elim has been shown to be one of the plural forms of El, of which the other is Elath or Eloth; and consequently, philologically speaking, we should be led to infer that the well-known port at the head of the Gulf of Akaba was known by these apparently dissimilar but really identical names, provided the traditional evidence pointed in the same direction. On quitting Elim, the Israelites entered the wilderness lying between that place and Sinai, and encamped at Rephidim.*

This word, only found in two places in the Hebrew records, is supposed to mean "props" or "supports," and to be

---

* Exod. xvii. 1.

derived from the root *Raphad*, to support, in the sense of refreshing a weary person. The cognate name Arphad is therefore deemed not ill applied to a fortified city.* This derivation, even if it be correct, gives us by itself no clue to the grounds upon which the place at which the Hebrews encamped was called by this singular name. The place of encampment was assuredly not a city, and we can only conclude that it was called Rephidim because there were there several *Rephids*, or whatever the singular of the word may have been.

In the tradition in the Book of Numbers we are told that the people journeyed from Kibroth-hattaavah to Hazeroth.† It was, however, at Kibroth-hattaavah that they suffered from eating the quails, which in the Exodus tradition were "sent" on the journey from Elim to Sinai, and immediately before the arrival at Rephidim; and on removing from Hazeroth they pitched in the wilderness of Paran,‡ or, as it is elsewhere in the Book of Numbers termed, the wilderness of Zin,§ in which place they obtained the miraculous supply of water. Now on turning back to the record in Exodus, we find that they removed from Rephidim where they received the water from the rock in Horeb, and came to the desert of Sinai, and pitched in the wilderness.‖ Judging by the similarity of the events recorded we would

---

* Hebraists are far from agreed upon the derivation of the word Rephidim, רְפִידִים. Thus Gesenius refers it to רָפַד *Raphad*, to spread out as a couch (*Thes.* s. v.). Fürst adopts the same view, whilst Buxtorf, accepting the apparent interpretation of the Targum of Jonathan, refers the word to the circumstance that at Rephidim the Israelites loosened their hands from the Law—*i.e.*, abandoned their God—thus deriving it from רָפָה *Raphah*, to loosen or to withdraw the hand from any one (*Lev. Chal. Talm et Rab.*, s. v.). See also for this interpretation Talm. *Bech.* 5b.

† Num. xi. 35.
‡ Num. xii. 16.   § Num. xx. 1–6.   ‖ Exod. xix. 2.

therefore be led to suspect that Hazeroth in the one tradition takes the place of Rephidim in the other.

Hazeroth is the plural of *Hazer*. It also occurs in the form Hazerim, the two words thus presenting a close analogy to the plural forms Elim and Elath.* Hazer, or more correctly Chazer, an "enclosure," is derived from the unused root *chazer*, to surround with a wall† or fence. This word also signifies "to be green," from whence its derivation may be used to mean "a pasture." The word Hazar is of sufficiently frequent occurrence in the Hebrew records, and is generally accompanied with another name. We find, for example, Hazar Addar "the village" or "enclosure of Addar;" Hazar Susah, also called Hazar Susim, Hazar Enan, Hazar Shual, &c. It has been suggested with much plausibility that the word may have been applied to those rude collections of temporary dwellings which are constructed by the Bedouins of loose stone walls, and serve to support canvas coverings;‡ and whether we accept this signification or that of "enclosures," we can equally understand how the Israelites should have applied the name to a place where some changes had been made to furnish a suitable resting-place, both as regards convenience and protection, for a nomad tribe. It was, however, between Elim and Sinai, apparently at Rephidim, that the Israelites met the Kenites under the guidance of their Sheikh Jethro, and concluded a league with them§ on the eve of proceeding into the wilderness of Sinai and encamping before the mount; and it was in Hazeroth they rested previous to pitching in the wilderness of Paran.‖ We should therefore be justified in inferring that the words Rephidim and Hazeroth were

---

* Deut. ii. 23.

† חָצֵר *Chazer*, signifies to enclose with a hedge or wall, and Hebraists are agreed in referring the words Hazerim–Hazeroth, to this root.

‡ Palmer's *Desert of the Exodus*, p 322.

§ Exod. xviii. 12.   ‖ Num. xii. 16.

used to convey the same idea—namely, "supports," or "fences," or "enclosures," and constituting a species of rude encampment in which loose stone walls and probably green bushes supplied the place of tents. This inference would, however, become irresistible if we found that the wilderness of Sinai and the wilderness of Paran, the former being contiguous to Rephidim and the latter to Hazeroth, were identical.

One of the names of the Mount of Elohim was Horeb (Choreb), so called, as we venture to think, from its caves. All the evidence at our disposal points, as we have shown, to the conclusion that it was in the Idumæan range; and we know that these mountains were inhabited by a people who were called Horites (Chorites), because they dwelt in caves.* The tradition that Jahveh appeared to Moses in a burning bush upon this mountain appears to have led some of those who settled in northern Palestine to substitute Sinai for Horeb, the latter name being, however, retained in southern Palestine. The sections into which the parent stock from Egypt split up were, however, numerous, and the name of the Mount of God was preserved by tradition in other forms than those of Horeb and Sinai. It was also called Mount Paran,† which was, however, only a different rendering of Mount Horeb. As, however, the identity of Horeb and Sinai is not contested, the *midbhar* of Horeb and the *midbhar* of Sinai would mean the same place; and if we are correct in concluding that Mount Horeb and Mount Paran were the same, and were identified throughout the Hebrew records with Mount Sinai, it necessarily follows that the wilderness of Paran—*i.e.*, of Horeb—must have been equally the wilderness of Sinai.

We have seen, however, that mention is made in the

---

* Deut. ii. 12.   † Deut. xxxiii. 2; Hab. iii. 3.

Book of Exodus of a *midbhar* of Sin, and also of a *midbhar* of Sinai; whilst in the Book of Numbers reference is apparently made to neither, though the *midbhar* of Zin is recorded as one of the places in which the Hebrews encamped. No difficulty whatever arises in respect to the *midbhar* of Zin. It is indisputably identified with the *midbhar* of Paran, which we have just seen was the *midbhar* of Sinai; but the fact that it was called in this tradition the *midbhar* of Zin shows that there were differences of dialect amongst those who had common traditions, and that the same *midbhar* which would be called Zin by some would be called Sin by others, just as the Shibboleth of the Gileadites was called Sibboleth by the Ephraimites.*
An interesting question still remains for consideration, whether there was any difference between the *midbhar* of Sin, mentioned in the tradition in Exodus as intervening between Elim and Sinai, and the *midbhar* of Sinai spoken of in the same tradition. This will be dealt with when referring more particularly to the topography of the region in which this or these *midbhars* were situated.

Kadesh, which in the Book of Numbers† is stated indifferently to have been in the *midbhar* of Paran and in the *midbhar* of Zin, is not referred to *eo nomine* in the Book of Exodus. The word, like the rest which have engaged our attention, is descriptive. It signifies "holy," or "dedicated to God." That such a title should be given to the region at the foot of the Mount of God—that is to say, to the portion of the *midbhar* of Paran where the Hebrews were dedicated to Jahveh by a solemn covenant—is at least probable.‡

---

* Jud. xii. 6. † Num. xii. 16; xiii. 21, 26.

‡ קָדֵשׁ *Kadesh*. This word has the meaning of "holy," but it is fairly open to doubt whether this was its original signification. Perhaps it meant simply "dedicated," and dedication to the service of God came in time to be considered synonymous with "holy." There

There are two other names in the record in Numbers which demand a passing remark. Taberah we know nothing of beyond the statement that in this place Jahveh consumed with fire some of his discontented people,* but it may possibly refer to the event recorded at greater length in the narrative of the rebellion of Korah and his associates.† The derivation of the word is unknown. Kibroth-hattaavah, the name given to the place where the people were punished by being afforded the opportunity of surfeiting themselves with the flesh of quails, is interpreted the "graves of lust,"‡ the place, according to the tradition, having been named after the graves of those who perished.§ If we are right in identifying the two traditions now engaging our attention, this place was between Elim-Elath and Sinai—that is, to the north of the Gulf of Akaba—across which, by means of a strong wind, the quails were carried to the camp of the Hebrews. It would also seem to follow that it could have been at no considerable distance from the sea.

Thus far, then, we have found that whilst every reference made to the Mount of God by those who lived subsequently to the settlement in Canaan places it in Idumæa, the traditions of those who quitted Egypt are alone intelligible on the

---

were a class of persons termed קְדֵשִׁים *Kedeshim* (male and female), so called because they were "dedicated," but whose service to the Deity was in the highest degree impure. The prophetic books are replete with protests against their practices. See also Deut. xxiii. 18. It seems probable that the place so frequently referred to by this name in the traditions of the Hebrew migration, was so called because the Hebrews were there dedicated to Jahveh.

* Num. xi. 3. † Num. xvi.

‡ תַּאֲוָה *Tavah*, if we accept as correct the interpretation given of the name in the Hebrew records, would thus be derived from אָוָה *avah*, a longing desire. The former word is frequently used in this sense. The rendering in the Authorised Version should be Kibroth-hat-Tavah, *hat* being simply the definite article, "Graves of the Tavah."

§ Num. xi. 34.

assumption that the mountain stood in the same region. By crediting the Hebrews with avoiding the Egyptian settlements which blocked up the entrance to the Sinaitic peninsula and following a direct track across the Tih, we have seen how they would have arrived at Elath at the time they are supposed to have arrived at Elim. We have also found that this tallies literally with the statement ascribed to Jephthah, that "Israel came up from Egypt, and walked through the wilderness unto the Red Sea, and came to Kadesh," which was in the *midbhar* of Paran or Zin or Sinai. We also know that between Elim-Elath on the Red Sea and Kadesh-Sinai certain events happened; which, since Kadesh was the place from which the spies were sent forth, and also from which the Hebrews turned in order to pass round the south boundary of Edom, must almost certainly have occurred on the east of the Tih steppe. The meeting with the Kenites; the battles with the Amalekites (one of which took place at Rephidim and the other at Kadesh); the flight of quails brought up from the sea; the miraculous supply of water, which according to one tradition flowed from the rock in Horeb to Rephidim, and in the other to Kadesh (hence Kadesh-Meribah), which must have been in close proximity to Hazeroth, and which in both is named the water of Meribah; in a word, all the evidence, whether considered in its entirety or its details, points in one direction, and in one direction alone.

Having now compared the opinions of the settlers in Canaan down to the commencement of the Christian era, respecting the locality of Mount Sinai, with the traditions which their ancestors brought with them from "the wilderness," let us acquaint ourselves more closely with the topography and the general features of the region in which, according to all the previous indications, the Mount of God was situated.

CHAPTER VII.

THE broad and desolate valley running in a direction almost due north from the head of the Gulf of Akaba, known apparently from very ancient times as the Araba, has been already described with sufficient particularity. It furnishes the natural highway for travellers passing between the Gulf and the Dead Sea, and is well known throughout its entire extent. The general features are everywhere the same. The sand and flint, of which its surface consists, are covered by the sparsest verdure; the Arabian acacia, the tarfa (or manna-bearing tamarisk), and an occasional stunted palm, with a scanty supply of sand-grass, furnishing the sole vegetation. It is almost waterless.*

The mountainous region which bounds this valley on the east is very little known. The area is inconsiderable, nowhere probably exceeding thirty miles in breadth; and of physical obstacles to exploration there are absolutely none. Yet it would be literally correct to say that the topography of Smith's Sound, leading to the North Pole, is more familiar to geographers than that of the picturesque hills and valleys of the land of Edom.

For many reasons this is to be regretted. No land, scarcely excepting Palestine itself, is richer in its historical associations and in its memorials of a mighty past than Idumæa. Occupied in the earliest times, at least on its western border, by a people who obtained the generic appellation of Horites

---

* See *ante*, p. 135, note.
P

(Chorites) from the fact of their dwelling in caves, it subsequently passed into the hands of nomadic tribes claiming descent from the eldest son of Isaac. To them it was given by Jahveh, and its fertility, especially when compared with the adjoining deserts, fully justified the description of its soil and climate as being "of the fatness of the earth, and of the dew of heaven from above."* In process of time, and as yet some centuries before the Christian era, the Edomites gave place to the Nabathæans—a very remarkable people, who brought with them from the east a high order of civilisation. Abandoning their nomadic habits, they not only developed to the utmost the industrial resources of the country, but established commercial relations with the Western world;† and when, at the commencement of the second century of the present era, the Romans secured possession of the country,‡ its capital, Petra Adriana, became the emporium through which passed the chief products of the East on their way to the principal cities of the Roman Empire.§ A few centuries later, the tide of Moslem in-

---

* Gen. xxvii. 39.

† Two expeditions were sent against the Nabathæans so early as the close of the fourth century B.C., by Antigonus, one of Alexander's successors. The first was commanded by Athenæus, the second by his son Demetrius. The inhabitants of Petra, happening to be absent at some fair, Athenæus carried off large quantities of frankincense and myrrh, and four hundred talents of silver (Diod. Sic., xix. 94–99).

‡ Under Trajan, A.D. 105, the kingdom of Arabia was subjugated by Cornelius Palma, the then Roman Governor of Syria (Dio. Cass., lxviii. 14; Amm Marcell., xiv. 8). Adrian, Trajan's successor, conferred on Petra certain municipal privileges, and many coins are still extant bearing the inscription, Ἀδριάνη Πέτρα Μητρόπολις (Mionnet, *Descript. de Medailles Antiques*, v. 587).

§ We learn from Strabo that the merchandise of Arabia and India was transported on camels from Leukè Komè (a port on the eastern coast of the Red Sea) to Petra, and thence across the Tih to Rhinoclura, a Mediterranean port at the mouth of the Wady-el-Arish (Strab. xvi. 4; xviii. 23).

vasion swept across the land. The blight was universal and complete. Everything not absolutely indestructible perished. The peaceful arts, of which so many rich memorials have been left, were extinguished; lawless hordes, the sole end of whose existence was rapine, and whose traditional instincts led them to regard as disgraceful every form of honest labour, speedily converted what was a garden into a wilderness, and what was an unrivalled city into a mass of ruins. But neither fanaticism nor barbarism, neither rapacity nor neglect, could obliterate the traces of the civilisation which had been only too completely superseded. The earliest inhabitants had excavated for themselves caves in the living rock; their successors had followed in their footsteps, and had hewn their temples and their palaces in the porphyry and sandstone precipices which encircled their city. It would need an earthquake to destroy Petra,* and so long as the mountains of Idumæa stand the relics of Horites, Edomites, Nabathæans, and Romans may be regarded as heirlooms secured to endless posterity.

In the early part of the present century Burckhardt, in the course of his travels, stumbled on the ruins of Petra. Since then it has been frequently visited, and the city, its approaches, and its most notable monuments are now familiar to those who study the records of Eastern travel. But, with the exception of its ancient capital, little is known of the interior of Idumæa. Travellers from the Sinaitic peninsula to the Holy Land, or *vice versâ*, when proceeding through the Araba, quit that great highway by some valley on the eastern side which conducts them to Petra; they thence return by a different route to the Araba, and having looked at, or in some cases ascended, the adjacent

---

* Arconati, *Diario di un Viaggio in Arabia Petræa.*

Jebel Harûn (Mount Hor), proceed on their travels. Laborde, who visited Petra more than half a century ago, and gave to the world a rich portfolio of drawings, together with a map of the mountain-embedded city, made his way back by a route on the eastern side of Idumæa, regaining the Araba near the head of the Gulf of Akaba, by a valley named the Wady El Yitm. Of the interior of the country, save at the capital, he appears to have seen little or nothing; nor have succeeding travellers been much more fortunate. The valleys of Idumæa still remain unexplored. The explanation is very simple. The country is occupied by tribes whose members pursue robbery as a fine art. The traveller must resign himself to being fleeced in order to avoid being violently plundered, and he must be prepared to risk his life if he desires to protect his purse. It requires no ordinary boldness to travel from the beaten track.

It will therefore be readily understood how valuable an acquaintance with the topography of this mountainous country would have proved in such an inquiry as that in which we are now engaged. We have now brought the Hebrews to an adjacent region, in which by the force of circumstances they were compelled to remain some time, and where some notable events took place which exercised an immense influence on their subsequent history. It was in this region that they met with the Kenite Sheikh whom tradition connects so closely with their great lawgiver; it was here that they were formally dedicated to their protecting God, and concluded with him a solemn covenant; it was from this region, as a base, that they first attempted to enter Canaan; it was equally from it that they set out by a circuitous route to seek possessions on the east bank of the Jordan.

The traveller proceeding from the head of the Gulf along the course of the Araba—at the same time a valley and a plain—reaches at nightfall,* or at an early hour on his second day's march, a swamp which compels him to skirt more closely the adjoining slopes. He notices in its vicinity the traces of a Bedouin cemetery.† The place is named El Daba.‡ Little presents itself to vary the monotony of the desert as the traveller proceeds onwards on his journey, treading his way over the gravelly soil, or crossing at no infrequent intervals the sand-dunes which intercept his path. The mountains on his right gradually diminish in altitude, but only to allow others still higher to rear themselves in the background.§ On the third day he reaches a valley debouching from the mountains into the plain. A few minutes' walk serves to convince him that he has quitted the desert. He sees a spring of clear water issuing from a cluster of acacias, whilst a few palm-trees invite him to repose beneath their shade.‖ If, instead of penetrating the Idumæan mountains at this point, he continues his course along the Araba, he passes a green meadow, the only patch of fertility to be found in the great valley,¶ and on the

---

* Deffieh was the first halting-place of Arconati after leaving Akaba, at least this was the name given to the place by his attendant Bedouins. He mentions nothing about it save that his party encamped close to a group of acacias. In a footnote, Arconati remarks that Deffieh is not mentioned by Buckhardt, Laborde, or Robinson. On the following morning he reached the swamp (*Diario*, p. 324).

† Un cimetière Arabe indique la continuation d'un ancien usage conservé par les tribus avec persévérance (Laborde, *Voyage de l'Arabie Petrée*, p. 53).

‡ Travellers vary considerably in the names they give to the places they visit. This arises from the difficulty of rendering phonetically into their own language the names uttered by the Bedouins. It seems to me that the place which Laborde marks on his map as El Daba is the Deffieh of Arconati, and in another map reappears as Taba. Any of these names would fairly correspond with the Tavah of the Hebrew tradition, the place of the *Kibroth* (graves).

§ Arconati, *Diario*, p. 332.

‖ *Diario*, p. 333; Laborde, *Voyage de l'Arabie Petrée*, p. 79.

¶ *Diario*, p. 334.

following day he comes to the entrance of another Wady, leading into the region on his right. The first-mentioned valley is called Wady Gharandel; the second, Wady Marhadè. The latter conducts the traveller to Petra.

Whilst still in the Araba, at the entrance of Wady Marhadè, the traveller sees to the north and on the east of the "plain" a mountain, towering above its neighbours. It presents the appearance of a truncated cone, and though still at a considerable distance it attracts notice by the singular richness of the colours reflected from its peaks.* This mountain is called Jebel Neby Harûn, the Mount of the Prophet Aaron, and is identified by tradition with that on which the High Priest died, and which in the Hebrew Scriptures is styled Hor Ha-Har, the Mount of Mounts—κατ' ἐξοχήν, *the mountain;* or, as it is rendered at the present day, Mount Hor.

Let us follow the traveller through the Wady Marhadè into Petra, not for the sake of examining its ruins, however magnificent and interesting, but solely to make ourselves acquainted with the natural physical characteristics of this region—characteristics which we may fairly conclude existed three thousand years ago. Winding his way through a labyrinth of passes, the traveller is struck by the contrast presented to the desert which he has quitted. The vegetation becomes gradually more and more luxuriant, and he picks his steps amidst thickets of oleanders, tamarisks, and red poppies.† Meantime the rocks forming the sides of the valleys assume the most varied hues, the sandstone, which here surmounts the porphyry, presenting the constantly

---

* "Alto e frastagliato che sorge al di sopra degli altri. È ancora lontano e velato di tinte cerulee" (*Diario*, p. 339).

† Arconati, *Diario,* p. 349.

changing tints of red and yellow, white and violet.* A day's journey serves to bring him into the heart of Petra, which, bounded on the east and west by precipitous mountains, lies in an expansion of a valley which to-day bears the name of Wady Mûsa—the valley of Moses.† The precipices partly enclosing the city are pierced with caverns hewn out of the rock, and of many of these excavations all that is known is that their antiquity must reach to the period when the inhabitants of this region were known as "dwellers in caves." To the west, and towering above the city of caverns and of rock-cut palaces, is seen the irregular summit of Mount Hor.

Most marvellous, however, of all the physical features of the valley of Moses is a chasm which pierces the mountains on the east, and leads into the city of Petra. This is called the *Sik*. As well to appreciate its natural beauties as to enjoy the surprise occasioned by the glories of the ancient city suddenly bursting on the view, the traveller should enter the gorge from the east.

Not far distant from the eastern mouth of the *Sik* is the

---

* "Le rocce che ci circondano sono di arenaria variegata, venata di rosso, di bianco, di giallo, di viola, tutte le tinte sono di una vivezza straordinaria. . . . . Le colorazeoni dell' arenaria sono veramente straordinarie, la venatura più frequente si compone di piccole onde bianche e rosso mattone, la venatura bianca si sfuma in viola chiaro, la rosa in color ruggine ed in bruno" (*Diario*, pp. 350, 352).

† Strabo thus describes Petra: "The metropolis of the Nabathæans is Petra so called, for it lies in a place in other respects plain and level, but shut in by rocks round about; precipitous indeed on the outside but within having copious fountains for a supply of water and the irrigation of gardens. Beyond this enclosure the region is mostly a desert, especially towards Judæa (Strabo, xvi. 4–21). Pliny gives the following description of the Nabathæan capital: "The Nabathæans inhabit the city called Petra, in a valley less than two miles in amplitude, surrounded by inaccessible mountains, with a stream flowing through it" (*H. N.* vi. 28, 32).

village of Elji, whose rude hovels are built with the broken fragments of the palaces of Petra.* A quarter of an hour's walk to the north-east of the village a stream of water may be seen bursting forth from beneath a rock. It bears the name of Ain Mûsa,† the Spring of Moses. The rivulet thus formed takes a westward course, where it is speedily joined by a stream from an adjacent Wady, and with the waters of some other springs it assumes gradually increasing proportions till it passes between some rocks. At this point the valley closes in, the sides being formed by sandstone cliffs some fifty feet in height and about fifty yards apart, the brook making its way along a bed thickly fringed with oleanders.‡ The sides of the cliffs are pierced with caves, which may have equally served the purposes of habitations for the living and tombs for the dead. Here also the evidences of the later rock sculpture of the Nabathæans and the Romans begin to manifest themselves. The valley continues to contract for about a quarter of a mile, and then suddenly expands into what appears to be a *cul-de-sac* closed in by cliffs of red sandstone. The brook crosses this space, and then disappears in a narrow cleft in the rocks hardly perceptible to the eye. This cleft marks the commencement of the *Sîk* of the Wady Mûsa.

---

* *Diario*, p. 375.

† "Ain Mousa is a copious spring, rushing from under a rock at the eastern extremity of the Wady Mousa. There are no ruins near the spring; a little lower down in the valley is a mill, and above it is the village of Badabde, now abandoned. Proceeding from the spring along the rivulet for about twenty minutes, the valley opens and leads into a plain about a quarter of an hour in length and ten minutes in breadth, in which the rivulet joins with another descending from the mountain to the southward. Upon the declivity of the mountain in the angle formed by the junction of the two rivulets, stands Elji, the principal village of the Wady Mousa" (Burckhardt, *Syria*, p. 420).

‡ Robinson, *Bib. Res.*, ii. 129; 3rd. Ed.

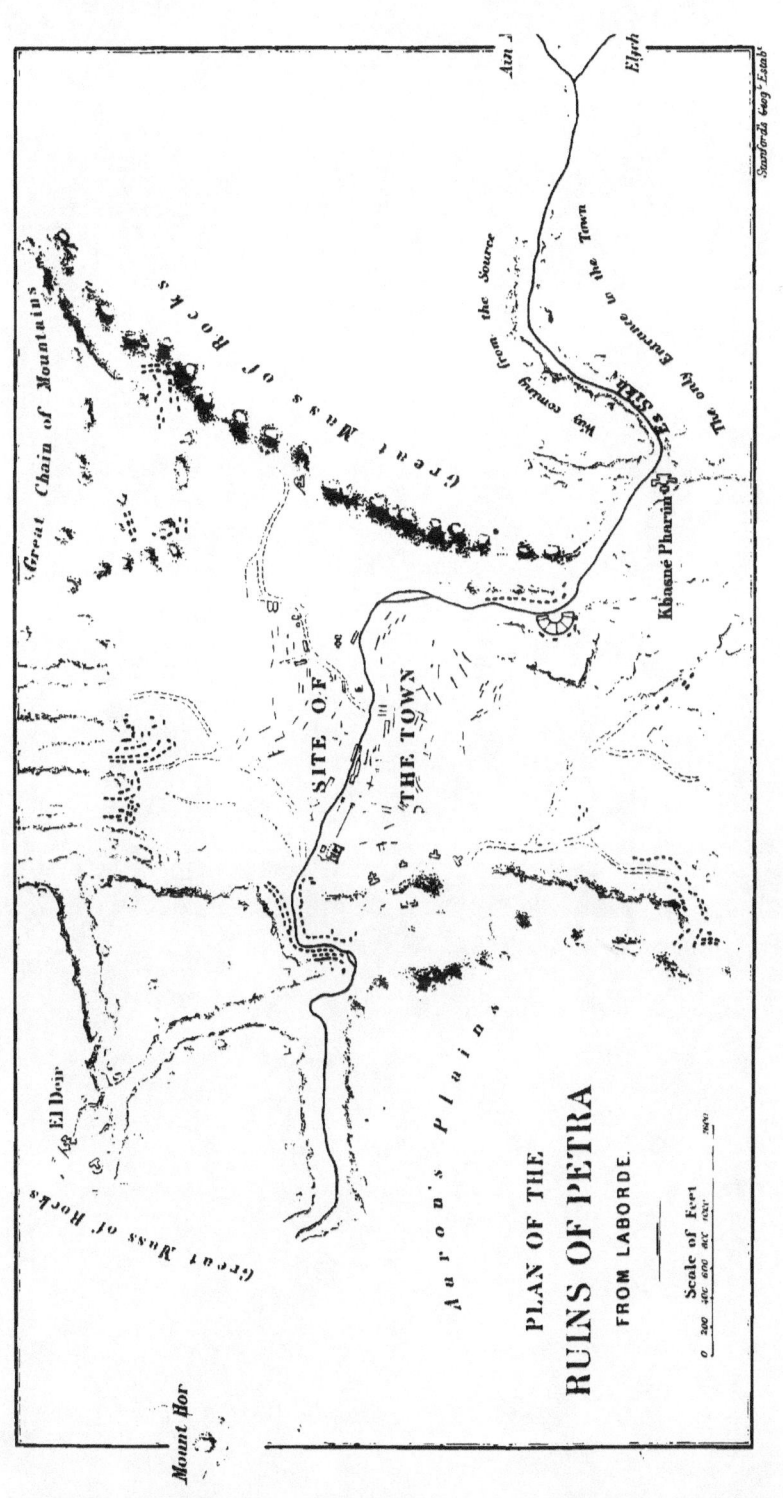

PLAN OF THE RUINS OF PETRA
FROM LABORDE.

The *Sîk* is a stupendous chasm, narrow and tortuous, of about a mile in length. It is probably the result of some natural convulsion which rent the sandstone cliff in twain, and apparently serves no other purpose in Nature than that of giving a free passage to the brook which flows from Ain Mûsa. Its course is westward. The descent of the bed of the gorge is somewhat rapid. The cliffs which form the sides are at the entrance not more than twelve feet apart, and about a hundred feet in height; but they gradually increase in altitude, and are supposed to attain at the western extremity of the ravine an altitude of two hundred and fifty feet.* The brook flows through the entire course of the *Sîk*, watering thickets of oleanders, which almost choke up the passage, whilst figs and tamarisks sprout forth between the crevices in the rocks, and rich festoons of creeping plants clothe the walls of the chasm. At some places the overhanging cliffs approach so closely as to intercept the view of the sky, and it is only on emerging from the opposite extremity of the gorge that the direct rays of sunlight again cross the field of the traveller's vision.† The *Sîk* terminates in a broader ravine, which it enters nearly at right angles. On emerging from the *Sîk* the traveller sees the marvellous façade of one of the principal glories of Petra, hewn in the face of the oppo-

---

* Robinson, *B. R.*, ii. 516. The height of the walls of the *Sîk* is still a matter of speculation, and travellers have varied considerably in their estimates. Robinson follows Burckhardt (*Syria*, p. 422) in his calculations. Irby and Mangles gave from 400 to 700 feet (*Egypt, Syria, and Holy Land*, p. 414); Arconati Visconti, 100 to 120 *métres* (*Diario di un Viaggio*, p. 362).

† "L'arenaria (del *Sîk*), è rossa tutta come mattone, ore più laccosa venata di strisce brune, violacee e bianche, strisce tortuose a desegni arabeschi i più bizarri: talvolta le pareti si accostano verso la cima e intercettano la vista del cielo" (*Diario*, p. 362; Stanley, *Sinai and Palestine*, p. 87).

site precipice, the rock-cut temple known as the Khuzneh Phar'ûn, the treasury of Pharaoh.*

Before quitting the *Sik* the traveller notices that the ancient inhabitants of the city took no ordinary pains to utilise the water which flows through the ravine. A channel is cut in the rock at the base of the southern wall, whilst the remains of a conduit are still to be seen high up on the opposite side of the chasm. Suitable provision appears to have been made by means of aqueducts, for not only carrying off, but turning to account, the excess of water in the rivulet during the rainy season.†

The brook follows the course of the broader ravine into which the *Sik* opens, and between precipices, pierced by caves, takes a north-westward course till, after passing the remains of an amphitheatre capable of accommodating upwards of three thousand spectators,‡ and whose benches are hewn out of the living rock (the ravine then turning to the west), it enters the area in which the city stood.

The cliff-bound valley here terminates, and opens into an irregular plain, bounded on the east and west by sand-

---

* The association by the Bedouins of many of the relics of Petra with the Pharaohs is very singular, and in truth inexplicable. The rulers of Egypt at no period occupied the Idumæan city; none of the structures, the traces of which still remain, can by any possibility have owed their existence to any of them. The Bedouins themselves can in no way account for connecting certain of the monuments with the Pharaohs. Thus, there are the Zub Phar'ûn, the Khuzneh Phar'ûn, &c., and hence in a general way the ancient city is associated with the Pharaohs. Arconati remarks: "Secondo gli Arabi, i Faraoni ed i Christiani sono gli autori di tutti i monumenti che non sono dell' epoca Musulmana. Non credo però che di Faraone se ne facciano un' idea abbastanza chiara" (*Diario*, p. 383). It appears to me, for reasons which will become apparent at a later stage of this inquiry, that the name Phar'ûn is a relic of the most ancient name of the city, Pharan, and that the objects now associated with the Pharaohs were originally spoken of as being in Pharan.

† Robinson, *B. R.*, ii. 131. ‡ Burckhardt, *Syria*, p. 427.

stone precipices, but extending to the north and south by constantly undulating ascents towards higher table-lands.* Through the midst of this plain the brook makes its way towards the cliffs bounding the city on the western side, and about midway across, the remains of stout walls bordering the banks give grounds for conjecture that its course was here bridged over. It pierces the western cliff by a chasm somewhat similar in character to the *Sik*, though somewhat broader and less regular. Its walls are full of tombs, and its sides are rent at frequent intervals by similar chasms in the sandstone rocks. The ravine is choked with oleanders and other shrubs, and beyond a comparatively short distance it has never been explored. It is unknown what direction is afterwards taken by the brook, or what ultimately becomes of the swollen waters of the stream which takes its rise in the Ain Mûsa.† For obvious reasons Petra has been visited by travellers in the summer, and at such time the brook is almost dry. It would be interesting to know its proportions in the rainy season.

The city of Petra, though bounded by lofty cliffs on the east and west, lies comparatively open towards the north and south. On the north, the ground ascends with many irregular eminences and seamed by various wadys towards the Sutûh Beida, or White Plains,‡ whilst on the south it equally mounts, but much more rapidly, to a plateau higher than that on the north, and named the Sutûh Harûn, or "Aaron's Plains."§ This plateau runs round the extremity of the western cliff of the city, and is gradually lost in the slopes of Mount Hor. A road emerges from the south-western corner of the area of Petra, and ascending a long

---

* Robinson, *B. R.*, ii. 135. † *Ibid. B. R.*, ii. 137.
‡ *Ibid.* ii. 138. § *Ibid.* ii. 129.

narrow gorge reaches this plateau, where, after skirting the southern slopes of Mount Hor, it divides into two paths leading to the Araba; that on the left being by way of the Wady Abu Kusheibeh, that on the right by the Wady Er-Rûbâ'y.*

The rocks which shut in Petra, and are rent by the various chasms and ravines which both from east and west lead towards the city, are of reddish sandstone, the softness of the material greatly facilitating those excavations and rock sculptures which have rendered Petra so famous. The forms of the cliffs are irregular and grotesque, and may be regarded as culminating in the adjacent pinnacles of Mount Hor. The most striking peculiarity of the rocks is, however, their bright and varied colourings. "They present," writes Robinson, "not a dead mass of dull monotonous red, but an endless variety of bright and living hues, from the deepest crimson to the softest pink, verging also sometimes to orange and yellow. These varying shades are often distinctly marked by waving lines, imparting to the surface of the rock a succession of brilliant and changing tints, like the hues of watered silk, and adding greatly to the imposing effect of the sculptured monuments." "This display of colours," he adds, "is strikingly exhibited along the paths leading to the Deir and to Mount Hor."†

---

* Robinson, *B. R.*, ii. 139.
† *Bib. Res.*, ii. 140. Stanley thus describes the rocks of Petra: "We found ourselves insensibly encircled with rocks of deepening and deepening red. . . . . The colours, though not gaudy, or rather because they are not gaudy, are gorgeous. . . . . When one comes in face of these very cliffs themselves, then they are a gorgeous though dull crimson, streaked and suffused with purple. . . . . The rocks are almost precipitous, or rather they would be, if they did not, like their brethren in all this region, overlap and crumble and crack as if they would crush over you" (Stanley, *Sinai and Palestine*. London: 1866. pp. 87-89).

The Deir, or "Convent," is a rock-cut temple hewn out of a cliff which springs from the plateau overlooking the north-west corner of the city. It is reached by a narrow and steep *Sîk*-like chasm which pierces the western cliff near its northern extremity. The Deir has a south-western aspect, Mount Hor towering above and in front of it. Its external architecture is florid, and too profusely ornamented; the interior consists of a single excavated chamber, square, and with perfectly smooth walls. In one side there is, however, a broad-arched niche, above which the traces of a cross have been discerned. The Deir may have been adapted to Christian uses, but there is no reason for doubting that it was a temple in pre-Christian times. But just as the niche and the cross are no evidence that the chamber was originally hewn in the rock to serve the purposes of a Christian temple, so the sculptured façade on the exterior does not necessarily refer its origin to the period of the Antonines. At what time it first acquired a character for sanctity is unknown, nor can we say whether the regular square chamber always possessed the same proportions. But one or two points in connection with the Deir are not unworthy of notice. It lay outside the city, in a place very difficult of access. The path to it leads through a steep gorge, with intricate windings, and is alone rendered practicable by steps hewn out of the rock with immense labour. It is not easy to understand what motive either Romans or Nabathæans could have had for constructing a temple in so strange a place. If it had an eastern aspect it might be connected with solar worship, and we might suppose that the priests of the cliff-girt city placed their temple on the summit of the western heights in order that they might adore the rising sun. But its aspect is south-west ; its occupants could see absolutely nothing but Mount Hor rising above them in all its solitary majesty. But why should Mount Hor have been kept in view? This supplies matter for curious speculation.*

The mountain Jebel Neby Harûn, as it is called by the Arabs, is situated on the eastern side of the Araba, about midway between the Gulf of Akaba and the Dead Sea, and almostly directly interposes between Petra and the great valley. It is roughly estimated at about 4800 feet above the level of the sea, but to the spectator standing in the Araba its isolation and rugged and precipitous peaks give it an apparently greater altitude. It presents the singular appearance of a mountain superimposed on another. The red sandstone of which it mainly consists is traversed by veins of red granite and porphyry, the effect being to give a rich and varied colouring to the bare and barren crags which seem piled upon each other in chaotic confusion.† Its ascent is unattended with any physical difficulty, but the jealousy and the rapacity of the Bedouins present obstacles which even to the boldest have frequently proved insurmountable. Burckhardt was compelled to turn back when he had reached "Aaron's Plains," which seemingly top the lower mountain from which the upper appears to spring. Robinson, one of the most indefatigable of travellers, in exploring every place invested with a real or fancied Biblical interest, was also obliged to quit Petra and return to Hebron, without ascending the celebrated mount. Arconati Visconti, a most careful and painstaking observer, and richly endowed with graphic power, was reluctantly compelled to resist

---

* Dean Stanley notices the peculiar position of the Deir and its difficult approach, and finds an explanation in its connection with the mountain hallowed as the burial-place of Aaron (*S. and P.*, p. 95). But independently of, nay even antecedent to, this tradition, this mountain was invested with a sanctity which may furnish a key to the site chosen for the Deir. It stands just outside "the borders" and "at the nether part of the mount." (Exod. xix. 12, 17.)

† Irby and Mangles, *Egypt, Syria, and Holy Land*, p. 133.

the exactions of the Arab Sheikh—the self-constituted custodian of the mountain—and deny himself the promised pleasure of ascending Mount Hor. Others have been more fortunate; and although the information at our command is far from being as precise as could be desired, we are still enabled to form a tolerably accurate idea of the general features of the Mount of Mounts.

The mountain proper rises from a lofty base or ridge commanding the Araba on the west, and overhanging on the east the city of Petra. This ridge may be reached with facility by more than one Wady, and thence the traveller by an ascent somewhat more arduous can make his way to the top of the mountain. The sides are plentifully covered with juniper-bushes, which are found even close to the summit. The rocks, with their strata of sandstone and porphyry, reflect the rays of the sun in every imaginable tint, and here and there flash them back with all the semblance of a lurid flame. Near the summit of the mountain is a cavern formed by an overhanging ledge of rock, and close by is a small building which is said to enclose Aaron's tomb.

It is not necessary to enter into any further details respecting the characteristics of this mountain. The base or nether part, from which the upper eminence springs, is a mountain in itself, and on the south-eastern side assumes the form of a plateau, which receives the name of Sutûh Hârûn, " Aaron's Plains."

It may, perhaps, appear that we have wandered far from the beaten track in entering the Idumæan mountains, with the object of throwing any new light on the direction of the Hebrew migration from Egypt. Kadesh, wherever situated, was, according to tradition, on the frontier of Edom; it was from thence the Hebrews addressed in vain their request for permission to pass through that country, and when that permission was refused, or when, according to one account, Edom came out against Israel with a strong hand,* the Hebrews retraced their steps towards the Ælanitic Gulf, and compassed Edom, in order to make their way towards the Trans-Jordanic region. It would seem, therefore, that if any point was established more conclusively than another, it is that the Hebrews did not enter Edom on their journey from Egypt to Canaan. But before accepting this conclusion, we must be careful not to confound the Edom of the Exodus with that of a much later period.

According to the accepted tradition, the western mountains of Idumæa (or, as they were collectively termed, Seir) were originally inhabited by a people styled Horites (Chorites), Troglodytes or cave-dwellers, who were ejected by the descendants of Esau. But the literal accuracy of this belief, if applied to the existing state when the Exodus took place, is open to grave doubt. The statement in Deuteronomy that the Horites were "destroyed" by the children of Esau, " who dwelt in their stead,"† if it could be referred to Moses or any of his contemporaries, would be undoubtedly entitled to great weight; but the concluding words of the sentence, "as Israel did unto the land of his possession, which Jahveh gave unto them," clearly indicates an authorship of an unknown date, but certainly subsequent to the settlement in Canaan. In the same chapter another allusion is made to the expulsion of the Horites by the Beni-Esau, where it is said that the latter "succeeded" the former, and "dwelt in their stead, even unto this day;"‡ a form of expression quite inconceivable if used at the time in reference to a people of whose possession of Edom, assuming that they did then possess it, the emigrants from Egypt could naturally entertain no doubt. The allusion to the Horites in "the battle of the kings,"§ is more to the

---

* Num. xx. 20.   † Deut. ii. 12.   ‡ Deut. ii. 22.
§ Gen. xiv.

purpose, as showing that they were a distinct people which preceded the descendants of Esau; because if we accept Abraham and Esau as historical personages, then the Horites were defeated by Chedorlaomer and his allies long before Esau was born. The latter question is, however, far too wide to be dealt with here.

That the Idumæan mountains were inhabited previous to the incursion of the tribes claiming descent from Abraham is very certain, but we have no evidence to fix the time when these tribes secured possession of the entire strip of territory intervening between the Araba, and the eastern desert. There are, however, very strong indications that this result had not been achieved at the time of the Exodus.

We know that, according to tradition, Moses was a son-in-law of Jethro, the Sheikh of Midian, elsewhere described as a Kenite; and that after quitting Elim, and between that place and Mount Sinai, the Hebrews were met by this Sheikh. We also know that an alliance was formed between the Kenites and the Hebrews; that the former aided in the invasion of southern Palestine,* and were rewarded for their co-operation; and that at a much later period this assistance was kept in kindly remembrance by Saul when about to make war against the Amalekites.† We are also aware that at the time of the Exodus the Kenites occupied the region in the neighbourhood of Mount Horeb,‡ and if we are right in our conclusions thus far in tracing the course taken by the Hebrews, we should place Jethro's land on the east of the Araba, and probably not far distant from that desert valley. Of the origin of the Kenites we are told nothing They are referred to as a people occupying a region to the south-east of Palestine. The most pointed allusion to the locality of the land of the Kenites is, however, that made in

---

* Jud. i. 16.   † 1 Sam. xv. 6.   ‡ Exod iii. 1.

the prophecy attributed to Balaam, the son of Beor: "And he looked on the Kenites, and took up his parable, and said, Strong is thy dwelling-place, and thou puttest thy nest in a rock." If this were a production of the period of the Exodus, it would furnish conclusive evidence that the Kenites then made their habitations in a precipitous region difficult of access. But although Biblical critics disallow to the prophecy of Balaam a greater antiquity than the eighth century B.C., it would still prove that the Kenites at that time were believed to have occupied such a region some centuries previously. But if the Kenites who made their nest in a rock were in effect Horites—Troglodytes, cave-dwellers—it is a significant fact that we discover, within a few miles of the Araba, a place which even to the present day furnishes indications that its inhabitants at some early period merited the designation applied to the Kenites.

In Balaam's prophecy a distinction is drawn between the Edomites, the Amalekites, and the Kenites, and to the writer's mind they were consequently separate peoples. It is not unreasonable therefore to conclude that the Kenites were the cave-dwellers who are referred to as having been dispossessed by the Beni-Esau, but who at the time of the Exodus occupied the mountainous region in the neighbourhood of the later Petra. They were clearly distinct from the Edomites, though probably, like the Midianites with whom they were confounded, they claimed a descent from Abraham. They were at all events at this period on terms of amity with their neighbours, and it was from Kenite territory that the messengers were sent on behalf of the Israelites, requesting permission to pass through Edom. It is said there were kings in Edom before there were kings in Israel; but although there is mention of a king of Edom in the traditions of the Exodus, we have no information as to the extent of his dominions. We know, however, that

one of the principal cities, if not the capital of Edom, in
early and in comparatively late times, was Bozrah ;* and
there is good reason for identifying it with the Arab village
Beszeyra, which lies in the mountainous region to the south
of the Dead Sea. Assuming that Bozrah was the capital of
the king of Edom at the time of the Exodus, it is quite conceivable that the Hebrews should have been amicably
received by a tribe occupying a district on the east of the
Araba, on the border of Edom, without being able to secure
a free passage through the territory in the heart of which
Bozrah was situated. But if Petra was occupied by the
Kenites at the time of the Exodus, it is worthy of note that
the only route from Petra to the region to the east of the
Dead Sea would have been through, or at all events very
close to, the city of Bozrah. It is not very surprising that the
king of Edom refused permission to the impoverished and
possession-seeking Hebrews to take this route. On the whole,
however, Edom did not treat his brother Israel badly; he
permitted him to pass through his borders, and supplied him
with food, a concession not only admitted, but relied on, by
Israel with some diplomatic skill on a subsequent occasion.†

If therefore the Hebrews, having quitted Elim-Elath,
proceeded up the Araba, there is not only nothing inconsistent with the traditions preserved to us in their having
penetrated one of the Idumæan valleys, but, looking to their
friendly reception by the Kenites, it becomes almost certain
they did so. The Araba furnished sustenance for neither
man nor beast. To find a suitable camping-ground on the
border of Edom, in which they could abide many days,
they must have entered one of the Wadys debouching from
the mountain range into the desert "plain."

---

* Gen. xxxvi. 33; 1 Chron. i. 44; Isa. xxxiv. 6; lxiii. 1; Jer. xlix.
13-22; Amos i. 12; Micah ii. 12.
† Deut. ii. 29.

CHAPTER VIII.

IF the Hebrews in the course of their migration from Egypt made their way in a direct course to the mountainous region on the east of the Araba; if they found there the Mount of Elohim; if some of the most remarkable events which marked the sojourn in "the wilderness" occurred in this region; then we might be led to expect that, even after the lapse of three thousand years, we should still find in tradition or in legendary lore some traces, however faint, of the associations said of old to have been connected with several of the places which the Hebrews visited. It becomes therefore our duty to inquire whether there are to be found in Idumæa any traditions or legends which support the inference that here the liberated captives made a temporary stay on their road from Egypt, and concluded or renewed a covenant with the Elohim of their fathers.

Should we discover the existence of such legends, it will subsequently be necessary to ascertain, through an examination of the patriarchal traditions and Egyptian records, whether Idumæa was the country to which those who quitted Egypt would not only in the natural course of things direct their steps, but where they would in all probability meet with a people claiming a common lineage, and if not actually prepared to give them a hospitable reception, not averse to speeding them on their way with good wishes for their future prosperity.

A tradition the origin of which is unknown, unless indeed it is to be found in those records we are now examining, but which can be traced from the present day to the early centuries of the Christian era, affirms that the singular chasm known as the *Sik* was effected by the rod of Moses, in order to give passage to the water which gushes forth from beneath a rock, and bears the name of Ain Mûsa. We are not now dealing with the credibility of the alleged miracle, but simply with the existence and the origin of the tradition which records it; and it is impossible to avoid being struck by the coincidence that in the very region in which, according to all the evidence supplied by Scriptural records, Horeb-Sinai, the Mount of God, was situated, and in whose vicinity water was said to have been miraculously supplied; and also the region into which, according to our interpretation of the records of the Exodus, the Hebrews would naturally have come; we find that a spring exists whose waters appear to force their way through a mighty, and, if the expression is permissible, an apparently supernatural chasm; that this source is known by immemorial tradition as the Spring of Moses, and the chasm as the cleft made in the rock by the Hebrew legislator in order that its waters might flow through to supply the wants of his exhausted followers.

Eusebius, Bishop of Cæsarea, has left in the *Onomasticon* a record of the received opinions in Palestine at the commencement of the fourth century, respecting the locality of a considerable number of the places mentioned in the Scriptures. The work was, even for that age, not distinguished by its research, precision, or exhaustiveness; and in describing the majority of the places enumerated, Eusebius contented himself with simply paraphrasing the account given in the Scriptures, without making any attempt to fix the locality. But in several instances the ecclesiastical historian was enabled, whether accurately or inaccurately of course we have no means of knowing, to identify with apparent confidence places referred to in the Hebrew records with others well known to those for whose information the *Onomasticon* was prepared. This descriptive catalogue of places, for which we are indebted to Eusebius, is therefore alone valuable as a probably correct representation, so far as it goes, of the opinions held in his time respecting the localities referred to. A century later the *Onomasticon* was translated and amplified by St. Jerome.

It would be very interesting to know what opinion was entertained by Eusebius respecting the locality in which the pious pilgrim would be enabled to find the Mount of God. It is, however, very easy to see that, beyond a hazy notion of the region where the holy mountain stood, Eusebius knew nothing whatever about it; and it may with some confidence be affirmed that he had never met with any one who had visited it, or who could with precision have described its situation. "Horeb, the Mount of God, in the region of Midian, near Mount Sinai, over Arabia, in the desert."* This is all that Eusebius has to tell us of Mount Horeb, whilst Sinai has neither place nor mention in the catalogue. To this brief description Jerome adds: "Adjoining the mount and desert of the Saracens, called Pharan. For my part, I think the mountain was known by the double name of Sinai and Horeb."†

Now let us contrast with this vague and unsatisfactory information the account which Eusebius and Jerome give of another mountain mentioned in the early records of the Hebrew nation—Mount Hor. "Hor, the mountain where Aaron died, beside the city of Petra, where unto the present day is shown the rock which, having been struck,

---

* Χωρήβ, ὄρος τοῦ θεοῦ ἐν τῇ χώρᾳ Μαδιάμ, παράκειται τῷ ὄρει Σινᾷ ὑπὲρ τὴν Ἀραβίαν ἐπὶ τῆς ἐρήμου (Euseb. *Onomast.*).

† "Cui jungitur mons et desertum Saracenorum quod vocatur Pharan. Mihi autem videtur quod duplici nomine idem mons nunc Sina, nunc Choreb vocetur" (Hier. *Onomast.* s. v. *Choreb*).

Moses supplied the people with water;"* or, again, where in describing Pharan (Faran) it is said to be "distant from Aila three days' journey towards the east."† In both these instances Eusebius and Jerome had perfectly clear ideas of the localities to which they were referring, and they took care to give their readers substantial information where to find them. Petra and Ailah were both places well known at that time to people in Palestine.

Now if Eusebius entertained, whether rightly or wrongly, the belief that Mount Horeb (which according to him was distinct from, since it was "beside," Mount Sinai) was, say in the Sinaitic peninsula, and, *à fortiori*, if he entertained a belief respecting the particular mountain in that peninsula which was in truth the Mount of God, it is impossible to suppose that he would not have given some unmistakable indication that the Sinaitic region was present to his mind, if he did not even go so far as to state the distance of the mountain from some well-known place. The fact that no such unmistakable indication is given, raises at all events a strong presumption that the Sinaitic region was absent from his thoughts; whilst the generality of his description, his statement that Horeb was beside Sinai (rightly treated by Jerome as an idle speculation, having no foundation in his own knowledge or that of his contemporaries), coupled with his silence about Mount Sinai, unmistakably prove that neither Eusebius, nor apparently any one whom he was enabled to consult, had any definite conviction respecting the precise situation of the celebrated mountain. And it is no

---

* "Ωρ. ὄρος ἐν ᾧ τελευτᾷ 'Ααρὼν πλησίον Πέτρας πόλεως, ἐν ᾧ καὶ εἰς ἔτι νῦν δείκνυται ἡ ἐπὶ Μωϋσέως ῥεύσασα πέτρα (Euseb.). Or, mons in quo mortuus est Aaron, juxta civitatem Petram, ubi usque ad praesentem diem ostenditur rupes, qua percussa Moyses aquas populo dedit (Heir. *Onomast.*).

† *Onomast.*, s. v. Faran.

less material to observe that Jerome, notwithstanding his desire to supplement the information given by Eusebius, was only enabled to add that the Mount of God was in the neighbourhood of the mountain and desert of Pharan, and to state simply as a matter of personal opinion that Sinai and Horeb were one and the same mountain. If there were any precise data at his command, if he knew or had heard of any mountain respecting whose identity with the Mount of God any definite opinion was entertained, he would never have supplemented the statement made by Eusebius that Horeb was beside Sinai, with his own personal speculation that they were identical, a speculation evidently based, not upon knowledge acquired respecting the mountain in question, but upon his interpretation of the Hebrew story.

Now let us ascertain through the *Onomasticon* what was apparently the common impression in Palestine, at the commencement of the fourth century, respecting the locality of the Mount of God.

According to Eusebius, Horeb was in Midian, over Arabia, in the desert, and, as Jerome adds, near Pharan of the Saracens. On referring to "Midian," we find that it is described as including a city and a country, the former of which was beyond (ἐπέκεινα) Arabia, towards the south, in the desert of the Saracens on the east of the Red Sea.* The region here indicated is unquestionably on the east of the meridian of Akaba, for had Eusebius been referring to the Sinaitic peninsula, he would assuredly not have described it as on the east of the Red Sea, that peninsula being actually wedged in between the Gulfs of Suez and Akaba. It may be objected that, although Midian when peopled by the illegitimate descendants

---

* Μαδιάμ κεῖται δὲ ἐπέκεινα τῆς Ἀραβίας πρὸς νότον ἐν ἐρήμω τῶν Σαρακηνῶν τῆς ἐρυθρᾶς θαλάσσης ἐπ' ἀνατολὰς (Euseb.). Madian est autem trans Arabiam ad meridiem, in deserto Saracenorum contra Orientem maris Rubri (Hier. *Onomast.*).

of Abraham, was on the east of the Araba and Ælanitic Gulf, its territory was subsequently extended into the Sinaitic peninsula; but it is not unreasonable to demand that some evidence should be forthcoming in support of such an allegation. There is nothing in the *Onomasticon* to show that Eusebius had ever heard of this westward extension of the land of Midian.

The term Arabia appears to have been applied in Palestine, not only previous to the Christian era but long afterwards, to the territory lying to the east of the Araba and Red Sea, or intervening between them and the inhospitable deserts and unknown regions which bounded on the east the comparatively narrow strip of territory with which the inhabitants of Palestine were acquainted. Josephus habitually speaks of the region which is now known as Idumæa as Arabia. Aretas the Idumæan is described by the Jewish historian as king of Arabia, whose capital was at Petra.* Even so late as the twelfth century the Crusaders only knew of three divisions of Arabia, designated respectively Prima, Secunda, and Tertia; the first, including the region to the east of the Jordan valley; the second, the country on the east of the Dead Sea; and the third, the territory extending southwards from Kerak to the Gulf of Akaba, which they also termed Syria Sobal.† It is unnecessary to repeat what we have already said on the early subdivisions of Arabia.

Now placing on one side the presumption that Eusebius used the word Arabia in the sense above referred to, we see in the description of a place on the east of the Red Sea as being on the other side of (ἐπέκεινα) Arabia, a natural and apposite description of a region which lay beyond the Idumæan mountains, whilst the qualification ὑπερ—trans

---

* *A. J.*, xiv. 1, 4.
† Jac. de Vit. c. 47, 96. Will. Tyr. xi. 26; xv. 21; xvi. 6.

Arabia, as applied to Mount Horeb, by a parity of reasoning equally indicates that the mountain was believed to be situated in or adjoining to Idumæa. But let us see what Eusebius has to say about the situation of some other places mentioned in the Hebrew records.

Kadesh is stated by Eusebius to be the place of the Spring of Judgment, whilst Kadesh-barnea is described as being in the desert contiguous to the city of Petra in Arabia, and as the same place where Miriam died, and where Moses supplied water to the people from the stricken rock.* Putting altogether on one side the value of the testimony of Eusebius, there can at all events be no doubt that he identified Kadesh-barnea, the oft-mentioned place on the border of Edom, the place from whence the spies were sent, where Israel abode many days, and where water was supplied from the rock, with a place in the neighbourhood of Petra, the well-known city in Idumæa, and where, as he observes in reference to the adjoining mountain, Hor, the riven rock from which the water was obtained, was shown even in his day.

But what is meant by describing Kadesh as the site of the Spring of Judgment? In order to understand this allusion, it is necessary to examine one of the oldest records in the Pentateuch in which reference is made to a spring which

---

* Eusebius apparently regarded Kadesh and Kadesh-barnea as distinct, at least he treats them separately. Of the former he simply states that at that place was the Spring of Judgment, whilst of the latter he writes: "Κάδδες Βαρνή, ἔρημος ἡ παρατείνουσα Πέτρᾳ πόλει τῆς Παλαιστίνης, ἔνθα ἀναβᾶσα ἐτελεύτησε Μαριάμ, καὶ Μωϋσῆς διαστὰς παίει τὴν πέτραν, καὶ ὕδωρ παρέχει διψῶντι τῷ λαῷ. καὶ δείκνυται εἰς ἔτι νῦν τὸ μνῆμα τῆς Μαρίας αὐτόθι, ἔνθα καὶ τοὺς ἄρχοντας ᾿Αμαλὴκ κατέκοψε Χοδολλαγόμωρ." Jerome, on the other hand, identifies Kadesh with Kadesh-barnea. "Cades ubi fons est judicii, et Cades Barnea in deserto quæ conjungitur civitati Petræ in Arabiâ, ibi occubuit Maria, (Miriam) et Moyses rupe percussa aquam sitienti populo dedit. Monstratur ibidem usque in præsentem diem sepulchrum Mariæ: sed et principes Amalech ibi à Chodorlaomor cæsi sunt" (*Onomast.*, s. v. Cades).

was thus designated long before the Hebrews settled in Egypt.

It is stated in the "battle of the kings"* that Chedorlaomer with his allies smote various tribes which there is reason to believe occupied Idumæa, and having done so returned (literally, "turned"), "and came to En-mishpat, which is Kadesh, and smote all the country of the Amalekites, and also the Amorites that dwelt in Hazezon-tamar." At this point, it is said the kings of Sodom, Gomorrah, Admah, Zeboim, and Bela (Zoar), went out against Chedorlaomer and the other kings, and joined battle with them in the vale of Siddim, which it is explained was "the Salt (*i.e.*, the Dead) Sea." There can be no reasonable doubt that the battle in question was fought in the neighbourhood of the Dead Sea, probably on its south side, and therefore En-mishpat or Kadesh, so far as the testimony of this record goes, was not far distant from Mount Seir, where the Horites are said to have been defeated by Chedorlaomer before "turning" to En-mishpat.

En-mishpat signifies the Spring of Judgment, and it would therefore seem that in very early times a spring was called by this singular designation which at a later period was known to flow in a place named Kadesh. Eusebius, however, on the faith of a tradition which must have existed in his time, declares that Kadesh, where was to be seen En-mishpat, the Spring of Judgment, was in the neighbourhood of Petra, where equally was to be seen the rock which had been struck by Moses. When the Bishop of Cæsarea wrote, "Barnea, the same is Kadesh; Barnea in the desert extending to the city of Petra," he must have meant the region on the east of the city and communicating with it through the *Sîk*, because Petra is confessedly separated from the Araba

---

* Gen. xiv.

by Mount Hor and the lower ridge of the Idumæan range.

We can only speculate on the reason why the spring referred to was called En-mishpat. There seems every reason to suppose that from times long antecedent to the Exodus, the spring in question, or the place whence the waters flowed, was reputed for its sanctity; and as it was the usage amongst the nomadic tribes to make inquiry of God* in the administration of justice, the spring in question probably came to be an accepted place for deciding causes. It was what in modern days would be called a "Holy Well," and if it was not used for the purpose of working miraculous cures, was doubtless supposed by its sacred associations to furnish a guarantee for the truthfulness of litigants, and for the attainment of strict justice. Its waters were therefore known for obvious reasons as those of Massah and Meribah, "contention" and "strife," long before the Israelites drank of them, though in after-times the latter found an explanation of terms, whose signification had long been lost in oblivion, in the fancied contention of their ancestors, or of those ancestors' leaders, with their protecting God.

The contiguity of Pharan to Sinai is indicated in the Hebrew tradition, and it is also stated that Kadesh was in the *midbhar* of Pharan.† Let us now note what is said by Eusebius and Jerome about the situation of Pharan, distinguishing the paraphrase of the Scriptural account from what was known to them respecting a place which apparently in their time bore a similar name.

"Pharan (Faran) is therefore, as we have said, on the other side of Arabia towards the south, and is distant from Aila eastwards three days' journey." It is also referred to

---

* Exod. xviii. 15; Num. xv. 34, 35; xxvii. 5; Lev. xxiv. 12.
† Num. xiii. 26; xxxiii. 36. Sept. Version.

as the place where Ishmael lived, whence were sprung the Ismaelites known in the time Eusebius and Jerome as the Saracens, and was the region which it was believed came within the sphere of the operations of Chedorlaomer and his allies.* But elsewhere, under the name Choreb, the Mount of God identified with Sinai, Jerome states that in its immediate neighbourhood was the mount and desert of the Saracens, called Pharan.† It is therefore incontestable that, whatever their opinions may have been worth, Eusebius and Jerome placed Pharan, which they knew to be in the neighbourhood of Kadesh, three days' journey (travelling eastwards) from Aila, the well-known port at the head of the Gulf of Akaba. But Kadesh they placed, as we have seen, in the *midbhar* adjoining the city of Petra, and consequently Pharan must have been, according to their views, in the same neighbourhood. This, however, completely tallies with the definite statement that Pharan was distant three days' journey from Aila towards the east. In the fourth century an excellent Roman road connected Aila with Petra, and three days' journey sufficed to enable the traveller to reach the region to the east of the Nabathæan capital.

The Peutinger table enables us to speculate on the place

---

* Φαραν, πόλις ἐστιν ὑπὲρ 'Αραβίαν, παρακειμένη τοῖς ἐπὶ τῆς ἐρήμου Σαρακηνοῖς, δι' ἧς ὥδευσαν υἱοὶ 'Ισραὴλ ἀπάραντες ἀπὸ Σινᾷ κεῖται δὲ καὶ ἐπέκεινα τῆς 'Αραβίας ἐπὶ νότον, ἀπέχει δ' Α'ειλὰ πρὸς ἀνατολὰς ὁδὸν τριῶν ἡμερῶν, οὖ φησὶν ἡ γραφὴ κατῴκησεν 'Ισμαὴλ. Λέγεται δὲ καὶ Χοδολαγόμωρ κατασκῆψαι εἰς τοὺς ἐν τῇ Φαρὰν, ἥ ἐστιν ἐν τῇ ἐρήμῳ (Euseb.). Faran, nunc oppidum trans Arabiam junctum Saracenis, qui in solitudine vagi errant. Per hoc iter fecerunt filii Israel cum de monte Sina castra movissent. Est ergo, ut diximus, trans Arabiam contra Australem plagam, et distat ab Aila contra Orientem itinere trium dierum. In deserto autem Pharan Scriptura commemorat habitasse Ismaelem, unde et Ismaelitæ qui nunc Saraceni. Legimus quoque Chodorlaomor regem percussisse eos, qui erant in deserto Pharan (Hier. *Onomast.*).

† *Onomast.*, s.v. *Choreb.*

which Eusebius and Jerome probably identified with the Pharan of the Hebrew traditions.

The Roman dominion having become securely established in what was then known as Arabia Petræa, a record was prepared of the principal stations on the main road by which the country was traversed. This record we now possess in the table of Peutinger.* It mentions two high roads from Aila, the ancient Elath, at the head of the Gulf of Akaba, to Jerusalem, the one taking an eastern course by way of Petra, and thence near the southern extremity of the Dead Sea, connected by a cross route with the Jewish capital; the other following a western direction across the desert of the Tih. It is with the former that we are concerned.

The eastern route from Aila as far as Petra is described as follows:—

	Mille Pass.
From Haila to Diana	16
„ Diana to Præsidio	21
„ Præsidio to Hauarra	24
„ Hauarra to Zadogatta	20
„ Zadogatta to Petris (Petra)	18

* The *Tabula Peutingeriana* was a compilation possibly begun in the reign of Augustus, and finished under the direction of the Constantines. It furnished in the form of a map the principal routes throughout the Roman Empire. The copy now preserved in the Imperial Library at Vienna was the work of a monk of Colmar in the thirteenth century, and in the sixteenth century it passed into the hands of Conrad Peutinger, an antiquary of Augsburg, whose name is now generally given to this curious relic. There is no ground for doubting that the monk of Colmar copied some similar map, with what accuracy we have no means of telling, but it is no less certain that he introduced "glosses" into the map, which were wanting in the original. Thus in the segment in which the route above referred to is laid down, the Tih is stated to be the desert in which the children of Israel wandered forty years, and Mount Sinai is delineated to the south of that desert, although unconnected with any of the Roman routes. It is also declared to be the place where the Israelites received the Law (*Tabula Peutingeriana*. Ed. Mannert Lips, 1824. *La Table de Peutinger*. Ed. Desjardins, Paris, 1869).

On the western route the first station is also Diana, so that the routes probably bifurcated at some point a short distance north of Aila.

On reading the list of stations on the eastern route, it strikes us that Hauarra, the third station, may have been identified by Eusebius and Jerome with the Pharan of the Israelites, the former name being regarded as the Roman rendering of the ancient Hebrew appellation. Now it may well be that in concluding that the Hauarra of the Romans was the Pharan of the Hebrews, Eusebius and Jerome were in error, but whether they so identified it or not, or whether such identification was right or wrong, it is equally apparent from the language in reference to Pharan and Aila and Petra that the Sinaitic peninsula, either in connection with the Mount of God or Pharan or Kadesh, was never present to their minds. That there was, however, a Pharan somewhere in the Idumæan mountains, and known by that name in the first century, is distinctly stated by Josephus.*

This collocation by Eusebius and Jerome of Kadesh and Pharan with the well-known city of Petra finds, however, a curious confirmation in the Chaldee Targums, and in the writings of Josephus. The historian tells us that the ancient name of Petra was Arke ('Αρκή) or Arekeme ('Αρεκέμη), and was so called after its founder Rekem, one

---

* *B. J.* iv. 9, 5. As the testimony of Eusebius and Jerome in respect to the situation of Pharan is hopelessly inconsistent with the location of the Mount of God in the Sinaitic peninsula, it is disposed of in a very simple manner. "When they placed Pharan three days' journey *east* of Aila, they evidently meant *west.*" It must be admitted to be a somewhat heroic mode of dealing with adverse testimony to contend that witnesses mean the direct contrary of what they say. It may be conceded that east might be inadvertently written instead of west, and that Hauarra was not the Roman rendering of Pharan; but putting aside the fact that the error of Eusebius was not corrected by Jerome, it is only necessary to examine what was written by both about Kadesh and Choreb to be satisfied that they made no such mistake as that so coolly attributed to them.

of the Midianite kings slain by the Israelites.* The former of these statements may have been matter of common knowledge in his time, the latter was doubtless idle speculation. If we now turn to the Chaldee versions of "the battle of the kings," we are struck by a very singular emendation on the Hebrew text. According to the Targum of Onkelos, Chedorlaomer and his allies, having vanquished the "Horites who were in the mountain of Seir, unto the plain of Paran, which lieth upon the desert, they turned and came to the plain of the division of judgment, which is Rekam;" whilst in the Targum of the pseudo-Jonathan the paraphrase runs that they smote "the Chorites (dwellers in caverns) who were in the high mountains of Gebala, unto the valley of Pharan, which was nigh upon the edge of the desert, and they returned and came to the place where was rendered the judgment of Moses the prophet, to the fountain of the waters of strife, which is Requam." Now, whether the correct date to be assigned to either or both of the Targums be the first century B.C. or the fourth century A.D., there can be little doubt, looking to the reference to the defeat of the Horites (the dwellers in caverns) on Mount Seir, subsequently known as Gebala, that the Rekam referred to was the same as that mentioned by Josephus, and declared by him to have been the city subsequently called Petra.

But this is not all that the Targums tell us of Rekam. In the rendering of Gen. xx. 1, they represent Abraham as dwelling "between Rekam and Hagra," which in the Hebrew version is "between Kadesh and Shur." Both Targums also agree in rendering Num. xx. 14,† "And Moses sent messengers from Rekam to the king of

---

* Josephus, *A. J.* iv. 4, 7; iv. 7, 1.
† "And Moses sent messengers from Kadesh to Edom." Num. xx. 14.

Edom;" and again, in the paraphrase of Num. xx. 22,* the Israelites are represented as journeying "from Rekam to Mount Hor" (called, in the Targum of Jonathan, Mount Umanom). In the opinion of the Targumists, Rekam and Kadesh were consequently regarded as substantially identical, thus furnishing a complete corroboration of the statements of Eusebius and Jerome; whilst the singular gloss in the Targum of Jonathan on the "En-mishpat" of the Hebrew version that it was "the place where was rendered the Judgment of Moses the prophet, the fountain of the Waters of Strife, which is Rekam," is conclusive that the Targumist was acquainted with the tradition mentioned by Eusebius, that near Petra was shown the rock which had been riven by Moses, and gave passage to the Waters of Strife, the latter being those which came from the "En-mishpat," the Spring of Judgment, which in the Hebrew tradition was identified with Kadesh.

The evidence supplied by the *Onomasticon*, separating carefully the information acquired by Eusebius and Jerome, through traditions accepted in their time from their personal inferences drawn from the interpretation of the Pentateuch, may be summed up as follows:—

A mountain stood close to the city of Petra, on which tradition declared that Aaron died, and at Petra was shown the rock from which Moses had caused the water to flow. Choreb, the Mount of God, was "over" or "in" ($\upsilon\pi\acute{\epsilon}\rho$) Arabia, to which Jerome added that it was near Pharan, so called by the Saracens, formerly Ishmaelites. Pharan was three days' journey from Aila, on the eastern road, and over, or otherwise expressed, in Arabia, consequently not far distant from the place where the smitten rock was

---

* "The whole congregation journeyed from Kadesh, and came unto Mount Hor." Num. xx. 22.

shown, and therefore, according to Jerome, in the neighbourhood of the Mount of God. Kadesh (En-mishpat) was in the desert adjoining Petra, where the celebrated rock was to be seen. To which we may add that Petra was identified by Eusebius and Jerome as the ancient Rekam, which, as we have seen, was treated by the Targumists as the still more ancient Kadesh, where was the Spring of Judgment with its Waters of Strife.*

It may perhaps be said that Eusebius and Jerome, accepting the Pentateuch as the work of Moses, regarded the account of the "journeyings" as a consecutive narrative, and therefore believed that the miracle of producing water from the rock, performed at the Mount of God,† was repeated after an interval of many years at a different place—Petra being the scene of the latter miracle; and that such was the view of these Fathers, their omission to fix with precision the situation of Mount Horeb-Sinai might be advanced with much plausibility.

Now there can be no reasonable doubt that Eusebius and Jerome did believe that the miracle was repeated after the lapse of many years, just as they believed much more that they would have thought it an unpardonable sin to entertain any doubt about. But though the mind may be reduced to apparent subjection by the will, there are times when it vindicates its independence and runs riot under the very eyes of its unconscious possessor. Eusebius and Jerome

---

* Dean Stanley, mainly on the strength of the evidence of Eusebius and Jerome, expressed the opinion that Petra must have been the Kadesh of the Hebrews (*S. and P.*, p. 97, 98); but as he nevertheless placed the Mount of God in the Sinaitic peninsula, his identification of the first-named places was open to numerous objections. "All that is clear," he writes, "is that they (the Israelites) marched northward from Mount Sinai (in the peninsula), probably over the plateau of the Tih" (*Sinai and Palestine*, p. 92).

† Exod. xvii. 6.

would have unhesitatingly anathematized any one who ventured to allege that it was the story of the smitten rock, and not the miracle, that was repeated; but nevertheless let us see what they wrote: "Rephidim, a place in the desert near Mount Choreb, where waters flowed from a rock, and where Joshua fought with Amalek, near Pharan."* With the exception of the two last words, the description is a mere summary of what is stated in Exodus to have occurred at Rephidim; but the concluding words fix the locality, at least according to the views of the Fathers. Rephidim was near Pharan, and Pharan was a three days' journey from Aila, on the road to Petra. It is therefore incontestable that, if they believed in two distinct miracles performed at different places, they were at all events of opinion that the first—that at Rephidim, near the Mount of God (juxta montem Choreb) —was performed near Pharan, in Idumæa; that is to say, at Petra, where the very rock was shown in their day. But the second miracle, that recorded in the Book of Numbers, was performed at Kadesh, where Miriam died; which place was, according to the testimony of Eusebius and Jerome, contiguous to Petra, and was treated by them and the Targumists as identical with Rekam. We arrive therefore at this striking and not unsatisfactory conclusion, that the Bishop of Cæsarea, and Jerome—not as the result of Scriptural interpretation, but of information acquired from their contemporaries, based upon existing traditions—concurred in the belief that the two reputed miracles were performed in the same place—namely, at or in the neighbourhood of Petra.

It would, however, be erroneous to conclude that either of the Fathers was acquainted with the precise locality of Mount Sinai. They had at best but a vague idea of the region in which it must have stood. But this idea was based, not

---

* *Onomasticon*, s. v. *Raphidim*.

upon any information derived from their contemporaries, but upon their own interpretation of the Scripture records, illustrated by existing traditions, respecting places which must have been in the neighbourhood of the celebrated mountain. If there had been, however, any mountain which in their time was pointed out as that on which the Tables of the Law had been given to Moses, no one can doubt it would have been as specifically mentioned as that on which, according to tradition, the High Priest Aaron died. We possess therefore in the *Onomasticon* very strong evidence that, at the commencement of the third century, the precise situation of the Mount of God was unknown.

When, in the seventh century, the tide of Mohammedan invasion overwhelmed Idumæa and Palestine, the former country quickly passed into historical oblivion. The Christian communities which had been established in the dioceses of Ailah, Petra, and Bozrah, appear to have made terms with the conquerors, and perhaps for a time were permitted to enjoy religious liberty.* But both the country and the inhabitants became speedily enveloped in an impenetrable cloud; and when, nearly five centuries later the cloud was temporarily lifted by the Crusaders, we see the country rich in so many historical associations, and in so many treasures of a great but forgotten past; inhabited—or perhaps,

---

* John, the Christian ruler of Ailah, agreed to an annual tribute of 300 gold pieces (Abulfeda, *Annales Muslemici*, 1789. i. 171). See *note* Gibbon's *Decline and Fall*, c. 50, on the doubtful authenticity of the "Diploma securitatis Ailensibus," which was attested by Ahmed Ben Joseph. The text of the charter was published, in 1630, by Sionita, but was disallowed by Grotius (Bayle, *Mahomet*). Mosheim pronounced against it. Even if the "Diploma" was spurious, it is historically true, to quote the words of Gibbon, that "to his Christian subjects Mahomet readily granted the security of their persons, the freedom of their trade, the property of their goods, and the toleration of their worship."

more correctly speaking, infested—by lawless nomadic hordes. But though the palaces of Petra had been reduced to ruins, though the commerce of the Nabathæan capital had long since been directed into other channels, neither fanaticism nor barbarism, nor even all-destroying Time, had obliterated the memory of those curious traditions recorded by the Bishop of Cæsarea and endorsed by Jerome.

In the last year of the eleventh century King Baldwin I. led an expedition from Hebron into the mountainous region lying to the south of the Dead Sea. Fulcher the monk of Chartres accompanied the expedition, and has left to us an account of the places visited, which if not so exhaustive as might have been desired, still conveys some interesting and valuable information. Directing their course round the south-western extremity of the Dead Sea, the Crusaders entered a mountainous country. In five days' time they arrived at a rich and fertile valley through which ran a brook, the water of which Fulcher declares was sufficient to turn a mill. This valley they were told was the Wady Mûsa, and was therefore named by the Crusaders the " Vallis Moysi." From this brook they could see the summit of a mountain, on which stood a monastery dedicated to Saint Aaron, which they appear to have been told was erected on the spot where God conversed with Moses and his brother the High Priest.* But, most extraordinary of all, they were informed that the brook was the same which issued from the rock struck by Moses. Fulcher not only records these local traditions without a suggestion that they clashed with his preconceived ideas, but clearly intimates that he fully believed them. In the mountain with the monastery he thought he saw Mount Sinai, and with a pious pride, not devoid of unconscious humour, he states that

* Num. xx. 23.

he watered his horses in the sacred stream that owed its
existence to the miraculous wand of Israel's legislator.
With respect to the natives, he observes that they fled at the
approach of the Crusaders, taking with them their flocks,
and seeking refuge in caves and ravines. The expedition
proceeded no further, and after a few days' rest returned to
Hebron.* It is stated however, on the authority of Albert
of Aix, that on this occasion Baldwin proceeded a day's
journey south of the Wady Mûsa, and came to a town
named Susum; but as Fulcher is silent on this point, it is
more probable that Susum was visited on a subsequent
occasion.

In the years A.D. 1115 and 1116, Baldwin led two suc-

* "Tunc invenimus vallem unam de omnibus frugibus opulentissi-
mam, in qua Moyses etiam Domino illuminante, virga scilicem bis
percussit, unde fons vivus statim, ut legitur, sic emanavit, ut populus
atque jumenta sufficienter ex eo adaquarentur. Qui etiam nunc
profluit non minus quam tunc, adeo ut molendini, rivuli ejus impetu
volubiles semper fiant, ubi ego ipse Fulcherius equos adaquavi meos.
Reperimus insuper in montis apice monasterium, quod dicitur sancti
Aaron, ubi Moyses, et ipse Aaron cum Domino loqui soliti erant;
unde valde lætabamur cùm loca tam sancta, et nobis incognita
intuebamur. Et quoniam ultra vallem illam, terra erat deserta et
inculta usque Babyloniæ affluitatem, ulterius progredi noluimus.
Vallis autem hæc bonis omnibus erat opima. Sed quia in aliis villis
prius morati fueramus, incolæ loci illius ablatis secum rebus suis atque
pecoribus, in montium diversoria et in caveas saxeas pro nobis fugientes
se intromiserant; ad quos cum appropinquaremus, audacter se defende-
bant" (Fulch. Carn. *Gesta Per. Franc*, xxiii. Bongars, *Gesta Dei*, i.
405. Han, 1611). The words, "loca tam sancta et nobis incognita,"
indicate that the Crusaders were solely dependent on the natives for
the information recorded. An unknown writer gives an account of the
expedition substantially identical with that of Fulcher. Skirting the
south-western extremity of the Dead Sea, which lay on their left
hand, the Crusaders passed through a district rich in date-palms, and
penetrating the mountains of Arabia, arrived at the "Vallis Moysi,"
where Moses produced the water from the rock; and on the top of a
neighbouring mountain they saw the "Oratorium" in the place where
it was said that Moses and Aaron had spoken with God (*Gesta
Franc. Expugn. Hier.* xxxviii., in the *Gesta Dei*, i. 581).

cessive expeditions into Arabia Tertia. Of the former we know comparatively little save that, having apparently crossed the Jordan and proceeded along the eastern side of the Dead Sea, he penetrated Idumæa to a point south of Vallis Moysi, and built a fortress, to which he gave the name of Mons Regalis.* In the second expedition he revisited this fortress, and proceeded onwards until he reached Aila, the modern Akaba. Fulcher did not accompany this last expedition, but he records what he was told by Baldwin and his companions on their return.† In Aila they identified Elim, the station remarkable for its wells and palm-trees, where the Israelites rested after the crossing of the Red Sea. Whether this identification was based on local traditions or upon their own inferences, we are not informed; but it is at all events curious that the conclusion, whether correct or erroneous, is recorded without any intimation that the discovery of Elim, on the east of what is now known as the Sinaitic peninsula, furnished matter for surprise. "We rejoiced greatly," says the monk, "in what they told us when they returned;" and no one was apparently found at Jerusalem to correct the supposed error of placing Elim at the head of the Gulf of Akaba. The expedition proceeded

---

* *Alb. Aq.* vii. 42, *Gesta Dei*, i. 307.

† "Invenerunt quidem Helim civitatem secus littus ejusdem maris (Maris Rubri) ubi populum Israeliticum, post maris transitum hospitatum legimus esse, quæ ab Hierusalem septem dierum equitis itinere distat. . . . . Qui cum expeditiohem sic factum nobis enarrarent, delectabamur etiam tam in dictis, quam in cocleis marinis, &c." Fulcher then proceeds to offer an opinion on the probable origin of the Red Sea—namely, that it is a tongue thrown up from the ocean on the south, and reaching as far as Helim, "non longe a monte Synai, sed quantum potest eques aliquis uno die profecisti." The monk of Chartres then goes on to speculate on the bearings of the Red Sea to the Garden of Eden, and, as might be expected, gets very rapidly out of his depth (Fulch. Carnot. *Gesta Per. Franc.* xliii.; *Gesta Dei*, i. 426).

no further than Aila, which Fulcher, on the faith of what he was told, says was not far distant from Mount Sinai, being about one day's journey on horseback, but in what direction is not stated. Keeping in mind, however, the impression formed by Fulcher sixteen years before, when at the Vallis Moysi, it would seem probable that he referred to the same mountain which he then saw, and which the Crusaders when at Aila were probably told could be reached by way of the Araba in a single day's journey. As none of the Crusaders, either on this or any subsequent occasion, had the courage or the curiosity to make the journey from Aila to the reputed Mount of God, the information they brought back as to its supposed distance from Aila is wholly unreliable. The monk of Chartres may not have been well versed in Biblical geography, but he appears to have recorded what he saw and what he heard with perfect candour.*

We obtain, however, from another source a more specific reference to Mount Sinai. In connection with Baldwin's expedition to Aila in 1115, Albert of Aix states that the king proceeded to Mount Oreb, which was commonly called

---

* "It does not argue highly," observes Robinson with much complacency, "for their (the Crusaders') skill in Biblical geography that they took the adjacent mountain (in the Vallis Moysi) with the tomb of Aaron for Mount Sinai, and the brook which flows down the valley for the water which came forth when Moses smote the rock." He then adds the foot-note, "The same error, however, goes back to the time of Eusebius and Jerome. Being once adopted by the Crusaders, it led them afterwards to take Ailah for Elim, with the twelve fountains and seventy palm-trees" (*Bib. Res.*, ii. 565). He might, if he had taken the trouble, have traced the *error* back to a much earlier period. Even the cautious and gentle Ritter expresses himself in similar language, and attributes the mistakes of the Crusaders respecting the mountain, the brook, and the town (Aila), to "the geographical ignorance of those times" (*Erdkunde*, xiv. 988).

Mount Orel.* He then refers to some project the king entertained of making an expedition eastwards, which however he abandoned, and continued his course southwards, through Arabia Tertia, till he arrived at Aila, identified as the Elim of the Israelites. This was on the Red Sea. The record then continues :†

"There, hearing that monks serving God dwelt on Mount Sinai, he decided to approach them by the slopes of the mountain for the purposes of prayer and conversation. But having been besought by the messengers they sent to him, he abstained from ascending, lest possibly the monks suspected by reason of the Catholic king, should be driven by the infidels from their habitation in the mountain."

This passage has been relied upon as indicating that Baldwin entertained the idea of visiting Jebel Mûsa, in the Sinaitic peninsula, but was dissuaded from doing so by the monks, who sent messengers praying him to desist. But this is open to very grave doubt. Aila was separated by an inhospitable desert from Jebel Mûsa, and it was in the highest degree improbable that the monks, if there, would have heard of the arrival of the Crusaders at Aila. But assuming that they had done so, and that they sent messengers to the camp, it is inexplicable that those messengers should not have corrected the error into which the Crusaders fell in identifying Aila with Elim. Nor is it by any means

---

* "In anno tertio postquam Rex Baldewinus nuptias supra dictas regaliter celebravit, tempore antumni ducentis equitibus et quadringentis assumtis peditibus, profectus est ad montem Oreb qui vulgò appellatur Orel" (*Alb. Aq. Hist. Hier.* xii. 21; *Gesta Dei*, i. 376).

† Ibi in monte Sina Monachos Dei servientes andiens commorari, ad eos per devexa montis causâ orationis et allocutionis, accelare decrevit. Sed rogatus eorum nunciis ad se præmissis, minime ascendit ne scilicet monachi suspecti propter Catholicum regem, a Gentilibus de montis habitatione pellerentur" (*Alb. Aq. Hist. Hier.* xii. 21; *Gesta Dei*, i. 376).

clear that the messengers were received at Aila, whilst Baldwin's project of reaching them "per devexa montis," "by the slopes of the mountain," seems singularly inapplicable to a journey from Aila to Jebel Mûsa, or any of the more distant mountains in the Sinaitic peninsula now claiming to be considered the Mount of God. Looking to the whole narrative, and especially to the introductory sentence "profectus ad montem Oreb," it would rather seem that either at Aila, or in the Wady Mûsa, Baldwin entertained the idea of visiting some monks dwelling on Mount Sinai; and that, in order to accomplish his object, all that was necessary was to ascend to them "by the slopes of the mountain." This might apply to the Araba, if the Idumæan chain was regarded as a single mountain; but it is more probable that when Baldwin was about to visit the monks he was already at the foot of what the chronicler calls Sinai, and that he was about to ascend it[*] when begged by the messengers to desist.[†] Fulcher of Chartres, however, states that they saw on the top of the mountain overhanging the valley of Moses a *monastery* dedicated to Saint Aaron, and if this word was used advisedly by Fulcher, who took part in the first expedition, we may have the key to the ambiguity in the narrative of Albert of Aix, who prepared his chronicle from the records of others, and unquestionably in more than

---

[*] "Minime ascendit" seems to imply that Baldwin forbore climbing up the mountain.

[†] Guibert in connection with this expedition says : " Primos suos post Regna recepta procinctus, et intra sinus exercuisse perhibetur Arabicos. Ubi dum ad Synai montis usque devexa procederet, repperit incultum, et Æthiopicis simile hominum genus. Ibi in ecclesia, quæ sancti dicebatur Aaron oravit, ubi sua Deus eum patribus oracula celebravit, et exercitus de contradictionis fonte potavit. Et istic presbyteri illius mei titubavit opinio : non enim Synai sed mons Or dinoscitur esse. Petræ quondam Arabum conterminus urbi ubi et Aaron hominem exuit, et aqua de intimo percusse rupis emergit" (Guiberti, *Hist. Hier.* vii. 36 ; *Gesta Dei*, i. 555).

one instance confused the accounts of different expeditions.
It is certainly remarkable that the monk of Chartres,
though in his records of Baldwin's expedition to Aila he
refers to the distance of Mount Sinai from Aila, yet makes
no allusion to the projected visit to the monastery. It
must, however, be stated, on the other hand, that there is no
intimation that the Crusaders in any of their expeditions
into Arabia Tertia (Idumæa) came into contact with any
Christian communities, and whether any such survived there
at that time can only be matter of speculation. If
Christianity had been crushed out in Arabia Tertia previous
to the twelfth century, then, assuming there was any
foundation for the statement that Baldwin I. knew of the
existence of a monastic community resident on Mount
Sinai, that mountain could not have been in Idumæa. But
was it, then, extinguished? We know that Christianity
survived and was tolerated in Idumæa for a considerable
period after the Mohammedan invasion in the seventh
century, and it may be that a monastery dedicated to the
High Priest of Israel, the Neby Harûn, held in equal
veneration by Moslems and Christians, long continued to
flourish, though the religion of its inmates possibly acquired
in time a Mohammedan tinge. It is easily intelligible how
such a community would view with apprehension the visit
of the Catholic king and his followers, and how they would
dread a demonstration of the identity of their religion with
that of the hated infidels. It is not easy to understand
how the monk of Chartres could have used the word
"monasterium," and stated that it was dedicated to Aaron,
unless he had been informed that monks actually occupied it.
Assuredly he never would have speculated on finding a
monastery in what, to him, was a Pagan land. The whole
question of the locality of the Mount Sinai referred to in
the chronicles of the crusades is not, however, free from

some difficulty. From the preceding remarks it will appear that the general assumption that Baldwin intended visiting a mountain in the Sinaitic peninsula is open to very formidable objections.

The evidence of those to whom we are indebted for chronicling the expedition made by the Crusaders through Idumaea must not, of course, be overrated. Much of it is only the hearsay repetition of information received by the Crusaders from the inhabitants, information the value of which the former naturally possessed little opportunity of testing. But when this allowance has been made, we must still concede to these records the merit of preserving with probable fidelity some notable facts connected with these expeditions. Thus no one can doubt that in his first expedition Baldwin and his followers reached a place south of the Dead Sea, by passing through a mountainous district; that this place was called by the inhabitants the valley of Moses; that a stream ran through it, which by local tradition was connected with that which Moses obtained from the rock; and that a neighbouring mountain was reputed to be that on which Moses and Aaron conversed with God. We also learn beyond all question from these records, that in the immediate neighbourhood of the valley of Moses was a mountain which, whether rightly or wrongly, the Crusaders took to be Mount Horeb or Sinai; and that on their arrival at the head of the Gulf of Akaba they believed that in Aila they found the original Elim of the Exodus. We also know that in this latter expedition some communications took place between the Crusaders and some holy men living on a mountain reputed to be Mount Sinai; and, independently of the reasons already stated, it is not an extravagant conclusion that this mountain must have been identical with that near the valley of Moses, which they unquestionably believed to be Mount Horeb, near whose foot flowed the Waters of Contradiction.

The allusions made by Arabian and Egyptian writers to the particular region now engaging our attention, furnish but little assistance in our inquiry; and, with the exception of some particulars respecting certain localities, which are of service for purposes of identification, we are told absolutely nothing about Idumæa. Isstachri, a writer of the tenth century, refers to Ailah (Akaba), and states that its inhabitants were Jews whose presence there was tolerated by virtue of a charter granted by Mahomet. This is confirmed by Macrizi, who wrote in the fifteenth century, but it is doubtful whether the Moslem writers may not have confounded Christians with Jews. Masudi, a contemporary of Isstachri, in his " Meadows of Gold and Mines of Gems," makes an allusion to Aaron's grave which, assuming that he believed the latter to be in the Idumæan mountains, raises a strong presumption that he held the same belief respecting Mount Sinai : " Harûn died, and was buried on the Mount Mowâb, which is not far from the mountains of Esh Sherah (Seir) and from the Mount Sinai. His grave is well known; it is in a frightful cavern, in which sometimes at night a great murmur is heard which frightens every human being."[*] There can be no doubt that Masudi here refers to Mount Hor, which by a singular unanimity of tradition is fixed on as Aaron's burying-place; and the statement that it was not far from Mount Sinai is irreconcileable with a belief that the latter was upwards of a hundred miles distant in what is now known as the Sinaitic peninsula. The substitution of Et Tohur for Sinai in what is believed to be a later text seems to indicate that Masudi's statement was subsequently modified, or rather interpreted (not necessarily in bad faith), in order to harmonise with the accepted Sinaitic theory. No particular

---

[*] El Masudi's *Meadows of Gold and Mines of Gems*. Translated from the Arabic by Aloys Sprenger, p. 92. London: 1841.

mountain in the Sinaitic peninsula bears the name of Sinai, though several claim to be so regarded. But one of these mountains has long been known as Mount Tur, or Tor, and is so named by Isstachri, and it would therefore seem that Tur was substituted for Sinai in a later text of the "Golden Meadows," on the assumption that Masudi must have intended to refer to it.*

Abulfeda mentions several places in Arabia Tertia, some of which have been identified with almost absolute certainty. He treats the Araba as the western limit of Arabia between the Red Sea and the Jordan valley, and consequently excludes from that country the Sinaitic peninsula and the desert of Et Tih.† Aila he refers to with a particularity which leaves no doubt that he is speaking of the modern Akaba, with its fort garrisoned by Egyptian soldiers for the protection of the Hajj. There are also some other places lying on the east of the Araba noticed by him, which demand a passing remark. He mentions Er Rakim as being one of the most celebrated towns of Syria, the dwellings of which, he says, are cut out of the living

---

* Sprenger adds a foot-note that in another text Et Tohur takes the place of Sinai (*Meadows of Gold*, p. 92).

† The Sea of Colzoum (the Red Sea), says Abulfeda, bounds the peninsula of Arabia from the confines of the country of Yemen as far as Ailah. Ailah is situated in the peninsula of Arabia, in the middle of its western region; the other part of Arabia that looks westward extends from Ailah to the frontiers of Syria. Abulfeda, describing the circuit of Arabia, makes the traveller start from Ailah southwards, with the Red Sea on his right hand, and thence round the peninsula till on the east side he leaves the Euphrates on his right hand, and thence passing to "the country belonging to Aleppo," he turns south by the Belka to Ailah, the point from which he started. All the region west of the Jordan valley, and of the Araba and of the Red Sea from Ailah southwards, is consequently excluded by Abulfeda from Arabia (*Description of Arabia*, translated by the Chevalier D'Arvieux, pp. 287-290. London: 1718).

rock.* This was, in all probability, Petra. Schaubekh is referred to as a small town rich in gardens lying to the east of the Ghor, inhabited by Christians, and watered by two brooks springing from separate fountains.† This has been supposed to be identical with a village lying between Petra and the Dead Sea, and to have been the site of Baldwin's fort of Mons Regalis. Moan, identified as Máan, a station of the Syrian Hajj nearly due east of Petra, is stated by Abulfeda to be but one stage distant from Schaubekh.‡ Al Khrakh (Kerak—Carracha Moab) is described as a town surrounded by walls and built on a hill.§ It is three stages from Schaubekh, and is undoubtedly the modern Kerak, which the Crusaders called Petra Deserti, and is situated a short distance to the east of the southern extremity of the Dead Sea.

Now, if we are correct in concluding that, under the title Er Rakim, Abulfeda referred to Petra, we discover in the writings of this distinguished Arabian a very singular confirmation of the statement of Josephus that Petra was known to the Syrians as Rekam, and it is at least probable that the Rekam which the Targumists identify with Kadesh may be the same place which Josephus and Abulfeda identify with Petra; in which latter place, according to the traditions brought to the knowledge of the Crusaders, the Waters of Contradiction, drawn by Moses from the rock, were to be found.‖ It has been suggested that by Er

---

* In celeberioribus Syriæ oppidis est etiam ar Rakim, oppidulum prope al Balkaam situm, omnes ejus domus sunt saxo vivo incisæ, quasi essent solidum saxum (*Tab. Syriæ*, p. 11; Lipsiæ, 1766. . . . . Isstrachri gives a similar description of the stone dwellings of Rekam (*Oriental Geography*, translated by Sir W. Ouseley, p. 46. London; 1800).
† *Tab. Syriæ*, p. 89.   ‡ *Ibid.* p. 15.   § *Ibid.* p. 89.
‖ The Targumists place Abraham's abode between Kadesh and Hagra. Schultens, in the *Index in Vitam Saladini*, s. v. *Errakimum*,

Rakim, Abulfeda meant not Petra but Kerak, but his explicit description of the latter place, which in almost every particular corresponds with those of modern travellers who have visited Kerak, negative this assumption. It is scarcely possible that Abulfeda could have overlooked so important a place as the celebrated Nabathæan capital in his description of this part of Syria.

In his allusions to the Sinaitic peninsula, Macrizi notices Mount Tor and a place called Faran, not improbably the modern Feiran, but makes the following significant remarks respecting them : " It is said that Faran is the name of the mountain of Mecca, and that it is the name of other mountains in the Hedjaz, and that it is the place mentioned in the books of Moses. But the truth is, that Tor and Faran are two districts belonging to the southern parts of Egypt, and that it is not the same as the Faran mentioned in the books of Moses.*

M. Quatremère first translated into an European tongue† an interesting account recorded by the Egyptian historian Nowairi, of an expedition made by Sultan Bibors into Idumæa in the latter portion of the thirteenth century. Having crossed the Tih and descended into the Araba, the Sultan proceeded as far as the entrance of the Wady Rubai to the

---

argues with much plausibility that Hagra and Rekam (Petra) were the same, relying apparently on a quotation from Ibn Haukel (Isstachri), a geographer of the tenth century, made by Abulfeda. The latter questions Ibn Haukel's accuracy as to the precise situation of Hagra. It was, according to the former, inhabited by the tribe of the Tsamondites, who are referred to in the Koran as making their dwellings in caves in the mountains. *Arkim* signifies in Arabic variegated in colour, hence the *Rekam* of the Hebrews having the same meaning. was doubtless applied to Petra in connection with the colouring of the rocks (*Index Geog. in Vitam Saladini*. Schultens, s.v. *Errakimum*. Leyden : 1732).

* Quoted by Burckhardt, *Syria*, p. 617.
† *Nouveau Journal Asiatique*, Paris, 1835.

west of Petra. Having encamped there for the night, he ascended the mountain on the following morning. It is described as consisting of a soft kind of sandstone agglomerate, with stripes of various colours—red, blue, and white—and marked by excavations capable of being traversed by a man on horseback. To the left-hand side were seen stone steps and the grave of Aaron, the brother of Moses, and close by a strong castle. The Sultan then explored the city of Petra with its rock-cut habitations, which receives in this narrative the singular designation of the "Villages of the Children of Israel." On quitting Petra the Sultan entered a valley called Medrah, and came to a place named Od-dema, where was a well, attributed by tradition to Moses, and from which blood at first issued, and was then followed by water. Quitting this place, Bibors arrived at Schaubekh on the following day, and continuing his journey he reached Kerak on the succeeding one at noon.

This curious record is important as showing that the Egyptian Sultan, dropping unexpectedly into the midst of the ruins of Petra, heard from the natives precisely the same stories which had been told to the Crusaders one hundred and sixty years before. The tomb of the prophet Aaron was still pointed out on the adjoining mountain, and the well was still shown which owed its origin to the blow struck by Moses' rod. But the designation of the rock-cut caves of Petra as the "Villages of the Children of Israel," however inappropriate and inaccurate, at all events goes far to support the conjecture that a tradition, whether well or ill founded, survived in that region to the effect that in the course of their journeyings the children of Israel had passed that way.

It will be seen that we gain not much information from the early Arabian and Egyptian authorities, but, such as it is, it confirms our previous conclusions. El Masudi is acquainted with the reputed tomb of Aaron, which he places on

s

a mountain near Es Sherah, a section of the Idumæan range, and also near Sinai. Abulfeda notices one of the most celebrated cities in Syria as Er Rakim, where the habitations are cut out of the living rock, and which there is no difficulty in identifying with the Petra Arekeme of Josephus, and, so far as we have the means of judging, with the Rekem Kadesh of the Targumists. Macrizi, though well acquainted with the Sinaitic peninsula and the Coptic pretensions that Mount Sinai was to be found there, takes care to state that, in his opinion, the Faran (Feiran) of that peninsula which is in Egyptian territory is not referred to in the books of Moses, and suggests that the Faran of the Hedjaz (which may be the Pharan of Idumæa) was the place visited by the Israelites. And finally, the somewhat earlier Egyptian writer, Nowairi, in his account of the expedition of Sultan Bibors, not only speaks of Aaron's tomb on the mountain overhanging Petra, but calls the cave-dwellings the "Villages of the Children of Israel," and finds the Ain Mûsa, the spring attributed by tradition to Moses, on the east of the city on the road to Kerak—namely, in the same place where it was said to be by Eusebius and Jerome, where it was found by the Crusaders, and where it is pointed out at the present day.

CHAPTER IX.

DURING the long interval which elapsed between the Exodus and the foundation of the kingdom of Israel, complete silence is preserved in the Hebrew records respecting Edom. If we are right in our conclusion that at the time of the migration from Egypt the nucleus of the latter kingdom—the Edom which in after-times extended to the Araba and the head of the Ælanitic Gulf—lay in the territory intervening between the eastern borders of Petra and the land of Moab, in the midst of which Bozrah was situated, we have still no means of judging at what time the subsequent changes may have taken place. It becomes necessary, therefore, to examine with great attention the earliest references which are made to this region subsequent to the Hebrew settlement in Canaan.

It is stated that Saul, by the direction of Samuel, made war on the Amalekites to punish them for having attacked the Israelites on their way from Egypt to Canaan.* The orders given by the prophet were comprehensive. The king was to utterly destroy every living thing—man and woman, infant and suckling, ox and sheep, camel and ass. In the traditions of the Exodus reference is made to two encounters with the Amalekites; in one the Hebrews are represented as being victorious, in the other they are said to have been utterly defeated.† They are most probably only two versions of the same event; but, however this may be, such fearful retribution as that commanded by Samuel was doubtless intended to avenge a defeat, and not

---

* 1 Sam. xv.   † Exod. xvii. 8; Num. xiv. 40; Deut. i. 44.

to punish an unsuccessful act of aggression committed many centuries previously. The reverse sustained at the hands of the Amalekites was one which might, however, well live in the recollection of Israel. Their ancestors had succeeded in reaching the frontier of Canaan in a comparatively short time after leaving Egypt, and having received the reports of the spies whom they sent to explore the land, attempted to enter it, when the Amalekites, aided by the Canaanites, repulsed them with great slaughter.* The after-effects were, however, even more serious than the immediate loss. The Israelites were compelled to alter their route to "compass Edom," and turn their steps towards the Trans-Jordanic region, from which as a base, many long years afterwards, they successfully forced their way into the promised land.

We have already alluded to the Amalekites, and to the singular statement of Josephus that they occupied the region of Gobolitis and Petra,† an assertion which amounts to no more than the expression of a belief on the part of the historian that the tribe which blocked the way of the Israelites inhabited the country to the south of the Dead Sea. In the report attributed to the spies, the Amalekites are said to dwell in the south (Negeb), wherever that may have been, the Amorites in the mountains, and the Canaanites by the sea and by the coast of Jordan.‡ The Amorites we know, however, occupied a portion of the Trans-Jordanic region to the north of Moab,§ far outside the field in which the spies operated. If, however, the Amalekites occupied the mountainous region between Petra and the Dead Sea, and the Canaanites the region to the west of that sea and

---

* In the record in Deuteronomy the Amalekites are called Amorites. It is, however, evident that the battle referred to is the same as that recorded in Numbers.
† *A. J.* iii. 2, 1.   ‡ Num. xiii. 29.   § Num. xxi. 13, 21.

the Jordan valley, it would be intelligible how an attempted invasion from Petra or its neighbourhood would be resisted by the Amalekites, or by a combination of that tribe and the Canaanites. It is, however, stated that such an alliance was actually formed to resist the Hebrews. The allies were successful, and it is noteworthy that the routed Israelites were pursued in Seir.*

Now let us follow the campaign undertaken by Saul for the punishment of the Amalekites. Having collected an army† (the figures, as usual, are preposterous), he proceeded to the Amalekite territory, and before commencing hostilities addressed a request to the Kenites to separate themselves from the Amalekites, being desirous of sparing the former on account of the kindness which they had shown to the Israelites on their journey from Egypt. With this request the Kenites complied. This connection between the Kenites and the Amalekites is, however, alone explicable on the assumption that they were neighbours; for it is not suggested that an alliance had been formed in consequence of the threatened attack by Israel, and consequently, if we are right in identifying the Kenites as the cave-dwellers about Petra, we find a corroboration of our inference that the Amalekites occupied the adjoining territory on the east or north-east.

It is then stated that Saul smote the Amalekites "from Havilah unto Shur, that is over against Egypt." Is it possible to ascertain where these respective places were which marked the limits within which Saul harried the Amalekites?

We may dismiss from consideration the Havilah referred to in connection with one of the four rivers formed by the stream which watered the Garden of Eden,‡ and also the

---

* Deut. i. 44.
† 1 Sam. xv. The army numbered 200,000 Israelites and 10,000 of the men of Judah.
‡ Gen. ii. 11.

Havilah mentioned in the genealogical table of Gen. x. A more precise indication is furnished in the statement that the descendants of Ishmael dwelt "from Havilah unto Shur, that is before Egypt, as thou goest towards Assyria;"* a region which precisely corresponds with that in which Saul smote the Amalekites. We will not dwell here on the singular light thus thrown on the identity of the traditions which respectively assign to the eldest son of Abraham (Ishmael) and to the eldest son of Isaac (Esau) the territory lying to the south-east of Canaan; but we must point out that the Amalekites are said to have constituted a branch of the Beni-Esau, and not unnaturally occupied a portion of the territory which was identified with Esau's possessions.

As no specific information is given respecting Havilah in either of the passages referred to, all that can reasonably be concluded from the former is that Havilah lay to the east of the Araba, as otherwise the Ishmaelites, to whom such great things were promised,† would have dwelt in the desolate wilderness lying between Egypt and that valley, and now universally associated with the wanderings of the Israelites.

It is not so difficult to determine the locality of Shur. In the passage just quoted it is spoken of as "before Egypt, as thou goest towards Assyria," and as "over against Egypt." If Shur was a town it might be possible to determine its distance from Egypt; but from all the indications in the Hebrew records it seems to have been treated in them as a region. Let us for a moment suppose that the broad expanse of desert now known as Et Tih was called Shur by the Israelites;‡ we will find that it would respond to the Biblical description of Shur as being before or over against Egypt. The

---

* Gen. xxv. 18.   † Gen. xvi. 10; xxi. 18.
‡ The precise locality of Shur will be considered subsequently.

Israelites on quitting Egypt made a three days' journey into the wilderness of Shur.* Abraham is said to have dwelt between Kadesh and Shur,† that is, in the region between Kadesh in Idumæa and the Araba, which marked the commencement of Shur. The Ishmaelites dwelt between Havilah and Shur —that is, between the Arabian desert and the desert of the Tih. Saul's campaign against the Amalekites was bounded on the west by Shur—that is to say, not by the Egyptian frontier, but by the barren waste of which all that the Israelites knew, or cared to know, was that it lay over against, or in the direction of, Egypt.

It is somewhat material to notice that Saul marshalled his army for this campaign at Telaim, which is reckoned in the Book of Joshua as one of the cities of Judah towards the coast of Edom southward,‡ and apparently not far distant from a city named Kedesh, which is equally included amongst the cities of Judah. In dealing with the statement that Saul smote the Amalekites from Havilah to Shur, "that is over against Egypt," we cannot suppose that the field of the campaign extended from the borders of the Arabian desert to the Egyptian frontier; and we may therefore treat it as an Oriental form of stating that the Amalekites were exterminated throughout the entire region which they were supposed to inhabit.

The Amalekites are constantly identified with the Edomites by Josephus, and we are tempted to inquire whether, in different traditions of the Exodus, Amalekites and Edomites may not have been convertible terms, as Amalekites and Amorites undoubtedly were.§ It is stated that when Israel sought permission to pass through Edom, it was not merely refused, but "Edom came out against Israel, with much

---

* Exod. xv. 22.   † Gen. xx. i.   ‡ Jos. xv. 24.
§ Num. xiv. 40-45; Deut. i. 41-46.

people, and with a strong hand."* In this narrative it is said that "Israel turned away" from Edom.† Is this the correct version of what occurred? Was there simply a demonstration by Edom, and did Israel prudently abstain from a trial of strength; or did Israel "go up" against Edom and sustain a defeat, which in the records that have come down to us is represented as an engagement in which the Amalekites and the Amorites are indifferently named as the adversaries of Israel?‡ The fact that the possessions of Amalek, who was said to be Esau's grandson,§ were identical with those given to Ishmael and his decendants,‖ raises a very strong presumption that Ishmaelites, Midianites,¶ Edomites, and Amalekites were designations indifferently given to one and the same people; and if so, Saul's raid on Amalek was in truth an invasion of Edom, with which nation it is elsewhere stated in general terms** that he made war. It is noticeable in the account of the campaign the narrator states that on his arrival at a city, probably the frontier of Amalek, Saul "laid wait in the valley,"†† and at this place addressed his request to the Kenites to separate themselves from the Amalekites. We shall subsequently find that a place called "the valley," *nachal*, lay to the east of Petra. After defeating the Amalekites, Saul "went down" to Gilgal, having previously set up a place at Carmel.‡‡ Dismissing for the moment the consideration of the locality of Carmel, all we may fairly infer from this narrative is that the tribes attacked by Saul inhabited a district to the south-east of Judæa, near, if not in, Edom; and if we are correct in identifying Shur with the Tih steppe, that this district lay to the east of the Araba. This would tally with the state-

---

* Num. xx. 20.   † Num. xx. 21.   ‡ Num. xiv. 40-45; Deut. i. 41-46.
§ Gen. xxxvi. 16.   ‖ Gen. xxv. 18.   ¶ Gen. xxxvii. 28; Jud. viii. 24.
** 1 Sam. xiv. 47.   †† 1 Sam. xv. 5.   ‡‡ 1 Sam. xv. 21.

ment that Saul "went down" with his spoil to Gilgal, which lay not far from Jericho in the Jordan valley.

It is related of David, that being apprehensive of being captured by Saul in Keilah, a Philistine town, he departed with his band, and sought refuge in a mountain in the wilderness of Ziph.* The Ziphites thereupon informed Saul that David was hidden "in strongholds in the wood, in the hill of Hachilah, which is on the south of Jeshimon."† Saul thanked them, adding, "I will go with you; and it shall come to pass, if he be in the land, that I will search him out throughout all the thousands of Judah."‡ Saul accordingly proceeded to seek for David; but the latter, having been informed of the king's design, "came down from the rock," and with his band entered "the wilderness (*midbhar*) of Maon, in the plain (*Araba*), on the south (or 'the right-hand') of Jeshimon."§ David succeeded in making his escape, by passing on one side of the mountain whilst the king went round the other; and Saul, having received information of a threatened invasion by the Philistines, was compelled to desist from the pursuit and to return home.|| It is stated that the rock received the name of Sela-hammahlekoth, and that David subsequently "went up and dwelt in the strongholds at En-gedi."¶

A different version of this episode in David's career is given in a subsequent chapter.** Saul is represented as going down to the wilderness of Ziph and encamping "in the hill of. Hachilah, which is before Jeshimon." Whilst there David spared Saul's life, whereupon the king acknowledged that he had sinned, and having blessed David they parted as friends. Is it possible to

---

* 1 Sam. xxiii. 13–15. † 1 Sam. xxiii. 19; *Lit.* "on the right hand."
‡ 1 Sam. xxiii. 23. § 1 Sam. xxiii. 24, 25. || 1 Sam. xxiii. 26, 27.
¶ 1 Sam. xxiii. 28, 29. ** 1 Sam. xxvi.

ascertain with any approach to probability the region in which this event is said to have occurred?

Of the hill of Hachilah* no mention is made save in the passage we have quoted, and we must therefore endeavour to fix its locality by that of the places said to have been in its immediate neighbourhood. In the one account it is said to have been " to the right of," and in the other " before" or in view of, Jeshimon, a place to which reference is made in several passages both of prose and poetry. The former are to be found in the Book of Numbers, exclusive of those now quoted from the First Book of Samuel. In Numbers xxi. 20 Mount Pisgah is said to look toward Jeshimon, and in Numbers xxiii. 28 Mount Peor is equally said " to look toward" the same place.† Pisgah and Peor (they may have been identical) were in the Trans-Jordanic region, probably on the east of the Dead Sea; and all we can fairly conclude from these passages is that Jeshimon was within view of Pisgah and Peor. The poetical allusions to Jeshimon are, however, more important, and have considerable significance in their bearing on the main object of our inquiry. In six different passages in which the word occurs, distinct reference is made to the region in the neighbourhood of Sinai, though the rendering of the word Jeshimon, " wilderness " or " desert," in the Authorised Version conveys no allusion to any specific place. The following are the passages:—

" He found him in a *desert land* (*midbhar*), and in the *waste howling wilderness* (Jeshimon)." Deut. xxxii. 10.

---

* I cannot help thinking that the Havilah which was the limit of the Ishmaelite and Amalekite territory, is identical with the Hachilah mentioned in connection with the pursuit of David by Saul, and that it is simply owing to an error in transcribing the original records that the names have now become dissimilar. חוילה *Havilah* and הבילה *Hachilah* might easily be mistaken for each other, and it is notorious that many similar errors occur in the accepted text.

† *Lit.* " in presence," or " in view of Jeshimon."

"O God, when thou wentest forth before thy people, when thou didst march through the *wilderness*, Selah (Jeshimon, Selah)." Ps. lxviii. 8; A. V., 7.

"How oft did they provoke him in the *wilderness* (*midbhar*), and grieve him in the *desert* (Jeshimon)." Ps. lxxviii. 40.

"But lusted exceedingly in the *wilderness* (*midbhar*), and tempted God in the *desert* (Jeshimon)." Ps. cvi. 14.

"They wandered in the *wilderness in a solitary way* (in the *midbhar in Jeshimon*)." Ps. cvii. 4.

"I will even make a way in the *wilderness* (*midbhar*), and rivers in the *desert* (*Jeshimon*)." Isa. xliii. 19.

It is of course open to question if Jeshimon, whether occurring in prose or poetry, be a proper name. If it be not, then the various passages in which it occurs may be dismissed from notice; if it be a proper name, then the materiality of the references to it cannot be overrated.

It is further stated that the *midbhar* of Maon where David took refuge was in the plain (*Araba*), on the south of Jeshimon. The significance of the employment of the term *Araba* must not be overlooked. The word is invariably used to designate the low region of the Jordan valley, and its continuation southwards beyond the Dead Sea, answering to the modern *Ghor*. As there is no other instance in the Hebrew records where the term is employed in which this application is not incontestable, it is reasonable to conclude that in the passage now under consideration the word is used in the same sense.

Of Maon and of its people the Maonites, or the Mehunims as they are called in the Authorised Version, sufficiently frequent mention is made to enable us with tolerable certainty to ascertain the locality and the people referred to. The Mehunims are bracketed with the Arabians as having been overthrown by King Uzziah,[*] and are spoken of in

---

[*] 2 Chron. xxvi. 7.

the reign of Hezekiah as settled of old in the valley of
Gedor,* whilst a subsequent reference connects this valley
with Mount Seir.† The most specific reference to this
people is made, however, in the narrative of an invasion of
Judah by some neighbouring tribes in the reign of
Jehoshaphat.‡ According to the Authorised Version the
story begins in the following words: "And it came to pass
after this also, that the children of Moab and the children of
Ammon, and with them other beside the Ammonites, came
against Jehoshaphat to battle." It is now generally considered that the reading "Ammonites" is incorrect, whilst the
translation "other beside" is undoubtedly wrong. The Septuagint gives οἱ Μιναῖοι, from which it would seem that the
Greek translators either found in their text the word for
Maonites, or else recognised an evident transposition of a
letter.§ The correct translation of the sentence supports the
LXX. version, as it should run, "and with them of the
Ammonites," or "Maonites," as the case may be. But as the
children of Ammon have been already mentioned as joining
in the invasion of Judah, the repetition would be unmean-
ing, and we may therefore conclude that the Maonites
were mentioned in the original record.

In the subsequent part of the narrative it is made
evident who were the people who had formed an alliance

---

* 1 Chron. iv. 41. † 1 Chron. iv. 42. ‡ 2 Chron. xx.

§ מעונים *Meonim*, instead of עמונים *Amonim*, the initial letters being
transposed. Such errors, it is supposed, were not of infrequent
occurrence in the text, and arose from oversights on the part of those
who acted as scribes. The Masorites notice sixty-two instances in
which they admit the error has been committed, and where the *Keri*,
or that which is *read*, differs from the text—the *Chetib*, or that which
is *written*. The above is, however, not one of the cases in which a
different reading from the text has the support of the Masorah.
Biblical scholars, amongst whom may be numbered Ewald and De
Wette, are of opinion that the correct reading is "Meonim."

with Moab and Ammon against Judah. In Jehoshaphat's prayer to Jahveh before the battle, the king says : " And now behold, the children of Ammon and Moab and Mount Seir, whom thou wouldest not let Israel invade, when they came out of the land of Egypt, but they turned from them, and destroyed them not." Here the Maonites are not only distinguished from the Ammonites, but they are called the men of Seir and identified with the Edomites, whom, in common with the Ammonites and Moabites, Israel was ordered to respect on the journey to Canaan. In subsequent passages the distinction is equally strongly marked, and when through the interposition of Jahveh the allies fall upon each other, thus effecting their common destruction, the men of Seir are the first to fall victims at the hands of the Ammonites and Moabites. When the news of the invasion was brought to Jehoshaphat, he was told " there cometh a great multitude against thee from beyond the sea on this side Syria (the Dead Sea), and behold they be in Hazezon-tamar, which is En-gedi." The inhabitants of the region to the south of that sea must therefore have co-operated in the invasion.

Maon is included in the Book of Joshua in a list of the towns of Judah, where it is joined with Carmel and Ziph among the cities which were "in the mountains;" but nothing is there said which can aid us in determining its locality.*

It is also mentioned in connection with David and Nabal, the husband of Abigail, David's future wife.† Whilst David was hiding from Saul in the wilderness of En-gedi the king pursued him, and having had occasion to enter a cave, David, who was concealed within, cut off Saul's skirt, thus proving to the king that he might have taken his life. Saul

---

* Jos. xv. 55.   † 1 Sam. xxv.

and David thereupon became reconciled, the former returning home, and the latter with his men going up into their "hold."* In a succeeding but distinct narrative it is recorded that David went down to the wilderness of Paran, and whilst there he heard that Nabal, a man of Maon, was then engaged at Carmel shearing his sheep. David thereupon sent a message to Nabal, requesting what would to-day be called *bakhshish*, and reminding Nabal that he and his men had respected Nabal's property : " Thy shepherds, which were with us, we hurt them not, neither was there ought missing unto them all the while they were in Carmel." Nabal refused compliance with the request, and David, incensed at his ingratitude—" in vain have I kept all that this fellow hath in the wilderness"—vowed to exterminate him and all his people. With the issue of the story we are not concerned.

Is the Maon, in whose wilderness David took refuge from Saul and to which Nabal belonged, the same as that which doubtless gave their name to the Maonites? Everything points to an affirmative reply. David's request to Nabal was based on the fact that he and his fellow-outlaws had for some time frequented the *midbhar* of Maon, and had abstained from plundering Nabal's flocks in the adjoining Carmel ; but when we find that David was in the wilderness of Paran when he addressed this request to Nabal—a region which, as we have already seen, was to the east of the Araba and probably near Petra—we must conclude that the Maon of Nabal was the Maon of the people who aided the Moabites and Ammonites in invading Judah. Too much stress should not be laid on the discovery of places bearing at the present day names similar to those which we find in the Scriptural records. It is, however, a curious coincidence that about

---

* 1 Sam. xxiv.

fifteen miles east of Petra is the town of Maan, to which Abulfeda refers in the fourteenth century, and which to-day marks one of the stations of the Syrian Hajj.

It will be noticed that mention is made in the preceding narratives of a place named En-gedi. David is said to have gone up from the *midbhar* of Maon, and taken refuge in strongholds at En-gedi.* Information is a second time given to Saul that David is "in the wilderness of En-gedi;"† and having spared Saul's life in the cave, David and his men "got them up unto the hold."‡ In the succeeding narrative of Nabal, David is represented as going down into the wilderness of Paran,§ whilst in the next chapter another version is given of the story of Saul and David at En-gedi, the scene of the occurrence being the wilderness of Ziph.‖ The points of resemblance between this last narrative, especially as regards the enumeration of the places referred to,¶ and that in which Saul's vain pursuit of David, when a threatened invasion by the Philistines compelled him to return home, is recorded, leaves no doubt that the *midbhar* of Ziph and that of Maon were regarded as practically identical; whilst equally strong indications are afforded, by a comparison of all these narratives, that the *midbhar* of Paran and that of En-gedi were not far apart.

It is supposed by modern travellers that the ancient En-gedi is found at Ain Jidy, a fountain situated about midway on the western shore of the Dead Sea.** Josephus says that En-gedi was a city on the Lake Asphaltites, and he gives its distance from Jerusalem, which is thought to correspond with that intervening between the Jewish capital and Ain Jidy.†† Jerome places En-gedi at the southern ex-

---

* 1 Sam. xxiii. 29. † 1 Sam. xxiv. 1. ‡ 1 Sam. xxiv. 22.
§ 1 Sam. xxv. 1. ‖ 1 Sam. xxvi. 13-25. ¶ 1 Sam. xxvi. 1-3.
** Robinson, *Bib. Res.* i. 508. †† *A. J.* ix. 1, 2.

tremity of the Dead Sea.* It appears in early times to have been identified with Hazezon-tamar† (which has been rendered the "pruning of the palms"), a place remarkable for its palm-trees; and although, owing to the improvidence of the inhabitants of the entire region, the palms have now almost everywhere disappeared, the Crusaders, in the twelfth century, were struck by their number and luxuriance on entering the country south of the Dead Sea.‡ In still earlier

---

* *Comm. Ezech.* xlvii. 10. † 2 Chron. xx. 2.

‡ Albert of Aix states that Baldwin, when on his expedition into Idumæa, reached a castle called after St. Abraham, which was situated close to the Dead Sea. Whilst there, and when about to penetrate the Arabian mountains, the Crusaders were informed that a neighbouring place, called that of "Palms," was well worth a visit. "Intimatum est eis a quibusdam incolis, quomodo, si paulo procederent ad locum qui dicitur *Palmarum*, plurimas opes et copias ciborum reperirent." Thither some forty of the Crusaders proceeded in the hope of carrying off booty, but with the exception of some food and sweet water (Albert expressly says, "nihil vero vini aut alicujus poculi præter fontes") they obtained nothing. Thence they arrived at the mountains of Arabia. " Illic quidem in loco palmarum refocillati, exurgentes ad montana Arabiæ pervenerunt" (Alb. Aq., *Hist. Hier.* vii. 41; *Gesta Dei*, i. 306). The expedition on its return again visited the city of Palms, "*Villa Palmarum*," where a profusion of dates were seen, and thence by St. Abraham's castle proceeded on its journey back to Jerusalem (Alb. Aq. vii. 42). Fulcher, who accompanied the expedition, gives more particulars respecting this place so noted for its palm-trees. Having passed round the Dead Sea on the south, " girato autem lacu a parte Australi," the Crusaders found a town which was said to be *Segor* (dicunt esse Segor), pleasantly situated, and great numbers of date-bearing palms, "situ gratissimam, et de fructibus palmarum quos dactilos nominant, valde abundantem." Thence the expedition ascended the mountains of Arabia, " Exhinc Arabiæ montana introire cepimus." The Crusaders thence proceeded to the "Vallis Moysi" (Fulch. Carnot. *Gest. Per. Franc.* xxiii; *Gesta Dei*, i. 405). An anonymous author, recording the same events, states that leaving the Salt Lake on their left hand, the Crusaders passed through a very steep region, having an abundance of date-palms, and entered the interior of Arabia. "Relicto itaque lacu a sinistrâ, per terram gratissimam et fructibus palmarum quos dactilos vocant, fertilissimam, interiorem Arabiam ingressi sunt" (*Gesta Francorum Expugn. Hierusalem*, xxxviii; *Gesta Dei*, i. 581).

times, the son of Sirach vaunted the palms of En-gaddi,* and in the traditions of Southern Canaan it was remembered that "the Kenites went up out of the city of palm-trees with the children of Judah into the wilderness of Judah."† It is therefore permissible to question the accuracy of the identification of the ancient En-gedi with the fountains bearing a somewhat similar name on the west coast of the Dead Sea. It is undoubtedly very singular that the En-gaddi of the son of Sirach may be rendered "Kadesh," and one is involuntarily led to speculate whether En-gedi may not be a corruption of En-kadesh of which the still earlier name was En-mishpat.‡

---

* Ecclus. xxiv. 14. † Jud. i. 16.

‡ The common assumption that "the city of Palms" from which Judah went up to invade Canaan was Jericho, rests on the statement in the Book of Joshua that all the tribes crossed the Jordan opposite that town. The apocryphal nature of this statement will be dealt with hereafter. The city of Palm-trees, from which Judah and the Kenites operated in invading Southern Palestine, was the Hazezon-tamar or En-gedi referred to as the point from which, in the reign of Jehoshaphat, the Moabites and Maonites threatened Judah (2 Chron. xx.). The statement of the Crusaders (in preceding note) that they found at the southern end of the Dead Sea a place known as the Villa Palmarum, which they were told was Zegor, receives a certain confirmation in the Talmud. "There is a story of some Levites who travelled to Zoar, the city of Palms, and one of them fell sick, and there he died" (*Jevamoth*, cap. xvi.; Lightfoot ii. 6). Zoar was by all accounts at the southern extremity of the Dead Sea. Abulfeda names this sea the Lake of Zogar (*Tab. Syr.* 12). Josephus describes it as "extending as far as Zoar in Arabia" (*B. J.* iv. 8. 4.) Jerome, in his commentary on Isaiah xv. 5, writes: " Segor in finibus Moabitarum sita est dividens ab iis terram Philistiim." En-gedi he placed at the southern extremity of the Dead Sea, "ubi finitur et consumitur" (*Com.* Ezech. xlvii. 10). Since Tamar and En-gedi were the same (2 Chron. xx. 8), and it was from Tamar that Ezekiel carried the southern boundary of the land to the waters of Meribah in Kadesh (Ezek. xlvii. 19), it appears almost absolutely certain that the Villa Palmarum of the Crusaders was the ancient city of Palms which is referred to in the Scriptural records. This also was, as I conceive,

Where was Ziph, and who were the Ziphites who informed Saul of David's hiding-place? Ziph is mentioned twice in the catalogue of the cities of Judah in the Book of Joshua. The first time it is classed with Kedesh and Hazor amongst "the uttermost cities toward the coast of Edom southward;"* and the second with Maon and Carmel, amongst the cities in the mountains. Whether two distinct cities of the same name were intended it is impossible to say, but there seem good reasons for concluding that one city was alone referred to.†

It is a very remarkable circumstance that not only is there a considerable difference between the Hebrew text and the Septuagint version of the passage in Joshua in which Ziph is first mentioned, but the name is converted by the Greek translators into $Μαιυάμ$ (seemingly Maon), whilst Bealoth is rendered $Βαλμαιυάμ$ (Baal-Meon). In the verse in which Ziph is named a second time the LXX. render Maon $Μαωρ$ (Maor) and Ziph $ΟΖιβ$ (Ozib).

In those passages in the Book of Samuel in which allusion is made to Ziph and the Ziphites, it is also remarkable that

---

the "Tamar in the wilderness" which was built by Solomon (1 Kings ix. 18). The Masorites have, in my humble judgment, incorrectly substituted the *Keri* (Tadmor) for the *Chetib* (Tamar) of the text, apparently to harmonise it with 2 Chron. viii. 4 (*Thenius Exeget. Handbuch*, 1 Kings ix. 18). This point is far from unimportant, because if the Tamar in the wilderness which was built by Solomon was the city of Palm-trees of Judah and the Kenites, and the Hazezon-tamar of the period of Jehoshaphat, the Tamar of Ezekiel, and the Villa Palmarum of the Crusaders, then the possessions of Judah indubitably extended to the east of the Araba. According to Pliny, the Essenes dwelt on the western shore of the Dead Sea, and "below these was the town En-gadda, the next to Jerusalem for fruitfulness and groves of palm-trees" (*Geog.* v. 17). Solinus confirms this, and adds "En-gadda is now destroyed, but its reputation for the famous groves that are there still endures, and in regard of its lofty palm-trees has suffered nothing through age and war" (Solin. xxxviii.).

* Jos. xv. 24. † Jos. xv. 55.

the Septuagint version differs considerably from the present Hebrew text. In two passages the "mountain" is substituted for the "*midbhar*" of Ziph, and in four the place is described as being in "the land of dryness" or "drought," or as being "a parched region;" whilst in one passage Ziph receives the qualification of ἡ καινὴ Ζειφ—the new Ziph, a rendering due to the Greek translators reading *Chadish*, or *Chadishah*, instead of *Chorishah*. The former word signifies "new," but it is a curious coincidence that it should be *idem sonans* with the name of a place which seems to have been in close proximity to Ziph.*

Coupled with the inferences which we are justified in drawing from the collocation of Ziph with other places mentioned in the narratives respecting David, we may conclude, from the preceding references, that the Ziph referred to as one of "the uttermost cities of Judah toward Edom southward," and which, by the Greek translators is rendered Maon, is the same in whose neighbourhood David took refuge from Saul, and was not far from En-gedi.

It still remains to offer a few remarks on Carmel, where Nabal the Maonite was shearing his sheep when David made an ineffectual appeal for a generous recognition of his abstention from "lifting" his cattle. The word signifies a cultivated or fertile place, and is applied as a proper name to the fertile promontory on the western coast of Palestine, which is supposed to be closely associated with the history of Elijah. This Carmel is clearly not referred to in the list of Judah's cities, or in the narrative about David and Nabal. It is even doubtful whether it should be regarded in the latter passages as a distinctive name. The word may have been used to designate the cultivated land which adjoined

---

* Kedesh, Jos. xv. 23. The confusion of *Daleth* ד with *Resh* ר is of frequent occurrence in proper names.

Maon. In the Book of Joshua, and in that of Samuel, Maon and Carmel are closely associated; but it is a matter of little importance whether the latter term was a proper name or simply descriptive of the place to which it was applied.*

Let us now review the preceding narratives respecting David, and see what light, if any, they throw on the boundaries of Edom at the time of the foundation of the Jewish monarchy. David and his men were fugitives; they constituted an organised band, setting the authority of Saul at defiance, and the scene of their operations—not to use too harsh a term—lay, at the time to which these narratives refer, within the territory of Judah. When Saul, acting on the information of the Ziphites, seeks David in the hill of Hachilah, on the south of Jeshimon, and close to the *midbhar* of Maon, he says : " If he be in the land, I will search him out throughout all the thousands of Judah."† There is no suggestion that Saul committed what would now be termed a breach of neutrality in pursuing David. But if the wilderness of Maon, or of Ziph, or of Paran; if the hill of Hachilah on the south of Jeshimon, or the celebrated rock which was called *Sela-hammahlekoth*,‡ lay on the east side of the Araba; then, as it is not pretended that David took refuge in what was then Edomitish territory, the latter must have been separated from the Araba by a tract then belonging to Judah. But that the region which was the scene of David's adventures with Saul and with Nabal the Maonite lay on the

---

* Saul, after the defeat of the Amalekites, is said to have set him up a place on Carmel before proceeding to Gilgal (1 Sam xv. 12). If we were right in concluding that Saul's operations were on the east of the Araba, the Carmel would be some noted place to the south of the Dead Sea, and the conclusion would correspond with the inference above drawn that Carmel was in the neighbourhood of Petra.

† 1 Sam. xxiii. 23.   ‡ 1 Sam. xxiii. 28.

east of the Araba, is supported by a very powerful combination of evidence. Ziph is named in the Hebrew text as one of the border cities of Judah on the frontier of Edom,* whilst in the Septuagint version the name appears as Maon. Amongst the cities of Judah " in the mountains " are Maon, Carmel, and Ziph,† a description which might at all events be suitably applied to the region on the east of the Araba. Jeshimon, if it be the proper name of a place, indicates some spot not far distant from Moab,‡ whilst its situation in the plain (Araba) is conclusive that it was in the continuation of the Jordan valley, and probably in the neighbourhood of the Dead Sea where the cities of "the plain" were believed to have been overwhelmed. The poetical allusions to Jeshimon, connected as they are with the incidents which happened during the migration from Egypt, all point to the Sinaitic region which, according to the evidence at our command, lay on the east side of the great valley separating the Tih from the Idumæan mountains. The Maonites are shown to have been a people occupying a city, or a district, south of the Dead Sea, since they joined with the Moabites and Ammonites in invading Judah from that quarter, and in the reign of Jehoshaphat were known as the men of Seir, and had then become absorbed by the Edomites, with whom they were identified.§ But in close connection with Ziph and Maon and Carmel were the *midbhar* of Paran,‖ and the mountain or the *midbhar* of En-gedi,¶ the former being in the neighbourhood of Petra,.and the latter in that of the Dead Sea ; and if we can rely on the testimony of Jerome** as to the situation of En-gedi and its ancient reputation for its palm-trees, probably at the south of that sea and identical

---

* Jos. xv. 24.   † Jos. xv. 55.   ‡ Num. xxi. 20; xxiii. 28.
§ 2 Kings xx.   ‖ 1 Sam. xxv. 1.   ¶ 1 Sam. xxiii. 29.
** Commen. Ezech. xlvii. 10. Jerome clearly indicates the south end of the sea by the words " Ubi finitur et consumitur."

with the Villa Palmarum of the Crusaders. Finally, the rock where David succeeded in making his escape from Saul, was known as *Sela-hammahlekoth*,* and Sela was the name given to Petra until it was changed by Amaziah into Joktheel.† We discover, therefore, a number of coincidences in respect to the several places referred to, all of which point to the region to the east of the Araba and to the south of the Dead Sea, and which tend to negative the assumption that in the time of Saul this territory was included in the kingdom of Edom.

But let us turn to the earliest evidence we possess respecting the limits of Judah, and ascertain whether it supports or negatives the above conclusions.

In the Book of Numbers the southern boundaries of the Promised Land are thus described:—"Your south *quarter* shall be from the wilderness of Zin, along by the coast of Edom, and your south *border*‡ shall be the outmost coast of the Salt Sea *eastward*; and your border shall turn from the south to the ascent of Akrabbim, and pass on to Zin; and the going forth thereof shall be from the south to Kadesh-barnea, and shall go on to Hazar-addar, and pass on to Azmon; and the border shall fetch a compass from Azmon unto the river of Egypt, and the goings out of it shall be at the sea."§ In the Book of Joshua, the south border of Judah is described in very similar language:—"To the border of Edom, the wilderness of Zin southward, was the uttermost part of the south coast, and their south border was from the shore of the Salt Sea, from the bay (or tongue) which looketh southward; and it went out to the south side to Maaleh-akrabbim, and passed along to Zin, and ascended up on the south side unto Kadesh-barnea, and passed along

---

* 1 Sam. xxiii. 28.   † 2 Kings xiv. 7.
‡ Note the distinction drawn between a *quarter* or region and a *border* or boundary.   § Num. xxxiv. 2–5.

to Hezron, and went up to Adar, and fetched a compass to Karkaa; from thence it passed towards Azmon, and went out into the river of Egypt; and the goings out of that coast were at the sea."* There are, however, in the Septuagint version of the last quoted passages certain variances which are deserving of notice. In Joshua xv. 1, the borders of Judah are said to extend "from the borders of Edom, from the wilderness of Zin, unto Kadesh, towards the south;" and in verse 3, the borders, after the ascent of Akrabbim, "pass around Sena (or Zena) and go up from the south to Kadesh-barnea, and go out to Hezron, and proceed up to Zarada, and go out by the way to the west of Kadesh, and they go out to Selmona," and thence to the river of Egypt. It is also noticeable that in the LXX. rendering of Num. xxxiv. 4, the word Zin appears as Εννακ in the Vatican Codex, whilst in the Alexandrine it takes the form of Σεεννὰκ—the name which, according to the Hebrew text, is repeated a second time in the enumeration of the boundary marks, thus curiously enough in the Septuagint version of both Numbers xxxiv. 4 and Joshua xv. 3 assuming the different forms of Εννάκ, Σεεννακ, and Σενά.

Many centuries later, and subsequent to the fall of the Jewish monarchy, Ezekiel, in prophecying the restoration, thus defined the southern limits of the possessions of Israel. The eastern boundary terminating on the south with the East Sea (Dead Sea) the southern border is carried "from Tamar, even to the Waters of Strife in Kadesh, the river to the Great Sea."† And in another passage, "from Tamar unto the Waters of Strife in Kadesh, and to the river towards the Great Sea."‡ In these passages, no less than in those in the Books of Numbers and Joshua, it is significant that Kadesh or Kadesh-barnea, or Meribah-kadesh, is

---

* Jos. xv. 1-4.   † Ezek. xlvii. 19.   ‡ Ezek. xlviii. 28.

specially included in the territory of Judah, and that from this place an undefined line is drawn apparently across the Tih until it reaches in the far west the river of Egypt, the Wady el Arish, which empties itself into the Mediterranean.*

If we now turn to the enumeration of the cities belonging to Judah towards the coast of Edom, we find, besides others not mentioned elsewhere, Kadesh, Ziph, Hazor, in two or three forms, Hezron, Dimonah, Adadah, and Amam, which in the LXX. appears as Σην. But if we revert to the boundaries of Judah,† starting from the south-eastern corner of the Dead Sea up to the point where "a compass is fetched," that is to say, an imaginary line is drawn across the Tih till it reaches the river of Egypt, we discover a number of places familiar to us in the traditions of the Exodus, and which, according to the route which the Israelites followed, must have lain on the east of the Araba. Amongst these are Kadesh and Hazeroth—the Hazors, elsewhere called Hazerim, and ultimately corrupted into Hezron. The Hazar Addar of the boundaries in the Book of Joshua, reappears as the Hazor Haddadah, or the Adadah, in the list of cities,‡ whilst the latter name is most probably identical, with the Adar mentioned amongst the landmarks in the Book of Joshua ;§ the Dimonah of the cities‖ may be the Azmon of the boundaries,¶ the starting-point of the border, which fetched a compass to the river of Egypt.

The Araba, it will be recollected, dips by a series of precipitate terraces into the hollow in which lies the Dead Sea, and viewing the physical characteristics of this region, and assuming that at the time of the settlement in Canaan the Araba constituted the western boundary of Edom, it is taken for granted that the southern border of Judah springing

---

* Jos. xv. 21-32. † Num. xxxiv. 2-5; Jos. xv. 1-4.
‡ Jos. xv. 25. § Jos. xv. 3; see note *ante* p. 275.
‖ Jos. xv. 22. ¶ Jos. xv. 4.

from the extremity of the Dead Sea mounted these terraces (the Maaleh Akrabbim) to the Araba (identified as the *midbhar* of Zin), and thence either immediately or after proceeding some fifty miles along the Araba ascended to the plateau of the Tih, and thence continued a westward course to the Wady-el-Arish—the river of Egypt. If this theory be correct, the several places noted subsequent to the ascent of Akrabbim must have been situated either in the Araba or on the west of that valley.

There is no ground for supposing that the main features of the Araba and the Tih have undergone any material change since the time of the Exodus. The former was then as it is now a barren, desolate, waterless valley, shut in by the cliffs of the Tih steppe on the one side and by the mountains of Idumæa on the other. It fails to-day, as it did three thousand years ago, to supply sustenance for either man or beast. That any tribe, however nomadic its habits, could have pitched its tents, or sought to pasture its cattle for even a few days together, in this gravelly unproductive waste, is scarcely within the limits of probability; that any people should have selected any portion of it as the site of a permanent abode is absolutely inconceivable. From the neighbourhood of the head of the Gulf of Akaba to the descent to the Dead Sea travellers search in vain for the traces of even the rudest town or village. It may with confidence be said that any tribe compelled to seek sustenance in the Araba would perish rapidly of famine.

It has, however, been suggested that Kadesh was situated on the western side of this wilderness, a short distance to the north of Mount Hor. This view was advanced by Robinson, who identified a fountain named Ain-el-Weibeh, with the waters of Meribah of the Hebrew traditions.* It

---

* *Bib. Res.* ii. 174-6.

is difficult to discover the ground upon which this conclusion was based, save that the Ain-el-Weibeh is the only spring of any importance found in this region, and that it may be described as on the border of Idumæa. It must not, however, be forgotten that Kadesh was expressly stated to be a "city"* (the only place which receives this designation in the traditions of the Exodus), that the Israelites remained there for a considerable time, and that its waters had from a much earlier period acquired a great reputation amongst the nomadic tribes. The description of Ain-el-Weibeh is not, however, such as to induce the opinion that at any period it could have enjoyed an exceptional character as a spring, or that its neighbourhood could have been selected as suitable for habitation by any class of people, whether nomadic or sedentary.

Ain-el-Weibeh consists of three fountains issuing from the foot of some limestone hills on the western side of the Arabа. The water is not abundant, and that supplied by two of the sources has the taste of sulphuretted hydrogen. That of the remaining fountain is described by Robinson as clear and limpid. "Below the springs is a jungle of coarse grass and canes, with a few palm trees, presenting at a distance the appearance of fine verdure, but proving near at hand to be marshy and full of bogs." "We could find here," continues the writer, "no trace of the remains of former dwellings."† Considering the description of the place it would certainly have been very wonderful if he did.

It needs great force of imagination to connect these fountains with the En-mishpat of the patriarchal period, or with the waters which, standing on the Mount of God, Moses

---

* Num. xx. 16.   † Bib. Res. ii. 174.

was declared by tradition to have obtained by striking the rock with his wand. But it necessitates a complete disregard of all the evidence of the senses to fancy that a spot such as that described by Robinson could at any period have been the site of even the humblest of cities, or the resting-place for any lengthened period of even a wandering tribe. Ain-el-Weibeh is well-known to the Bedouins, because it is the only place for many miles round where water can be obtained in a region which they are anxious to quit as soon as possible. But it offers no temptations to remain. There is no reason for supposing that it was any different at the time of the Exodus.

If, however, on the assumption that the Edom of the Exodus and of Saul and David extended to the Araba, we find ourselves compelled to reject this hypothesis that Kadesh or any of the other places enumerated on the southern border of Judah were in the Araba, we must seek for them to the west of that valley. In doing so, however, we are met at the outset by some very formidable obstacles. If Kadesh was a city which could be correctly described as on the border of Edom, and from which messengers would have been despatched requesting a passage through that country, then it must have been situated in some part of the table-land of the Tih overhanging the Araba. But there is no spot in this region which by any amount of straining can be made to correspond with Kadesh. Nor would it be possible, following the traditions of the · Exodus, to account for the Israelites finding themselves there. It has accordingly been suggested that Kadesh was situated not far from the middle of the Tih steppe, and that it was reached by the Israelites on quitting the Sinaitic peninsula by following a northerly course, through one of the defiles in the Jebel-et-Tih.

This view was broached by Mr. Rowland,* and has since received considerable support. It is open, however, to (amongst others) the very serious objection that the place identified as Kadesh was not only not on the border of Edom, even supposing that the latter extended to the Araba, but was separated from it by a tract of rugged wilderness of even greater extent than that which lay between it and the Egyptian frontier. It is inconceivable that from such a spot messages should have been sent to Bozrah, the then capital of Edom, and lying at the opposite side of the mountains, forming the eastern wall of the Araba, for the purpose of demanding a free passage to the Trans-Jordanic region. No object could be served by preferring such a request before arriving at the Edomitish frontier, as, *ex hypothesi*, no permission was necessary to enable the Israelites to proceed as far as the Araba. It may also be remarked, that, according to this theory, Kadesh was situated in the very region where the Israelites are supposed to have wandered purposely about in order to kill time, whilst they themselves died off, which implies an amount of stupidity on their part, for the traces of which one seeks in vain amongst their descendants. It is needless to say that if our view of the direction taken by the Israelites on quitting Egypt be correct, they never even approached the region in which, according to this theory, Kadesh was situated.

If, however, Kadesh was not in the Araba, and not in the Tih plateau, then since it was on the border of Edom, it must have lain to the east of that valley, from which the western boundary of Edom must have been separated by an interval more or less great. And it also follows that this intervening district must have been that into which the

---

* G. Williams, *The Holy City*. Mr. Rowland's speculations on the site of Kadesh will be found in the *Appendix*, 488-492.

Israelites penetrated without opposition on their way from Egypt, where stood the Mount of Elohim, and where, in obedience to the stroke of Moses's rod, flowed the waters of Contention and Strife, where for the first time, after quitting the land of their servitude, they came to the "villages" (Hazeroth, Hazerim) of a semi-nomadic and friendly people, and where they found a town of sufficient importance to be designated a city, in which they established their headquarters, whilst they projected an invasion of Canaan from the south, and failing in that, made an ineffectual attempt to secure a free passage through the neighbouring country on the East which lay across their direct path to the pastures beyond the Jordan.

But as the result of our investigation we acquire something more valuable than a better knowledge of the western limits of Edom at the time of the Exodus. We are able to correct our impression respecting the extent of Judah. We are able to appreciate the significance of the statement that the southern *quarter* or region—not *border* of Judah—lay between the *Midbhar* of Zin and Edom, and that the southern *border* commenced at the outmost coast of the Salt Sea *eastward*, and after ascending the heights, passed southward to Kadesh-barnea, and having included Hazar Addar, and Azmon, swept across the Tih, a region equally unknown and uncared for, until it struck the Wady-el-Arish.* In drawing this, like the other boundaries, care was alone taken to name places where disputes might arise with an adjoining people as to the precise limits of territory. Thus, for example, the boundaries on the north and east are very carefully drawn down to the point where the Jordan empties itself into the Dead Sea.† The southern boundary is then taken up at the lower end of that sea, and several

---

* Num. xxxiv. 3–5.   † Num. xxxiv. 6–12.

places are named on the confines of Edom; but then the broad interval extending to the Egyptian frontier is treated like "the great sea"* which marked the western frontier. As the seaport towns are not mentioned on the coast of the latter, so the possessions of Judah on the edge of the wilderness are unnamed. The Tih was then, as it is now, an uninviting, waterless, unproductive waste. Judah was at perfect liberty to push her possessions into it as far as she pleased, there were none who had either the right or the temptation to challenge her frontier in that direction.

* Num. xxxiv. 6.

CHAPTER X.

THE ramifications which we are tempted to pursue, as a consequence of placing a portion of the territory of Judah to the south of the Dead Sea are, however, too numerous and too various to be followed in this treatise. We should be compelled to reconsider the accepted opinions respecting the situation of the Negeb, or south country, which is universally regarded as lying exclusively on the northern border of the Tih. We should be forced to examine in detail the patriarchal traditions, and possibly to alter our views respecting the first home of the ancestors of the Hebrew nation, when they migrated westwards from the land of the Chaldees. We should be obliged to anticipate the story of the invasion of Canaan, and to explain how, politically and strategically, the possession of territory by Judah on the east of the Araba was as much a matter of necessity as the possession of territory by Israel on the east of the Jordan. We should have to inquire into the fortunes of the tribe of Simeon, so closely linked with Judah, yet playing apparently so small a part in Judah's history, and finally disappearing from the scene on the confines of the Arabian desert at the close of the eighth century.* We should be forced, in the absence of the records of Edom's history, and aided alone by those of the hostile kingdoms of Israel and Judah, to follow the territorial changes which took place, and to trace the steps by which Edom, taking

---

* 1 Chron. iv. 41–43.

advantage of Judah's weakness, and at a later period of her overthrow, appropriated not only the territory lying between Edom proper and the Araba, but extended her conquests to the neighbourhood of Jerusalem. But inquiries such as these, however interesting in themselves, and however calculated to fortify our conclusions respecting Judah's possessions in what are now known as the Idumæan mountains, would necessarily lead us too far afield in an investigation having for its object the solution of the enigma of the Hebrew migration from Egypt to Canaan.

It will, however, be necessary, though at the cost of a digression, to take notice of some of the earliest allusions to the Negeb, and some of the places contained in it, and to ascertain whether the region referred to lay to the south of the highlands of Judea, or to the south of the Dead Sea; and in doing so, we must, so far as it is possible, endeavour to distinguish the original elements of the patriarchal traditions from the accretions and modifications which they underwent subsequent to the settlement in Palestine.

The tide of Semitic migration from the East appears to have been temporarily arrested by the comparatively rich pastures and fertile valleys which fringe the Arabian desert on the west, and extend from the Jordan valley southwards along the coast of the Red Sea. In this region we are told that the descendants of Terah* settled, having, as it would seem, dispossessed or absorbed the original inhabitants. The kinship between the various peoples of Terahitic descent was generally acknowledged *inter se*, though their respective rivalries and animosities led to claims of precedence on the one hand and imputations of spurious origin on the other, which severally had no more solid foundation than the promptings of vanity or the suggestions of malevolence.

---

* Gen. xi. 27.

Thus the Moabites and Ammonites were declared to have sprung from the incestuous intercourse of Lot with his daughters.* Ishmael,† who, like Esau‡ and Jacob, was the ancestor of twelve great families, was declared to be the son of a slave.§ Esau, whose identity with Ishmael is apparent, was said to have sold his birthright to Jacob.‖ The Midianites and others who, equally with the rest, claimed descent from Abraham, were, like Ishmael, derived from children born to the patriarch by a concubine,¶ and not a wife. Unfortunately, however, all this information is derived exclusively from the records of Israel and Judah, and we have no opportunity of knowing what these various tribes would have had to say in respect to their own or their kinsmen's genealogies.

But there is one great fact conveyed to us by these several traditions—namely, that an important section of the descendants of Abraham settled in the region to the south of the Dead Sea, and here the Israelites found a powerful people on their road from Egypt—a people whom they claimed as brethren,** and whom they were forced to admit belonged to the elder branch of Abraham's descendants.†† Despite all that could be said to the contrary, the Beni-Esau multiplied and prospered, and apparently succeeded in establishing a kingdom‡‡ whilst the Beni-Jacob were making bricks for Egyptian taskmasters in the land of Rameses. It is not unreasonable to conclude, therefore, that the Beni-Esau took, or at all events believed that they took, the possessions of their reputed ancestor.

Now, it is a very singular fact that in the story of the settlement in Egypt, although Jacob and his family

---

* Gen. xix. 30-38.   † Gen. xxv. 16; xvii. 20.   ‡ Gen. xxxvi. 11, 13, 14.
§ Gen. xvi. 3, 6.   ‖ Gen. xxv. 33.   ¶ Gen. xxv. 6.
** Num. xx. 14.   †† Gen. xxxiii. 3.   ‡‡ Gen. xxxvi. 31; Num. xx. 14

are represented as coming from the land of Canaan, there is no suggestion that they left any possessions behind them.* Nor is it at all probable, if the number of the family be correctly given—seventy souls—that they could have done so.† When, some centuries later, Israel and Judah successfully invaded the Promised Land, it was exclusively inhabited by hostile peoples; they nowhere met any claiming a common descent with themselves, nor did they seize on a single place which they claimed, not by right of conquest, but as having originally belonged to their ancestor Abraham. They appropriated the entire country by virtue of a covenant which they alleged had been made between Jahveh and their ancestor, but they did not believe that any portion had been reduced into possession until they by force of arms expelled or vanquished the inhabitants. If, on the removal of Jacob's family from Canaan to Egypt, any "possessions" had been left behind, the fact would assuredly have been preserved by tradition; and when we find not only no trace of such possessions, but that the elder branch of Abraham's descendants peaceably acquired and continuously retained the possessions south of the Dead Sea, we have a further reason for concluding that these possessions were traditionally believed to have been obtained by Abraham, and by him to have been transmitted to his eldest son (Ishmael—Esau). The acquisition of Esau's birthright by Jacob was a comparatively late invention, in order to give Israel precedence over Edom, for unquestionably Jacob and his family derived no material advantage from that discreditable transaction.

The traditions which connect the patriarchs with the land of Canaan expressly admit that the original in-

---

* Assuming the land of Canaan to be Palestine. † Exod. i. 5.

habitants then possessed it; and although, if we regarded these personages as historical, their temporary or even permanent residence in that country would be perfectly intelligible, still it is more natural to suppose that they were believed to have inhabited the region which came to be occupied on their supposed decease by those who claimed to be their descendants. We must, however, for reasons into which it would here be impossible to enter, reject the historical character of the patriarchs. In any event, however, we see reason to conclude that those who not only claimed descent from Abraham but who believed that they directly inherited his possessions, credited him with living in the same region in which they themselves dwelt.

The close resemblance between the traditions connected with Abraham and Isaac must strike every one. The family likeness throughout is complete, and many of the incidents related in the biography of the one are in almost identical language related in that of the other. We are, however, told much less about Isaac than about Abraham. We are justified in suspecting that Abraham was a creation of the nomadic mind, whilst Isaac was, so to speak, of Phœnician or Canaanitish extraction.

Passing over the alleged visits of Abraham to Canaan and Egypt, a tradition tells us that Abraham and Lot, respectively the son and grandson of Terah, prospered so greatly that " the land was not able to bear them that they might dwell together," and they accordingly separated.* In more prosaic language, the nomads who had come from the East found the region in which they first settled insufficient for their wants, and a section moved on into a new country. Lot selected " the plain of Jordan." " He journeyed east," and the uncle and nephew separated ; or, in other words, the

---

* Gen. xiii.

people which in after-times claimed descent from Lot—the Moabites and Ammonites—forced their way into the region lying to the east of the Dead Sea. But Lot having made this choice, what was the territory which was left to Abraham? We are informed that Abraham dwelt in the land of Canaan, but if "the Canaanite was then in the land" this was not possible, and we are therefore led to suspect that the country in which the patriarchs were unable to subsist together was on the south of the Dead Sea; and if this region was occupied by the parent stock of the nomads, the tide of migration, if withstood by the inhabitants of Palestine, would naturally roll up the eastern side of the Dead Sea and into the Jordan valley.

In the ancient record of the battle of the kings,* Abraham the Hebrew appears as the confederate of Mamre the Amorite and others aiding the kings of the Plain against Chedorlaomer and his allies, and in a much later production he is represented as "pitching his tent in the plain of Mamre," which by a still more recent gloss is said to have been identical with Hebron.† From this we would gather that in very early times the nomads formed an alliance with a section of the original inhabitants against a common enemy, who from whatever quarter operating ravaged the country between the lower Jordan and the Ælanitic Gulf. But the most definite information handed down respecting the habitation of Abraham is that which places his abode in the Negeb or south country, and even localises it with much apparent precision. He "dwelt between Kadesh and Shur, and sojourned in Gerar."‡

Before proceeding to consider the respective situations of these places, let us briefly notice some of the events related

---

* Gen. xiv.   † Gen. xiii. 18.   ‡ Gen. xx. 1.

of Abraham and of those who were, according to tradition, closely connected with him.

At the time when Abraham was sojourning in Gerar, Abimelech, the king of that country, conceived a passion for Sarah, Abraham's wife.* The same story is told of the patriarch on the occasion of a visit to Egypt,† and again of Isaac and Rebekah, when the same Abimelech, under precisely the same misapprehension that the wife was the sister, sought her in marriage; ‡ but in the last-mentioned narrative the king of Gerar is called the king of the Philistines. But this was not the only incident in Abraham's relations with the king of Gerar which repeated itself in the history of Isaac. Whilst Abraham was in Gerar a quarrel arose between his servants and those of the king, respecting the possession of a well, and subsequently Abraham made a covenant with Abimelech respecting a different well, giving to the king seven ewe lambs as witness that he had dug it. "Wherefore," it is added, " he called the place Beer-sheba, because there they sware both of them."§ In like manner we are told that when Isaac dwelt in "the valley" of Gerar, he digged again the wells which it is said had been dug in the days of his father Abraham, but which the Philistines had stopped, and gave to them the same names which had been given by Abraham. Disputes arose between the herdsmen of Gerar and those of Isaac respecting the wells, whereupon Isaac called the name of one well *Esek*, " because they strove with him," and the name of the other *Sitnah*, because they contended for the possession of it also. Isaac thereupon " removed from thence" and digged another well, to which he gave the name of Rehoboth, and " he removed from

---

* Gen. xx. 2–16.   † Gen. xii. 10–20.   ‡ Gen. xxvi. 6–11.
§ Gen. xxi. 22–32.

thence and went up to Beer-sheba;" and there Jahveh appeared to him, telling him to fear not, and that his seed would be multiplied for his father's sake. Whilst at Beer-sheba, Abimelech came to him from Gerar. This proceeding elicited from Isaac the question, "Wherefore come ye to me, seeing you hate me, and have sent me away from you?" Thereupon Abimelech, with "Phichol the captain of his army," proposed a league, which was concluded with the usual formalities, and Abimelech and his companions departed in peace. On the same day Isaac's servants, having dug a well and found water, Isaac called it "Shebah," the well of "the oath," and "therefore the name of the city was called Beer-sheba unto this day."*

In reviewing these narratives, we have no difficulty in detecting the ascription of the same legends to different individuals. There was, for instance, some noted well which received the name of Shaba or Sheba, and different accounts were given how it obtained this name. According to one, it was because Abraham dug it and purchased the undisputed title to it, by giving to Abimelech the king of Gerar seven ewe lambs, *Shaba* signifying seven; whilst, according to another, it was so named by Isaac because it was dug by his servants on the same day on which Abimelech, having found him in the land to which he had removed, made a covenant of peace with him, *Sheba* signifying an oath. But whilst still in the valley of Gerar, and before "he went up to Beer-sheba," we are told that Isaac reopened wells which had been originally dug by Abraham, and again gave to them the names which they received from his father. In the narrative of Abraham we look in vain for any mention of these names, but we discover the singular circumstance that disputes arose between Abraham's servants and those of Abime-

---

* Gen. xxvi. 15–33.

lech respecting some wells, and that there were similar differences between those of Isaac and the herdsmen of the king. In consequence of the latter, Isaac named the wells *Esek* and *Sitnah*, "contention" and "strife," and it is not an unreasonable conclusion that in the tradition of Abraham as it originally stood, these or names having a similar meaning found a place. We are, however, here brought once more into the presence of the celebrated "Waters of Contention and Strife," "of Massah and Meribah," the waters of Kadesh. These waters had evidently a tradition attached to them, which was carried back prior to the Exodus, and which connected their names with the disputes which arose between the reputed ancestors of the Hebrews and the original inhabitants of the land.

It is related of Hagar, that having conceived by Abraham, she despised Sarah, and fearing punishment at the hands of the latter, fled from the patriarch's house. The angel of Jahveh found her "by the fountain in the *midbhar*, on the way to Shur," ordered her to return, and told her that she was with child, and that her seed would "be multiplied exceedingly, that it should not be numbered for multitude." It is added that "she called the name of Jahveh that spake unto her, Thou God seest me; for she said, Have I also here looked after him that seeth me? Wherefore the well was called Beer-lahai-roi; behold, it is between Kadesh and Bered."*

Elsewhere we find a different version of the same tradition. Ishmael is a full-grown boy, and in consequence of Hagar's "mocking" Sarah she and her son are turned out of doors. It is related that she departed and wandered in "the wilderness of Beer-sheba" (a place, by the way, according to the sequence of events recorded, not yet thus named).

---

* Gen. xvi. 4-14.

The contents of her water-bottle being exhausted, she laid the boy under a shrub, and removed some distance off to avoid seeing him die. The angel of "Elohim thereupon spoke to her from heaven, promised that her son would become "a great nation," and "Elohim opened her eyes, and she saw a well of water," where she filled her bottle and gave the lad to drink. The narrative concludes: "And Elohim was with the lad, and he grew and dwelt in the wilderness, and he became an archer, and he dwelt in the wilderness of Paran, and his mother took him a wife out of the land of Egypt."*

Mention is again made of the fountain to which, according to tradition, Hagar had given the name of Beer-lahai-roi. It is related that Isaac "came from the way of the well Lahai-roi, for he dwelt in the south country (Negeb), and went out into a field to meditate," when lifting up his eyes he saw the camels of his father's servant approaching. The steward had returned from the house of Bethuel, in Mesopotamia, bringing with him Rebekah.† It is also stated that on Abraham's death Isaac inherited his possessions, the illegitimate offspring having been sent into the East country

---

* Gen. xxi. 9–21. We have here another indication of the tendency to impeach the purity of Abraham's descendants through Hagar. It was not sufficient that she should be a slave, but she must also be an Egyptian; or, according to another tradition which makes Ishmael the ancestor of his race, his wife was an Egyptian.

† Gen. xxiv. 62, 63. The accepted view that a country so distant as Mesopotamia, that is, the region between the Tigris and Euphrates, is here referred to is, I venture to think, erroneous. *Aram-Naharaim*, "Aram of the two rivers," was probably the country to the north-east of Edom and Moab. It was there that the king of Moab sought Balaam the seer (Num. xxii. 5; Deut. xxiii. 4), and it was the ruler of the same country who oppressed the Israelites (Jud. iii. 8). It was also known as Padan-aram, the house of Jacob's father-in-law, Laban, the land of the Beni-Kedem (Gen. xxix. 1). May it not have been Aram-Nahorim, Aram of the Nahorites (Gen. xxii. 20, 21), ח *Cheth* being transcribed ה *He*.

(*Kedem*) with gifts, and that he dwelt by the well Lahai-roi.*

Now it is a matter of some interest to ascertain, if possible, where this fountain was supposed to be situated. With the explanation of its name we need not trouble ourselves, but it is more probably supplied by the second than by the first of the two narratives to which we have referred.† It was "between Kadesh and Bered;" it was in the Negeb, or south country. It was in the possessions which Isaac was said to have inherited from his father Abraham, and if we are correct in treating the two narratives of Hagar as different versions of the same tradition, it was apparently in the neighbourhood of the wilderness of Paran.

That Hagar could not have been supposed to have journeyed far from Abraham's house when her water-bottle was exhausted, is a reasonable assumption, and it would therefore appear that the fountain or well of Lahai-roi was at all events in the region where Abraham dwelt. The patriarch, as we know, having "journeyed to the south country (*Negeb*), dwelt between Kadesh and Shur, and sojourned in Gerar," and the well of Lahai-roi was between Kadesh and Bered. The place Kadesh is common to both descriptions, but where, it will be asked, was Bered? The names Gerar and Bered are extremely dissimilar in English characters, but it is far different in Hebrew. The occurrence of the name Bered only furnishes one out of many instances in which in deciphering and copying the ancient scrolls in which the Hebrew records were preserved, the same name came in different places to assume different forms.‡

There is every reason for believing that the Bered which

---

* Gen. xxv. 5, 6, 11.

† In connection with the Elohim opening Hagar's eyes and causing her to see the well.

‡ גרר *Gerar*, ברד *Bered*. In the Rabbinical Hebrew characters the *Beth* and *Gimel* resembled each other still more closely.

in the tradition concerning Hagar is associated with Kadesh, is identical with the Gerar where Abraham sojourned, and which apparently lay between Kadesh and Shur; and it therefore becomes material to ascertain where Gerar was, with the view of fixing more precisely the locality of Kadesh, in which we are so much interested, and incidentally of throwing some light on the situation of the Negeb where Abraham is believed to have dwelt.

The statement that Abimelech, after concluding the covenant with Abraham at Beer-sheba, "returned into the land of the Philistines," and in the narrative of Isaac the allegation that he was "king of the Philistines," have not unnaturally led to the conclusion that the Philistines of the patriarchal traditions were the same as the well-known people who inhabited the seaboard between Judæa and the Mediterranean, and as a result of this assumption Gerar has been placed in this region. There are, however, strong reasons for calling in question the soundness of this reasoning.

Without allowing ourselves to be entangled in a disquisition on the origin of the extremely interesting people who play so prominent a part in Hebrew history, it may suffice to point out that the name, in its etymological signification, means simply the "wanderers" or "strangers," and is frequently rendered by the Greek translators $\alpha\lambda\lambda o\phi v\lambda o\iota$—that is to say, "other," or "strange tribes." That it was in this generic, rather than in its later specific sense, that the designation was used in the patriarchal narratives, appears from the surrounding circumstances. Abimelech, though said to be accompanied on his visits to Abraham and to Isaac by "Phichol, the chief captain of his host," is pre-eminently the chief of a pastoral people. He is rich in flocks and herds, and the differences which arise between his servants and those of the patriarchs relate to the possession of wells, whose acquisition would be specially valuable in the eyes of a nomadic or pastoral people. It is manifestly difficult to reconcile these characteristics with those of any nation which occupied the rich agricultural region forming the south-western portion of Palestine.

We find, in the Book of Chronicles, a reference to a place apparently having the same name as that of which Abimelech was king. In a passage to which we have already directed attention, it is related that in the reign of Hezekiah, the Simeonites " went to the entrance of Gedor, unto the east side of the valley, to seek pasture for their flocks." There they found good pasture, " for they of Ham had dwelt there of old," and they smote the Mehunim (Maonites) who were found there, " and dwelt in their rooms," and " some of them went unto Mount Seir."* There can be no reason for doubting that Gedor and the valley here referred to lay to the east of the Araba, and that the Maonites who were expelled were the same people who united with the Moabites and Ammonites in the invasion of Judah in the reign of Jehoshaphat.†

But on turning to the Septuagint version, we find that Gedor of the above passage appears as Gerar, or literally Γέραρα (Gerara); and on reverting to the Greek rendering of the name of the place of which Abimelech was king, we find it is reproduced in the same form.‡ This coincidence would in itself be entitled to but little weight, because, even assuming that Gerar was the name of the place to which the Simeonites went, it may have been quite distinct from

---

* 1 Chron. iv. 39–43. † 2 Chron. xx.
‡ The names Gerar and Gedor in Hebrew resembled each other so closely that it may have been impossible, in the absence of anything to assist him, for the scribe to distinguish one from the other. גרר *Gerar*, גדר *Gedor*.

the Gerar of the patriarchs. But there are some points of resemblance between these independent and far-distant references to Gerar or Gedor which cannot fail to arrest our notice.

Gedor was rich in pastures, and pre-eminently fitted for a pastoral people; and the same description equally applied to Gerar. Gedor had been inhabited of old by a people said to be the descendants of Ham, and therefore of a different race from the Hebrews, who claimed descent from Shem. Gerar was the country of the *Phelisti*, "the wanderers," "the strangers," the "other tribes;" it was the strange land in which Abraham sojourned on coming from the far East. Gedor had a valley which separated it from the adjoining territory on the west; for it is said that the Simeonites "went to the entrance of Gedor, even unto the east side of the valley, to seek pasture for their flocks;" and this valley, or *Gé* (strictly "ravine"), was apparently some well-known defile, in order to merit this specific mention. But in the narrative of Isaac[*] we are informed that when the patriarch quitted the country of the king of Gerar, "he pitched his tent in the valley of Gerar, and dwelt there," and reopened the wells of Abraham; and here in this valley arose the disputes respecting the possession of springs, which led to their being named Esek and Sitnah, the synonyms of Massah and Meribah. "The valley," here called *Nachal*, not *Gé*, is also treated in this passage as an important and distinctive place. These points of resemblance in the description of Gedor and Gerar, it must be admitted, are entitled to great weight, and go far to establish the accuracy of the LXX. rendering of the name in the Book of Chronicles, and the identity of the region in which the patriarchs were believed to have sojourned as strangers, with that which was suc-

---

[*] Gen. xxvi. 17.

cessfully invaded by the Simeonites in the reign of Hezekiah.*

It may possibly be objected that the tradition connected with Beer-sheba cannot be reconciled with the location of Gerar to the east of the Araba. It is believed that the site of the ancient Beer-sheba has been found at a place some thirty miles south of Hebron, and almost equi-distant between the head of the Araba and the Mediterranean.† Without discussing the accuracy of this identification, we may remark that there are as many difficulties in bringing to that place for the purposes of a covenant concerning a well, the king of the Philistines, properly so called, as the king of a pastoral people inhabiting the region between the Araba and the Arabian desert. But we must direct attention to the fact that, according to both the traditions connected with the "well of the oath" or the "well of the seven," it was not situated in the country of Abimelech. That which ascribes its nomination to Isaac‡ is the more complete of the two. According to it Isaac, when dwelling in Gerar, became so prosperous as to excite the apprehensions of Abimelech,—"Go from us, for thou art much mightier than we;" in other words, the Hebrew nomads became so numerous, that they were compelled to move onwards. Isaac then quitted Gerar, and "he pitched his tent in the valley of Gerar," but subsequently "he went up from thence to Beer-sheba." To this latter place he was followed by Abimelech, not for the purpose of raising any question about the right of possession in a well, but to make a friendly

---

* It may be only a curious coincidence, but Stephen of Byzantium notices a plain called *Syrmæón* (Συρμαῖον) as lying between the Nabathæans and the nomads (s. v.), and a place named *Gea* (Γέα), as being in the neighbourhood of Petra (s. v.). *Stephani Byzantii Ethnicorum quœ supersunt.* Ex recens. Aug. Meinekii. Berolini, 1849.

† *Bir-es-Sebá*, "the well of the lion." ‡ Gen. xxvi.

alliance. "We have not injured you whilst you were with us," said Abimelech, "swear now that you will not injure us." An alliance was accordingly concluded between Isaac and Abimelech—that is to say, between the Hebrew nomads and the people of a different race, who had permitted them to abide for a time in their country, but had ultimately compelled them to seek a home outside their frontier. To suppose that these people of a different race were the inhabitants of the maritime region bordering on Palestine, would be to contend that the original Terahitic migration came from the West.

In the narrative of Abraham in connection with the naming of Beer-sheba,* there is less completeness. We are not told where Abraham was when Abimelech and Phichol came to him and proposed a covenant, but it is noticeable that the king makes the same proposal as that ascribed to him in the tradition of Isaac—namely, the conclusion of a friendly alliance—"according to the kindness that I have done to thee thou shalt do unto me, and to the land wherein thou hast sojourned." The use of the past tense in the concluding words raises a presumption that Abraham had then quitted the country of Abimelech, which is confirmed by the statement that on the conclusion of the covenant Abimelech and Phichol "returned into the land of the Philistines." Abraham is said to have reproved the king in consequence of a well having been forcibly taken from him by the king's people; but this occurrence was evidently not recent, for Abimelech replied that he had never been informed of it, and only heard of it then for the first time. Then follows the account of the transfer of the seven ewe lambs to Abimelech as a witness that Abraham had digged the well where they made the covenant, and which on that

---

* Gen. xxi. 22–32.

account was named Beer-sheba. It is, however, not difficult to see that in this mode of accounting for the name of the well a confusion has taken place between the real covenant concluded between the patriarch and the king, and the previous contention respecting the possession of wells when Abraham was still in Gerar. It seemed a fitting ending to the story to make Abraham establish his title to the well which was named because of the covenant made there between him and Abimelech.

Where was "the well of the oath" which tradition associates with the covenant between Abraham-Isaac and Abimelech? If we accept the belief which in later times became established in Judæa, it was situated not improbably in the region to the south of Hebron. Isaac, having quitted Gerar, settled in "the valley," and having been expelled from the latter, "went up to Beer-sheba," a description which would tally with the course of a migration from the east towards the west, and would be the reverse of the course taken by the Simeonites, who, quitting the region in which Beer-sheba was situated, passed through the valley of Gedor in order to reach the country of that name. But there is an obvious difficulty in supposing that the ruler of a pastoral people inhabiting a district amongst, or on the eastern side of, the Idumæan mountains would have visited a nomadic tribe on the southern borders of the hills of Judæa for the purpose of making an alliance. Assuming the tradition of the friendly convention to be well-founded, we should rather be inclined to look for this *Beer-sheba* in the region in which, as we have shown, Abraham had his possessions where he became mighty and powerful, and where it might well be that the ruler of the pastoral people in the adjoining region on the east would seek him for the purpose of concluding a treaty of friendship in consideration of the kindness which had been shown to him—that is, to the migrating nomads on their arrival from the far East. Whether there was a well associated with such a tradition in the region to the south of the Dead Sea we have no means of knowing; but the statement that, on quitting the house of Abraham, Hagar found herself in the *midbhar* of Beer-sheba when her water-bottle was exhausted, would justify such a presumption—a presumption further strengthened by the allusion to the wilderness of Paran.* Subsequent to the settlement in Canaan, owing to the operation of causes which in themselves open up a vast and interesting field of inquiry, the scenes of some of the early nomadic traditions became transported into the new home, whilst still other traditions grew up equally foreign to the usages, both political and religious, of the parent stock from which Israel and Judah claimed descent. Whether from similarity of name, or from some other cause, it would therefore seem probable that a place or well lying between the hills of Judæa and the plateau of the Tih came to be associated in later times with the covenant between Abraham and Abimelech—an error which became all the more easy when the generic sense in which the denomination *Phelisti* was originally employed came to be confounded with the special appellation of the powerful people who inhabited the region between the highlands of Judæa and the Mediterranean Sea.†

In tracing the course of the Terahitic migration from the East, it is generally taken for granted that the Haran where the migration westward was temporarily arrested, was situated between the Euphrates and the Tigris. It seems

---

* Gen. xxi. 21.
† Jerome's description of Segor (Zoar) as being on the borders of Moab and separating it from the "terra Philistiim," would seem to support the above view (*Com.* Is. xv. 5).

more probable that Haran was the volcanic region which runs nearly parallel with the eastern coast of the Red Sea at a distance of some forty miles, extending between 28° and 25°, or even 24° North latitude. This region is still known as El Harrah, the name signifying the same as the Hebrew Haran, or more properly Charran, a place which is burnt or parched. Very little is known about this singular tract, owing to the predatory habits of the tribes by which its borders are inhabited.* If, as we are inclined to think, the Terahitic migration rolled up the eastern borders of the Red Sea, and effected settlements to the south of the Dead Sea previous to overrunning the Trans-Jordanic region and the "land of Canaan," "the Harrahs" would not improbably constitute the region in which Abraham was believed to have sojourned for a time, and where Terah died on the long journey from Ur of the Chaldees.† It is noteworthy that at the time of the Exodus no descendants of Abraham were settled in Palestine or in the Trans-Jordanic region. The northern border of Moab was formed by the Arnon,‡ which emptied itself into the Dead Sea. The Amorites who occupied the territory on the north bank of the stream were not of Terahitic descent. Behind them, and farther to the north, were none claiming that lineage. It seems therefore inconceivable, assuming the parent stock of the Hebrew nation to have come from the land of the Chaldees, that having crossed Arabia or Syria the tide of migration could have flowed from the north to the south. The direction must have been quite the contrary, a conclusion which is corroborated by the fact that the land which lay on the east of the Red Sea and Araba was, from the patri-

---

* For a description of El Harrah, see Burton, *Land of Midian Revisited*, i. 325; ii. 104, 144.
† Gen. xi. 26–32.   ‡ Now named the Wady-el-Mojeb.

archal period, inhabited by tribes claiming descent from Abraham.*

It is universally assumed that by "the land of Canaan" was always meant, even in the earliest traditions of the patriarchs, the country lying between the Jordan valley and the Mediterranean. The accuracy of this conclusion is very questionable. We have seen that, so far as we have the means of judging, Abraham, or the parent stock of emigrants from the East, with which he was traditionally associated, settled in the region to the south of the Dead Sea, and therefore if the traditions in their original shape stated that he quitted Haran and came into the land of Canaan,† then his land of Canaan must have been in Idumæa. In dealing, in however cursory a manner, with this interesting question, we are beset with the difficulties arising from the modifications undergone by the patriarchal traditions subsequent to the settlement in the Cis-Jordanic region, owing to the natural tendency of the settlers to associate their reputed ancestors with places which had already acquired a high reputation for sanctity. For example, if we treat as historical and connected the narrative contained in Gen. xii., Abraham on quitting Haran entered Canaan, commonly so called, from the north-east, passed through the region to the east of Jericho, and travelled southward, and thence, owing to a famine, went into Egypt. We cannot, however, for reasons already stated, accept this as an accurate account of the course of the Terahitic migration. The statement that on the occasion

---

* It must be understood that these observations do not apply to the general tide of Semitic migration from the East, but only to the advance of that section which is known as the Terahitic branch of the Semitic race.

† Gen. xii. 5. The Septuagint (Cod. Vat.) differs from the Hebrew text of Gen. xii. 5 in omitting the last clause, " and into the land of Canaan they came." In the Alexandrine Codex the passage is similar to that in the Hebrew.

of this journey Jahveh promised to give this territory to Abraham's seed, indicates that the record now before us is of a creation posterior to the settlement on the west of Jordan by tribes claiming descent from that patriarch.

The emigrants from the far East were probably well content when, partly by sufferance, partly by violence, they succeeded in establishing themselves in the pleasant valleys of Idumæa. For them the region lying to the west of the Dead Sea and stretching towards the Mediterranean was a *terra incognita*, save so far as the fame of its fertility and its resources may have been conveyed by itinerant merchants. That it excited their cupidity we have no evidence; certainly there is no tradition of any attempt being made to take it by conquest. At the period to which we refer—namely, previous to the Hebrew bondage in Egypt —the region south of the Dead Sea was the land of the Hebrews. It was there that the possessions of Abraham's descendants were to be found; there was situated the Mount in which the God of the Hebrews had his abode; and it was from thence that came the stock whose descendants subsequently quitted Egypt under the circumstances which furnish the subject-matter of the present inquiry.

In the account of the Hebrew settlement in Egypt, it is stated that Jacob and his family were driven by famine to quit Canaan and accept the protection and hospitality of the Pharaoh. Here, again, we are compelled to reject the accepted belief that the land between the Mediterranean and the Jordan was referred to. The stock from which the Hebrew captives in Egypt was derived had no possessions in this region, and therefore if the name Canaan occurred in the tradition in its early form, some other country must have been intended—namely, the territory lying on the east of the Araba, the land of the Hebrews.

Let us now turn to the records of Egyptian history, and

ascertain whether they throw any light upon this interesting question.

From a period long anterior to the Exodus, the nomad tribes of Arabia were known to the Egyptians as the Shasu, and their principal home was called the land of Aduma, probably the Edom and Idumæa of later times. At the commencement of the nineteenth dynasty these tribes, either trespassing on the indulgence of previous Pharaohs in tolerating their settlement in the region adjacent to the Delta, or emulating the prowess of the Hyksos, assumed so formidable an attitude as to provoke a war at the hands of Seti, the first king of that dynasty and father of Ramses II., the celebrated Sesostris. The records of this war are still preserved in the illustrations and inscriptions which adorn the walls of the great hall of the temple at Karnak.

Egyptologists have deciphered and interpreted the inscriptions, whilst the illustrations furnish a key by which it is possible to form a general idea of the nature of the country in which the campaign took place. The inscription which records the first victory, states that "in the first year of King Seti there took place, by the strong arm of Pharaoh,* the annihilation of the hostile Shasu, from the fortress of Khetam of the land of Zalu, as far as Kan'aan;" and in the accompanying illustration the boundary of the land of the Shasu is marked by the hill-fortress of Kan'aan, near which a stream is represented falling into a lake.

There can be no question that the illustration of the lake with the river flowing into it was intended to represent the Dead Sea with one of its affluents, and we are therefore forced to conclude that the hill-fortress of Kan'aan was in the vicinity of that sea. Brugsch Bey suggests that it was in the Araba, but it seems much more probable that the

---

* Brugsch Bey, *Egypt under the Pharaohs*, ii. 13.

stronghold of the Shasu of the land of Aduma lay between the Araba and the Arabian desert, and near the southern extremity of the Dead Sea. Specific mention of this hill-fortress of Kan'aan is made in the great Harris papyrus, where it is spoken of as being in the land of Zahi. The name Aduma appears to have been applied in the same wide sense in which Edom and Midian were used in the early Hebrew traditions; or like Kedem—the east country. The Shasu were from the land of Aduma, so, without necessarily implying any connection between the words, they were the Beni-Kedem, the children of the East. The land of Zahi was a region which evidently included the districts to the south of the Dead Sea.

It is at all events a significant fact, that not only are no traces to be seen in the Egyptian records of the application of the name Canaan to the country lying between the Mediterranean and the Jordan valley, but we invariably find that this country is termed the land of the Ruthen, or Rutennu or Lutennu. It was thus known in the time of Thutmes III., a Pharaoh of the eighteenth dynasty (circa 1600 B.C.), and it was similarly designated so late as the period of the Exodus. There is no mention of the Rutennu seeking sustenance in Egypt, or yielding to the temptation of effecting a settlement on the Egyptian frontier. The case is far different with the Shasu. Independently of the hostile incursions which provoked the first Seti to war, there are unmistakable proofs that the nomads obtained from time to time permission to enter the rich pastures on the east of the Delta. In the very curious and interesting document of the reign of Mineptah, the successor of Ramses II., already referred to, we find almost a paraphrase of what was stated to have occurred when Jacob and his family came from Canaan to Egypt, It is apparently the report of a high Egyptian official.

"Another matter for the satisfaction of my master's heart. We have carried into effect the passage of the tribes of the Shasu from the land of Aduma through the fortress (Khetam) of Mineptah (Hotephima) to the lakes of the city Pitom, which are situated in the land of Thuku, in order to feed themselves and to feed their herds on the possessions of Pharaoh, who is there a beneficent sun for all peoples."*

From this curious record we learn not only how the Hebrew settlement in Egypt came to be effected, but we have unmistakable proof who the relieved nomads were, and from what region they came. They came from the land of Aduma, and that land beyond all question was not Palestine. They were termed generically Shasu, and half a century previously they, or the people with whom they were identified, possessed a hill-fortress called Kan'aan in the neighbourhood of the Dead Sea. It is not easy to carry further the demonstration that the nomadic tribes which from time to time obtained relief from the Pharaohs, and which were permitted to pasture their flocks on the north-eastern frontier of Egypt—or, as the Hebrew records express it, in the land of Goshen—came from the country lying on the east of the Araba; and it is at least probable that the Canaan referred to in the earliest patriarchal traditions was the same to which reference was made in the Egyptian records.

In the patriarchal traditions we find two allusions to a place named Shur. Hagar was found by the angel "by the fountain on the way to Shur,"† which she afterwards named Lahai-roi, and which we are further informed lay between Kadesh and Bered; and Abraham is said to have dwelt between Kadesh and Shur.‡ In the account of the

---

* Pap. Anastasi, vi. pp. 4, 5. The above is Brugsch Bey's translation of the passage (*Egypt under the Pharaohs*, ii. 127).
† Gen. xvi. 7. ‡ Gen. xx. 1.

twelve tribes descended from Ishmael it is stated that "they dwelt from Havilah unto Shur, that is before Egypt, as thou goest toward Assyria,"* and elsewhere we learn that Ishmael settled in the *midbhar* of Paran.† In dealing with these traditions we should, in the absence of other evidence, be inclined to conclude that Shur was the name of a place or region familiar to those amongst whom these traditions grew up—a presumption which would, however, be rebutted if it could be shown that the traditions underwent modifications in later times. *À priori* we should therefore infer that Shur was known *eo nomine* to the nomads who had come from the East, and that it admitted of being spoken of for the purpose of fixing, as in the case of Hagar, the way or road in which she found the fountain of Lahai-roi; or in that of Abraham, one of the limits of the district within which he dwelt; or in that of Ishmael and his descendants, the region in which they exercised dominion. But it is obviously in the highest degree improbable that the nomads could in any of these instances have referred to an insignificant Egyptian fortification known to its possessors by an entirely different name,‡ and with whose existence it is not unreasonable to conclude they were wholly unacquainted; whilst if we are correct in placing the scenes of the events referred to in the patriarchal traditions to the east of the Araba, it would have been equally delusive and uninstructive to refer to a place in a foreign country, distant upwards of one

---

* Gen. xxv. 18. † Gen. xxi. 21.

‡ Brugsch Bey states that a small fortification existed on the Egyptian frontier not far from the Serbonian lake, to which the Egyptians gave the name of Anbu, signifying a "wall" or "fence," and he suggests that the Hebrews translated Anbu, Shur, which in their language had the same meaning. "It is this Shur," says the Bey with confidence, "which is mentioned in Holy Scripture" (*L'Exode*, 14).

hundred and twenty miles, and separated from the scene of events by an inhospitable desert. Let us see if no other explanation can be found which is more reconcilable with the probabilities of the case and with the evidence at our command.

The nomads who made their way westwards across the steppes and deserts of the Arabian peninsula found their further advance arrested in the more southerly region by the Red Sea. On following its shore in a northerly direction they saw beyond its waters lofty mountains, and finally they discovered that it terminated in a narrow gulf, the opposite side of which was formed by precipices descending to the water's edge. Above the head of this gulf opened a broad and desolate valley, apparently a continuation of the chasm in which were contained the waters of the narrow sea, and bounded on its western side by a continuous but rugged wall of rock. If they had the curiosity to scale this wall, they saw stretching before them, towards the setting sun, a barren waste seared by the fissures of streamless *wadys* and dotted by eminences covered with a sparse vegetation. But though further advance was thus repelled, the nomads learned that on the opposite side of that desert lay a powerful kingdom teeming with wealth, whose people could supply from their granaries sufficient to meet the wants of the famished tribes which were from time to time compelled to seek their help, and whose merchants were ever ready to purchase slaves and every costly product conveyed to them from the East. That kingdom was Egypt, and with that kingdom was necessarily associated the forbidding wilderness by which it could alone be approached. To the pastoral tribes which settled amongst the mountains of Idumæa the vast uninhabitable table-land was simply known as a region which was over against Egypt—a region whose precipitous wall reared in front of their mountain slopes seemed a visible protest against any advance in that direction.

The word Shur in ancient Hebrew and in modern Arabic signifies "a wall," and it is certainly no extravagant presumption to suppose that the inhabitants of the region on the east of the Araba gave this name to the long line of cliffs supporting the table-land across which lay the road to Egypt. If we accept this explanation, there is no difficulty in understanding the reference to Shur in the patriarchal traditions, and reconciling them with those conclusions already forced upon us respecting the region in which the events related are supposed to have taken place. If Abraham was said to have dwelt between Kadesh and Shur, it would be another way of saying that the nomads settled in some portion of western Idumæa. In like manner, the fountain of Lahai-roi would be in the same region, and lie in the path of any one proceeding westwards or in the direction of Egypt. And, again, Ishmael and his descendants, who dwelt from Havilah unto Shur, that is before Egypt, were thought to have occupied a region lying between Havilah, some unknown place to the east of the Araba, and Shur the great wall which was reared as it were a rampart before Egypt. In all these instances, assuming the traditions to have had their original home in the region where the descendants of the patriarchs undoubtedly settled previous to the Hebrew captivity in Egypt, the Shur thus treated as a well-known and clearly marked boundary; and "objectively" referred to by the inhabitants of that region as being "before Egypt," was therefore in all probability the great natural barrier extending from end to end the entire length of the western side of the Araba.

The next allusion to Shur is in the traditions of the Exodus. On quitting Egypt the Israelites traversed the wilderness of Shur, and proceeded three days without finding water.* It is, however, apparent that a wilderness so extensive could have been none other than that now known as the Tih, and we are therefore justified in concluding that the immense wilderness stretching from the western wall of the Araba to Egypt was known, at all events to the nomads, as the *midbhar* of Shur. This is undoubtedly the wilderness referred to by Jephthah as having been "walked through" by Israel on the way from Egypt to the Red Sea.†

An account is given of a fillibustering raid made by David, when under the protection of the Philistines, on some tribes which apparently enjoyed the friendship of the latter.‡ It is recorded that "David and his men invaded the Geshurites, and the Gezrites (Gerzites, *Heb.*), and the Amalekites, for those nations were of old the inhabitants of the land, as thou goest to Shur, even unto the land of Egypt." On his return, David exhibited his prudence at the expense of his candour, by telling Achish that he had come from attacking "the south of Judah, and the south of the Jerahmeelites, and the south of the Kenites." In effect he "saved neither man nor woman alive, lest," to quote his own words, "they should tell on us." From the name of the tribe first mentioned it would seem that it was called after the territory on whose border it lived, and that it and the others on which David made the raid inhabited the comparatively fertile strip of land intervening between southern Philistia and the wilderness. The references to Shur in connection with Saul's campaign against the Amalekites§ have been already alluded to.‖ They, like the others, equally point to the conclusion that Shur embraced the table-land extending from the Egyptian frontier to the Araba.

---

* Exod. xv. 22.
† Jud. xi. 16. ‡ 1 Sam. xxvii. 8–12.
§ 1 Sam. xv. 7. ‖ See *ante*, p. 262.

In reviewing our cursory examination of this portion of the patriarchal traditions we conclude that Abraham and Isaac were supposed to have settled permanently or ultimately in the same region, which was called the Negeb, or south country; that this was in the vicinity of a district known as Gerar; and while in the case of Abraham the place of permanent abode was localised between Kadesh and Shur, in that of Isaac it was placed near the well of Lahai-roi, which was between Kadesh and Bered, and must have been in the same region where Abraham dwelt. In respect to the locality of the Negeb here referred to, and the places enumerated, we infer that the Gerar-Bered of the patriarchal traditions was identical with the Gedor of the Simeonite emigration, and lay to the east of the Araba, and probably consisted of the rich pastures found on the eastern borders of southern Idumæa, and was separated from the region bounding it on the west by a remarkable valley or ravine, in or near which were springs which were known as the waters of "strife" and "contention." But regarding the Kadesh and Gerar of Abraham as identical with the Kadesh and Bered of Hagar, we conclude that the first-named of these places (Kadesh) could not have been far distant from the second, and was therefore in or near "the valley" adjoining Gerar, where, according to tradition, the herdsmen of the ruler of that country disputed with those of the patriarchs respecting the user of certain springs. But the patriarchal place of abode near the well of Lahai-roi was in the same region, and was in the neighbourhood of the *midbhar* of Paran, where Ishmael removed and settled on his expulsion from his paternal home; and we therefore infer that all these places were situated on the east of the Araba, and that the Negeb in which lay the possessions of the patriarchs was in the same region, on the south of the Dead Sea.

CHAPTER XI.

LET us once more return, and take up the broken thread of the narrative of the migration from Egypt. If, on the one hand, following the traditions of the Exodus, we have been constrained to lead the Hebrews across the table-land of the Tih to the head of the Ælanitic Gulf, on the other we are gratified by finding that this route corresponds with the ancient traditions respecting the locality of the Mount of God. But as the result of our further investigation of traditions which still live in Idumæa, and which may be traced with unbroken continuity to the dawn of the Christian era, we see that the region lying on the east of the Araba was regarded as the scene of the great miracle attributed to Moses in the neighbourhood of the Mount of God, and that there was situated the *midbhar* from which the spies were believed to have been sent forth to explore the land of Canaan. Pursuing our inquiries into the early history of Edom and its situation relatively to Judah, we have seen that there is nothing incompatible with the tradition that the emancipated Hebrews never penetrated beyond its borders, in supposing that they entered and temporarily occupied the region in immediate proximity to the Araba on the east; whilst our brief review of the patriarchal traditions points to the same quarter as that in which the released captives would find tribes claiming a common descent, prepared to sympathise with them in their misfortunes, and possibly to assist them with material aid. If the records of the Exodus, fragmentary and disconnected though they be, indicate in no uncertain fashion the course taken by the liberated Hebrews, the still earlier traditions of the Hebrew race point with no less certainty to the region to which they would direct their steps on quitting the land of their bitter servitude, and where they would find the Mount of Elohim, already sacred to the Hebrews' God.*

On quitting Elim, the Israelites entered the wilderness of Sin, which lay between Elim and Sinai; but if Elim lay at the head of the Ælanitic Gulf, the *midbhar* of Sin was unquestionably the Araba; and if the latter lay between Elim and Sinai, the mountain must have been contiguous to it. As, however, the Araba terminates at its upper extremity by dropping into the hollow of the Dead Sea, and as on the western side the cliffs, though precipitous, nowhere present the appearance of a distinct mountain, Sinai must be sought for on the eastern border, and probably at some distance from Elim, because a wilderness interposed which was not traversed in a single day, and in which some notable events took place. Here—that is to say, on the journey between Elim and Sinai—the Israelites for the first time obtained manna,† and here, according to tradition, were the graves of those who perished from eating the quails which had been carried by the wind across the adjoining sea.‡

There can be little doubt that some spot in the wilderness between Elim and Sinai came, by reason of some physical peculiarities, to have attached to it the legend that there the Israelites perished in great numbers, and that the place of their sepulture was there to be seen. The legend had possibly some foundation in fact. But, however this may be, it is somewhat curious that at about a day's journey from Akaba the bed of the Araba is converted into a marsh, which is known to the Arabs as El Daba, or Taba, or

---

* Exod. iii. 1.
† Exod. xvi. 12-15.
‡ Num. xi. 34.

Deffieh, and is chosen for a cemetery. It would seem to correspond with the Kibroth-hat-tavah of the Hebrew tradition.

According to the narrative in Exodus, the Israelites next arrived at Rephidim;* whilst, according to that in Numbers, the next station was Hazeroth;† and in the former record the succeeding events take place in the vicinity of the Mount of God, whilst in the latter they occur in the *midbhar* of Paran.‡ Where was or were Rephidim-Hazeroth? To this question it is impossible to give a positive reply. Looking to the plural forms of the words, it is doubtful whether any precise spot was thus designated; and all we can fairly conclude is that the Rephidim-Hazeroth were reached through some valley opening from the mountain range on the right-hand side of the Araba. But it was at or near these places that the Kenite Sheikh met Moses and the Israelites when they were encamped before the Mount of God; and as we have identified the Kenites with the Troglodytes (cave-dwellers), we can have no hesitation in regarding them as the then inhabitants of Petra. Moses was, however, the Sheikh's son-in-law, and we here find an additional reason why he should have led them to this spot, and why the people under his leadership should have been so well received by the Kenites. The Israelites would therefore seem to have quitted the Araba in the neighbourhood of Petra, and to have established themselves, at least for a time, in or near what was afterwards the site of the Nabathæan capital.

When we picture to ourselves Petra with the *Sik*, and the brook winding its way through chasms apparently cleft expressly to give it passage through mountains of living rock, we can have no difficulty in understanding how either

---

* Exod. xvii. 1.   † Num. xi. 35.
‡ Num. xii. 16.

at the time, the thirsty wayfarers, emerging from the Araba, came to believe that their leader had gone on before them to the Mount of God,* and with his wand had cleft the mountain in order to give passage to the water of which they stood in so much need; or how, in after-times, the legend that he had done so came to be suggested by the extraordinary physical peculiarities of the region. The course of the brook on quitting Petra is unknown; it is not necessary that the Israelites should have penetrated as far as the cave-abounding city before slaking their thirst in its waters.

We have now, following the traditions, arrived in the immediate neighbourhood of the Mount of Elohim, indifferently called Sinai, Horeb, Paran; and we can no longer postpone the attempt to ascertain, if possible, its locality. It is perhaps needless to say that our investigations point but to one conclusion—namely, the identification of the Mount of God with Mount Hor, the *Har-Ha-Har*, the Mount of Mounts.

Assuming that we have rightly followed the track of the Hebrews, we can have no hesitation in arriving at this conclusion, because there is confessedly no mountain in the region where, *ex hypothesi*, the emigrants have now arrived, which so fully satisfies the requirements of Mount Sinai. It is the loftiest of the mountains which overhang the Araba, and lying to the west of Petra its position corresponds with that of the mount to which Moses led the flock of his father-in-law on "the back side of the desert."† But there are other reasons why, independently of the conclusions already arrived at respecting the track of the Hebrews, we are led to identify Mount Hor with Mount Sinai.

We have already pointed out that as on quitting Elim the

---

* Exod. xvii. 5. † Exod. iii. 1.

Israelites entered the wilderness between that place and Mount Sinai, the latter mountain must almost certainly have stood on the border of the Araba. We have, however, a somewhat singular confirmation of this inference in the narrative of the first occasion on which the liberated slaves were gratified and encouraged by seeing "the glory" of their God.

The Israelites had journeyed across the great wilderness of Shur by the direct and well-known route, and, descending through the steep defile overhanging Elim-Elath, had encamped for a time at the head of the gulf. They then turned their footsteps towards their promised home, the attractions of which had been held out to them by their leaders as an inducement to brave the terrors and perils of their journey on leaving Egypt.* Until they quitted the desolate table-land of the Tih, and left the track familiar to the caravans trading between Egypt and the East, they scarcely regarded themselves as having left the land of their bondage; and on setting out from Elim they seem to have expected to enter at once into that country of figs and pomegranates which was their promised haven. On entering the Araba, and looking onwards over its desolate waste, their disappointment was immense, and the crushed spirit of the slaves induced a bitter regret at having left the country in which they were at all events sufficiently fed. They murmured, and apparently hesitated to proceed, when their leaders encouraged them by saying, "At even, then ye shall know that Jahveh hath brought you out from the land of Egypt, and in the morning, then shall ye see the glory of Jahveh."† Then followed a specific promise: "Jahveh shall

---

* This strongly corroborates the inference that the liberated captives were accompanied by leaders well acquainted with the region to which they were taking them —namely, the land of Aduma.

† Exod. xvi. 6, 7.

give you in the evening flesh to eat, and in the morning bread to the full,"* and, on the following day, " Aaron spake unto the whole congregation of the children of Israel, and they looked toward the wilderness, and behold, the glory of Jahveh appeared in the cloud."† In order to fully appreciate the meaning of this narrative, it is necessary to collate it with the corresponding tradition recorded in the Book of Numbers.‡ The Israelites obtained manna for the first time on entering the Araba, and they appear to have been dissatisfied with it as a substitute for the food to which they had been accustomed. They rebelled, and possibly threatened to return; and then it was that Moses told them that if they only proceeded on their journey they would be rewarded at even by finding themselves in a region where they would obtain everything necessary for their wants; when they would be practically convinced that they had in very truth quitted the land of Egypt, and entered the fertile and productive country to which he promised to conduct them. And furthermore, he promised them that on the morning of the following day they would witness with their own eyes tl e glory of the God who was prepared to take them under his special care. The slaves yielded, and proceeded on their journey. At nightfall they reached one of the valleys opening into the fertile region on the east of the Araba, and on the following morning, when " they looked towards the wilderness,"§ they saw the first rays of the rising sun dissipating the cloud which enveloped the summit of Mount Hor, and producing on its striated rocks that marvellous play of brilliant colours which still continues to arrest the attention of the traveller ascending the Araba from the south.

It will be recollected that when Moses received his mission from Jahveh to proceed to Egypt, with a view to the libera-

---

* Exod. xvi. 8.   † Exod. xvi. 10.   ‡ Num. xi.
§ Exod. xvi. 10.

tion of the Israelites, certain difficulties presented themselves
to the mind of the former. In the first place, the captives
might refuse to accept his leadership; and in the next, the
Pharaoh might refuse to allow the people to depart. It became necessary, therefore, that the appointed leader should
be armed with conclusive credentials, and that he should be
in a position to offer an adequate inducement to the Hebrews
to quit Egypt under his guidance.* The credentials consisted mainly in the gift of thaumaturgy, but one of the
"tokens" indicated was that when the captives had been
led out of Egypt they should serve the Elohim on the particular mountain where Moses received his mission.† The
inducement offered to the Israelites to quit Egypt, independently of the natural desire to acquire freedom, was that
they should be led into a land flowing with milk and
honey. In after times, when the successful invasion of the
Trans- and Cis-Jordanic regions had been effected, it was
assumed that the occupation of these extensive territories was
the prize held up before the eyes of the oppressed slaves.
But not only is this opposed to probability, but it is nega-
tived by indelible traces still found in the ancient
traditions. We know, as a matter of history, that during
the period of the Hebrew settlement in Egypt wars were
not infrequent between the powerful Pharaohs and the inhabitants of Palestine, and that treaties were concluded on a
footing which recognised the prowess and the dignity of
the respective adversaries.‡ It would therefore have been
perfectly preposterous for Moses, however great his command
of magical powers, to have sought to persuade the elders of
Israel, and through them the people, to quit Egypt in the

---

* Exod. iii. 11-22; iv. 1-17.   † Exod. iii. 12.
‡ See the treaty between Ramses II. (Sesostris) and the king of
Khita, translated by Goodwin (*Records of the Past*, iv. 25).

hope of being able forthwith to overrun and occupy a country whose people and whose resources were not despised by their masters, the Egyptians. And so far as we can judge from the evidence before us, Moses did nothing of the kind. There was not the slightest suggestion that the Israelites were about to exchange the hardships of captivity for the perils of an arduous invasion. What they did anticipate was that they would find a home amongst kindred tribes, and possibly, with the assistance of those whom they regarded as brethren, be enabled to establish themselves in some region where the struggle for existence would prove less keen than in the country where they had forfeited their political freedom, and where they were compelled to eat the bitter bread of servitude. But Palestine was far removed from their thoughts. So little did they know about it, that they were at a later period obliged to send spies to acquaint themselves with the nature and character of the inhabitants, and with the resources of the country. They had absolutely no connection with its people. The only land of which the son-in-law of Jethro could tell them was that where he himself had lived, a land which supplied the wants of a pastoral people—a land in which they would receive a welcome, and where they would find the mountain on which dwelt the God who grieved for them in their affliction, who bethought him that they were of the same kindred with those who lived and prospered in the well-watered and fertile region which that mountain overlooked; who was prepared to take them under his gracious protection, and to renew with them the covenant he had made with their fathers. From the land of the Hebrews they had come; to the land of the Hebrews, the abode of the God of the Hebrews, they were about to return. " Thou shalt come, thou and the elders of Israel, unto the king of Egypt, and ye shall say unto him, Jahveh, God of the Hebrews, hath met with us; and now let us go, we beseech thee, three days' journey into the wilderness, that we may sacrifice to Jahveh our God."*

A consideration of Ark worship, which from the records in the Pentateuch would seem to have been so intimately connected with the religion of the Hebrews during their migration from Egypt, does not come within the scope of the present inquiry. It is generally assumed that the visible manifestation of the glory of God, the Shechinah of the Targumists, appeared over the Ark of the Covenant, or in the Tabernacle. Without entering into the inquiry how or when Ark worship came to be established, it will be universally conceded that the visible manifestation of the Deity could not have taken place above the Ark before the latter was constructed, and it is not suggested that the Ark, or the Tabernacle which contained it, was introduced until subsequent to the promulgation of the Law on Mount Sinai. The word Shechinah is derived from the Hebrew *schachan* (to dwell), and as applied to the Deity, means the place of his abode. The object in constructing the Tabernacle was that Jahveh might "dwell" among his people.† Again, there is the promise, "I will dwell among the children of Israel, and be their God;"‡ and in the decree of Cyrus for the building of the second temple at Jerusalem, the Persian monarch is represented as saying, "The God that hath caused his name to 'dwell' there."§ But whilst the released Hebrews were still on their way to the Mount of God, they naturally entertained the belief that Jahveh "dwelt" there, and they were not improbably led to expect that some manifestation would take place upon that mountain in order to justify the story which Moses had told them of his mission. But all doubt is removed on this point by the statement that, on the conclu-

---

* Exod. iii. 18.
† Exod. xxv. 8.   ‡ Exod. xxix. 45.   § Ezra vi. 12.

sion of the covenant between Jahveh and the people, "Moses went up into the mount, and a cloud covered the mount, and the glory of Jahveh abode ('dwelt') upon Mount Sinai, and the cloud covered it six days."* It is then added, that on "the seventh day he called unto Moses out of the midst of the cloud, and the sight of the glory of Jahveh was like devouring fire on the top of the mount in the eyes of the children of Israel."† This is not, however, the only version of what is said to have occurred on the conclusion of the solemn covenant. In the same chapter, but coming from a different source, the record of the tradition takes the following form:—"Then went up Moses and Aaron, Nadab and Abihu, and seventy of the elders of Israel; and they saw the God of Israel; and there was under his feet as it were a paved work of a sapphire stone, and as it were the body of heaven in his clearness. And upon the nobles of the children of Israel he laid not his hand: also they saw God, and did eat and drink."‡

We are now able to appreciate what took place on the journey from Elim to Sinai, where Aaron called on the children of Israel to appear for the first time "before Jahveh," and when they "looked toward the wilderness, and behold, the glory of Jahveh appeared in the cloud."§ They then saw what in after-times came to be known as the Shechinah, and what they were readily induced to believe was the manifestation of the glory of their protecting God. But the voice of tradition afterwards represented in varied language the astounding phenomenon. Whilst some, in whom the sentiment of awe was predominant, pictured to themselves the Divine manifestation under the semblance of "devouring fire;" others, with a keener sense of the Beautiful,

---

* Exod. xxiv. 15, 16.
† Exod. xxiv. 17.   ‡ Exod. xxiv. 9–11.   § Exod. xvi. 10.

and a closer approach to the True, treasured up the recollection that the glory of their God seemed to rest on a pavement of sapphire, and to be lost above in the azure vault of heaven.

It has been noticed that the expression *Hor-ha-Har*, rendered "Mount Hor," is the only instance in the Hebrew where the name precedes the designation. This fact, coupled with the notorious unreliability of the Masoretic pointing in proper names, may well induce a doubt whether in thus describing the mountain the relaters of the early traditions intended to give it a specific name. What they did call it was much more probably *Har-ha-Har*, "Mount, the Mount," which would seem to have been an idiomatic form of denoting a mountain pre-eminently distinguished. It is thus used to denote the range of the Lebanon, on the northern border of Israel;* and in the traditions of the Exodus, if used in this sense, could alone have been applied to the Mount of God. This conclusion, however, corresponds with the chain of reasoning which, as has been shown, points to the site of Sinai, on the east of the Araba. Mount Hor overlooks this valley, and if Mount Sinai stood in the same region, it is impossible to suppose that the voice of tradition would have given to any neighbouring mountain the proud designation of *Har-ha-Har*—*the* mountain, κατ' ἐξοκήν. At the commencement of the Christian era, the situation of the mountain on which tradition declared that Aaron had died was well known in Judæa; but it is significant, and to a certain extent corroborative of our reading of its Hebrew designation, that the great Jewish historian does not name it as Hor, but simply describes it as a very high mountain overlooking the metropolis of the Arabs, previously known as Arke, but then called Petra.†

---

* Num. xxxiv. 7. † *A. J.* iv. 4. 7.

To the identification of Mount Hor with Mount Sinai it will be objected with much force that it is strange, and apparently unaccountable, that the Mount of God should have been termed in certain traditions Sinai or Horeb, and never by the peculiar designation *Hor*, or *Har-ha-Har*, whilst in those connected with, or referring to, the death of Aaron the latter expression should be invariably employed. It would be no less idle than disingenuous to attempt to ignore the gravity of this objection. It must therefore be carefully considered.

It will be seen that it rests *primâ facie* on the assumption that the Pentateuch is the work of a single hand, and that the various traditions we have found it necessary to examine form a continuous narrative. But its fragmentary character has been already demonstrated, and if the Mount of God came to be known in different traditions as Sinai and Horeb, it is certainly not impossible that in still another tradition it should, in connection with a particular event, be referred to, not by either of its specific names, but by an expression denoting its pre-eminence. It will be admitted that " the Mount of Mounts " would have been no inappropriate mode of describing the Mount of God, and it is important to note that the mountain on which Aaron was said to have died, and from which the Israelites set forth to compass the land of Edom when they failed to obtain permission to pass through that country, is by a number of circumstances very closely connected with the Mount of God.

It was at Kadesh the Israelites abode many days, and from that point they turned and took their journey by the way of the Red Sea. Kadesh was, however, in close proximity to Mount Hor, and both equally stood on the border of the kingdom of Edom.* But Kadesh was also,

---

* Num. xx. 16, 22, 23.

as we have seen, in the immediate neighbourhood of Mount Sinai, and we are consequently left to choose between two difficulties—namely, to identify Mount Hor with Mount Sinai, notwithstanding the objection above referred to, or to regard them as distinct mountains but in the same region. For many reasons it seems preferable to adopt the former alternative. If Mount Sinai stood in Seir, everything points to its identification with that lofty mountain, associated by a still existing tradition with the death of Israel's High Priest.

It is related of Miriam that she died in Kadesh,[*] and of Aaron that he died on Mount Hor.[†] We have elsewhere stated our reasons for suspecting that in some of the early traditions which in later times became, so to speak, absorbed by others possessing greater elements of vitality, Miriam played a much more prominent part in the migration from Egypt than from the materials now at our command would seem to be assigned to her. It is at all events somewhat curious that, according to the voice of tradition, she and Aaron vanish from the scene apparently about the same time, and at or near the same place; and from this, no less than from other circumstances, we might be tempted to inquire whether we might not find Miriam connected in the traditions of some of the sections of the Hebrew nation with much that is associated in the existing records with Aaron. This inquiry cannot, however, owing to absence of materials, be now instituted.

That Josephus possessed sources of information in dealing with even the earlier portions of the history of his people which are no longer available there can be no doubt, and there would seem to have been still preserved at the commencement of the Christian era traditions of which we seek in vain the traces in the Biblical records. What he tells us respecting the death of Miriam is somewhat curious.

---

[*] Num. xx. 1.   [†] Num. xx. 28.

"Miriam," writes Josephus, "was buried upon a certain mountain which they called Sin."* We have it, however, not only on the authority of the Biblical records, that she died at Kadesh, which is identified by the Targumists with Rekam—the latter being in its turn identified by Josephus and others with Petra—but we have the statement of Eusebius that in his time the place of her sepulchre was shown at Kadesh.† We are consequently brought face to face with the very singular fact that, according to a tradition extant in the time of Josephus, Miriam was buried on a mountain named Sin, which must have been close to the supposed place of her death, Kadesh-Rekam-Petra. It is impossible to avoid the conclusion that "the mountain," *Har-ha-Har*, was believed to be the last resting-place of Aaron according to one tradition, and of Miriam according to another; and that this mountain was said to be named Sin, a name in the Hebrew practically indistinguishable from Sinai.

A much more formidable objection may be advanced to the identification of Hor with Sinai, on the ground that if these mountains were the same, some intimation to that effect would appear in the Scriptural records, or in the writings of Josephus. Mount Hor must at all events have been perfectly familiar to the inhabitants of Judæa, if, indeed, it was not actually included within the south quarter of Judah; and it may well seem incredible that the traditions connected with the deaths of Aaron and of Miriam should have survived in connection with the mountain, and should have apparently overshadowed, nay, completely obliterated, the recollection of the far more striking associations connected with the Mount of God.

In order to deal completely with this objection, it would be necessary to undertake a more minute examination of the reli-

---

* *A. J.* iv. 4, 6. † *Onomasticon*, s. v.

gion of the nomad tribes which had settled on the western fringe of Arabia at the period of which we are now treating than is possible in this essay. But, without entering into details, it may be possible to explain a break in the traditions of Israel which *primâ facie* would seem incredible.

However extraordinary the fact may seem, everything indicates that the Hebrew settlers in the fertile regions, on both sides of the Jordan, forgot everything connected with the locality of the Mount where they had concluded a covenant with their protecting God. They never performed pilgrimages to it, they never referred to it except in general terms as being in Seir, and, so far as the Biblical records can be trusted, it passed into complete oblivion. The account of the visit of the prophet Elijah is a transparent parable drawn on the lines of the narrative of Moses, and at the commencement of the Christian era all that Paul and Josephus knew about the mountain was that it was somewhere in Arabia—that is, east of the Araba. Two centuries and a half later Eusebius was unable to give more specific information respecting the Mount of God, and when, a little later, the Copts found it convenient to place the mountain in the Sinaitic peninsula, there was no one in a position to oppose their pretensions. If, however, there was a Mount Sinai, it must have stood somewhere, and whether it was in the peninsula so called, or in the Idumæan range, or elsewhere, we are equally compelled to face the oblivion and neglect into which it unquestionably fell.

The causes of this oblivion were various. They were due, however, mainly to the principles on which the religion of the Semitic tribes rested, and on the anthropomorphism and localisation which characterised their conception of the Deity.

The religion of the Semites, not excluding the races then settled in Palestine, rested exclusively on contract. A covenant was made, with all the necessary formalities observed in ordinary contracts, between the protecting deity on the one hand and the protected people on the other. But for this ceremony it was indispensable that there should be a *locus* where the protecting deity would be believed to be actually present, and where the covenant might be duly concluded. But the beliefs entertained by distinct independent tribes in distinct independent deities, necessarily led to the multiplication of these *loci*, an effect further enhanced by the variety of superstitions respecting the character of the *locus* in which the deity was supposed to dwell. Thus, the deity might be found on a mountain, or in a tree, or in a stone, or at a well. The multiplicity of holy places had, however, an obvious tendency to detract from the reputation of each, regarded individually, whilst the necessity of having the deity ready at hand for the purposes of consultation, for the renewal of covenants, for the decision of causes, &c., led, amongst other consequences, to the conception that he might accompany a nomadic tribe, and dwell like its members in a tent. If the Israelites were led to believe that they would find the God who was prepared to take them under his special care on a particular mountain, it was totally opposed to their conceptions, that after having entered into an engagement to serve him, they could proceed on their journey and leave him behind. It was part of the covenant that Jahveh should accompany his chosen people, fight their battles for them, and destroy their enemies. We find Moses addressing Jahveh—" If thy presence go not with me, carry us not up hence. For wherein shall it be known here that I and thy people have found grace in thy sight?" And Jahveh promises—" My presence shall go with you."* Elsewhere the promise takes the form—" Behold, I send an angel before thee, to keep thee in the way;" and " I will send my fear before thee, and will destroy all the people to whom thou shalt

---

* Exod. xxxiii. 14, 15.

come."* But in those records which deal with the construction of the Tabernacle, however late their date, we have a complete recognition of the existence in early times of the belief that on quitting Sinai the protecting Deity personally accompanied his people—" Let them make me a sanctuary, that I may dwell among them ;"† and in the reign of David the words of Jahveh are conveyed through the prophet Nathan—" Whereas I have not dwelt in any house since the time that I brought up the children of Israel out of Egypt, even to this day, but have walked in a tent and in a tabernacle."‡

The generally accepted doctrine that the Almighty concluded on Mount Sinai a covenant with a numerically small and insignificant section of the human race, and that he there promulgated a religion which, save for His intervention, would never have been known to mankind, has necessarily tended to invest the mountain with an importance which pre-eminently distinguishes it above all the mountains in the world. To those who entertain this view, it seems perfectly unaccountable that the people so highly favoured should have apparently consigned to oblivion the mountain on which so unexampled a manifestation of the Divine interest in their welfare took place, standing as it must have done within comparatively easy reach of their own frontier; and it may at once be conceded, that if the Hebrew emigrants from Egypt entertained the belief with which they are credited, their subsequent treatment of Mount Sinai furnishes the most striking instance in the history of the world of human indifference and neglect. But, on the other hand, the undoubted historical fact that when the Israelites turned their backs on Mount Sinai (wherever situated) they troubled themselves no more about it, would, even if it stood alone,

---

* Exod. xxiii. 20, 27. † Exod. xxv. 8. ‡ 2 Sam. vii. 6.

go far to prove that they did not view what took place at the mountain in the same light in which it came to be regarded long centuries afterwards.

It has been observed by Bishop Butler that passive habits grow weak by repetition,* and undoubtedly the passive habit of reverence for a place in which a deity was supposed to temporarily abide, or where some visible manifestation of his actual presence had taken place, would become considerably weakened by a belief that his place of abode was being continually shifted, and that visible manifestations of his presence were of frequent occurrence. But this is precisely the belief that was entertained by the Israelites, and not only by them, but by the various tribes with which they came in contact. The "places" where one protecting deity or another could be found, and where the people might be summoned to appear "before," that is, in the actual presence of their god, were almost countless; and consequently events, however awe-inspiring, if of solitary occurrence, came by the force of repetition to lose that character, and the places with which they were associated naturally fell into oblivion or contempt. How much the Henotheism of the Hebrews contributed to the same result can alone be dealt with in an examination of their religion subsequent to the settlement in Canaan.

And thus it happened that when accompanied, as they believed, by "the presence" of their protecting God, the Israelites set forth from Mount Sinai, the then abandoned home, the then deserted shrine, ceased to occupy a place in their thoughts. The Tabernacle supplanted the mountain, and the latter was forgotten, save by the poets, who in later days called to mind the original dwelling-place of the God of Israel, and in spirit-stirring language represented him

---

* *Analogy of Religion.*

sallying forth from it like a mighty warrior to fight the battles of his people.

But the reputation for sanctity which, however arising, so to speak, made Mount Sinai, never entirely deserted it. Those who went away might forget it, but those who remained could never divest themselves of a reverence for the Mount of Elohim. It continued to be a holy mountain. When after the lapse of time the settlement in Canaan had been effected, and it was recollected that not even the leaders of those who had quitted Egypt had been permitted to enter the Land of Promise, some consolation was found in the reflection that they were at least permitted to see, though at a distance, the pleasant hills and smiling valleys afterwards to be peopled by the descendants of those whom they had brought out of the house of bondage. The lofty mountain overhanging the Araba (the mount of the Bush, the mount of the Covenant), had been ascended by their leaders, and from its summit they must have beheld the highlands of Judæa. Accordingly, in the tradition of Judah it was related that Jahveh had spoken to Moses and Aaron in "the Mount of Mounts," and had told the latter that he should die there, and on account of his misconduct should not be permitted to enter the Land of Promise.* It is, however, noticeable that throughout the traditions of the migration from Egypt the only mountain on which Jahveh is ever represented as speaking with Moses or Aaron is the mountain on which he dwelt, Mount Sinai; and keeping this fact in view, and coupling it with the descriptive designation of the mountain on which this conversation took place, *Har-ha-Har*, we find a further confirmation of our belief that the mount of the Bush and the mount of Aaron's disappearance were identical. But subsequent to the settlement in the Land of

* Num. xx. 23, 24.

Promise, and when the mountain had ceased to be the abode of the protecting Deity, it still kept a place in the memory of the people as the scene of their High Priest's death, and as the spot from which he had been enabled to view the land he was not permitted to enter. The situation of this mountain was never forgotten. It stood "by the coast of the land of Edom."* The recollection of what, according to our ideas, was the less striking event, eclipsed that of the seemingly more important of the two, but centuries elapsed before this result was accomplished. In the traditions relating to the death of Aaron, and to the turning-point at which the emigrants from Egypt were compelled to change their route, the mountain is distinguished by a title of honour. It is, *par excellence*, "*the* Mount." But as time rolled on this archaic mode of expression ceased to be intelligible, the mountain was presumed to have been called Hor, and the last link by which it could be connected with Mount Sinai was thus snapped asunder.

But let us see what the Deuteronomist has to tell us on the subject of Aaron's death. He states, evidently on the authority of some old record, that "the Israelites journeyed from Beeroth of the children of Jaakan to Mosera (A. V.), there Aaron died and was buried."† The parallel statement in the tradition recorded in Numbers is that they proceeded from Kadesh to *Har-ha-Har*, where Aaron died.‡ We have no difficulty, therefore, in identifying with Kadesh "the wells (*Beeroth*) of the children of Jaakan." But Jaakan was the grandson of Seir,§ that is to say, Jaakan, or the place in which the Beni-Jaakan lived, was in Mount Seir. The springs of Kadesh, the waters of Massah and Meribah, the wells of Esek and Sitnah, had, it would seem, still another name by which they were known—namely, the

---

* Num. xx. 23.   † Deut. x. 6.   ‡ Num. xx. 22, 28.
§ Gen. xxxvi. 27; 1 Chron. i. 42.

wells of the Beni-Jaakan.* Now, it is very remarkable that the Deuteronomist inserts this little scrap immediately after giving an account of the second pair of Tables, and their consignment to the Ark previous to the departure from Mount Horeb.† It is thus perfectly clear that in the seventh century B.C. the opinion, whether right or wrong, obtained in Judah that the tradition of the Law took place near "the wells of the Beni-Jaakan," otherwise known as Kadesh, and situated in Seir, on the border of Edom. But where did Aaron die? Following the Authorised Version, it would appear that from "the wells of the Beni-Jaakan" the Israelites proceeded to a place called Mosera, where Aaron's death took place. The conflict between this statement and that in the Book of Numbers awakens our suspicion. Nothing can be more circumstantial or precise than the account of Aaron's death on *Har-ha-Har*, which was unquestionably a mountain. Where, it will then be asked, was Mosera, and how came this name to be employed apparently as a synonym for *Har-ha-Har*?

If we turn to the Septuagint version, we shall find that the Greek translators interpreted this passage differently and more correctly. They failed to see any ground for inserting the preposition "to" between the words "Beni-Jaakan" and "Mosera," and accordingly rendered the passage—"And the

---

* May not Jaakan be a corruption of Isaac, the ע Tsade having been transcribed ע Ain? If this were so, we should have conclusive confirmation that the wells of Isaac, afterwards known as the wells of the Beni-Isaac, were in Idumæa. According to Eusebius, the wells here referred to were in his time pointed out in the neighbourhood of Petra (*Onomasticon*, s.v. Βηρώθ), and were unquestionably, according to Hebrew tradition, close to, if not identical with, the place where Aaron was last seen by the people. Eusebius says that Aaron died at the Beeroth Beni-Jaakan, but, apparently to harmonise this statement with the tradition of Mount Hor, places the wells on the top of the mountain.

† Deut. x. 1-5.

children of Israel took their journey from Beeroth of the children of Jaakim Misadai; there Aaron died, and there he was buried .... from thence they journeyed to Gadgad."* In what sense the word Misadai or Mosera, whichever it may be, is to be understood we have no means of knowing. We can, however, have no hesitation in following the example of the LXX. in interpreting the Hebrew text, and coupling it with the preceding words Beni-Jaakan; we thus discard the suggestion that Mosera was a distinct station, as not only unsupported, but in direct conflict with the unequivocal tradition that the place of Aaron's death was *Har-ha-Har*. But if this be the true reading of the passage, what a flood of light is thrown on the identity of Mount Horeb and *Har-ha-Har*. According to the Deuteronomist's conception, after Moses came down from the Mount of God with the second set of Tables and placed them in the Ark, the Israelites made their first journey from the Beeroth of the Beni-Jaakan (Mosera-Misadai); but before the narrator mentions the next station he says that "there"—where?—at the place where the Israelites were encamped when Moses came down from the mount—"the wells of the Beni-Jaakan"—Aaron died and was buried. But the general expression "there" is not inconsistent with the belief that Aaron died on the mountain at whose foot the Israelites were encamped. It was "there," at "the wells of the Beni-Jaakan"—*i.e.*, Kadesh—that the people saw Aaron for the last time, when he was summoned to ascend the mount.

* Καὶ οἱ υἱοὶ 'Ισραὴλ ἀπῆραν ἐκ Βηρὼθ υἱῶν 'Ιακίμ Μισαδαί, ἐκεῖ ἀπέθανεν 'Ααρών, καὶ ἐτάφη ἐκεῖ, ... ἐκεῖθεν ἀπῆραν εἰς Γαδγάδ. The LXX. here, as in so many other instances, saw ד *Daleth* where the Masorites saw ר *Resh*, hence *Misadai* instead of *Misarai*. They also gave the vowel point *i* to the *Vau* where the Masorites supplied an *o*, and an *a* after the *Samech* where the Masoretic pointing is *e*. When names fell into oblivion, their original vocalisation was naturally lost.

The author of the Itinerary in the Book of Numbers apparently treats Mosera as a distinct station, and his authority may possibly be cited to overthrow the conclusion at which we have arrived. An attentive perusal of the Itinerary will, however, show that in this, as in so many other instances, the scribe was totally ignorant of the materials which he was manipulating. According to him, the Israelites followed the route Hashmonah—Moseroth—Beni-Jaakan—Hor-hagidgad—Jotbathah—Ebronah—Ezion-gaber—Kadesh—Mount Hor.* The juxta-position of Moseroth to Beni-Jaakan, Hor-hagidgad and Jotbathah—the two latter being evidently the Gudgodah and Jotbath of the Deuteronomist†—places it beyond a doubt that the Moseroth of the one is the Mosera of the other; but it is no less clear that Mosera-Moseroth is separated by seven stations from Mount Hor, and not only was it impossible for Aaron to have died at two places so far apart, but it is inconceivable that any one ever could have thought he did. We are also struck by the curious fact that the author of the Itinerary takes the Israelites in the wrong direction—namely, from Moseroth to Beni-Jaakan, instead of, according to the present interpretation of Deut. x. 6, from Beni-Jaakan to Mosera. How this wonderful production found its way into the Hebrew records can only be accounted for by the supposition that at the time of its compilation (probably during the Captivity) there were none sufficiently conversant with the true interpretation of the traditions of the Exodus, or with the topography of the region traversed by the Israelites, to point out its many inaccuracies.‡

* Num. xxxiii. 30–37.
† Deut. x. 7. This Gudgodah is probably the Zadogatta of the *Tabula Peutingeriana* (see *ante*, p. 238), close to Petra.
‡ It is somewhat singular that the compiler of the Itinerary leaves out the word Beeroth, which precedes Beni-Jaakan in Deuteronomy, and brings in Moseroth out of its order. This affords matter for

We may now finally dismiss from our consideration the locality of the Mount of God. It has stood forth prominently as a beacon to guide us on our path, and we have been directed towards it by the rays still reflected from its earliest traditions, though they are upwards of three thousand years old. We have seen as the result, not of a balance of evidence, but of an accumulation of all the testimony which possesses any real value, that Mount Sinai stood in what was afterwards known as Idumæa, and we have also seen that it was to Idumæa that the emigrants from Egypt immediately directed their steps. Our road has not been free from difficulties, but by patience, we believe, that they have been successfully surmounted. Absolute exactitude cannot be hoped for even by the most sanguine in such an investigation as that in which we have been engaged; but if doubtful points still remain which seem to demand further elucidation, if obstacles still obtrude themselves which seem to need

---

curious speculation. It seems highly probable that in the original text of the Deuteronomist, the sentence ran—"And the children of Israel journeyed from Beeroth Beni-Jaakan; there Aaron died." The compiler of the Itinerary, or some one whose materials he used, may have mistaken in the scroll before him מבארת, *mi Beeroth* (from Beeroth, "the wells") for מסרות, *Moseroth*, which latter he presumed was the name of a station which preceded that of Beni-Jaakan, and he thus made Beni-Jaakan, "the children of Jaakan," serve as the name of a separate stage on the journey. The record preserved by the Deuteronomist is far more intelligible, from "the wells of the children of Jaakan" (mi Beeroth Beni-Jaakan). But at a later date the text of the Deuteronomist became corrupted by the interpolation of what was intended by the scribe to be a spécies of marginal note. Seeing the conflict between the account in the Itinerary and that in Deuteronomy, he apparently inserted in the latter after the words Beeroth Beni-Jaakan, the word *Moserah* in a suggestive way as a place mentioned in a different record, and which seemed to him to have been confounded by another writer with "Beeroth" Beni-Jaakan. The Masorites give eight instances in which entire words have crept into the text (Ruth iii. 12; 2 Sam. xiii. 33; 2 Sam. xv. 21; 2 Kings v. 18; Jer. xxxviii. 16; Jer. xxxix. 12; Jer. li. 3; Ezek. xlviii. 16).

removal, we believe that they are few and insignificant compared with those which even the warmest supporters of existing theories are obliged to admit beset their own path. It is unnecessary, either for the vindication of God or in the interests of historical truth, to make the divinely-led people visit the desolate wilderness which constitutes the greater portion of the Sinaitic peninsula. They not only had no business there, but they never went there; and not a single passage can be cited from the Scriptural records, from the time of the Exodus to the Apostolic age, to show that any person, whether Jew or Gentile, ever thought they entered that region. To quote once more the concise language, put into the mouth of Jephthah, on quitting Egypt "they walked through the wilderness unto the Red Sea, and came to Kadesh;"* and at or near Kadesh they must have found the Mount of God, if it played any part in the history of the emigration from Egypt. To Jephthah's mind, Kadesh and Sinai were identical; or, in other words, Kadesh was the place where the emigrants took up their temporary abode in the neighbourhood of the Mount of God, which it would have been a desecration for any of the people to have ascended.

There is something amusing in the anxiety which has been always manifested by the diligent searchers after "the true Mount Sinai," to find standing-room for the two or three millions of people who were supposed to have encamped at its foot, and to have there heard the Ten Commandments uttered by the voice of the Almighty. Perhaps, if their reverence for the Deity was somewhat keener, they might be struck by the profanity of suggesting that God actually uttered for the exclusive benefit of a few of his creatures the precepts contained in the Decalogue.† Man did not then

---

* Jud. xi. 16.

† In the 125th chapter of the Egyptian Ritual of the Dead, which existed long before the Exodus, the soul of a dead man is represented

want to be made acquainted with the social obligations contained in the latter portion, whilst the remainder imposed special duties towards the protecting Deity which were then familiar to all the nomadic tribes. But though the more thoughtful might give up the preposterous idea of the Deity speaking to a number of people with the voice of a man, they may not so readily abandon the numerical estimate of the released captives. To them it may be a consolation to know that there was ample accommodation for their numerous host, either in the Araba or on the east side of Mount Hor, in the mountain enclosed plain which became the site of the Nabathæan capital.

The peculiar conformation of Mount Hor—a mount imposed upon a mount—tempts one to inquire whether the upper portion may not have been exclusively "the Mount," so frequently referred to as the place where Jahveh dwelt. It will be recollected that the plateau overhanging Petra on the south-west is known as *Sutuh Harân,* "Aaron's Plains." According to an old tradition, Moses inadvertently led his flock to the back side of the *midbhar*, and came to the Mount of God. This would seem to indicate that he was pasturing his flock on the table-land referred to when he saw the phenomenon of the burning bush. It is not necessary to suppose that this occurrence existed only in the inventive imagination of the original narrator of the story. The play of the sun's rays on the red sandstone produced the appearance of fire, whilst the bushes on the rocks remained unconsumed. The optical illusion is one which any curious traveller might doubtless easily witness for himself. When

---

as declaring in presence of Osiris that he has not committed a variety of sins. Amongst the number of declarations the following may be cited: "I have not borne false witness in a place of justice. I have not killed. I have not committed adultery. I have not stolen."

the covenant was subsequently concluded, it is possible that the people may have been assembled upon "Aaron's Plains," and that from thence Moses and his brother went up to take part in the final ceremony by which the compact between the protecting God and the protected people was supposed to have been sealed in nomadic fashion.*

---

* Exod. xxiv. 11. "And they did eat and drink." One of the oldest relics of nomadism, preserved by the Bedouins to the present day, is the custom of eating together on the occasion of a league or covenant between different individuals. A number of illustrations are afforded in the Scriptural records. In the covenants between Isaac and Abimelech (Gen. xxvi. 30), between Laban and Jacob (Gen. xxxi. 46), between Jethro the Sheikh of the Kenites and the leaders of the Israelites (Exod. xviii. 12), between Judah and Israel, when the sovereignty over both kingdoms was secured to David by a covenant of salt (2 Chron. xiii. 5), and in other instances the contracting parties partook of food together.

CHAPTER XII.

WHEN the captive Hebrews quitted Egypt they had very confused ideas, if indeed they had any ideas at all, where they were going. They placed themselves exclusively in the hands of their leaders, and at times they bitterly regretted what they came to think was misplaced confidence. The toilsome journey across the desert of Shur, with its attendant hardships, exhausted their strength and damped their spirits, and when they toiled over the sand-dunes of the Araba their patience at length gave way. But on entering the valleys of Seir the aspect of things became brighter, and from this point we hear no more of their murmurings, at least against natural privations.* Here they would seem to have obtained all that was sufficient for their simple wants, and to have secured the friendship of the Kenites, in whose territory they temporarily sojourned. But this stay could not be perpetual. Although their numbers were far less than those popularly supposed, they found the narrow strip between the Araba and the eastern desert already occupied by tribes more or less closely connected with them by descent. It was necessary to continue their migration, and one of two courses lay open— namely, to push their way in a north-westerly direction round the southern extremity of the Dead Sea into Canaan, or to proceed eastwards towards the pastures lying beyond the Jordan. This alternative was forced upon them at a

---

* Save possibly when they had to quit Kadesh, and retracing their steps descend the Araba to the Gulf of Akaba (Num. xxi. 4, 5).

time after their arrival in Seir, the duration of which we have no means of estimating.

As soon, however, as it became apparent that the onward movement should be continued, their leaders adopted the prudent step of despatching spies for the purpose of ascertaining the resources of the neighbouring regions, and acquainting themselves with the denominations and physical characteristics of the tribes which inhabited them. These spies would appear to have been sent into the country which subsequently was occupied by the tribe of Judah, and they are said to have made a report favourable as regarded the resources of the land, but unfavourable as regarded the difficulties to be surmounted.* Tradition records that "the people" were unanimous in declaring that the project of invasion entertained by their leaders was hopeless, and once more they bitterly reproached Moses and Aaron for having induced them to quit Egypt.† But this version of what actually happened is open to grave suspicion, and conflicts with another tradition. If the people did in fact refuse to invade Canaan from the south, we should have expected that they would thereupon have directed their attention towards the Trans-Jordanic region, to which, as we know, they ultimately turned their steps. But beyond all doubt the attempt at invasion was made. If they refused to listen to the exhortations of their leaders, it is impossible to account for the attack made upon the Amalekites and Canaanites who occupied the region barring the entrance to the Cis-Jordanic region.‡ An endeavour is made in Deuteronomy to explain the inconsistency on the ground that, when the people were reproached by Moses for their want of confidence in Jahveh, and told that in consequence of their

---

* Num. xiii. 27, 28. † Num. xiv. 1-4.
‡ Num. xiv. 40-45.

misconduct they should not be permitted to enter the Land of Promise, they repented, and set themselves in battle array, but were then told that Jahveh was no longer with them; and so, having rashly attacked their foes, were utterly routed.* The record in Numbers, though not so explicit, will bear the same interpretation. But it is easy to see that in later times, when the settlement in Canaan had been accomplished, the traditions naturally moulded themselves into a form which made the defeat of the Hebrews not inconsistent with the might of their protecting God, and at the same time gave a plausible explanation of the notorious fact that the emigrants from Egypt did not live to enter Canaan. The so-called Waters of Strife and Contention supplied the basis for the tradition that Moses and Aaron were excluded from the Land of Promise, and the serious reverse sustained by the Hebrews on their first attempt to force an entrance into the land which subsequently became theirs, furnished a convenient foundation for the story that the attack had been made in direct opposition to the expressed will of their God, through his displeasure at their previous refusal to do that to which they subsequently gave their assent. The Israelites were much too superstitious to have ventured to attack their enemies in the teeth of an assurance from Moses that Jahveh would not give his assistance, and we must therefore conclude that the response of the oracle was propitious, but the result disastrous. The Israelites were, however, very indignant at being defeated, and seem to have contemplated putting their leaders to death, electing a new captain, and returning to Egypt.† The phenomena attending the conclusion of the covenant at Mount Sinai must have been very highly coloured by the voice of tradition since their effect was so speedily forgotten.

---

* Deut. i. 41-44. † Num. xiv. 4, 10.

An apparently different account of this battle is given in a very curious fragment contained in the Book of Numbers. It is stated that when King Arad the Canaanite heard that Israel followed in the footsteps of the spies, he fought against the invaders, and took some of them prisoners; and thereupon Israel made a vow to utterly destroy the Canaanites and their cities, if Jahveh would deliver them into their hands. Jahveh hearkened to the voice of Israel, the Canaanites were overcome, and they and their cities were destroyed, wherefore the place was named Hormah.* This was, however, the place to which, according to the other accounts, the Israelites were driven after their defeat, and was situated in Seir; and the doubt is raised in our mind whether the invasion may not have been partially successful—that is to say, whether a portion of the invading force may not have effected a lodgment in the enemies' country. It is about this time that the severance between the two great sections, which subsequently came to be known as Judah and Israel, took place. This is, however, a matter which cannot be dealt with in this treatise. It is somewhat singular that the author of the 78th Psalm,† repeating the "dark sayings of old," and

---

* Num. xxi. 1, 3.
† Ps. lxxviii. 9. The translation of this verse is confessedly very difficult. Ewald renders it, "The children of Ephraim, carrying slack bows, turned back in the day of battle." From the Targum of the pseudo-Jonathan, it would seem that the affair referred to was a cattle-lifting expedition, conducted against the Philistines by no less than two hundred thousand of the Ephraimites whilst still in captivity in Egypt. The latter were all killed, because they transgressed the word of Jahveh in quitting Egypt three years before the appointed termination of their servitude. It was in order to avoid the shock which would have been sustained by their brethren on seeing their bones, that Moses did not lead the Israelites by the direct road into Canaan. It is as well to make an explanation exhaustive when one is about it, and the Targumist adds that these are the dry bones restored to life by the word of Jahveh through the instrumentality of the prophet Ezekiel (*Targ. Pal. Ex.* xiii.). The raid of the Ephraimites is probably alluded to in 1 Chron. vii. 21.

referring to the incidents of the migration from Egypt, records that "the children of Ephraim, being armed and carrying bows, turned back in the day of battle." There is no reference to such an occurrence elsewhere in the Scriptural records, but as it is possible that in this invasion of Canaan from the south, the Ephraimites—that is, the stock of the future Beni-Israel—"turned back;" and as they unquestionably abandoned the project of forcing their way by this route into the coveted territory lying to the west of the Dead Sea, this may be the episode referred to.

The attempt to invade Canaan from the south having failed, the position of the emigrants became one of serious embarrassment and peril. They found it impossible to break through the hostile tribes which barred their advance in that direction. They could not remain where they were, and no course seemed open to them but to elect a captain, under whose guidance they might retrace their steps to Egypt. For their part, they had no apprehensions about the reception they would receive from their former masters. They bore no enmity to the Egyptians, and they knew of no reason why the Egyptians should bear any enmity to them. They were unacquainted with the marvellous stories which in after-times national pride and piety conjured up, to represent their God compelling the Pharaoh to let his people go, and luring him on from day to day to certain destruction. They had been sojourners in Egypt, they had been strangers in that land, and long centuries afterwards the hospitality they had received was kept in kindly remembrance.* It was not, therefore, petulance or despair which at this crisis prompted a return to Egypt. On grounds of expediency, many of the Hebrews may well have thought that it was the wisest course to adopt. Their descendants, looking back

---

* Deut. xxiii. 7, 8.

from the theatre of accomplished facts, judged them harshly, and posterity has made it a point of religious duty to endorse that verdict. But the impartial historian will form a different opinion of the men who quitted Egypt. Enervated by their servitude they may have been, and many amongst them were no doubt easily discouraged. But there was sterner and stouter stuff to be found amongst their ranks. They had leaders endowed with indomitable energy, and the very nature of the existence led by the mass of the people in Egypt, rendered the latter all the more docile instruments in their hands.

It was known to the tribes then settled in Idumæa that fertile and well-watered plains stretched to the north-east over the table-land which overhung the Jordan. When some centuries previously the Terahitic settlers to the south of the Dead Sea found the land insufficient to supply their wants, the surplus population forced their way into the plain and adjoining highlands.* Their inroad was probably not unresisted by the then occupants of this region, but at a later period a warlike tribe known as the Amorites succeeded in driving the intruders back, deprived them of a considerable portion of their recently acquired territory, and obliged them to withdraw behind the Arnon, an insignificant river emptying itself into the Dead Sea.† ' But what had been done in times past by the descendants of the emigrants from the far East might be done again. The Israelite leaders formed the project of obtaining permission to pass through the intervening territory of Edom and Moab, trusting by further negotiation to secure a passage through the land of the Amorites to the sparsely populated region stretching towards the Syrian desert. It was necessary, in order to attain this object, to give assurances to the kings of these

---

* Gen. xiii. 11. † Num. xxi. 26–30.

countries to respect their territory. Ties of kindred, no less than motives of expediency, prompted this course in dealing with Edom and Moab. The Elohim of the Hebrews had given to the children of Esau and to the children of Lot their then possessions,* though he was not known to them by the name of Jahveh,† and they held their territory by virtue of covenants similar to that concluded between Jahveh and the Israelites.

The proposals made to the Edomites were not favourably received. According to one account, Edom came out with a high hand against Israel,‡ but perhaps this was only another way of saying that the Edomites refused permission to pass through their territory, and took measures for its defence in the event of the Israelites attempting to effect their purpose by force. The effect of this refusal on the emigrants was disheartening, and for some time at least they were obliged to continue at Kadesh.§

If we trusted to the accounts which were drawn up many centuries afterwards, with the view of harmonising the traditions of the Exodus with the belief that the specific term of forty years elapsed between the departure from Egypt and the crossing of the Jordan, we would conclude that nearly the whole of that period was passed at or in the neighbourhood of Kadesh. But we know that much hard work had to be done in the region on the east of the Jordan, that some powerful tribes had to be conquered and dispossessed, and we cannot therefore accept the theory that all this was accomplished in the course of a few months. No account of

---

* Deut. ii. 5, 9, 19.
† The name of the tribal God of Moab and Ammon appears from the earliest time to have been Chemosh. In fragments of great antiquity, and dealing with occurrences antecedent to the Exodus, this is fully recognised (Num. xxi. 26-30). According to Josephus the God of Edom was named Kozeh (*A. J.* xv. 7, 9).
‡ Num. xx. 20.   § Deut. i. 46.

time was kept in the traditions of the migration; all that was known was that a very long period, expressed *more Hebraico* as forty years,* elapsed between the Exodus and the crossing of the Jordan.

We are therefore unable to form any opinion how long the Israelites remained at Kadesh, or when it was that they decided on once more entering the Araba, retracing their steps towards the Red Sea (Akaba), and marching round the country which they were not permitted to traverse.† The term may have extended over several years, or only over a few months. According to tradition, the links which connected the emigrants with some of those who took a prominent part in the Exodus from Egypt were here broken. Aaron according to one tradition,‡ Miriam according to another,§ died whilst they were at their place of temporary sojourn. Moses is represented as accompanying the Israelites to the banks of the Jordan; under his leadership a number of important battles are said to have been fought, but he too lies outside the limits of the Land of Promise.|| The circumstances of his death closely resemble those of Aaron's. Whether the son-in-law of the Kenite Sheikh accompanied the Israelites to the Trans-Jordanic region will be considered at a later stage of this inquiry.

It would be absurd to suppose that during the stay in the mountains on the border of the Araba the Hebrews maintained a complete isolation and formed no connections with the friendly tribes amongst whom they sojourned. It is probable that social alliances were formed, and we know that the Kenites and the tribe of Judah became closely united.¶ When at length the resolution was taken by at least a section of the emigrants to make the toilsome journey round

---

* See *ante*, p. 8.   † Num. xxi 4; Deut. ii. 1.
‡ Num. xx. 28.   § Num. xx. 1. || Deut. xxxiv. 5.
¶ Jud. i. xvi.

the mountains of Seir, they were doubtless accompanied by some of the people amongst whom they had lived.

Tradition has preserved for us but little connected with this journey. The Israelites descended the Araba, and having approached the Red Sea, they probably turned off by the Wady-el-Yitm. They proceeded for some miles along the valley, until they were enabled to face northwards and skirt the eastern border of Edom.* This they did without molestation, and they not improbably received some assistance from their brethren.† At all events, no further record appears of complaints on account of want of food. Having passed the limits of Edom, they followed in like manner the borders of Moab until they reached the Arnon, which river at that time constituted the frontier line between Moab on the south and the country of the Amorites on the north.‡ From the time of emerging from the Wady-el-Yitm to their arrival on the border of the Amorites the Israelites seem to have followed a route parallel to, and slightly to the west of, that taken for centuries past by the Syrian Hajj.

At this point the journeyings of the Israelites may be said to terminate. Here commenced the invasion and conquest of that rich tract of country lying to the north of the Arnon, which was said to have been appropriated by tribes respectively styled Reuben, Gad, and Manasseh. With the circumstances under which that conquest was effected we are not concerned, nor indeed have we any materials for the construction of its history. It is briefly stated, in a record of Judah, that a request was addressed to Sihon, the king of the Amorites, for permission to traverse his territory, in order to enable the Israelites to cross the Jordan above the Dead Sea, and thus to "go in and possess the land" which Jahveh

---

* Deut. ii. 3.   † Deut. ii. 29.   ‡ Num. xxi. 13; Deut. ii. 24.

had covenanted to give them.* But there is no difficulty in detecting the late origin of this version of what really occurred. Even if "the land" was promised, it had yet to be conquered; and however great the confidence of the Israelites in their protecting God, the king of the Amorites could not be expected to share it. His territory bordered on the Jordan and the upper portion of the Dead Sea, and it would have been preposterous to have asked him to allow it to be converted by the possession-seeking Israelites into a base of operations against the people inhabiting the region on the right bank of the river. If permission was sought at all, it was to follow the course taken in respect to Edom and Moab—namely, to skirt the border of the Amorite territory, and to push onwards through Gilead.† The permission was refused, and we are briefly told that the Israelites thereupon made war on the Amorites, dispossessed them of their entire territory, and then invaded Bashan, a region lying to the north of the land of the Amorites, and including Gilead. This latter campaign was equally successful, but no details are given. "We took," writes the Deuteronomist, "at that time out of the hands of the two kings of the Amorites the land that was on this side of Jordan, from the river of Arnon unto Mount Hermon, all the cities of the plain, and all Gilead and all Bashan,"—in a word, the entire Trans-Jordanic region.‡

This absence of particularity in respect to the conquest of an extensive region—a conquest, moreover, which gave to

---

* Deut. ii. 27, 29.

† This is the fair construction of the older account which is recorded in Num. xxi. 22. Nothing is here said about crossing the Jordan.

‡ Deut. iii. 8, 10. The employment of the expression "this side of Jordan," as applied to the east bank of the river, is due to the assumption that it is Moses who is speaking. The account in Numbers is even more brief (Num. xxi. 24, 25, 33, 35).

the emigrants from Egypt rich and almost boundless pastures—apprises us that we have reached a phase in the history of the migration which held an insignificant place in the traditions of those who subsequently established their home in Palestine. The latter came to regard their conquests as the great and sole end aimed at when their ancestors were led out of Egypt. But if we possessed the traditions of those who remained in the Trans-Jordanic region we should find these conquests, so summarily disposed of in the records of Israel and Judah, dealt with in a far different manner. The settlers on the east of the Jordan had then entered what was *their* Land of Promise; they had come into the possessions which from their stand-point their God had covenanted to give them, and their ambition was satisfied. In the struggle for existence—the motive cause of all migrations—they had succeeded, and they were content. The part, if any, which they took in the conquest of Canaan must be treated of elsewhere. The Trans-Jordanic tribes are referred to by Deborah, but only to reproach them for holding aloof from the struggle in which their kindred were engaged with the Canaanites.* Jephthah the Gileadite is represented resisting the pretensions of the Ammonites to recover the region to the north of the Arnon, and denying the charge that it had been taken from Moab by Israel. It had, in fact, been wrested by the Amorites from the Moabites, and was in turn taken from the Amorites by the emigrants from Egypt. An undisputed possession of three hundred years was, as Jephthah urged, sufficient to obliterate whatever title Moab might originally have had to the coveted territory. Jahveh had given it to the Israelites, just as Chemosh

---

* Jud. v. 16, 17.

had given to Moab the possessions south of the Arnon, and from a religious, no less than from a political, point of view there could be no ground for reopening the question.*

How were these extensive conquests effected on the east of the Jordan, and how could a body of men, such as the released captives of Egypt must have been, have succeeded in overthrowing the Amorite kings? On these points, in the dearth of materials, we can offer no definite replies. In the movement to the north-east, it is probable that many took part who had not quitted Egypt. We must not conclude that the Israelites proceeded, like an eastern caravan, past the borders of Edom and Moab, only halting for a few hours' rest at stated intervals. We have indications that connections, exercising important influences over themselves, were formed between them and the tribes with which they came in contact.† Whether these influences were pernicious or not, it is difficult to believe that they could have operated at all unless the emigrants were largely recruited from the tribes to which we refer.

And it is necessary here to recall to mind the broad features of the religion which the Israelites took with them. They had made a covenant with Jahveh, by which they agreed to serve him exclusively, in consideration of his being to them a protecting God, giving them the victory over their enemies, and bringing them into a land suitable to their wants. There was nothing in this religion new or original: it was the religion of the Kenites, and, for that matter, the religion of the various tribes inhabiting the region through which the Israelites passed. The protecting deities might vary like the patron saints of Christian communities, and the mode of service—that is, the religious rites—might differ considerably amongst distinct tribes; but the foundations of

* Jud. xi. 14 26. † Num. xxv.

religion were everywhere the same. The members of a tribe, and the strangers who sojourned amongst them, were under an imperative obligation to render exclusive service to the God whose protection all equally shared and in whose bounty all participated.* It is needless to point out how the very act of migration, with the accompanying necessity of accepting the hospitality of friendly tribes, tended to promote a conflict between the services of different deities, and to induce the adoption of novel religious rites.

In the narrative of some occurrences which took place whilst Israel was in the land of Moab, we have an illustration of the operation of the causes to which we allude. It is stated that the Moabites "called the people unto the sacrifices of their gods, and the people did eat, and bowed down to their gods; and Israel joined himself unto Baalpeor, and the anger of Jahveh was kindled against Israel."† In what appears to be a continuation of the same narrative, the Moabites are called Midianites, and very strong indications are afforded of the licentious nature of the rites incidental to the worship of Baal-peor.‡ But, however consonant with established usage it may have been for strangers to render service to the national—that is to say, the local—deities, there were amongst the leaders of Israel zealous observers of the covenant with Jahveh who felt that, as the people were migrating *en masse*, with their God amongst them, it was impossible to join in the service of any other deity without offence to Jahveh, and a consequent violation of the contract on the strict observance of which they relied for his assistance in dispossessing their enemies of the territory which they coveted. Jahveh was a jealous

---

* Lev. xvi. 29; xvii. 12, 15; xxiv. 16, 22; xxv. 6; Num. ix. 14; xv. 14-16, 29, 30, &c.
† Num. xxv. 1-3.   ‡ Num. xxv. 6-18.

God, and it was well understood that he would punish the people collectively for individual apostasy. In the case of Zimri and Cozbi the offence was of the grossest, for it was committed in the camp within sight of the tabernacle, and therefore, in the strictest sense of the term, before the face of Jahveh.* In their case, the punishment was prompt and signal; the atonement they made for the entire people was accepted by Jahveh, and Phinehas was rewarded for his zeal by being made by special covenant the head of an everlasting priesthood. The importance of jealously watching and severely punishing any infraction of the covenant may be appreciated from the fact that, according to the religious conceptions of the time, the offence was visited by the Deity, not alone on the guilty individuals, but on the people collectively.

It is stated that these events occurred at Shittim. This place is generally supposed to have been situated on the left bank of the Jordan, opposite to Jericho. This conclusion is based on the precise statement in the Book of Joshua that it was from Shittim that the spies were sent to Jericho,† and that there the Israelites encamped before crossing the Jordan.‡ For reasons which will be stated hereafter, we must reject the testimony of the author of the introductory chapters of Joshua. The territory of Moab at the time of the Exodus did not extend north of the Arnon, and if the apostasy referred to took place at the instance of the Moabites, it must have been within their country. We shall have occasion presently to notice in detail the localities south of the Arnon referred to in the traditions of the migration. We must, however, direct passing attention to the meaning of the word Shittim. In the Hebrew it is preceded by the definite article, and

---

* Exod. xx. 3; Deut. v. 7.   See *ante*, p. 11.
† Jos. ii. 1.   ‡ Jos. iii. 1.

signifies "the acacias," and in the Itinerary (Num. xxxiii. 49) we find mention of Abel-has-Shittim, "the meadow" or "plain of the acacias." Here Baal-peor was worshipped, and, as will be shown by-and-by, here, or in the immediate neighbourhood, were performed the sacrifices directed by the seer Balaam, the son of Beor. Allusion is made by the prophet Micah to this place of "the acacias," in connection with the last-mentioned occurrence.* Independently of the consequences, both religious and political, resulting from the contact of the emigrants with the Moabites, it must not be forgotten that the former, on forcing an entrance into the Trans-Jordanic region, necessarily absorbed, or were absorbed by, the tribes which they found there.

The stereotyped expressions which tell us that the conquests of the Israelites were invariably followed by the indiscriminate slaughter of entire populations, must not be construed prosaically. The narrators never intended that they should be understood literally, nor did those whom they addressed fall into the absurd error of thinking that they did so. When the Israelites succeeded in establishing themselves on the left bank of the lower Jordan, they coalesced with the former inhabitants, just as at a later period the invaders of Canaan coalesced with the native population. The individuality of the parent stock of emigrants suffered by the frequent accretions, and even before the Jordan was crossed the social and religious character of the people underwent a considerable change. Large numbers adapted themselves to the pastoral habits of the tribes which they found feeding their flocks on the undulating downs stretching to the north-east from the table-land of Moab; others

---

* Micah vi. 5.

mingled with the sedentary population of the Jordan valley. The religion of these settlers became in time different from that of their kindred who crossed that river—that is to say, they worshipped different Elohim. Whether they or the settlers in Canaan were the apostates may be open to discussion, but a writer of the third century B.C., referring to the Trans-Jordanic tribes, states that they adopted the worship of the Elohim of the people amongst whom they dwelt, and that in consequence they were carried away into captivity by the king of Assyria.*

The successes attained by the Israelites on the left side of the Jordan appear to have given grave cause for apprehension to the people of Moab. The emigrants had been permitted to pass through Moab's borders in search of possessions, but they had prospered so amazingly that the Moabites became seriously alarmed lest they, like the Amorites, should be "licked up as the ox licketh up the grass of the field."† But this state of things did not arise till long after the settlement in the Trans-Jordanic region. Without entering into the question of the date and authorship of the narrative of Balak and Balaam,‡ it is noticeable that Jephthah, in his negotiations with the king of the Ammonites, asks him whether he is mightier than his predecessor Balak (who appears to have been a celebrated Moabite monarch), and whether the latter ever strove against Israel whilst dwelling in Heshbon, and in Aroer, and by the coasts of Arnon, during three hundred years.§ Jephthah's chronological estimate may have been faulty, but respecting the traditions of the region in which he lived, he most assuredly did not believe that Balak was the contemporary of those who quitted Egypt.

---

* 1 Chron. v. 25, 26. † Num. xxii. 4.
‡ Num. xxii., xxiii., xxiv. § Jud. xi. 25, 26.

CHAPTER XIII.

ACCORDING to the accepted account, the people of Israel, composed of distinct, well-defined tribes, crossed the Arnon under the leadership of Moses, overthrew the Amorite kings, and possessed themselves of the whole Trans-Jordanic region from the Arnon to the Lebanon in the course of a few months.* We are also told that within the same brief period they not only dispossessed, but exterminated the inhabitants.† It is further stated, that when the Trans-Jordanic region was thus conquered, the tribes of Reuben and Gad, and (impliedly) half the tribe of Manasseh, preferred to Moses the modest request that this region should be given to them because it was eminently suited for pastoral purposes, and that Moses gave his assent without eliciting any protest from the remaining tribes, who were thus left to find possessions for themselves on the opposite side of the Jordan.‡ The narrator, conscious of the injustice of such a mode of proceeding, has made the assent of Moses dependent on an engagement on the part of the favoured tribes to aid the others in the conquest of Canaan, and the engagement, we are told, was subsequently fulfilled.§ Whether, however, we examine the story told in the Book of Numbers or its apparent confirmation in the Book of Joshua, it requires no extraordinary perspicuity to become aware that we have passed into the region of romance.

---

* Num. xxxiii. 38; Jos. v. 6, 10; Deut. iii. 8. † Num. xxi. 24, 35.
‡ Num. xxxii. 1–33.   § Jos. i. 16–18.

In after-times, when the Hebrew settlement in Canaan had taken place, and when it was notorious that many who preserved the traditions of the Exodus had remained behind in the region beyond the Jordan—when, in a word, the existence of tribes with common traditions, and holding possessions on both sides of the river, was an established historical fact—it became necessary, from a religious stand-point, to reconcile all that had occurred with the prevalent conception of the Divine intervention in every detail affecting the future welfare of the chosen people of Jahveh. That Jahveh had driven out the Amorites on one side of the Jordan, as he subsequently drove out the Canaanites on the other, in order to make room for his peculiar people, none could doubt; and it was therefore reasonable to conclude that he provided for the easy and peaceable partition of these possessions amongst distinct and—so far as they were apparently incapable of coalescing with each other—conflicting tribes. But inasmuch as these tribes undoubtedly possessed so strongly marked an individuality, and as their members were probably not uninfluenced by those selfish feelings which have guided the actions of all communities, whether large or small, since the world began, we must regard with suspicion an account which represents them as acting in concert to secure a specific end, and subsequently abstaining from equal participation in the benefits obtained.

Whatever family distinctions may have existed amongst the Hebrew emigrants who forced their way into the pastures on the east of the Jordan, there can be no doubt that the entire community was acting with a common purpose—namely, the desire of finding the means of existence—and that all equally shared in the advantages resulting from their successful movement. But, owing to circumstances the consideration of which does not come within the scope of this essay, the tide of migration was subsequently forced westwards across the Jordan valley. The pleasant pastures on the east of the river were not, however, deserted. Many of those who had quitted Egypt remained in that region. These latter, owing to circumstances easily intelligible, formed quasi-national or tribal communities, and became known by distinctive names. This subdivision into tribal communities was, however, a universal feature wherever the descendants of Terah set foot. The nomadic instincts of the race conflicted with the ideas of national union, and could only be overcome when the nomadic habits were entirely abandoned. That which had already happened in Idumæa and to the south-east of the Dead Sea, was repeated on the left bank of the Jordan. The tide rolled on, receiving an additional impetus through the migration of the Egyptian captives. But the comparatively small territory lying between the Arnon and the Jabbok was insufficient to satisfy the wants of the newcomers. Many still pushed forward towards the north and east. Following the accepted account, those who settled on the north of the Arnon were termed the tribe of Reuben or Reubel, and in after-times they were not inappropriately regarded as the descendants of the eldest born of Israel,* since they constituted the first section of those who, after quitting Egypt, secured distinct possessions. This tribe was not, however, composed exclusively of those who had been born in Egypt, or their descendants. The population which it already found in the country in which it settled must have largely outnumbered it, and it may well be doubted whether it did not receive its distinctive appellation because its members served the deity who was worshipped in the region which they acquired. Reuben is said to have been the eldest son of Leah, who so called him, because "God had

---

* Gen. xxix. 32.

seen her affliction," owing to her previous barrenness.* But it is a very curious fact that, so late as the first century of the present era, a man well conversant with the Hebrew Scriptures unquestionably believed the name to have been Reubel.† That this was the original form of the name, and that it was subsequently corrupted into Reuben, has been maintained by a German scholar of great eminence, who has further contended that it must be interpreted "the flock of Bel," or "Baal."‡ This deity, or perhaps more correctly one of the numerous Baalim, was worshipped in the region on the east of the Dead Sea, and appears to have had a sanctuary near the Moabite frontier.

A tribe of Israel, with the appellation of Gad, is said to have settled in the pastoral region lying to the north of that occupied by the Reubenites.§ That it included some of those who had quitted Egypt (or their descendants) is very probable, but in time it became absorbed by or confounded with the Gileadites. Jephthah is represented as a Gileadite, and though speaking on behalf of his people, he still speaks in the name of Israel; at least the title to the territory in dispute is based upon the right of conquest, acquired by those who came up from Egypt.‖ But in later times, when the kingdom of Israel was established, this identity between Israel and the Gadites, or Gileadites, seems to have disappeared; for we find in the celebrated inscription on the Moabite stone, which records a war between Moab and Israel, a special acknowledgment that the men of Gad (clearly distinguished from the Israelites) possessed from of old certain towns near the Moabite frontier. This was about 900 B.C.

---

* Gen. xxix. 32.
† Josephus invariably gives the name as 'Ροὔβηλος, and interprets it ἔλεον τοῦ θεοῦ, "the pity of God."
‡ Redslob, *Die Alttest. Namen*, 86.
§ Jos. xiii. 24–28.   ‖ Jud. xi. 12–28.

To the north of the region occupied by the Gadites was the portion which we are told was formally allotted by Moses to half the tribe of Manasseh.* It included the upper part of Gilead, and appears to have extended northwards to Hermon, and eastwards, with no well-defined limits, over the plains stretching towards the Euphrates.† A more probable account of the mode in which these rich possessions passed into the hands of the Beni-Manasseh is preserved in an historical fragment of earlier date.‡ This region was said to have been conquered by Jair, the son of Manasseh, though elsewhere the son of Manasseh is called Machir, who was the father of Gilead.§ Nothing of importance turns on the names, but it is material to observe that we possess here the record of an old tradition that the people or tribe known as Manasseh conquered this region; that Gilead —the place inhabited by the tribe—came, according to a common practice in the Hebrew genealogies, to be regarded as one of the descendants of Manasseh; and that the term Gileadite in time superseded the earlier appellation of Manassite. But Manasseh and Ephraim were said to have been the two children of Joseph,|| and the descendants of both represented those who were in after-times specially known as the children of Israel. In this sense an Ephraimite and an Israelite were convertible terms after the settlement in Canaan, and in the Trans-Jordanic region, in Jephthah's time, a Gileadite and an Israelite were equally treated as synonymous. Manasseh was, according to tradition, the first-born of Joseph, and we may rest confident that this claim was maintained without any qualification on the east of the Jordan. But on the west bank, although the reputed fact of Manasseh's seniority was not questioned, it was found

---

* Jos. xiii. 29-31. † 1 Chron. ii. 21-24. ‡ Num. xxxii. 39-42.
§ Num. xxvi. 29, 30. || Gen. xlvi. 20.

convenient to give to Ephraim—that is to say, to the offshoot of the same stock which crossed the river—precedence over the elder branch.* The transposition of Isaac for Ishmael, of Jacob for Esau, was again repeated. The tide of migration kept rolling onwards; but, as we possess alone the records of those who were carried to the furthest point, it is the last in order who are represented as held in the highest honour.

In the narrative of the allocation of the Trans-Jordanic region, the Reubenites and Gadites are represented coming to Moses and setting forth their claims to "the country which Jahveh smote before the congregation of Israel," and which would seem to have included all the territory of the kings of the Amorites.† To the objection raised by Moses that they were bound to aid in the conquest of Canaan, the supplicants promised to leave their wives, children, and flocks, in fenced cities and sheep-folds, behind them, and to join the children of Israel in the invasion of the territory on the opposite side of the Jordan.‡ Moses thereupon yielded, and said that if they did as they promised they should have the land of Gilead for a possession.§ The sequel to the narrative is curious, for we find that not only the Reubenites and the Gadites obtained their coveted possession, but the half-tribe of Manasseh, which did not appear as a supplicant, was made a sharer with the other two tribes in the land of Gilead. "And Moses gave unto them, even to the children of Gad, and to the children of Reuben, *and unto half the tribe of Manasseh*, the son of Joseph, the kingdom of Sihon, king of the Amorites, and the kingdom of Og, the king of Bashan."‖ That this half-tribe should be so specially favoured, and that without having advanced any request, or

---

* Gen. xlviii. 14. † Num. xxxii. 4.
‡ Num. xxxii. 16–19. § Num. xxxii. 20–22. ‖ Num. xxxii. 33.

accepted any conditions, it should have obtained possessions from Moses, necessarily excites our suspicion.

The Cis-Jordanic origin of this story is very manifest. We know that in not any age, and least of all in one so barbarous as that with which we are now dealing, could those who had just conquered and occupied a country act in the manner attributed to the settlers on the east of the Jordan—namely, leave their families and flocks defenceless, and assist in the invasion of a neighbouring country for the exclusive benefit of others. But we further notice that the Reubenites and Gadites are distinguished from "the children of Israel," which could hardly have been the case if this had been a contemporaneous record. "Wherefore discourage ye the heart of the children of Israel?"* is the language in which Moses at first replies to their request; and the Reubenites and Gadites answer, "We will build sheepfolds for our cattle and cities for our little ones, and we ourselves will go ready armed before the children of Israel until we have brought them into their place."† This "objective" way of speaking of the children of Israel does not conflict with the possibility of Reubenites, Gadites, and "children of Israel" having come from the common stock which quitted Egypt, but it tends to confirm our doubts whether at the time of the migration the title "Beni-Israel" had come into use. The author of the narrative clearly regarded the Beni-Israel on the west of the Jordan as essentially distinct from the Reubenites and Gadites on the east, and he went so far as to make the title of the latter to the possessions dependent, not on the immediate grant of Moses, but on the approval by Joshua and the fathers of Israel of their subsequent conduct. "And Moses said unto them, If the children of Gad and the children of Reuben will pass

---

* Num. xxxii. 7.   † Num. xxxii. 17.

with you over Jordan, every man armed to battle before Jahveh, and the land shall be subdued before you, then ye shall give them the land of Gilead for a possession ; but if they will not pass over before you armed, they shall have possessions among you in the land of Canaan."* The concluding sentence is unintelligible. It would have been absurd to punish the Reubenites and Gadites for their disobedience by making them sharers in possessions which they did not aid in securing.

The most singular feature in the narrative, at least in its present shape, is, however, the mention of the half-tribe of Manasseh as sharing with Reuben and Gad in the Trans-Jordanic possessions. No explanation is given why this disposition was made, or why a distinct tribe should, without any apparent cause, have divided itself in half, one portion electing to remain on one side of the river, whilst the other was prepared to seek possessions on the opposite side. An explanation may be found in the corruption of the original text by the interpolation of the words, "and unto half the tribe of Manasseh;" but this inference, though possibly correct, does not indicate how this interpolation became necessary. In order to solve the mystery, let us devote a few moments' further consideration to these Trans-Jordanic tribes.

Excepting the statement that the Reubenites and Gadites fulfilled their engagement of assisting in the invasion of Canaan, these tribes to all appearances vanish into obscurity after this event. Neither, apparently, gave a judge to Israel, nor played any part in its history; and when we are told by the compiler of the Books of Chronicles† that they were carried into captivity by the king of Assyria, we may be excused for suspecting that his statement was prompted by

---

* Num. xxxii. 29, 30. † 1 Chron. v. 26.

his own idea of what ought to have taken place.* This singular disappearance of two important tribes demands explanation, and all the more so if the theory be upheld that the emigrants from Egypt consisted of twelve, or rather thirteen, distinct tribes, pursuing a common purpose, having a common religion, and with, to a great extent, a common future before them.

We have had frequent occasion to point out how the same tradition came to assume different forms; how sometimes the story varied, whilst at others the actors were changed. The fate that befell individuals was shared by tribes, and in some cases a tribe or people came to be known by totally different designations. Thus we have seen how the Amalekites of one story† are the Amorites of another;‡ how the Moabites and the Midianites are confounded together;§ how the same tribe is now treated as Midianite,‖ and now as Kenite;¶ and how the region said in one record to have been occupied by the Beni-Moab** is in another assigned to the Beni-Ammon.†† It is unnecessary to explain the causes which led to this confusion; it is simply sufficient to note its existence.

But amongst those who settled in the region beyond the Jordan, and who together with the original inhabitants formed communities more or less distinct, appellations arose which, in the course of time and owing to change of circumstances, became confounded together or superseded by other titles. According to one tradition, the land of Gilead, as the Trans-Jordanic region was commonly termed, was apportioned between Reuben and Gad;‡‡ whilst, according to another, it was conquered by the tribe of Manasseh.§§ Both

---
* The older records in the Books of Kings are silent on the subject.
† Num. xiv. 40–45.   ‡ Deut. i. 41, 44.   § Num. xxv.
‖ Exod. iii. 1.   ¶ Jud. i. 16.   ** Deut. ii. 9–12.   †† Deut. ii. 18, 21.
‡‡ Num. xxxii. 1.   §§ Num. xxxii. 39.

stories, however, only recounted in different language the same event. The emigrants from Egypt effected by their united efforts a settlement in Gilead, and at least two sections of them acquired different designations: one that of Reuben or Reubel, the other that of Gad. But when the territory on the west of the Jordan was invaded, the original stock which quitted Egypt was presumed to have been split in two, one half remaining on the east of the river. Those who went westwards, and who subsequently adopted the distinctive title of Beni-Israel, were at first content with a different and less comprehensive patronymic. They were the descendants of Joseph, of whom some had remained behind on the other side of the Jordan. It is in this manner that we can understand how half Manasseh was supposed to have taken Gilead, and how the rights of Reubenites and Gadites, and even their names, pass into oblivion. It is not suggested that the Trans-Jordanic Manasseh dispossessed Reuben and Gad, but nevertheless in that most interesting record of Jephthah we find the Gileadite chief vindicating the rights, not of the Reubenites or the Gadites, but of the Gileadites, to that very territory north of the Arnon which was said to have been given to the former tribes.* But it is no less clear that Jephthah and his people were identified *eo nomine* with the Manassites, and not with the Reubenites or Gadites. When the Ephraimites—that is to say, the section of the original stock which passed to the west of the Jordan—heard of Jephthah's victory over the Ammonites, they sought a quarrel with him because he had not invited them to join in the war. A battle ensued, in which the Ephraimites were worsted, and the Gileadites having seized the fords of the Jordan, slew forty-two thousand of the Ephraimites when attempting to retreat into their own territory. In a passage, which is

---

* Jud. xi. 12-28.

unfortunately very obscure, we are told of something which passed before the conflict began. According to the Authorised Version, "the Gileadites smote Ephraim because they said, Ye Gileadites are fugitives of Ephraim among the Ephraimites, and among the Manassites: and the Gileadites took the passages of the Jordan before the Ephraimites," &c. This rendering is, however, generally condemned. The better interpretation would seem to be, "The Gileadites smote Ephraim, for they (the Gileadites) said, Ye (the Ephraimites) are fugitives from Ephraim: Gilead to his place between Ephraim and Manasseh! And the Gileadites took the passages of the Jordan," &c.* As Ephraim and Manasseh occupied the opposite sides of the Jordan, the battle-cry of the Gileadites, together with their subsequent manœuvre, becomes intelligible, whilst at the same time we discover a singular proof of the contempt in which the elder branch of the Beni-Joseph (Manasseh) affected to hold the younger which had crossed the Jordan. But for the purpose of the question we are now considering it is sufficient to note that the Gileadite chief and his followers, and the heads of the people whom he represented, are completely identified with the Manassites, and that the existence of Reubenites and Gadites, whose territory was at issue in the war with Ammon, is entirely ignored. It is across Gilead and Manasseh that Jephthah advances to invade the Ammonite territory, not across Reuben and Gad; and it is between Ephraim and Manasseh that his army threw itself when he seized the fords of the Jordan. The designations of Reuben and Gad had become overshadowed, if not almost entirely extinguished, by the style of Beni-Manasseh, the descendants of Joseph, the original stock which had come from Egypt— the Beni-Israel in its strictly limited sense, of whom indeed there were offshoots, which had crossed the Jordan.

---

* See Reuss, *La Bible Trad., Nouv.* Jud. xii. 4.

In the celebrated lyric of Deborah*—a production certainly anterior to the Monarchy—allusions are made to the Trans-Jordanic tribes. In the conflict between the Hebrew settlers on the west of the river and the Canaanites, in which Deborah and Barak were victorious, these tribes took no part, and their inactivity is referred to by the poetess in terms of pointed sarcasm. It is important to observe how they are noticed. Gad is not mentioned; the section of the Manassites is not mentioned; the only names we find being Reuben and Gilead. Let us see how these names are employed.

The passage in the Authorised Version runs: "For the divisions of Reuben there were great thoughts of heart. Why abodest thou among the sheep-folds to hear the bleatings of the flocks? For the divisions of Reuben were great searchings of heart. Gilead abode beyond Jordan." This translation, whilst failing to do justice to the original, is incorrect in rendering the Hebrew word *Pelagoth*, "divisions." It means "rivulets." With this alteration, it would appear that Deborah was referring to the great pastoral region appropriated by those who remained on the left bank of the Jordan comprehensively known as Gilead, and that the result of the mighty deliberations by the rivulets of Reuben to which she ironically refers, was that Gilead remained inactive on the other side of the river. Deborah ignores any tribal distinctions on the east bank of the Jordan, and speaks collectively of those who settled there as Reuben-Gilead. But what renders this mode of designation all the more striking is, that she makes special mention of Machir as one of those who joined her in the struggle with the Canaanites. Now, Machir was said to have been the eldest son of Manasseh,† who was the eldest

---

* Jud. v.   † Jos. xvii. 1.

son of Joseph; and Joseph is reported to have seen Machir's children before his death.* Machir was, according to one account, the conqueror of Gilead;† but the name came in time to be convertible with Manasseh. Thus we find the territory beyond the Jordan which, according to one account, was given to half the Beni-Manasseh,‡ was, according to another, assigned to half the Beni-Machir.§ The other section, whether called Manasseh or Machir it matters not, crossed the river into Canaan, and is referred to by Deborah by the latter name. It was from this Cis-Jordanic portion that she received assistance, and even in her time the severance between the two sections had become so complete that she felt there was no danger of being misunderstood in saying that Machir (without any other qualification) was one of her allies. To her and to those whom she addressed on the west of the Jordan the section of the parent stock which remained behind on the east was Reuben-Gilead. But when we listen to the representatives of Reuben-Gilead∥ the language is different. To them the designation Reuben is apparently unknown. The people are Gileadites-Manassites, and their leader vindicates their rights on the strength of conquests made by the children of Israel, the original emigrants from Egypt.

We see therefore that in the settlement on the east of the Jordan, the emigrants acted with a common purpose, and secured an end by which all equally benefited. Nor is this conclusion affected by the circumstance that the tide subsequently rolled westward across the river. But there was no division or allotment of the conquered territory between particular tribes or families. The conception that

---

* Gen. l. 23. † Num. xxxii. 39. ‡ Jos. xiii. 29.
§ Jos. xiii. 31. ∥ Jud. xi.

such a course of procedure was adopted, was the creation of a later age, when even the designations given to the Trans-Jordanic settlers came to be confounded and misunderstood. In the oldest traditions, collected respectively on opposite sides of the river, it was found that these settlers were spoken of as Reuben and Gad, Manasseh and Gilead, and it was supposed that they must have been distinct tribes. According to the traditions on the west of the river, Reuben and Gad divided the Trans-Jordanic conquests between them; whilst, following the memories preserved on the eastern bank, Machir, son of Manasseh, had conquered this region, and Gilead was his son.* But tradition also preserved the fact that men, claiming descent from those who had quitted Egypt, had crossed the Jordan and effected a settlement in Canaan; and as these latter also claimed descent through Machir Beni-Manasseh, the conqueror of the Trans-Jordanic region, the conception arose that half the tribe of Manasseh remained beyond the river. The substantial identity of this half-tribe with those who were known as Reuben (Reubel) and Gad was, however, forgotten; and it became historically necessary to apportion the Trans-Jordanic region, not only between Reuben and Gad, but to give a share to the half-tribe of Manasseh.† But this apportionment was unknown to the authors of the earliest records. Jephthah the Gileadite —that is, the Manassite, since Gilead was reputed to be the grandson of Manasseh—not only speaks and acts on behalf of the whole body of settlers on the east of the river, but he is unconscious that they are other than Manassites or Gileadites. In the traditions of his people, Manasseh is said to have been the eldest son of Joseph, who was personally identified with the Hebrew captives in Egypt.‡ But, in the Cis-Jordanic region, Reuben is made the eldest son of

* Jos. xvii. 1.   † Num. xxxii. 33.   ‡ Exod. i. 8.

Jacob,* who, in a more extended sense, is identified with the captives. The two traditions are substantially the same, and record the same fact—namely, that the first great section of those liberated from Egypt, who succeeded in permanently establishing themselves, were those who settled on the east of the Jordan, and who were known on the opposite sides of the river by the respective designations to which we have referred.

---

* Gen. xxix. 32.

CHAPTER XIV.

OUR task approaches its conclusion, and it will probably be asked, with some feeling of disappointment, "If this be a substantially correct version of the Hebrew migration from Egypt, what becomes of the traditional wanderings of the children of Israel?" The only reply must be, that they are not traditional, if by that term be meant narratives transmitted from hand to hand, from the time at which the events recorded are supposed to have taken place. The history of the human race is replete with traditions, but it may not be out of place to remark that all traditions are not true. Some are the mere creations of the fancy; some are the expressions of pious fraud; whilst others, again, are simply the illustrations of the fallibility of human judgment and the vitality of undetected error. A mistake is made; it is endorsed, and in course of time acquires a position which it is equally inconvenient and impracticable to assail.

That "the wanderings" found no place in the early traditions of the Hebrew race, is apparent from the attentive study of all the records which reproduce the impressions which were first formed respecting the migration from Egypt. By the collation of these records, the broad track taken by the released captives may be followed with almost absolute certainty, and it is precisely the track which, having regard to the physical peculiarities of the region traversed and the political conditions existing at that time, one would *à priori* have expected the Hebrews to take. Whether the special intervention of the Deity in their favour be admitted or denied, there is at all events nothing repugnant to probability in supposing that they acted like rational beings. When they quitted Egypt they were under the necessity of seeking a new home, and they naturally concentrated their energies to secure that end. If it be contended that during the greater part of forty years they did nothing of the kind, but simply roamed to and fro in a desolate wilderness, dependent for their sustenance on the daily recurrence of a miracle, their conduct is alone explicable on the assumption of a faith unparalleled in the history of religion, or an hallucination unsurpassed in the records of human folly. Before, however, we impute to the Deity so whimsical an adaptation of means to an end as that attributed in the now accepted story, or to the Hebrews a course of conduct irreconcilable with the canons which govern the actions of sane men, let us briefly consider the foundations upon which this marvellous romance reposes.

The emigrants from Egypt and their immediate descendants knew nothing of the wanderings with which it pleased posterity to credit them; indeed, if we may be permitted so to express it, it was inconsistent with their religious conceptions that they could wander. They believed in an everpresent protecting deity, one of whose obligations by virtue of the covenant was to lead them in the right path through a region with which they were unfamiliar, but whose aid they deemed it not inconsistent with prudence to supplement by human precautions.* The patience and the confidence of such a people in the judgment and good faith of their God, would have been exhausted before the termination of one year, much less forty, if they found out that he was virtually leading them nowhere.

But those who insist that by God's special providence the

---

* Num. x. 29-32.

Israelites did wander for close on forty years, are not released from the obligation of finding a wilderness in which the wandering took place, and the plateau of the Tih has naturally supplied the scene for this grotesque manifestation of the Divine Will.* But one may be permitted to doubt whether any of the upholders of this view have ever seriously considered the consequences which it involves. The Tih was not then, any more than now, in the moon. It lay on the borders of a powerful and highly civilised people, and it supplied the only route by which the communications of that people could be maintained with the Eastern world. Were those communications suspended during forty years? did Arabia cease to send her products to the banks of the Nile? were the Ishmaelite caravans discontinued? and did the powerful Pharaohs tacitly assent to an unexplained and unaccountable blockade of close on half a century, in order that by God's providence those whom he had taken out of Egypt with a high hand should wander, wander, wander, until—they had died out?

But what is this steppe which was thus singularly utilised, and which we are gravely told was suitable for the *bonâ fide* wandering of the Israelites, who, be it remembered, are, according to the accepted view, estimated at between two and three millions? In size—its length or breadth nowhere exceeds one hundred and twenty miles, and it can be traversed in a week. If they numbered two millions, and had formed a column of ten abreast, allowing a yard in depth for each rank, the caravan, exclusive of cattle, would have reached from Suez to Akaba. In respect to physical characteristics, the

---

* It has been said that the name Desert of "et-Tih," given to this region, signifies the Desert of the Wandering, and that the title is a quasi-memorial of the antiquity of the tradition. I am assured by an eminent Arabic scholar that the name *Tih* is not uncommon, and that elsewhere it confessedly has not the signification here given to it.

Tih probably differs but little from what it was three thousand years ago. Its condition may have been better; it could scarcely have been worse. But if it was then less desolate and barren than now, it had inhabitants who must have come in contact with the wanderers. The significance of the fact that "the divine historian" tells us nothing of what happened during this long period of straying, has been singularly overlooked, or intentionally put out of sight. "It was not the object of the inspired leader of the Israelite host to preserve a chronicle of events devoid of interest or of religious instruction for posterity." But this is to invert the order of reasoning. One must be satisfied of the conclusiveness of the evidence in support of a given proposition, before explaining away or disregarding the evidence which is apparently irreconcilable with it. This has not been done by those who so flippantly treat as of no importance the silence of "the divine historian" in respect to the eccentric peregrinations of the host of which he was the responsible leader.

It would be idle to attempt to ascertain the time when the belief in the "wanderings" first gained a footing in Judæa, though happily it is not impossible to explain the manner in which the belief arose. Let us review the evidence still remaining at our disposal upon this interesting point.

The settlers in Canaan preserved the recollection that a long period which, following an early nomadic custom was called "forty years," had elapsed between the Exodus from Egypt and the crossing of the Jordan.* Canaan was, in their eyes, the Land of Promise—the land which Jahveh had covenanted to give to their fathers; but, presumably for their rebellion and disobedience, this long period was per-

---

* Deut. i. 3; Jos. v. 6.

mitted to elapse before they, or rather their children, were brought into their promised home. In the punishment thus meted out even Moses and Aaron were made to share, and although the former was represented as leading the Israelites to victory in their wars against the kings of the Amorites, and as allotting the Trans-Jordanic region amongst certain tribes, he was still presumed never to have set his foot in the Promised Land. It would therefore appear that, however rich and fertile the region on the east bank of the Jordan may have been, and however worthy of acceptance by a section of the children of Israel—nay, however positively it may have been included within the possessions covenanted to be given to those who were led out of Egypt—it came to be regarded by those who made their home to the west of the Jordan as not included in the Land of Promise. That such an opinion should have arisen goes far to disprove the existence of that *solidarité* between the settlers on the opposite sides of the Jordan (whether they be called Hebrews, Israelites, or by specific tribal designations) which is commonly supposed to have subsisted from the time of the Exodus down to the Assyrian captivity.

But such of the parent stock as settled in Gilead could never have entertained the view that the land covenanted to be given to their fathers lay on the opposite side of the Jordan, because then *ex hypothesi* they would never have entered into possession of it. They obtained what they wished for, and what satisfied them, on the east bank of the river; or, in their own religious phraseology, they possessed the land which Jahveh their God gave unto them.* Taking a retrospective view of the period which elapsed during the migration from Egypt, the traditions of the Trans-

---

* Jud. xi. 24.

Jordanic tribes might declare it to have been of indeterminate length; but that period, whatever its duration, would undoubtedly be regarded as brought to a conclusion as soon as their ancestors entered the territory which became theirs, and which they were content to possess. And if these settlers held the belief that Moses was denied the satisfaction of accompanying his followers—*i.e.*, their fathers—into their future possessions, they could never have entertained the idea that he took a prominent part in the conquest of Gilead.

Now let us recur once more to that invaluable record of Jephthah's negotiations with the king of the Ammonites.* Having noticed the vain attempt of the Israelites to obtain permission to pass through Edom and Moab on their road from Egypt, Jephthah states that Israel abode in Kadesh. At a later but unnamed period he declares that the Israelites compassed Edom and Moab, and "pitched beyond the Arnon," and that then followed the conquest of the territory of the Amorites, "from the wilderness to the Jordan," the land which was given over by Jahveh to Israel for a possession. We should not lay much stress on the absence of any allusion to the possessions acquired on the west of the Jordan, because they were not in dispute between the Gileadites and the Ammonites; but it is evident from Jephthah's language that the period of journeying through the wilderness terminated, in his opinion, when the Israelites crossed the Arnon and entered into the possessions the title to which he was then vindicating.

But we have more precise information respecting the stage at which the journeyings through "the wilderness" were, according to the earliest traditions, supposed to have come to a close. In a record preserved in the Book of

---

* Jud. xi.

Numbers, it is stated that the Israelites, after compassing Edom, rested at a place called Oboth, from whence they proceeded to "Ije-abarim, in the wilderness which is before Moab, toward the sun-rising,"*—*i.e.*, on the eastern border of Moab. "From thence they removed and pitched in the valley of Zared, from whence they removed and pitched on the other side of the Arnon," which formed "the border of Moab, between Moab and the Amorites."†

We find the valley of Zared, or Zered, also referred to in the introductory portion of Deuteronomy. The Israelites are directed to "rise up and cross over the brook (*nachal*) Zered ;"‡ and it is then added that the space of time which had elapsed between the departure from Kadesh-barnea and the crossing of the *nachal* Zered was thirty-eight years, in which time "all the generation of the men of war were wasted out from among the host."§ The valley of Zered has been generally identified with the Wady-el-Ahsy, which formed the southern boundary of Moab, and through which a stream flows into the lower end of the Dead Sea. This is an error, and has arisen from treating Deuteronomy ii. 9-25 as a continuous narrative, instead of recognising two distinct fragments (9-15; 16-25), the one being merely a different version of the other. In the latter a reference is made to Ammon which is not in the former, and the *nachal* Zered of the one is replaced by the *nachal* Arnon of the other. "Rise ye up, take your journey, and pass over the river Arnon . . . . this day will I begin to put the dread of thee and the fear of thee upon the nations."∥ That the Zered and the Arnon were substantially identical appears, however, still more clearly from the previous record to which we have referred.¶ Ije Abarim is distinctly stated to

---

* Num. xxi. 11. † Num. xxi. 12, 13. ‡ Deut. ii. 13.
§ Deut. ii. 14. ∥ Deut. ii. 24. ¶ Num. xxi. 11.

have been between Moab and the wilderness towards the east, and could not possibly have been reached by the Israelites without previously crossing the Wady-el-Ahsy, which is supposed to have been the boundary between Moab and Edom. The expression "they pitched in the *nachal* Zared, from thence they removed and pitched on the other side of Arnon,"* is perfectly consistent with an encampment in a valley, and the subsequent crossing of the stream or river flowing through it. The valley (*nachal*) of Zered, or of Arnon, constituted the boundary line which in the earliest traditions, and notably in those preserved on the east of the Jordan, was believed to have marked the termination of the journeyings in the wilderness.

We have seen, therefore, that between the traditions preserved by those who settled to the east of the Jordan and the views subsequently entertained by the descendants of those who entered Canaan, respecting the terminal point of the journeyings through the wilderness, a very important difference existed. The former considered that their trials came to an end when they crossed the *nachal* Zered, or Arnon; the latter, on the other hand, made the Jordan the boundary line which had to be crossed before they entered into the possessions which Jahveh had covenanted to give them, and they may or may not have believed that "forty years" were exhausted when they passed this river and entered the land of Canaan.

But in the course of time the views entertained by the inhabitants of Judæa respecting the migration from Egypt underwent an extraordinary change. In the pious romance which constitutes the first portion of the Book of Joshua, we find "the wilderness" and its privations assume marvellous proportions. The writer lived at a period so far re-

---

* Num. xxi. 13.

moved from that whose events he professed to record, and was so wholly unacquainted with the physical features and characteristics of the country about which he wrote, that he not only made the forty years terminate when the Jordan was crossed, but he actually brought "the wilderness" up to the bank of that river, and declared that the Israelites were recipients of manna until they set foot in Canaan.* It is needless to point out that the Amorites who were vanquished on the left bank of the Jordan must have had the means of subsistence, and that the region coveted by the Reubenites and Gadites was not one in which it was essential to disturb the laws of Nature in order to supply the inhabitants with food. Besides we know, from other sources, that the emigrants from Egypt were willing to purchase from friendly tribes the supplies of which they stood in need,† and they could not have even temporarily consorted with Kenites, Edomites, Moabites, Midianites, and others, without partaking of the food at the disposal of those tribes. But considerations such as these were overlooked or disregarded by the writer to whom we refer. He probably found it stated in an ancient record—to which we shall have occasion to refer—that the children of Israel were for their disobedience made to "feed" for forty years in the wilderness,‡ and as the forty years were supposed by him to have terminated at the crossing of the Jordan, he probably thought he would be historically correct in representing the Israelites as having been fed on manna until they passed that river. But, whatever may have been the

---

* Jos. v. 10 12.   † Deut. ii. 6, 28, 29.
‡ Num. xiv. 33. The record in Exodus (chap. xvi.) containing the statement that the children of Israel ate manna forty years (Exod. xvi. 35), is of very late date. It brings in the "Testimony"—that is, the Ark—at a time when it did not exist, and gives an explanatory gloss on the nature of an omer.

impressions which he formed or the motives which actuated him, he succeeded in giving to the migration from Egypt a complexion it never originally possessed, and laid the foundation for those unintelligible wanderings which have for more than two thousand years perplexed the minds of the earnest believers in the providence of God, and driven to despair the painstaking and confiding thousands who have vainly endeavoured to follow the track of the Heaven-conducted host.

It is needless to observe that in the oft-quoted address of Jephthah to the king of the Ammonites, there is no suggestion that the children of Israel "wandered" on their way from Egypt. There is an intimation of a break in the journey at Kadesh, but nothing more. They "walked through the wilderness to the Red Sea, and came to Kadesh;" they "abode in Kadesh;" and, again "they walked through the wilderness, and compassed Edom and Moab." And if we refer to the only records we possess respecting the migration, we not only discover nothing inconsistent with this simple statement, but everything which confirms it. The traditions preserved in the Books of Exodus and Numbers respecting the movements of the Israelites, as we have already shown at great length, tally with Jephthah's description. There is confessedly no account given of the wanderings themselves, and we are therefore reduced to the simple inquiry whether it is stated in the Scriptural records as a matter of fact that the Israelites did wander in the wilderness, and, if so, on what authority such statement rests.

In the first place, we must take precautions against being misled by words, and before adopting the term "wander," which is of tolerably frequent occurrence in the Authorised Version in connection with the Israelites' movements in the wilderness, we must ascertain whether the idea implied by that term was conveyed by the Hebrew words so translated.

In an address which Caleb is said to have made to Joshua subsequent to the successful invasion of Canaan, the former refers to his life having been preserved while "Israel wandered in the wilderness."* In the margin of the A. V. the correct translation "walked" is to be found. The Hebrew word† is of very frequent occurrence, and signifies to "go," to "walk," and occasionally implies a simple state of continuance. Thus, "Jahveh thy God *walketh* in the midst of thy camp, to deliver thee;"‡ meaning, Jahveh "accompanies" or "is with" his people. "For the children of Israel *walked* forty years in the wilderness, till all the people that were men of war were consumed,"§ does not mean that they wandered, nor even that they "walked," in the sense of constant motion, from place to place, but simply that they passed their time in the wilderness during "forty years," until a certain result was brought about—a result which, it is important to remark, needed for its realisation the simple evolution of time, and not any particular occupation on the part of the Israelites.

It is stated that when the Israelites murmured against their leaders, and refused to invade Canaan, Jahveh was very angry; and, to punish them for their disobedience, told them they should be consumed, and that their children should "wander" in the wilderness forty years.‖ The word here translated "wander"¶ has no such meaning. It signifies (as, indeed, is stated in the A. V. margin) to "feed" or to "pasture," and the passage was in the original never intended to convey any other idea than that the rising generation of the Israelites would be (or rather were) compelled to live for forty years in the wilderness, until the

---

* Jos. xiv. 10. † הָלַךְ *hâh-loc'h*. ‡ Deut. xxiii. 14.
§ Jos. v. 6. ‖ Num. xiv. 33. ¶ רָעָה *Râh-yâh*.

adults who were responsible for the rebellion had died out. That this is the correct interpretation appears from the other version of the tradition which is contained in the same chapter.* In it there is no mention of "wandering" or "feeding," but Jahveh simply declares, " Surely they shall not see the land which I sware unto their fathers; neither shall any of them that provoked me see it."† The Israelites believed that, in consequence of their disobedience in the wilderness, the adults were not allowed to live long enough to enter into the promised possessions, whilst the rising generation was, according to the Hebrew conception of vicarious punishment, obliged to expiate such disobedience‡ by remaining in the wilderness—*i.e.*, in the region outside their future home, until their fathers died. But there is nothing here to support the suggestion that they ever thought they whiled away their time in objectless straying in a region assumed to be uninhabitable by man, under the ordinary conditions of nature.

It is related that when the tribes of Reuben and Gad sued for the possessions which had been conquered on the east of the Jordan, Moses reproached them, and reminded them of the consequences which followed the rebellion of the Israelites on the return of the spies. "And Jahveh's anger was kindled against Israel, and he made them wander in the wilderness forty years, until all the generation that had done evil in the sight of Jahveh were consumed."§ Moses then continues : " Behold, ye are risen up in your fathers' stead . . . . for if ye turn away from after him, he will yet again leave them in the wilderness; and ye shall destroy all this people."|| We have already stated our reasons for assigning a comparatively late date and a Cis-Jordanic origin

---

* Num. xiv. 11–25.   † Num. xiv. 23.   ‡ Num. xiv. 33.
§ Num. xxxii. 13. || Num. xxxii. 14, 15.

to the narrative of the allotment of Gilead to Reuben and Gad, and we find in the passage here quoted a confirmation of this conclusion. The Trans-Jordanic region had been already acquired when Reuben and Gad preferred their request; the Israelites had entered, and then held by right of conquest a rich and fertile country; and yet we find the narrator representing Moses warning Reuben and Gad that their anxiety to obtain possessions before their brethren had entered into their promised home might excite the anger of Jahveh, and induce him to punish the people—how?—by "yet again leaving them in the wilderness." But as at this time the Israelites were no longer in a wilderness, in the general acceptation of that term, but in the highly productive region of which they had dispossessed the Amorites, we have further proof that the word *midbhar* was used to denote the entire region which on their way from Egypt the Israelites were obliged to traverse before reaching their final homes. The wilderness of the Trans-Jordanic tribes terminated at the Arnon, that of the settlers in Canaan at the Jordan. But in what way was the anger of Jahveh, according to the conception of the narrator, to be manifested? Clearly in the same form in which it had been manifested before. Jahveh would assuredly treat those who had risen up in their fathers' stead as he had already treated their fathers, and "yet again leave them in the wilderness." But the wildest imagination could never conceive the possibility of a people wandering about in the country bordering Jordan on the east; and it must be taken that the warning put in the mouth of Moses by the narrator was simply intended to convey the idea that Jahveh would probably punish the people by detaining them for another long period outside the limits of the land which he had promised to them, or might possibly abandon them altogether.

These considerations consequently lead us to examine with

some caution the word employed by the narrator, which in the Authorized Version is rendered "he made them wander."* This word† is stated, on the high authority of Gesenius, primarily to signify "to move to and fro," "to vacillate." It is applied to the motion of the drunk, and of the blind, to the rustling of leaves, and by the prophet Amos it is twice used to convey the idea of fruitless journeying.‡ In the causative form it is employed in the Book of Daniel in allusion to the movement of "reeling;"§ it appears in the 59th Psalm‖ in the same sense in which it is used by Amos; and in Numbers (in the passage now under consideration), and in the Second Book of Samuel, with significations to which we are about more particularly to refer. It is nowhere employed to convey the idea of "straying," or of objectless motion from place to place.

When David quitted Jerusalem in consequence of the rebellion of Absalom,¶ he was accompanied by a Gittite, named Ittai. As Ittai was a foreigner, and presumably uninterested in the change of government, David advised him to return and abide with the new king—"Whereas thou camest but yesterday," said David, "should I this day *make thee go up and down* with us [in the margin of the A. V., "make thee wander in going"], seeing I go whither I may: return thee with thy brethren." David with his followers fled across the Jordan, and having been pursued by Absalom with the army of Israel, a battle took place, in which the latter was vanquished, and Absalom was slain. The meaning of David's expression, italicised in the above passage, is tolerably apparent. He was uncertain what would be the issue of the impending struggle between himself and his son.

---

* Num. xxxii. 13.   † נוֹעַ *Noo-ay*.   ‡ Amos iv. 8; viii. 12.
§ Dan. x. 10.   ‖ Ps. lix. 15.
¶ 2 Sam. xv. 13-23.

and he knew not in what direction he might be compelled to turn his steps. He therefore sought to dissuade Ittai from accompanying him. But he had no idea of wandering, or of being the cause of Ittai's wandering, in the ordinary acceptation of that term.

But in the passage in Numbers which immediately occupies our attention, is there any justification for concluding that the word employed has any larger signification than that of a change of movement consequent on the non-realisation of the object originally prompting it? The prominent feature of the migration from Egypt, exhibited in all the traditions, was the check received on the return of the spies, through the failure to enter Canaan from the south, with the subsequent refusal of the Edomites to allow a passage through their territory, the consequent abode at Kadesh, and the retracing of their steps by the Israelites, when they once again proceeded to the Red Sea (Akaba) previous to passing around Edom and Moab. It was at Kadesh, at this turning-point, that Jahveh caused the people, in consequence of their disobedience, to abandon that direct route by which he had led them from Egypt to the possessions which he had sworn to give to them. But from the Hebrew religious stand-point, Jahveh naturally could not commit any mistake. If the Israelites did not immediately enter Canaan, and if they were obliged to abandon their original route and retrace their steps, the fault was exclusively theirs; and it was Jahveh who, in consequence of their disobedience or want of faith, obliged them to turn back and seek their future destination by another route. But as the change of purpose and of route involved a long delay before Canaan was ultimately entered, the change of route and the consequent delay came to be combined in one complex idea, and hence the employment of a form of expression calculated to convey the impression that the change of route was an ever-continuing process coincident with the whole period of forty years. In one sense it was so, because the adoption of the altered route involved the subsequent delay ; but the construction that the Israelites were made during a long period to change their course continuously, without ever having any objective point to which they were tending— now moving north, now south, now east, now west—only to find themselves at the end of many years at the place from which they started, is one which the passage will not bear, which the writer never intended it to have, and which, moreover, would never have been put upon it by sane men in search of historical truth, if the passage so construed occurred in writings for which the authority of inspiration had not been claimed. It is, however, only just to the author of this passage to say that he is not responsible, because a love of the marvellous, together with a fantastic conception of the ways of Providence, have led pious men to attribute to him a meaning which he never intended to convey.

The author of Ps. cvii.* employs a word† which is rendered " wander," but independently of the ambiguity of the allusion which may or may not refer to the journey from Egypt, and the uncertain date of the composition, it is to be observed that the same word is elsewhere used in a different sense. When Abraham said to Abimelech, " God caused me *to wander* from my father's house,"‡ he used the term simply in the sense of departure from the paternal domicile in search of another but as yet undetermined home. In a similar sense, it would seem to be employed in the narrative of Hagar's expulsion from Abraham's house.§

At the close of the seventh century B.C., the date assigned to the composition of the Book of Deuteronomy,

---

* Ps. cvii. 4, 40. † תָעָה *Tah-yah.* ‡ Gen. xx. 13.
§ Gen. xxi. 14.

the conception entertained respecting the migration from Egypt assumed another form. The religion of Israel had become purer, and the author of this Book formed a higher and a grander idea of Jahveh. Monotheism began to supplant Henotheism; the tribal deity gave place to the Lord of the Heavens and the Earth. In dealing with the traditions of the migration from Egypt, the writer adopted the literal construction of the forty years' stay in the wilderness, but purified the conception of the care manifested by the protecting God for his people. "He led them in the wilderness during forty years*—that is to say, he watched over them, he was with them, he directed their steps so that ultimately they should reach their promised destination. But the writer says nothing to make one suppose he thought that the Israelites were literally made to stray in the wilderness during the period to which he refers. On the contrary, in the language of Oriental imagery, he exaggerates the provident care of the Deity, by representing the raiment of the Israelites as not wearing out, and their feet as unaffected by their long and arduous journey.† That he magnified the toil and the dangers incidental to the physical task of proceeding from Egypt to Canaan, even with the *détour* round Edom, is very possible; and that the forty years' stay in the wilderness, unexplained as it was, had created in Judæa the impression that many and grievous hardships had been borne by the emigrants of which no record was kept, is tolerably certain; but there is really no evidence that, even so late as the fall of the Jewish monarchy, any clearly defined idea was entertained that the Israelites had occupied the greater part of the traditional forty years in straying about. How the time was passed was unknown, and this ignorance, coupled with the fantastic notion that the Israelites ate

---

* Deut. viii. 2; xxix. 5.   † Deut. viii. 4; xxix. 5.

nothing but manna from the time they quitted Egypt until they crossed the Jordan, laid the foundation for the marvellous superstructure of the wanderings. If men received a miraculous supply of food daily, it was reasonable to suppose that they stood in need of it, and this necessity could only have arisen in a wilderness. But a stay of forty years in such a region was alone comprehensible on the assumption that such a period was indispensable to traverse it, or that owing to exceptional circumstances the Israelites were unable, or were not permitted, to cross it in a shorter time. That in consequence of their disobedience they were not permitted to quit it any sooner, was the universal belief amongst the settlers in Canaan; or, to borrow the language of the author of the concluding chapters of the Book of Joshua, they "dwelt in the wilderness a long season."* But in time the idea arose that, although one portion of a completely barren region would be no better than another, occasional motion would be preferable to continuous rest; and hence came the conception of the movements of the Israelites from one part of the wilderness to another—a conception which became strengthened through misunderstanding the records in which were preserved the traditions of the migration. Their fragmentary and unconnected nature was lost sight of, and they came to be treated as a continuous narrative. There seemed to be two arrivals of the Israelites at Kadesh, separated by a long series of years. What could be more natural than to fill up the interval by making the people expiate their rebellion by wandering about until their appointed punishment had been fulfilled?

---

* Jos. xxiv. 7. The same writer uses language which excludes a belief on his part that the Israelites passed the forty years wandering in a desolate, uninhabited region. "For Jahveh, our God, he it is that brought us up and our fathers out of the land of Egypt, and preserved us in all the way wherein we went, *and among all the people through whom we passed*" (Jos. xxiv. 17).

CHAPTER XV.

IN treating of the history of the Hebrew migration from Egypt, it is of some importance to ascertain, if possible, whether those who forced an entrance into the Trans-Jordanic region secured their "possessions" within a comparatively short period after quitting the place of their captivity, and also whether they accomplished this great work under the leadership of Moses. In dealing with this part of our inquiry, we are equally embarrassed by the scantiness and the imperfection of the materials at our command. The records which preserve the Trans-Jordanic traditions are far from numerous, and such as they are they have passed not uninjured through Cis-Jordanic channels. We are compelled therefore, as best we can, to distinguish the original stories from the later embellishments and glosses, in order to ascertain what were the beliefs entertained by those who established themselves on the left bank of the Jordan.

It is no doubt specifically stated that Moses led the Israelites against the kings of the Amorites, and, having dispossessed them, that he partitioned Gilead between the Reubenites, Gadites, and half the tribe of Manassites. We have already set forth the grounds upon which we must reject this story of the partition, and it will therefore cause us the less effort to withhold our acceptance of the statement that Moses was the conqueror of Gilead until we have examined the traditions respecting the circumstances of his death. It will further be recollected that the account of the conquest of the Trans-Jordanic region is extremely bald, and that according to one statement it is said to have been accomplished under the leadership of Machir, and according to another under that of Jair.

In the Book of Numbers it is recorded that Jahveh said unto Moses, " Get thee up into this mount Abarim, and see the land which I have given unto the children of Israel; and when thou hast seen it, thou shalt be gathered unto thy people, as Aaron thy brother was gathered."* In Deuteronomy there is a somewhat different version : " Get thee up into this mountain Abarim, unto mount Nebo, which is in the land of Moab, that is over against Jericho ; and behold the land of Canaan, which I give unto the children of Israel for a possession."† " And Moses went up from the plains of Moab (*Araboth Moab*), unto the mountain of Nebo, to the top of Pisgah, which is over against Jericho : and Jahveh showed him all the land of Gilead, unto Dan, and all Naphtali," &c.‡ " So Moses died in the land of Moab, and he buried him in a valley in the land of Moab, over against Beth-peor ; but no man knoweth of his sepulchre unto this day."§ Where was this Mount Abarim (*Har-ha-Abarim*) ?|| Are we to look for it opposite and in sight of Jericho, or are we to seek for it to the south of the Arnon ? We are not now inquiring whether as a matter of fact Moses ever accompanied the Hebrews as far as the land of Moab, even as limited on the north by the Arnon, but whether a tradition arose that he did so, and from a mountain in that country viewed the possessions he was not permitted to enter. That there was such a tradition there can be no doubt ; but the statement that the mountain from which

---

* Num. xxvii. 12, 13.   † Deut. xxxii. 49.   ‡ Deut. xxxiv. 1, 2.
§ Deut. xxxiv. 5, 6.
|| The word Abarim is preceded by the definite article, "the mount of the Abarim," whatever that may have meant.

Moses was said to have viewed the future home of his followers was placed in Moab, and not in Gilead, the newly acquired territory on the east of the Jordan, and that he was permitted to see Gilead, which according to other accounts he is said to have conquered, raises a strong presumption that Mount Abarim was to the south of the Arnon. If Moses had accompanied his followers into Gilead, and had died there, it is inconceivable that tradition should not have preserved so important a fact; and no less so that the Trans-Jordanic settlers should have forgotten the place where they buried their great leader, though his grave necessarily lay within the limits of their lately acquired possessions.

We have already stated our reasons for identifying the *nachal* Zered with the valley of the Arnon. Let us inquire whether the heights of Abarim have any apparent connection with the border which separated "the wilderness" from the possessions of those who settled on the east of the Jordan.

In one of the Targums the *nachal* Zered is called "the valley of willows,"* and Isaiah makes mention of a "valley of willows"† as lying within the territory or on the borders of Moab. In the construction of "booths," at the Feast of Tabernacles, "willows of the brook" were used, together with "branches of palm-trees:"‡ and there is good reason for supposing that the willow was associated in the Jewish mind, at all events previous§ to the Babylonian captivity, with happiness and prosperity. That this was due to the tradition that the "valley of willows" marked the final

---

* "Thence they journeyed, and encamped in a valley abounding in reeds, osiers, and mandrakes," or "lilies" (*Targ. Pal.*, Num. xxi. 11; Etheridge's Translation).
† Isa. xv. 7.   ‡ Lev. xxiii. 40.   § Ps. cxxxvii. 2.

encampment of the children of Israel before quitting the wilderness is, to say the least, not improbable.

The valley or brook referred to by Isaiah is called in the Hebrew text *nachal Ha-Arabim*, which is probably rightly construed "the valley of willows," and would seem to be identical with the *nachal* Zered,* "the valley of willows" of the Targumist. But we know that before quitting the wilderness the Israelites rested at Ije-Abarim, then moved into the valley of Zared, and then crossed the Arnon;† and we are therefore led to inquire whether the word Abarim may not be the result of the transposition of a letter by a scribe—Abarim for Arabim. There are instances in which there can be no doubt that such errors have occurred in the Hebrew text, and this would seem to have been one of them.‡ The name Abarim occurs elsewhere, but this furnishes no proof that the word appeared originally in this form, because, putting out of sight the later date of the records in which the name is repeated, it must in any case have been necessary to harmonise the several passages so far as regarded the name of the place, if any discrepancy existed. The point is of some importance, because, if this speculation should be well-founded, it would furnish a curious corroboration of the identity of independent traditions in bringing the migration through the wilderness to a close at a "valley of willows," known respectively as *nachal* Zared and *nachal Ha-Arabim*, the heights commanding which

---

* זָרַד *Zarad*, an unused root = to prune trees, hence זֶרֶד *Zered*, which signifies the luxuriant growth of trees. We find, consequently, that the *nachal Zered* and the *nachal Ha-Arabim* have a similar meaning—a valley remarkable for its trees, or adjoining a place having this characteristic.

† Num. xxi. 11-13.

‡ The Masorites give sixty-two instances in which, in their opinion, this error has crept into the text.

furnished a resting-place for the Israelites before descending into the Wady.

An allusion is apparently made to this celebrated valley in a narrative told of Elijah, which merits a passing reference as illustrating the way in which miraculous legends are formed.

Elijah, who was a Gileadite—that is, an inhabitant of the Trans-Jordanic region—is said to have foretold to Ahab, king of Israel, a long-continued drought. He then was commanded by Jahveh to turn eastward, and hide in the *nachal* Cherith, which was "before the Jordan," to drink of the waters of the brook, and food would be brought to him by ravens. Elijah did so; bread and meat were brought to him night and morning by ravens, and he drank of the water of the brook until it dried up, and then he received the commands of Jahveh to go to Zeraphath, in Zidon.*

The word which is translated "ravens" is, save in the Masoretic vowel punctuation, identical with that which is rendered "willows,"† and it would seem therefore that Elijah was told to proceed to the *nachal* Cherith, which was noted for its willows; and this supposition is strengthened by considering the direction which Elijah was supposed to have taken when quitting Ahab, who probably was at the time in his capital, Samaria. He went eastwards to a valley which was "before," that is, to the east of, the Jordan. Now, if he was seeking to avoid Ahab's vengeance, it was natural that he should go beyond his reach; and the "valley of willows," the *nachal* Zared, lying as it did outside the Trans-Jordanic possessions, would supply to the Gileadite a suitable place of refuge. If this view be correct, Cherith would be the

---

* 1 Kings xvii. 1–9.

† עֲרָבִים *Arabim* (willows), עֹרְבִים *Orebim* (ravens). It is needless to remind the reader that in the original text there were no vowel points, and that the two words were absolutely identical.

corruption or Cis-Jordanic evolution of the more ancient name Zered.

The story of the ravens was too strong even for St. Jerome, and he suggested that the providence of God, and a due regard for probabilities, might be reconciled by reading Arabim for Orebim, and translating the word Arabians.* Having been commanded to take refuge in a valley on the frontier of Arabia, it seemed a natural explanation of what subsequently occurred that the Arabians should, by the Divine command, have fed the fugitive prophet. Another and more probable explanation of the supposed miracle, however, presents itself. It has been noticed by travellers that a tree grows on the banks of the Jordan and in the neighbouring valleys, named the *Gharrob* or *Gharb*, which produces on its leaves and branches a gum that closely resembles the *manna* of the Bedouins which is found on the *tarfa* or tamarisk.† The *Gharrob* has, however, been iden-

---

* In the Comm. on Isa. xv. 7, Jerome writes: "Pro salicibus in Hebræo legimus *Arabim*, quod potest et Arabes intelligi et legi *Orbim*, id est villa in finibus eorum sita cujus a plerisque accolæ in Monte Oreb Eliæ præbuisse alimenta dicuntur: quod nomen propter ambiguitatem transfertur et in *corvos*, atque *Occidentem*, *loca que campestria*." The reference to Mount Horeb shows how completely the Sinaitic peninsula was absent from the mind of Jerome, since the *nachal Arabim* of Isaiah, however the designation be understood, was declared by the prophet to be on the borders of Moab.

† "One of the most interesting productions of this valley" (Burckhardt is referring to the Ghor and the eastern side of the Dead Sea) "is the Beyrouk honey, or, as the Arabs call it, Assal Beyrouk. I suppose it to be the manna, but I never had an opportunity of seeing it myself. It was described to me as a juice dropping from the leaves and twigs of a tree called Gharrab, of the size of an olive-tree, with leaves like those of the poplar, but somewhat broader The honey collects upon the leaves like dew, and is gathered from them, or from the ground under the tree" (*Syria*, p. 393). It is to be regretted that Burckhardt had not an opportunity of seeing this product or collecting it. The Gharrab has been identified with the *Salix babylonica*, or willow (Sprengel, *Hist. Rei. Herb.* i. 270); and it is found in the valley of

tified with the *Salix babylonica* or willow, and it would therefore seem that, according to the original story, Elijah was commanded to proceed to the well-known "valley of willows," where he would be fed by the "willows," and drink water from the brook. Either a later writer, mistaking the word Arabim for Orebim, amplified the story by declaring that the *Orebim* (ravens) brought bread and flesh to the prophet morning and night, or the original narrator simply desired to state that each morning and night the *Arabim* (willows) produced by the Divine command what was necessary for Elijah's sustenance.

Taking it, then, as an established historical fact that between the Trans-Jordanic possessions and Moab there was a valley known descriptively as the *nachal Ha-Arabim*, and having also satisfied ourselves that the emigrants from Egypt must have reached this valley immediately before entering the country of the Amorites; and finding, further, that they encamped on the *Ije-ha-Abarim* (the heights of Abarim) before entering the *nachal* Zered, and thence "pitched on the other side of Arnon," it is difficult to avoid the conclusion that the *Ije-ha-Abarim* were the *Ije-ha-Arabim*; that the heights overhung the valley famed for its willows; that on descending from those heights the Israelites encamped in the valley on the Moabite side of the stream; and that they thence removed and pitched their tents *on the other side* of the Arnon, the name borne by the river. But these conclusions derive support from other sources.

Some half-dozen miles to the east of Kerak, the ancient Kir of Moab, a hilly range extends in a north-easterly

---

the Arnon and in those running into it. The Hebrew name of this manna-bearing tree has been preserved unchanged, ערב *Gh'rb*, the initial letter *Ain* being a guttural. The source from which Elijah derived his sustenance phonetically rendered in English is *Gh'rebim*.

direction, overhanging the main tributary, or rather the principal source of the Arnon. This ridge is called to-day Jebel-et-Tarfûyeh, the mountain of the tarfa-trees. At its base flows a stream, known in its upper portion as the Seyl Sayde, but which a little lower down bears the name of Seyl Szefye.* The word Szefye signifies a willow,† and it is at least noteworthy that we find even to-day the principal source of the Arnon bearing a name in Arabic which corresponds with the *nachal Ha-Arabim* of the Hebrews, identified by us with the *nachal* Zered. We find, in addition, that this valley is overhung by a hilly range, which bears the name Jebel-et-Tarfûyeh, which not inaptly corresponds with the Ije-Abarim; or, as we contend it should be written, Ije-Arabim—"the heights of the willow-trees" of the Hebrew tradition. When it is further added that the willow is found in the valley of the Arnon,‡ we have a combination of coincidences which go far to support the conclusion that the modern Seyl Szefye is the *nachal* Zered, or *nachal Ha-Arabim* of the Biblical records, and that the Jebel-et-Tarfûyeh is the Ije-Abarim (Arabim?) of the earliest tradition preserved in the Book of Numbers, and which is in the strictest sense "before Moab, toward the sun-rising," or east

---

* "The principal source of the Mojib is at a short distance to the north-east of Katrane, a station of the Syrian Hajj. There the river is called Seyl Sayde; lower down it changes its name to Efm-el-Kereim, or, as it is also called, Szefye" (Burckhardt, *Syria*, p. 373).

† Ezekiel uses the word Zaphzapha in this sense (Ezek. xvii. 5).

‡ Burckhardt describes the valley of the Arnon, the Wady Mojib, when viewed from above, as resembling a deep chasm, formed by some tremendous convulsion of nature, the distance from the edge of one precipice to the opposite one being about two miles. On descending into the valley he found some Defle and willow-trees growing on its banks (*Syria*, pp. 372, 373). Burckhardt also mentions a Wady through which flows an affluent of the Arnon. It is the Wady Wale. "The banks of the rivulet are overgrown with willows, Defle, and tamarisks" (*Syria*, p. 370).

of Kerak, the chief city of Moab at the time of the Exodus.*

It may perhaps appear that we have been at unnecessary pains to determine the precise point at which, according to the earliest traditions, the Hebrews believed that they quitted "the wilderness," and entered into their possessions on the east of the Jordan; and that it is a matter of little importance whether the name given to a particular range of hills was Abarim or Arabim. But the point we have been discussing has an important bearing on the not uninteresting question whether, according to the traditions of those who settled in the Trans-Jordanic region, the leader under whose guidance they quitted Egypt accompanied them into their possessions.

The many curious travellers who have sought to identify the Mount Nebo, or the Pisgah, from whose summit Moses

---

* In further confirmation of the conclusion that the Abarim of Num. xxi. 11, was in the original tradition Arabim, attention is directed to the Hebrew text of Deut. xxxiv. 1. The opening verses of this chapter seem to furnish the sequel to those at the conclusion of Deut. xxxii. In Deut. xxxii. 49, we find Jahveh giving these directions to Moses: "Get thee up into this mountain Abarim, unto mount Nebo, which is in the land of Moab, that is over against Jericho, and behold the land of Canaan." In accordance with the usual style of Hebrew composition, we should expect to find it related that, in compliance with Jahveh's command, "Moses went up into the mountain Abarim, unto mount Nebo, which is in the land of Moab, that is over against Jericho." But instead, we read, "And Moses went up from the plains of Moab, unto the mountain of Nebo, to the top of Pisgah, that is over against Jericho." This, it must be admitted, is a very important variation, the *Har-ha-Abarim* of the injunction disappearing, and "the plains of Moab" taking its place. On looking at the Hebrew, we see that the word rendered "plains" is ערבת *Araboth*, a word which is simply a different form of ערבם *Arabim*. We cannot help suspecting that in the text of Deut. xxxiv. 1, as it originally stood, the word Arabim was to be found; but when the record came to be incorporated, the meaning and significance of the words were forgotten, and the text was altered in order to give expression to what may have been supposed to be the meaning of the original author.

is said to have seen the possessions of Israel and Judah on both sides of the Jordan, have been compelled to admit that they could nowhere discover a mountain fulfilling all the conditions set forth in the Scriptural records. Josephus describes Nebo as a very high mountain opposite Jericho, and commanding a prospect of the greatest part of the land of Canaan.* According to Eusebius and Jerome, the mountain stood between Heshbon and the Jordan,† and would therefore be an eminence of the mountain range which constitutes the western wall of the plateau of Moab. There is, however, confessedly no prominent peak in this range which can with plausibility be selected as the mountain which Moses ascended for the purpose of viewing the Promised Land. Seen from the west of the Jordan, the table-land of Moab presents the appearance of a wall, with an upper skyline which is perfectly unbroken.‡ The traveller approaching the river from the east, proceeds across the plateau till, arriving at the edge of the steppe, he looks down into the plain of the Jordan. It is not necessary for him to ascend any mountain in order to obtain a prospect of Canaan. It breaks upon him as soon as he reaches the line where the table-land begins to drop into the Jordan valley.

It is easy to explain how the posterity of those who settled on the west of the river, when they came to interpret the earliest traditions of the migration from Egypt, brought themselves to believe that from some point on that mountain wall which bounded their view on the east, Moses must have looked down on the land he was not permitted to enter, and that there he must have found his unknown grave. They

---

* *A. J.* iv. 8, 48.   † *Onomast.* s. v. *Nabau.*

‡ "On ne distingue pas un sommet, pas la moindre cime; seulement on apercoit cà et là de legères inflexions comme si la main du peintre qui a tracé cette ligne horizontale sur le ciel eut tremblé dans quelques endroits" (Chateaubriand, *Itineraire*, iii.).

did not care to inquire whether this belief was compatible with historical truth.

If any fact can be regarded as more conclusively established than another, it is that the kingdom of Moab was at the time of the Exodus bounded on the north by the Arnon,* and the Arnon is admitted beyond all question to be the river which flows through what is now known as the Wady-el-Mojib, and empties itself into the Dead Sea fully five-and-twenty miles south of Jericho. It is also, if we accept the authority of the record in the Book of Numbers, beyond question that the Ije-Abarim were reached by the emigrants from Egypt before they crossed the Zered or the Arnon,† and consequently these heights were situated in the land of Moab, as that country was defined at the time of the migration, and long after the Hebrew settlement on the east of the Jordan.‡ The only point about which there can be any dispute, is whether the Har-Abarim which Moses was commanded to ascend in order to see the land given to the children of Israel§ was distinct from the Ije-Abarim, and situated in a different region.

The command to ascend Mount Abarim‖ is apparently separated by a long interval of time and by several important events from the arrival at the Ije-Abarim,¶ and it might therefore be unhesitatingly concluded that the one place was not only distinct from the other, but that they were far apart. But this conclusion would depend on the assumption that the Book of Numbers was a consecutive narrative, and that the parts of which it is made up were of equal antiquity. The fragmentary nature of the Pentateuch has, however, been sufficiently demonstrated to render it

---

* Num. xxi. 13, 15. † Num. xxi. 11. ‡ Jud. xi. 18, 22.
§ Num. xxvii. 12. ‖ Num. xxvii. 12. ¶ Num. xxi. 11.

needless to say that we must demur to inferences which rest upon such a basis.

The statement of the arrival at Ije-Abarim is followed by the account of the movement across the Arnon;* then follows an extract supposed to have been made from the Book of the Wars of Jahveh;† and this is succeeded by an enumeration of certain journeyings, not mentioned elsewhere, terminating at the Pisgah, in the land of Moab, looking toward Jeshimon.‡ We next have an account of the message sent to Sihon, king of the Amorites,§ followed by a brief account of the conquest of the Trans-Jordanic region;|| and then follows the Book of Balaam the Seer,¶ introduced by the statement that the Israelites set forward, and pitched in the plains of Moab, by Jericho.** Next in order comes the account of the apostasy of the Israelites with the Midianites or Moabites;†† then the record of the census taken in the plains of Moab;‡‡ and then, after an account of a judgment given affecting the law of inheritance,§§ we meet the disconnected fragment which tells us that Moses was commanded to ascend Mount Abarim, to see the land given to the children of Israel.|||| There is no record in the Book of Numbers to the effect that Moses did so. We are, however, subsequently told that he obtained a brilliant victory over the Midianites,¶¶ and apportioned the Trans-Jordanic region between Reuben, Gad, and half the tribe of Manasseh.***

Now let us briefly notice the contents of some of the records which interpose between the account of the arrival at Ije-Abarim with the subsequent crossing of the Arnon,

---

* Num. xxi. 12, 13. † Num. xxi. 14, 15. ‡ Num. xxi. 16–20.
§ Num. xxi. 21, 22. || Num. xxi. 24-35. ¶ Num. xxii. 23, 24.
** Num. xxii. 1. †† Num. xxv. ‡‡ Num. xxvi.
§§ Num. xxvii. 1–11. |||| Num. xxvii. 12. ¶¶ Num. xxxi.
*** Num. xxxii.

and the mention of the command to Moses to ascend the Har-Abarim, and view the land given to the children of Israel.

It is undoubted that when the emigrants crossed the Arnon, or probably that portion of the stream which runs in a north-westerly direction, now known as the Seyl Szefye,* before it enters the Wady-el-Mojib, they arrived on the frontier of the Amorite king. They then sent the message which was rejected, and at this point the invasion of the Amorite territory began. In no sense therefore can it be said that there were any further "journeyings" by the emigrants, and least of all journeyings subsequent to their message to the Amorite king, which would have conducted them through their enemy's territory as far as a point, "the Pisgah," in view of Jericho. It was through this very region that they requested to be permitted to pass, which permission was refused. We know therefore that we have, in Numbers xxi. 18-20, a separate and independent fragment, about which we shall presently have more to say. The statement in respect to the message to Sihon is clearly consecutive upon that recording the crossing of the Arnon.

The conquest of the Trans-Jordanic region followed the unsuccessful mission to the king of the Amorites, and when it was completed the Israelites found themselves masters of Gilead, their possessions reaching from the desert on the east to the Jordan on the west. On the south, the Arnon continued to be the boundary of Moab. At some period, the date of which we have not the means of deter-

---

* It is not improbable that the Seyl Szefye was the Zered, whilst the valley into which it flows, now called the Wady-el-Mojib, was known in early times as the valley of the Arnon. Although the Szefye may be the principal source of the Arnon, it changes its name as soon as it enters the valley running due west to the Dead Sea, in which it unites with another stream which flows down the eastern portion of the valley.

mining, the Moabites appear to have taken alarm at the increasing power of the Israelites on their northern frontier; and, if the narrative in the Book of Balaam is to be relied upon, they took measures to arrest their tide of prosperity. For this purpose they had recourse to an expedient which, perhaps rather owing to the facility of its application and the terror which it inspires, than to the necessary efficacy of its operation, has in all ages recommended itself to the clergy of every religion. They engaged the services of an individual, noted for his sanctity, to mould the designs of Providence in accordance with their own views of expediency. They employed Balaam to curse their neighbours. The danger which threatened the infant nation was, however, happily averted; Balaam, to the astonishment and disgust of the king of Moab, blessing instead of anathematising Israel.

Whatever may be the date of this remarkable composition,[*] it is based upon an old tradition, in which Balaam was represented as carrying out the behests of the king of Moab, and cursing Israel with all becoming ceremonial.[†] But, however this may be, it is reasonable to conclude that the places to which Balak was supposed to have taken Balaam for the purpose of "seeing" the people of Israel, and cursing them, were in his own territory, and close to the common

---

[*] See an able Essay by Dr. Kalish on the Book of Balaam (*Bible Studies*, part i.).

[†] This would appear from Deut. xxiii. 4, 5, which excludes the Moabite and the Ammonite from the congregation, "because they hired against thee Balaam the son of Beor of Mesopotamia, to curse thee; nevertheless, Jahveh thy God *would not hearken unto Balaam*, but Jahveh thy God *turned the curse* into a blessing unto thee" (see also Jos. xxiv. 9, 10). It is stated that Balaam was slain by the Israelites (Num. xxxi. 8), and that it was through him that they were led into apostasy (Num. xxxi. 16). Josephus puts a gem of a speech into the mouths of the Midianite maidens, beginning Ἡμῖν, ὦ κράτιστοι νεανιῶν, "O illustrious young men, we have homes of our own," &c. (*A. J.* iv. 6, 8).

frontier. And accordingly we find that, on the arrival of the seer, Balak goes to meet Balaam "in a city of Moab, in the borders of Arnon, in the utmost coast;* and subsequently they proceed to the high places of Baal (*Bamoth-Baal*), from whence to "see the utmost part of the people."† Sacrifices are duly offered, and Balaam in vain endeavours to curse Israel.‡ The king then proposes to try another place, and they proceed to the field of Zophim, to the top of the Pisgah, where the intentions of the seer are again frustrated;§ and, lastly, they go to "the top of Peor, which looketh toward Jeshimon," where a final and equally unsuccessful effort is made to carry out the wishes of the Moabite king.‖

If, according to the original tradition, Balaam actually cursed Israel, it is probable that the sacrifices were said to have been offered in only one place. And there are strong reasons for believing that the Bamoth-Baal and the Zophim on the Pisgah, and the summit of Peor, were only different descriptive names of a single place, noted in Moab for its sanctity, and where sacrifices were offered to the tutelary deity, here styled *Ha-Baal-Peor*—the Lord Peor, though probably also having the specific name Chemosh. In the tradition recording the death of Moses, he is said to have ascended Mount Nebo, to the top of the Pisgah,¶ and to have "died there in the land of Moab," and to have been "buried in the land of Moab, in a valley against (or close by) Beth-Peor."** In any case, it is apparent that the Pisgah where Moses was supposed to have died, was in the land of Moab; and that the Pisgah, or the top of the Peor, where Balaam offered sacrifices, and did or did not curse Israel, was also in the land of Moab, and that the land of Moab at the time

---

* Num. xxii. 36.   † Num. xxii. 41.   ‡ Num. xxiii. 1–13.
§ Num. xxxiii. 14–24.   ‖ Num. xxiii. 27; xxiv. 25.
¶ Deut. xxxiv. 1.   ** Deut. xxxiv. 5, 6.

of the events referred to, and for many centuries afterwards, extended no further north than the Arnon.

A curious fragment of an itinerary, taken doubtless from some ancient record, is, as we have seen, interposed between the notice of the arrival at the Arnon, and the mission to the king of the Amorites.* It, like other fragments in this chapter, was probably taken from an early historical compilation,† now unfortunately lost. It apparently states in detail some of the movements of the Israelites immediately preceding their arrival at the Amorite frontier. It is there recorded that the Israelites proceeded to Mattanah, thence to Nahaliel, thence to Bamoth in the valley, in the field of Moab, and thence to the top of the Pisgah, which looketh toward Jeshimon. We have no means of identifying Mattanah or Nahaliel, but we can have no difficulty in recognising the Bamoth as the Bamoth-Baal in the field of Moab referred to in the narrative of Balaam, and in close proximity to the Pisgah, or hill looking towards *Ha-Jeshimon* —the wilderness. It is unquestionable therefore, so far as the authority of this fragment goes, that the Bamoth and the Pisgah reached by the Israelites were in Moab, and south of the Arnon.

This, however, is not all the evidence at our command respecting the locality of the Pisgah. Reference is made more than once in the Scriptural records‡ to Ashdoth-hap-Pisgah,§ which is rendered in the Authorised Version in one place "the springs of Pisgah."‖ In all these passages Ashdoth-hap-Pisgah is or are placed on the east side of the Dead Sea. Thus a boundary is drawn from "Chinnereth

---

* Num. xxi. 18-20. † Num. xxi. 14.
‡ Deut. iii. 17; iv. 49; Jos. xii. 3; xiii. 20.
§ Pisgah is in all these instances preceded by the definite article "Ashdoth of the Pisgah."
‖ Deut. iv. 49.

(the Sea of Genesareth or Galilee) even unto the sea of the plain (*Araba*), even the Salt Sea, under Ashdoth-hap-Pisgah eastward;* and again, "all the plain on this side Jordan eastward, even unto the sea of the plain under Ashdoth-hap-Pisgah."† As, however, in these passages the boundaries of the Trans-Jordanic possessions are indicated, and as the Arnon is admitted in them to have been the border of Moab, the inference is irresistible that the Ashdoth-hap-Pisgah could not have been far distant from that river.

Ashdoth is probably the plural form of the unused word *Ashd*, which is found in the singular only in the passage quoted from the Book of the Wars of Jahveh.‡ It has been rendered "a pouring out," and in this quotation is deemed to refer to the streams of the valleys (*nachalim*) going down to Ar, and lying on the border of Moab. That the Arnon and its tributaries are referred to in this most ancient fragment no one entertains a doubt, and as we find elsewhere in the passages above referred to, the same archaic word employed (*Ashd-Ashdoth*) in reference to brooks emptying themselves into the Dead Sea on its eastern side, and denominated Ashdoth-hap-Pisgah, we must regard the demonstration as complete that the Pisgah from which the Ashdoth proceeded must have been identical with the mountains or hills in which the sources of the Arnon are to be found. It is only necessary to glance at a map of the region on the east of the Dead Sea to observe that the valley of the Arnon, or the Wady-el-Mojib, is the main channel through which the adjoining watershed is drained.

The remaining records interposing in the Book of Numbers, before we come to the command to Moses to ascend Mount Abarim, call for no particular comment. One

---

* Deut. iii. 17.   † Deut. iv. 49.   ‡ Num. xxi. 15.

is a record of Israel's apostasy in serving the Elohim of Moab at Shittim;* another is an account of a census taken of the several tribes,† a composition probably not earlier than the fifth century B.C.; and the third is the judgment in the case of the daughters of Zelophehad.‡ We then find the brief and disconnected fragment which tells of the command to Moses to ascend Mount Abarim, view the land given to the children of Israel, and die.§ Is it possible to resist the conclusion that it originally followed in order the record of the arrival at Ije-Abarim, and that in the traditions of the Trans-Jordanic tribes Ije-Abarim was or were regarded as the place from which Moses viewed the land Jahveh had given to the children of Israel—that is to say, the land of Gilead.‖

The last chapter of Deuteronomy contains, though in a mutilated and corrupted state, the record in which was originally preserved the tradition of the Trans-Jordanic tribes, in respect to the death of their great leader. The story begun in the Book of Numbers is here completed, and, notwithstanding the alterations the record has undergone,

---

* Num. xxv. We are here struck by the curious coincidence that the scene of Israel's apostasy bore a name having a meaning closely resembling that of the word which, as we suggest, should stand instead of Ije-Abarim—namely, Ije-Arabim, "the heights of the willows." *Has-Shittim* signifies, or is supposed to signify, "the acacias;" Ha-Arabim signifies, or is supposed to signify, "the willows." Has-Shittim and Ha-Arabim were, therefore, the names apparently given in different traditions to places noted for a luxuriant growth of trees (groves) where Baal-peor was worshipped. The modern Jebel-et-Tarfûyeh would consequently be the Arabic rendering of Has-Shittim and Ha-Arabim.

† Num. xxvi. ‡ Num. xxvii. 1–11. § Num. xxvii. 12, 13.

‖ It is especially noticeable that the command given to Moses is, "Get thee up into *this* mount Arabim," clearly denoting a reference to a mount Abarim already mentioned. But the only apparent antecedent allusion to such a mount is in the reference to the Ije-Abarim (Num. xxi. 11), "the heights of Abarim," which were in close proximity to the *nachal* Zered. We have here a further proof that Num. xxvii. 12–14 in the original record followed Num. xxi. 11.

sufficient of its original tenor remains to fix with absolute certainty the region in which was situated the mount traditionally associated with the death of Moses, and to demonstrate the groundlessness of the conception which arose in comparatively late times amongst those who settled in Palestine, that Moses died on the eve of crossing—not the Arnon, but the Jordan.

The opening verse of this chapter states that Moses went up from the plains (Araboth) of Moab unto the mountain of Nebo, to the top of the Pisgah, that is over against Jericho,* whilst in later passages it is said that he died there, and was buried in a valley in the land of Moab, against Beth-peor, but that his sepulchre was unknown.†

We have already set forth our reasons for suspecting that the word here appearing as Araboth was another form of Arabim. Mount Nebo is here mentioned, although unnamed in the Book of Numbers; and then follows the specific reference to the top of the Pisgah, which is stated to have been *al-peni*, in sight of or looking toward Jericho. Now, if our conclusions respecting the locality of the Pisgah be correct, it could not have been accurately described as being in sight of or in front of Jericho. How are we to explain this error or misstatement?

In the first passage in which the top of the Pisgah is referred to, it is described as looking towards (*al-peni*) Jeshimon.‡ This is in the fragment of the itinerary which brought the journeyings of the Israelites to a termination on the border of the Amorites. In the narrative of Balaam, the second place selected for the sacrifices was the top of Pisgah,§ and the third was " the top of Peor, which looketh toward (*al-peni*) Jeshimon."‖ We have stated our reasons for

---

* Deut. xxxiv. 1.   † Deut. xxxiv. 5, 6.
‡ Num. xxi 20.   § Num. xxiii. 14.   ‖ Num. xxiii. 28.

regarding the top of Peor and the top of Pisgah as identical; at all events they are both described in the same language as "looking toward" (*al-peni*) Jeshimon. But if the Pisgah in the land of Moab which Moses ascended to die, and which must have adjoined the valley in which he was supposed to have been buried, which valley was described as being against Beth-peor ("the house of Peor"),* was, as it is impossible to doubt, the same Pisgah on which Balaam was said to have offered sacrifices, then it was in sight of Jeshimon (probably the wilderness on the eastern border of Moab), and was in all probability so described in the original record of the tradition which told of the death of Moses. But when this record came to be dealt with centuries afterwards by the descendants of those who settled on the west of the Jordan, they found it impossible to reconcile its terms with their traditional belief that the Jordan was the Rubicon which they crossed in order to enter the possessions which Jahveh had given to them, and which marked the termination of their journeying through the wilderness. Moses never accompanied them, but Moses must have been permitted at least to see the pleasant land which became theirs by virtue of the covenant made with Abraham, and renewed at Sinai. In order to do this, he must have accompanied their fathers to the banks of the Jordan, and must have seen the land of Canaan from the eastern heights commanding the valley. This being so, it became evident to the compiler that an error was committed in describing the Pisgah as being *al-peni*, in front of, Jeshimon, and the latter word (probably honestly regarded as a clerical error) was altered to Jericho.

Having ascended to the top of Pisgah, it is recorded that Jahveh showed to Moses all the land of Gilead unto Dan,

---

* Deut. xxxiv. 6.

and all the possessions on the west of the Jordan, and the Negeb, and the Araba of the valley of Jericho, to Zoar. It is needless to repeat that the conqueror of Gilead, as Moses is in the Scriptural records represented to have been, did not require to be shown the country which he subjugated; nor, indeed, is there any eminence on the edge of the table-land overhanging the Jordan valley, which, however magnificent the prospect commanded of the country on the west of the river, affords an extensive view of the Trans-Jordanic possessions of Israel. But we are not the less grateful to the compiler for having left uncorrected the reference to Gilead. In the original record, it is probable that it was the only region mentioned. Moses, according to the belief of those who settled on the east of the Jordan, was permitted to see the land of Gilead, which he was not permitted to enter. For this purpose he was directed to ascend Mount Abarim (Arabim?), in Moab,* to the top of the Pisgah, looking toward Jeshimon, an eminence equally turned to account when Balaam was taken by the king of Moab to a suitable place† to hurl his maledictions against the Israelites. Moses was there supposed to have died, and, his death occurring in a strange land, the precise place of his burial was forgotten. In the record, as it originally stood, possibly the name of the individual was mentioned‡ who was supposed to have rendered the last rites to the great leader of the Hebrews on their departure from the house of bondage.§

---

* Num. xxvii. 12, 13. † Num. xxiii. 13. ‡ Deut. xxxiv. 6.

§ This passage has in all seriousness, even to the present day, been interpreted as meaning that God actually buried Moses. "God buried him. The penalty of Moses' sin was fully paid by his death, and this signal honour conferred on him after his death was doubtless designed to sustain the lawgiver's authority, which without it might have been impaired with the people in consequence of his punishment" (*Speaker's Commentary*, Deut. xxxiv. 6). But did the people see God bury their leader, or was there any eye-witness of this remarkable proceeding; or,

Whether the precise mountain or hill, the top of the Pisgah or of the Peor, associated by the Trans-Jordanic traditions with the death of Moses, can be determined, may depend on the research of future travellers. The task should be one of no considerable difficulty. The limits of the region through which the Israelites passed before quitting Moab are circumscribed within so small a compass, and the information afforded by the traditions of the emigration and by the narrative of Balaam are, considering all the circumstances, so precise and exhaustive, that it should be comparatively easy to ascertain the Pisgah from which Moses was supposed to have seen the land of Gilead. It doubtless lay between Kir of Moab, the Kerak of to-day, and the desert on the east, or the Wady Mojib on the north. It may have stood between that town and the Seyl Szefye, the main source of the Arnon. If so, it is to be found in the range which is now known as Jebel-et-Tarfûyeh, between which and the Har-Abarim (Arabim?) we have noticed a resemblance. This range is continued on the opposite side of the Seyl Szefye, under the name of Jebel-el-Ghoweiteh, as far as the Wady Enkeileh, which is the eastern continuation of the Wady-el-Mojib. There is nothing in the traditions to lead one to suppose that the top of the Pisgah or of the Peor was the summit of a lofty mountain. In the narrative of Balaam it is stated that the seer could not view the whole of the people of Israel, but only their utmost part*—that is to say, only the border of their territory.†

---

if not, were the people content to take the statement of some one who was not present that the Creator committed the creature to the ground? Are there really no limits to the disrespect which may, in the supposed interests of religion, be shown to the Almighty?

* Num. xxiii. 13.

† A somewhat singular mountain stands between Kerak and the Wady Mojib, and but a short distance from the latter. The ruins of a temple near the summit indicate that in past times it may have

The identification of the mountain or of the range associated by tradition with the death of Moses is, however, a matter of minor importance, even if the search should prove successful. There are many reasons which would lead us to question the grounds on which the tradition rested. But what does concern us is, that the existence of the tradition proves beyond all question that the settlers on the east of the Jordan were not accompanied there by Moses. The story of Mount Abarim (Arabim ?) and the Pisgah, and the unknown place of burial in a valley in the land of Moab, is of Trans-Jordanic origin ; for had it been created on the west side of the river, we should not have found localities indicated which were, without exception, south of the Arnon; it would have been told of places familiar to all, in the region overhanging the lower portion of the Jordan valley. But the narrative is not a Cis-Jordanic invention : it is simply a novel application of an ancient tradition. The names could not be altered, but they received a different signification. The land of Moab was carried up the left bank of the Jordan, and the Pisgah was declared to be in sight of Jericho.

Should we then be justified in concluding that the settlers in Gilead preserved a tradition that the migration from Egypt to their new possessions occupied a period which, in nomadic style, they called forty years ? Not necessarily. Cis-Jordanic Israel and Judah undoubtedly believed, and probably with truth, that a very long and undetermined period elapsed between the departure from Egypt and the conquest by them of their respective possessions. But we have nothing to justify us in concluding that the

been noted for its sanctity. It is described by Burckhardt as an insulated mountain, standing about three-quarters of an hour's distance to the west of the road leading from Kerak across the Arnon. It is named Jebel Shihan (*Syria*, p. 375). The Bamoth-Baal may have been here, and it is possible that this mount was the Pisgah.

belief was shared in Gilead. Jephthah is silent on the subject. He refers to a protracted stay at Kadesh, but says nothing about forty years in the wilderness. The ground of Moses' exclusion from the future home of his followers is stated to have been his misconduct at the waters of Meribah in Kadesh.* But this must have been shortly after the departure from Egypt. On the other hand, the forty years' punishment fell on "the people" in consequence of their refusal to invade the region which had been explored by the spies on the west of the Jordan,† an episode on which the settlers on the eastern bank could afford to look back with indifference. On the whole, therefore, it seems reasonable to conclude that the period which elapsed between the liberation from Egypt and the crossing of the Arnon was comparatively brief, possibly not exceeding a few years; but, on this point we have no data. That Moses did not accompany the emigrants to the Trans-Jordanic region is apparent from the tradition we have noticed above.‡ Those who effected a settlement north of the Arnon were acquainted with the fact, and their descendants discovered a plausible explanation of his non-participation in the fruits of their labours, by attributing to him grave misconduct on the celebrated occasion when he produced the water from the rock. But though he was punished by Jahveh in not being permitted to accompany "the congregation of Israel" into their promised possessions, it was reasonable to suppose that he was allowed to proceed as far as the highlands of Moab, and from some eminence on the south of the Arnon view at least a portion of the undulating plains which Jahveh gave for a possession to the first-born of Israel.

---

* Num. xx. 12; xxvii. 12-14. † Num. xiv. 11-39.

‡ How it was he came not to do so, cannot be conveniently brought within the limits of the present treatise. The history of Moses can best be dealt with in an examination of the religion of the Hebrews in the wilderness.

CHAPTER XVI.

THE story of the Exodus has now been again re-told. To the critical and impartial must be referred the duty of determining whether the amended narrative is in accordance, not with preconceived notions which may be erroneous, but with the only trustworthy materials which lie at our disposal. Whatever may be the value which different persons may be inclined to attach to the Scriptures, the traditions, or the nuclei of the traditions, taken with them to the regions in which they ultimately settled, by those who quitted Egypt, can supply the only true foundation upon which the story must rest. If these men did not care to preserve at least an outline of the circumstances under which they were released from servitude and made their way to their future homes, posterity cannot hope to supply the void. If they did preserve some materials for the historian, then the task of the latter is lightened in proportion to their extent and their integrity. In dealing with such materials, it becomes, however, incumbent to take into careful consideration the circumstances under which they were formed, and the ever-varying conditions to which they were ultimately subjected, before they assumed their present shapes. The historical elements of an illiterate nomadic tribe cannot in the necessity of things resemble those of a cultivated and civilised people. History, like everything else, has its beginnings, and those beginnings, according to the experience of mankind, have been found to be universally the same. Events happen which are sufficiently notable to attract attention and to retain a place in the memory. If those events affect the fortunes of the tribe or people, their memory is transmitted from father to son, and then the story-teller and the bard take up the chain. But the later links that are forged differ in character from those of earlier construction. The first made are rude and uncouth; the last exhibit more care, and more polish. The naked narrative of even an interesting event does not attract in the same degree as a judiciously adorned account of the same transaction. The untutored barbarian demands, even more earnestly than civilised man, that his feelings shall be appealed to, and the story-teller met the required want. If he contented himself with being dry and accurate and prosaic, his occupation would be gone. He was expected to excite the emotions of his listeners, and he did so.

The historical *origines* of the Hebrew nation presented these characteristics. The different sections or offshoots of the parent stock which quitted Egypt preserved, in somewhat dissimilar forms, accounts of what were in truth the same transactions. The stories were told differently; the names of the same places varied according to the dialects of the different tribes. Those who quitted Egypt were of diverse elements, though of a common lineage. There were captives, liberated from a long and galling servitude. There were also nomads, who had only temporarily visited Egypt in search of food. That the one and the other should call the same places by different descriptive names, and that even the sections into which the captives were subsequently split up, should in time vary the common language which they spoke by the introduction of new dialects, cannot surprise us. The mountain credited with being the abode of the Elohim was known to some as the Mount of Caves, whilst by others it was distinguished as the Mount of the Bush. Of the former, some expressed their meaning by calling it Mount Choreb, and others named it Mount Paran, whilst the latter gave it the designation of Mount Sinai. Again, in the memories preserved of some of the more notable places at which the emigrants rested on their journey, some styled a spot, remarkable for its palm-trees, Elim; others, by a very slight variation of dialect, Elath; and others, again, possibly Elish.* The Hazerim of one section, in like manner, became the Hazeroth of another; whilst a similar idea was conveyed by a third under the name of Rephidim. The place where the emigrants halted for a considerable time in the neighbourhood of the Mount of Elohim, where they planned and from which they made their unsuccessful attempt to invade Southern Palestine, was variously named Kadesh and Paran; those who gave it the former title not improbably connecting it in their minds with their dedication to their protecting God, whilst others associated it with the rock excavations by which it was surrounded. But although in different narratives the names varied, the broad features of the stories have been shown to be alike; and thus by coincidences, which must have been undesigned, we obtain a mass of corroborative evidence which enables us to unravel the tangled skein, and with something approaching certainty to reconstruct the very simple story of the Hebrew migration from Egypt.

To this heterogeneous character in the elements out of which the early history of the Hebrew nation came to be formed, the nomadic habits of the parent stock, and the tribal divisions into which that stock became again and again split up, mainly contributed. Those who claimed descent from Terah became, by the force of circumstances and the necessities of their pastoral life, divided into distinct clans or "nations." The younger inherited the traditions of the

---

* The Alush of the Masorites (Num. xxxiii. 13).

elder, but those traditions were made to accommodate themselves to the altered conditions under which they were preserved. The greatness of the parent stem was not unnaturally presumed to be overshadowed by that of the branch; the deeds of the ancestor were transferred to the descendant, and history was made to repeat itself with fantastic precision. This incongruity was not, however, apparent to those who occasioned it. The story-teller addressed himself exclusively to the members of his own tribe, and the latter only heard, or only interested themselves, in what they were told under their own tents. If the traditions of but one tribe had survived, they would doubtless have been consistent with each other, and the incongruities which we have noticed would not have appeared. But the elements out of which the Jewish nation was formed were so diverse, and the tribal distinctions so clearly marked, that the same stories, though told of different individuals or narrated with trifling modifications, have been preserved to us among the historical records of this interesting people. We have seen how the Abraham of one set of stories is the Isaac of another; how Esau and Ishmael are counterparts; how the descendants of the one obtain from Jahveh the same possessions which are accorded to the other; how in still another tribal tradition Ishmael appears as Midian, and how the descendants of the one are regarded as identical with those of the other; how Moab and Ammon are interchangeable; how the Amorites of one narrative are the Amalekites of another; how, in fine, in every page of this singular mass of historical fragments the conclusive evidences of their varied origins is made apparent.

But in lifting the veil which covers the legends of the patriarchs, we have done more than obtain a confirmation of the soundness of the analytical method we have adopted in dealing with those records which refer to the migration from Egypt. We have thrown no inconsiderable light on the important question of the region inhabited by the stock of those who were reduced to slavery in Egypt, and, inferentially, on the region to which the latter directed their steps on recovering their liberty. Notwithstanding the local colouring which the patriarchal traditions acquired in Judæa, we have had no difficulty in showing that the land of the Hebrews, the land of Abraham and his immediate descendants, lay between the Araba and the Eastern desert, and was, in fact, the land of Aduma of contemporary Egyptian records, the same land in which the only tribes with which the released captives claimed lineage were to be found when the latter quitted Egypt. It was the land of Edom or of Midian in the broadest sense, though, with a more limited signification, the kingdom of Edom was regarded as interposing between the western mountains of Idumæa and the Arabian desert.

Independently of the variety of sources from which the materials are supplied for the construction of the early history of the Jewish people, the singular religion of the parent stock contributed to colour the traditions with a hue which, owing to the subsequent spiritualisation of that religion, is eminently calculated to mislead. If even the least observant traveller were at the present day to meet with a tribe or a people entertaining the religious views of the Hebrew shepherds, he would have no hesitation in recognising its utterly selfish character and demoralising tendency. But the force of habit and a superstitious reverence for the teachings of childhood, lead men of even the highest order of intelligence to ignore the mighty chasm which separates the religion of the Hebrew prophets from that of the barbarous and ruthless nomads who effected a settlement in Palestine. The Monotheism of a more spiritual age is carried backwards in defiance of history, and the Almighty is invested with the vanity, the passions, and weaknesses of a tribal God.

According to the Henotheistic conception of the Hebrew shepherds, their God was distinct from, and superior to, all other gods; whilst they, in like manner, were a distinct and peculiar people, separate from other peoples, and dedicated to His service. The relative duties of the Deity and the people were accurately determined by covenant, the former being expected to interpose in all matters affecting the interests of the latter. With these ideas, it necessarily followed that when the main incidents connected with the migration from Egypt came to be related by those who in a primitive age discharged the duties of historians, the elements of the marvellous became multiplied and developed, and almost every fact related by those who quitted Egypt came to be referred to the direct interposition of Jahveh, either for the purpose of aiding or of punishing his people.

It has been remarked that the miracles recorded in the Old Testament, for the most part, admit of a rational explanation, and this holds specially true of those connected with the departure from Egypt and the migration to the region beyond the Jordan. The story of the plagues is simply a description of phenomena familiar to those who quitted Egypt, but which, when the story of Israel's liberation came to be told, was not only highly coloured, but was made a means of glorifying the national Deity. It was Jahveh who released the captives from their bondage, and a ready explanation of the means that were employed was found in occurrences which in the land of Canaan would be regarded as supernatural. Everything which conflicted with the broad idea that the Israelites were specially protected, and that the Egyptians were specially ill-treated, was toned down, eliminated, or distorted, in order to produce a narrative gratifying to the national vanity and tending to glorify the national God. The true story of the cause of the liberation, or possibly the expulsion, of the Hebrews from Egypt became forgotten, and in its place was substituted a far different narrative. But even this record has not remained unaltered. The story-tellers of at least one section of the Hebrew nation, attributed to Jahveh a miracle in connection with the Exodus from Egypt of whose occurrence those of the remaining sections were entirely ignorant. The first-born of Israel—that is to say, the settlers beyond the Jordan, and their kinsmen who forced their way westwards across that river—were unacquainted with the story of the passage of the Red Sea.

The materials for future history brought with them by the emigrants from Egypt were, in all important respects, the same, only they came to be dealt with somewhat differently by the settlers in different regions; different names were given to the same places, and the same occurrences were apparently represented as happening at different places and different times. But it is only just to say that this confusion was not due to the first narrators. The stories which the Hebrew shepherds and their immediate descendants delighted to listen to may have abounded in the marvellous, but they must have possessed the element of simplicity; they must have been easily understood. A Bedouin would not object to a narrative because its incidents were incredible—in fact, he would be all the more delighted on that account; but he would require that the incidents should follow each other in natural succession, that the story should have a beginning and an end, and that the one should in a natural way lead up to the other. Even a fairy tale must be drawn on simple lines, not only that it may be easily understood, but as easily recollected and transmitted by one to another. It is perhaps needless to say that a narrative which in its present form is hopelessly unintelligible, and which no one has hitherto attempted to present in a simple form, never could have satisfied the requirements of the children of the emigrants from Egypt when they desired to be told of the liberation of their fathers, and of their successful conduct by their protecting Deity across the wilderness which interposed between the land of their captivity and their future home.

The story of the migration from Egypt, as told originally to the settlers beyond the Jordan and in Southern Palestine, was extremely simple. There was not much to relate, but it was told in a fashion which recommended itself equally to the comprehension of young and old. Divested of the marvellous, it was as follows:—A number of Hebrews were driven by famine to settle in Egypt, and were reduced to servitude. After the lapse of a long period, they obtained their liberty, and were permitted to quit Egypt. Accompanied by a section of a friendly tribe, they made their way across a desert to the land which their ancestors had quitted, and at a mountain in that land, reputed to be the abode of the Elohim of their people, they concluded a covenant with their protecting God. They subsequently from this region endeavoured to force an entrance into Palestine, and having failed, they then sought permission to traverse a country immediately interposing between them and the extensive pastures on the east of the Jordan. Their request having been refused, they marched round this country, and then successfully invaded the Trans-Jordanic region. The story of those who afterwards were known as the men of Judah, differed as regarded what happened subsequent to the arrival in the land of the Hebrews. They were unacquainted with the journey round Edom and the conquest of the Trans-Jordanic region. They, with the assistance of the inhabitants of the country about the Mount of Elohim, forced their way into Southern Canaan.

Such was the plain, unadorned story. But it received considerable embellishments before it assumed the form in which it was ultimately committed to writing. The arrival of the parent stock of Israel in Egypt in search of food, was made to be consequent upon a special interposition of Jahveh in favour of a Hebrew boy. This boy was sold by his brethren into captivity, but after many vicissitudes raised to the highest office under the Pharaoh, on account of his skill in interpreting a dream, and by this means enabling the Egyptian Government to make provision during a period of plenty for a succeeding period of scarcity. Joseph was made the favourite son of Jacob, and by his invitation his father and his kinsmen were represented as quitting their home in order to receive, according to the command of Pharaoh, " a possession in the best of the land, in the land of Rameses." But this state of prosperity was speedily exchanged for a condition of servitude. The famine-stricken Hebrews were obliged to make such terms as they could in order to secure the means of subsistence, and they quickly lapsed into slavery. In the narrative taken with them from Egypt, the emigrants told the simple truth respecting this transaction; but when, at a later period, the Egyptian Viceroy was made the son of Jacob and the progenitor of the tribes of Israel (Ephraim and Manasseh), it was necessary to give a different colouring to this mournful chapter in the history of those who were represented as entering Egypt under the most favourable auspices. The Egyptians, and not the Hebrews, were made the victims of the Viceroy's policy; it was the people which gave succour to the famished shepherds, and not the latter which was reduced to servitude. This ingenious variation of the original story obtained easy acceptation from hearers who were neither inclined nor competent to criticise tales in which their credulity was largely appealed to. We have seen, however, that in the total absence as well of any allusions to the circumstances under which the Hebrews lost their liberty, as of any protest on their part against being treated as slaves, the proof that in the story of Joseph's negotiations with the Egyptians we possess the nucleus of the tale which the released captives took with them to the land of their settlement.

The condition of the Hebrews in Egypt was no doubt almost intolerable, and their cry must have often been raised to the Elohim of their fathers to restore them to liberty. But they were not so foolish, or so ignorant of the usages of the time in which they lived, as to suppose that the king of Egypt oppressed them merely for oppression's sake, or through apprehension of their proving a formidable danger to his people. Slavery was a recognised institution even amongst their own people, and they could not have failed to see in Egypt many slaves pertaining to races different from their own. But in later times, when it was thought expedient to be silent as to the manner in which the parent stock had parted with their liberty, explanations were devised in order to account for what would otherwise have been unintelligible. It gratified the national pride to represent the captives in Egypt as having become so numerous and powerful as to inspire the Egyptian Government with dread, and it was related that Pharaoh "set taskmasters over them, to afflict them with their burdens," with the object of checking their increase. Such was the account given by the *raconteurs* of the tribes claiming the title of Israel. But a different version obtained amongst other sections of the descendants of the captives. In a fragment, which unfortunately is incomplete, we are told that to attain the desired end the Pharaoh ordered the male children of the Hebrews to be slain. This would seem to have been the story which survived in Judah.

As soon as the descendants of the captives succeeded in

establishing themselves in their possessions on the opposite sides of the Jordan, they necessarily felt grateful to their protecting Deity for enabling them to deprive the former inhabitants of their territory. Their religion was based upon contract, and they willingly recognised the fact that Jahveh had observed his engagements. But by a very intelligible process the bards and story-tellers carried backwards the Divine intervention in favour of the protected people, and made the various incidents in their early history so many means towards the accomplishment of the final end. The covenant with Abraham and his seed for the acquisition of Canaan, which was even at the period of the bondage in Egypt regarded by the inhabitants of Idumaea as accomplished, was advanced a step for the benefit of those who entered Palestine; and the later covenant which was made when the invasion of that country was contemplated, was treated as a simple renewal of the preceding engagement. Those who were reduced to slavery in Egypt claimed descent from Abraham, and as it was inconsistent with the Semitic idea of the majesty and might of the tutelary deity to suppose that any misfortunes could happen to the people save by his permission or direction, it was related that even at the time of the conclusion of the covenant with Abraham the servitude in Egypt was predicted by Jahveh. We have seen, however, that although a tradition to this effect grew up amongst the descendants of the emigrants from Egypt, yet it assumed different shapes in different tribes, the period of servitude being represented in one version as at least twice as long as in the other. That even when the people were geographically separated from their God, he should feel for them in their affliction, was a not unreasonable assumption; and the part played by the tribe of shepherds which accompanied the captives from Egypt supplied a fitting illustration of the Divine intervention.

A mountain stood in the land of the Hebrews which had long been sanctified as the abode of the Elohim. Here Jahveh grieved for the children of his servant Abraham, who groaned in bondage on the opposite side of the great wilderness of Shur, and here he entrusted the leader of a tribe about to visit Egypt with the mission to liberate his people. This individual so highly honoured was Moses, and, according to the traditions of Southern Palestine, he was born in Egypt, narrowly escaped death as a Hebrew boy, was brought up in the palace of the Pharaoh, and was subsequently compelled to fly from Egypt and take refuge with a people dwelling in the land of the Hebrews, in the neighbourhood of the Mount of Elohim. The real circumstances under which the captives obtained their liberty were no doubt sufficiently prosaic. They were probably not only unattractive, but such as the liberated people were only too willing to consign to oblivion. If they were turned out of Egypt because they were regarded as leprous and unclean, and because their presence was, either rightly or wrongly, interpreted as the cause of pestilence amongst the Egyptians, it was not very likely that their descendants would represent the matter in this light. It was gratifying to the national pride, and more consistent with the fitness of things, to represent the influences at work as supernatural, and specially called into operation by the emissary of Jahveh. In this manner the stories of the plagues, and of the struggles for supremacy between the Elohim of the Hebrews and the Elohim of the Egyptians, as represented by their respective champions, came to be told.

The mountain where the God of the Hebrews dwelt was the point to which the liberated captives naturally directed their steps. Their Elohim had sent for them. He required that they should come and serve him at that place. This was the substance of the message which Moses was represented as conveying to the elders of Israel, and to the king of Egypt; it was in order that this object should be realised that supernatural pressure was put upon the Pharaoh and his people to let the captives go. As soon as the Israelites quitted Egypt, they made their way to the sacred mountain. That this mountain stood in the country in which their kinsmen dwelt, that the sacred associations connected with it could alone have grown up amongst the people of whom they were a section, and that they should find in the same region the home of their fathers and the reputed abode of their God, is only what we should look for in the narratives of the Exodus. That this celebrated mountain should have been sought for in a land which not only was never part of the possessions of the descendants of Abraham, but was beyond all doubt subject at that time to Egyptian sway, and that in this unknown region the Elohim of the Hebrews should have been supposed, for ever so brief a period, to have taken up his abode, is not only opposed to all probability, but was so completely at variance with the religious conceptions of the Hebrew shepherds, that no such story could ever have been told. It would never have entered the mind of a Hebrew to represent his God as dwelling in a strange land.

At the period of the Exodus the tribes claiming descent from Abraham inhabited the region lying to the east of the Arabа, and as the Egyptian captives were of the same lineage they turned their footsteps towards this country. Not only is there a complete absence of any suggestion that they went anywhere else, but the stories originally related are alone intelligible when read as descriptive of the movement having taken place in this direction.

The migration from Egypt to the Trans-Jordanic region may be said to have had three stages. The first, from Rameses to the Red Sea; the second, from that sea to Kadesh; the third, from Kadesh to the frontier which separated Moab from Gilead. Of the first of these, we possess but one account; of the second we have two, if not three, accounts; and of the third, we have more than one account, besides the fragments of some others.

The narrative of the journey from Rameses to the Red Sea is very simple. The captives, having been thrust out, proceeded to Succoth, and thence to the edge of the wilderness. Through this wilderness they proceeded for some days without finding water; continuing their journey, they came to Marah, where the water was bitter; and subsequently to Elim, with its palm groves and fountains, on the shore of the Red Sea. In other words, they crossed the Tih from Egypt to Akaba.

The second stage of the journey, from Elim to Mount Sinai and Kadesh, was accomplished by marching up the Araba to the foot of Mount Hor, and proceeding by one of the lateral valleys to what in after-times was the site of the Nabathæan capital. The region traversed, and that where the emigrants made a considerable stay, were not only well known to the Hebrew shepherds, but continued to be more or less comprehended within the territories of the settlers in Palestine down to the overthrow of the Jewish monarchies. Our information respecting this stage is therefore more extensive than in regard to the first, and the legends connected with it are more numerous. The fountains and palm-trees of Elim-Elath came to be respectively numbered so as to correspond with the tribes of Israel and the Sanhedrin. The curious product found on the shrubs of the Araba, known to the Bedouins as *manu*, supplied the groundwork of the story that the Israelites were miraculously fed by their protecting God. The singular marsh in the lower Araba, possibly known even at the time of the Exodus as the Tavah or Tabah, gave rise to the narrative that, dissatisfied with manna, the Hebrews demanded more solid food;

that their God in his anger sent them quails in abundance; that they ate to excess, and perished in great numbers; and that in consequence the place was named Kibroth-hat-Tavah, which was interpreted the "graves of lust." In a different tradition Tavah is unnoticed, whilst the supply of quails, like that of manna, is said to have been intended for the natural sustenance of the people. In a third, the destruction of large numbers of the Israelites is referred to; but the name of the place is apparently changed to Taberah, and is explained on the ground that the disaffected people were destroyed by fire; whilst in still a fourth, the physical peculiarities of the place apparently suggest the account that the earth opened and engulfed the malcontents.*

Pre-eminent in the narratives dealing with this stage of the migration, were the descriptions of the phenomena attendant on the manifestation of the glory of Jahveh on the Mount of Elohim, and the accounts of the miraculous supply of water from the smitten rock. But the phenomena witnessed on the Mount where Jahveh dwelt, were, by a very simple operation, presumed to have been equally inseparable from the Tabernacle in which he "walked" in company with his people, and the imaginative powers of the narrators sufficed to conjure up the picture of the tutelary deity leading his people in the alternate 'manifestations of fire and cloud. But some time elapsed before this version of the journeyings through the wilderness was presented. In the earliest story of the departure from Kadesh, for the purpose of descending the Araba and passing to the east of Edom, it was related that an ineffectual appeal was made to Hobab the Kenite, to guide the Israelites upon their way.†

---

* In the narrative of Korah's rebellion, as now presented to us, we discover the traces of the three original stories—the destruction by fire, by engulfment, and by pestilence (Num. xvi.).
† Num. x. 29-32.

The region where the celebrated waters flowed was specially rich in traditions, and many of these were still ancient when the released captives from Egypt approached the Mount of Elohim. Situated in the neighbourhood of this mount, the spot where these waters sprang shared in its sanctity. The source was named the En-Mishpat, or "Spring of Judgment," and there, "before" the Elohim, causes were decided. The waters were also known as those of Massah and Meribah, or, in the language of another tribe, Esek and Sitnah, names supposed to signify respectively Contention and Strife. It became necessary for the early story-tellers to explain these terms, and even anterior to the migration from Egypt they were accounted for by connecting them with the disputes between rival sheikhs for the possession of the wells. When the stories of the "journeyings" came to be told, another explanation was found. Moses was declared to have produced the waters with his staff, and caused them to flow through the rocky cliffs, whilst the contention and strife were attributed to the leaders or to the people in their relations with Jahveh.

Of the third stage in the migration there are but few traces left, but such as they are they deal mainly with occurrences at the commencement and termination of the journey. This does not surprise us. The region on the east frontier of Edom was unfamiliar to the settlers in Canaan, and any traditions connected with this portion of the journey were speedily forgotten. It was different with Kadesh, the point at which the movement commenced, and the northern frontier of Moab, where it ended. We are told, in connection with the former, of the ineffectual invasion of Southern Canaan, of the futile request for permission to traverse Edom, and of the deaths of Aaron and Miriam; and, in connection with the latter, of the apostasy of the Israelites, and of the death of Moses on the borders of the land he was not permitted to enter. That more ample and more accurate accounts of this final stage were preserved by Trans-Jordanic Israel we may feel perfectly assured, but they, together with the detailed history of the settlement in Gilead, are now lost for ever. That we possess so much of the story of Israel's passage through Moab and of the death of Moses, is due to the necessity imposed upon the story-tellers of Cis-Jordanic Israel of relating the events connected with the termination of the journeyings through the wilderness. At a later period, when the scribe took the place of the verbal narrator, the original story was preserved but modified, in order to suit the supposed requirements of those who settled on the west of the Jordan. Moses was represented as the conqueror of Gilead, and from a mountain overhanging the Jordan was pictured, in his dying moments, viewing the land of Canaan.

Those who, operating whether from the Idumæan hills or from the table-land overlooking the left bank of the Jordan, forced their way into Palestine, thus carried with them a number of traditions bearing a close family likeness and betraying a common origin, but nevertheless differing, sometimes in the names of individuals, sometimes in the names of places, sometimes in the periods at which the alleged events took place. This confusion was, however, intensified by the gradual amalgamation of traditions having a Canaanitish origin, and by the natural tendency of a new race of story-tellers to associate some of the traditions with the region in which the tribes had been settled.[*] But in such an age, and amongst an illiterate and semi-barbarous people, this process had a natural tendency to impair the value of the materials with which the future historian had to deal. Original distinctions became lost and forgotten, and a

---

[*] This is specially the case in the history of Jacob.

heterogeneous mass of independent and apparently disconnected records was collected. For after the story-teller came the embryo historian, who contented himself with committing to writing the narratives hitherto transmitted by oral tradition. But there were such men both in Israel and in Judah, on the right bank of the Jordan and on the left bank, in Edom and in Canaan; and these scribes, acting independently of each other, produced records which, if read separately, were probably fairly intelligible and far from confused, but which, when in a later age amalgamated and dovetailed, became a hopeless compound of irreconcilable contradictions and needless repetitions. The stories of one tribe were welded with those of another; too glaring inconsistencies were pared down, according to the judgment of the manipulator; and the whole shaped, with the aid of additions and emendations, into what was intended to pass for consecutive history.

But this was not the whole extent of the evil. Long before the final redaction took place, a variety of causes— partly natural, partly political, and partly religious—conspired to distort and corrupt these early records. The effluxion of time caused the identity of tribes and places, originally distinguished by somewhat different though cognate names, to be forgotten; and dialects changed, whilst the fact that they did so was ignored. The rivalry and antagonism which grew up between the various sections of the people claiming descent from Abraham, led to the distortion of traditions in the interests of particular tribes, and the complexion of history was varied in order to suit political requirements, or to conform with the necessities of a religious scheme. The severance between those who settled on the opposite sides of the Jordan was politically and religiously complete before the establishment of the monarchy, though at a later period the successful campaigns of the kings of Israel may have given to their people, possessions on the left bank of the river. But, according to the conceptions of Cis-Jordanic Israel, theirs was the land of Canaan, theirs was the Land of Promise. They could not deny the fact, that the first-born of those who quitted Egypt held the Trans-Jordanic possessions by virtue of a covenant with the Deity who had led them through the wilderness; but they found it convenient to represent them as nevertheless receiving it as a reward for their services in aiding the younger but favoured branch to expel the Canaanites. The foundations were thus laid for the superstructure of pious romance of which nearly half the Book of Joshua is composed. The story of the migration from Egypt, many of the details of which had become confused and obscure, was travestied for the greater glorification of God, and the higher exaltation of those who established themselves in Canaan. The liberated people were made to subsist exclusively on manna until they crossed the Jordan, during a period which came to be definitely fixed at forty years. The meaning of the ancient nomadic expression, though understood on the left bank of the Jordan in the ninth century B.C.,* had then been completely forgotten in Judæa.

Those who believe—or, more correctly speaking, who fancy that it is their duty to believe—that the narrative of the Exodus and of the journeyings to the Promised Land was contemporaneously committed to writing by Moses under the direct inspiration of the Deity, will probably dismiss the views expressed in this Essay, and the arguments by which they are supported, as unworthy of consideration. The candid inquirer cannot, however, refuse to recognise inaccuracies and inconsistencies and repetitions; he cannot ignore the proofs that the records before him are the produce of dif-

* The Moabite Stone inscription.

ferent people and different times, because he is told upon no evidence whatever that these *disjecta membra* form a perfect and consistent narrative, whose author is the Almighty. Indeed, if he is not devoid of reverence for the Deity, such a preposterous and profane assertion cannot fail to awaken his just indignation.

It is to those to whom historical truth is dear, and who can distinguish reliance on God from blind subservience to the teachings of men, that this work is addressed. If religion be worth anything, it cannot treat truth as of no account; nor should its professors affect to be horror-struck because what their reason tells them is truth is incompatible with what they have been taught it is their duty to believe. It has been well observed, that men should take care not to confound faith in God with faith in somebody else's faith. This error is, however, much more frequently committed than is commonly supposed.

In addressing ourselves to our task, we set before us two objects—to ascertain whether it was possible to present an intelligible account of the Hebrew migration from Egypt, which would be consistent with the historical records at our command; and to explain the introduction of those elements of the grotesque, the repulsive, and the impossible, which, though the creation of a barbarous and superstitious age, being endorsed even at the present day by teachers of religion in both Jewish and Christian communities, bring the Almighty into contempt and derision. The champions of what passes for orthodoxy, must be well aware that the most deadly weapons employed against them are supplied out of their own armoury. They are guilty of the inconceivable weakness of selecting positions which invite attack, and are hopelessly untenable; and yet they express amazement when they are assailed, and bemoan the strides made by the scepticism which they provoke. In a word, they drag their God through the gutter, and then raise their hands in pious horror because men refuse to fall down and worship the hideous object they have set up.

The annals of religious fanaticism tell us how much more serious in past times were the consequences of thus vilifying the Deity. But even now they are such as cannot be contemplated without serious apprehension. If the highest object of religion be to attain to conformity with the Divine will, the standard of conformity becomes equally repulsive and demoralising when the Almighty is invested with the attributes which upwards of three thousand years ago the nomad tribes of Western Arabia gave to their tribal Elohim. But this is what is done by those who claim to be the vindicators of religion. The order of creation is reversed —and man makes God in his own image.

INDEX.

AARON'S Plains, 219
  Abarim, Mount, 293, 398, 402, 409 *note*
Abiar Alaina, 181 *et seq.*, 184 *note*
Abijah, 116 *note*
Abimelech, 293
Abraham, Traditions of, 291 *et seq.*
Abulfeda, 254, 256
Aduma, 199, 308
Ælanitic Gulf, 171, 173
Ailah, 237, 243, 244 *note*, 247-254
Ain-el-Weibeh, 281
Ain Mûsa, 216, 229, 258
Akaba, 77, 78, 153-159, 171, 181
Alush, 190 *note*, 418
Amalekites, 173-178, 195, 259-263
Amaziah, 103 *note*, 146, 154
Amorites, 167, 260, 352
Anbu, 311
Anthropomorphic conception of God held by Hebrew Shepherds, 10 *et seq.*
Araba, 134, 135, 161, 192, 209, 213, 281
Arabia, 153-155, 197, 233, 254
Arabia Petræa, 155
Arabim, 395, 396 *note*, 400 *note*, 409 *note*
Araboth, 400 *note*
Arke, 240
Arnon, 348, 380
Ashdoth-hap-Pisgah, 407, 408
Avaris, 27, 94

BAAL-PEOR, 162, 355
  Baal Zephon, 68
Balaam, 162, 226, 358, 405
Baldwin I., 245, 251
Bamoth Baal, 407
Battle of the Kings, 144, 224, 235, 240, 292
Beer-lahai-roi, 296
Beer-sheba, 147, 293, 301-304.
Bered, 297, 315
Bibors, Sultan, 256
Bozrah, 227

Brugsch Bey, theory of Passage of Red Sea, 70 *et seq.*; identification of places connected with Exodus, 89, 91, 98, of Shur with Anbu, 311 *note*

CANAAN, Land of, 306 *et seq.*
  Carmel, 270, 275
Casius, Mount, 68
Chemosh, 12, 20, 349
Cherith, 396
Choreb, 193 *note*
Cis-Jordanic Traditions of Death of Moses, 401 *et seq.*, 414
Crusaders, 233, 244.

DABA, 213, 317
  David, 265, 269, 387
Deborah, 103, 115, 138, 140, 145, 370
Decalogue, 340
Deffieh, 213
Deir, the, 221
Deuteronomist on Aaron's Death, 335
Deuteronomy, date of Composition, 62 *note*, 139
Dialect, differences of, 201
Dophka, 190 *note*
Dumah, burden of, 145

EDOM, 135, 136, 152, 224, 209, 259
Elath-Eloth, 135, 170, 171, 184
Elim, 164, 170, 179, 184, 247, 317, 320
Elijah, 140, 147-152, 396
Elji, 216
El Paran, 144, 170
En-gedi, 265, 271, 272
En-Mishpat, 144, 235, 241
Ephraimites, 346 *note*
Era, 33 *note*
Esek and Sitnah, 293, 295, 335
Etham, 90, 99 *note*, 164
Et Themed, 182
Eusebius, *Onomasticon*, 229 *et seq.*
Exodus, date of, 32, 33
Ezion-gaber, 73, 165

F ARAN, 256
Forty Years, its signification, 8 *note*
Fulcher, 245 *et seq.*
Future State, Hebrews had no belief in, 16

G AD, 359, 362-372, 385
Gebalena, 197
Gedor, 268, 299, 300, 315
Gerar, 293, 297, 299, 300, 315
Gharrab, 397 *note*
Gileadites, 362, 368 *et seq.*
Gilgal, 177
Gobolitis, 197
Goshen, 36, 37 *note*

H ABAKKUK, 145
Hachilah, 265, 266
Hagar, 153, 295
Hagra, 240, 256
Hajj Route, 129, 185 *note*
Haji Khalifeh, 182
Harau, 305
Har-ha-Har, 326, 334, 337
Harrah, El, 305
Hanarra, 238
Havilah, 168, 261, 266
Hazeroth, 191, 204 *note*, 318
Hazezon Tamar, 238, 269, 272
Hebrews, early religion of, 10 *et seq.*; sojourn in Egypt, 34; how reduced to servitude, 39-43; diverse elements of those who quitted Egypt, 102 *et seq.*; distinction between Hebrews and Israelites, 107; occurrence of word in traditions of Exodus, 111, and in historical books, 112 *et seq.*; probable way in which liberation from Egypt obtained, 119 *et seq.*
Henotheism of Hebrews, 10, 21, 355
Hobab, 430
Hor, Mount, 212, 214, 223, 230, 241, 319, 321, 326
Horeb, 138, 147, 193 *note*, 205, 230
Horites, 136, 144, 205, 210, 224, 240
Hormah, 166, 178
Hyksos, 27, 9 b, 94

I JE-ABARIM, 380, 398, 402
Isaac, traditions of, 291 *et seq.*
Isaiah, Book of, work of two persons, 61 *note*
Ishmael, 153, 161
Israel distinct from Judah, 103 *et seq.*; contempt for Judah, 104 *note*; Israel's version of bondage in Egypt, 108, 109; distinction between Israel and Judah very old, 114; no connection between them save for a brief period under Monarchy, 115; counted separately in time of Samuel, 116
Itinerary (Numbers xxxiii.), 165, 189, 338

J AAKAN, Beni, 335, 336, 339 *note*
Jahveh, distinctive name of God of Israel, 19; error in its rendering as Lord-God, 20
Jam Suph, accepted interpretation of the name, 75 and *note*; probable derivation, 76-78; possibly synonymous with present Arabic name of Gulf, 76 *note*
Jebel-et-Tarfâyeh, 399, 409 *note*, 413
Jebel Shiban, 414 *note*
Jehoshaphat, 268
Jephthah, 81, 82, 208, 340, 368, 379, 383
Jerome, *Onomasticon*, 230 *et seq.*, 397
Jeshimon, 265-268
Jethro, 162, 164, 195, 197, 225
Jordan Valley, 134
Joseph, story of, 39, 153, 161
Josephus, 26, 152, 159, 177, 196, 239, 271, 329, 401
Joshua, Book of, 382
Judah, silence respecting, 103; contempt in which held by Israel, 103 *note*; Judah's version of Egyptian oppression, 109; and of Moses' early life, 110; boundaries of, 278
Justice, Divine, rests on same foundation as Human, 5
Justinian, 156

K ADESH, 142, 144, 166, 180, 206 *note*, 234, 236, 239, 279, 281, 283, 315, 327, 340, 349
Kân'aan, 308
Kedem, 153, 161
Kenites, 162, 198, 225
Kerak, 255, 398
Keturah, 153
Kibroth-hattaavah, 191, 200, 203, 207 *note*, 213 *note*, 317
Korah, 430
Kozeh, 349

L OCALISATION of Deity, belief in, 331

M A'AN, 255, 271
Macrizi, 253, 256
Maghara, W., 175
Manasseh, 359, 363 *et seq.*
Manetho, 27, 28, 94
Manna, 192 *note*, 317, 382, 397

INDEX. 439

Maon, 265, 267, 270, 277, 299
Marah, 164, 169, 179, 181, 183 note
Massah, 144
Meribah, waters of, 126, 186-189, 236, 255
Meribah-Kadesh, 142, 279
Mesopotamia, 296 note
Midian, slaughter of, 146, 153
  ,,   land of, 159, 163, 198, 232
  ,,   son of Abraham, 161
Migdol, 66-68
Mineptah II., 33, 37, 117
Miriam, 328
"Mixed Multitude," how composed, 106 et seq., 117-120
Moab, 356, 402
Mokkateb, W., 175
Monotheism, unknown to Hebrews, 10
Mosera, 336, 339 note
Moses, story of early life, 110; his mission, 111, 162, 322; probable part he played as Sheikh of tribe visiting Egypt, 119 et seq.; blessing of, 139; flight of, 158-162, 198; traditions respecting death, 393 et seq., 409 et seq., 412 note
Mount of Elohim, interest attaching to its identification, 133; region where situated, 137; different names, 138, 335
Musa, Jebel, 174

NABATHÆANS, 210, 215 note
  Nakhl, 181-183
Nebo, 400 et seq.
Negeb, 287, 292, 298
Nowairi, 256
Numbers, book of, 125-127

OM SHOMAR, 179
  Oreb, 146, 249
Orebim, 396, 397 note

PALMS, city of, 272 note
  Paran, 142, 143 note, 145, 152, 160, 165, 179, 193, 205, 218 note, 230, 236, 243, 271, 296, 315, 317
Pelusium, 67
Peor, 406, 409, 413
Petra, 154, 197, 211, 215, 243, 257, 317
Peutinger Table, 148, 237, 238 note
Philistines, 112 et seq., 298 et seq.
Pi-hahiroth, 66, 69
Pisgah, 400 et seq., 410, 413
Pithom, 88
Poetry, Hebrew, 141, 142
Polytheism of Hebrews, 10

QUAILS, supply of, 126, 430

RAMESES, 88, 89
  Ras Sufsaveh, 179 note
Red Sea, names of, 73, 75, 76 note, 77-79, 85
  ,,   passage of, 50 et seq., 58, 59, 61-65, 79, 82, 84
Rekam, 240, 255
Religion of Hebrews, 10-17
Rephidim, 164, 176, 203 note, 243, 318
Reuben, 359, 364-372, 385
Ritual of the Dead, 340 note
Rutennu, 309

ST. CATHERINE, Mount of, 179
  St. Paul, 153, 156
Sanhedrin, 126, 199, 430
Saul, 168, 177, 259
Sarbut-el-Khadem, 174, 176
Seir, 141, 157
Sela-ham-mahlekoth, 276, 278
Serbal, 179
Serbonian Lake, 69
Seti, 308
Seyl Szefye, 399, 404 note, 413
Shasu, 37 note, 117, 199 note, 308, 310
Shechinah, 320, 324, 325
Shibboleth, 206
Shihan, Jebel, 414 note
Shittim, 356, 409 note
Shur, 164, 168, 180, 240, 261, 310 et seq.
Sihon, 351
Sik, the, 215-219, 229, 318
Simeon, 287
Sin, 164, 185, 191, 193
Sinai, Mount, 138, 141, 145, 153, 156, 159, 193 note, 236, 243, 248, 317, 319, 327, 330, 339
Sinai, Wilderness of, 165
Sinaitic Peninsula, 131, 155
Succoth, 90, 98
Sutûh Beida, 219
  ,,   Harûn, 219, 341

TABERAH, 207, 340
  Tanis, 89
Tavah, 213 note, 429
Teman, 145
Temple, building of, date, 32
Terah, 288
Tetragrammaton, 19, 20
Tih, Desert of the, 128-130, 376
Tih, Jebel-et-, 131
Timsah, Lake, 100

INDEX.

Tor, Mount, 254, 256
Traditions of Israel and Judah, 108
Trans-Jordanic Conquests, 354, 359, 378
Trans-Jordanic traditions respecting stay in the Wilderness, 392, 414; respecting Moses' death, 409-414
Troglodytes, 158, 198, 224

VALLIS MOYSI, 245, 247

WADY-EL-ARISH, 280
  ,, Gharandel, 214
  ,, Marhadè, 214
  ,, Mûsa, 215, 245
  ,, Rûbai, 220, 256
  ,, -el-Yitm, 192 note, 212, 351
Wander, words so interpreted, 384 et seq.

Wanderings of Israelites, 122, 124, 374
Wilderness, different beliefs concerning its extent, 379, 380
Willows, Valley of, 394-397, 399

YITM, Wady-el-, 192 note

ZAHI, 308
  Zalu, 308
Zered, 380, 394, 395 note, 404 note
Zin, 186, 187, 191, 206, 278
Zini, 194 note
Ziph, 265, 274
Zoan, 89, 92, 94, 96
Zoar, 273 note, 304 note

THE END.

PRINTED BY BALLANTYNE AND HANSON
LONDON AND EDINBURGH

www.ingramcontent.com/pod-product-compliance
Lightning Source LLC
Chambersburg PA
CBHW022135300426
44115CB00006B/193